For Dear Life

For Dear Life

AND

SELECTED SHORT STORIES

by Belinda Jelliffe

edited by Virginia Pruitt and Howard Faulkner

The Kent State University Press ▣ Kent & London

Frontis: This drawing of Belinda Jelliffe by Charles T. Mayer was used on the cover of *For Dear Life* when it was published by Scribner's in 1936. *Thomas Wolfe Collection, Aldo Magi Series, North Carolina Collection, University of North Carolina Library at Chapel Hill.*

© 2003 by The Kent State University Press, Kent, Ohio 44242
All rights reserved.
Library of Congress Catalog Card Number 2002001853
ISBN 0-87338-747-3
Manufactured in the United States of America

07   06   05   04   03   5   4   3   2   1

Grateful acknowledgment and thanks to Charles Scribner III.

Library of Congress Cataloging-in-Publication Data
Jelliffe, Belinda Dobson, 1892–
For dear life and selected short stories / by Belinda Jelliffe ;
edited by Virginia Pruitt and Howard Faulkner.
p.   cm.
Includes bibliographical references.
ISBN 0-87338-747-3 (pbk. : alk. paper)
1. North Carolina—Fiction. 2. Rural families—Fiction. 3. Poor families—Fiction.
4. Poor women—Fiction. 5. Nurses—Fiction. I. Pruitt, Virginia D., 1943–.
II. Faulkner, Howard J., 1945–. III. Title.
PS3519.E427 F67 2003
813'.52—dc21   2002001853
British Library Cataloging-in-Publication data are available.

Contents

Acknowledgments

We would like to thank Donna Park for her intelligent and meticulous word processing of the text; Robert Stein, chair of the Department of English at Washburn University, for his continuing enthusiasm and encouragement; and especially Aldo Magi, for his unflagging help, expert knowleges, and extreme kindness.

We shared equally in the pleasures of preparing this book, and the ordering of the names reflects nothing more than the exigencies of printing.

Introduction

In August of 1936, Belinda Jelliffe published her thinly disguised autobiographical novel, *For Dear Life,* to generally favorable reviews. A year later, it appeared in England, where the reviewer for the *London Observer* wrote "this book is too fine a thing to be the shooting star of a publishing season. But it will be there next year, and the next, glittering like Jupiter for all who have eyes to see."[1] Despite the reviewer's prediction, *For Dear Life* had disappointing sales. Jelliffe frequently complained that if all the people who wrote her telling her they had read the book had actually bought it instead of borrowing it from friends or a library, she would have been a rich woman. Scribner's, her publisher, allowed the book to go out of print, and although the now-defunct Arno Press (then a division of the *New York Times*) reprinted the original in 1980 (complete with the mistakes of the earlier version) as part of its "Signal Lives: Autobiographies of American Women" series, sales were again disappointing, and the novel once more quickly vanished. Shamefully.

This is a story that deserves an audience, a story realistically portraying life among the rural poor in the early part of the twentieth century and the tough-minded woman who fought her entire life to overcome the obstacles that confronted women, the poor, the isolated. The novel has mythic resonances: it reads like a woman's version of the legendary American success story. As in the autobiographies of Benjamin Franklin and Booker T. Washington or the novels of Horatio Alger, a protagonist—through her own pluck and luck—works her way from an existence of poverty to a fairy-tale resolution when she leaves behind, apparently for good, the miseries of her

---

1. J. S. Collins, *London Observer,* Oct. 10, 1937.

previous life after meeting a world-famous doctor. There the novel ends for Belinda Dan, the autobiographical protagonist, concluding on what seems a hopeful note, though after the many false starts followed by disappointments that the character has experienced, perhaps the ending is not so unambiguously optimistic as it first seems. Belinda Dobson Jelliffe's story parallels that of her persona in the novel. From the few published accounts of Jelliffe's life after her marriage to the famous doctor, Smith Ely Jelliffe, the match seems worthy of the rags-to-riches stories of Cinderella or Alger. The truth, however, is as double-edged as a wary reader's response to the tale's abrupt finish.

Belinda Dobson was born in a barn on July 16, 1890, in Leicester, North Carolina, a small town near Asheville (called Carleton in her novel), the youngest of eleven children, two of whom died at birth. Her parents were desperately poor, and Jelliffe does nothing to romanticize them or their existence of unending labor, eking out a living from the land. Though late in the book Belinda is unforgiving of a brother who returns to North Carolina after years of absence, she makes clear early in the novel her assumption that when the children grew up, they would move away to try to make a better life for themselves, and Bee's (Belinda Jelliffe was usually known as Bee or even Lady Bee) own insistent pleas from childhood on were that she be able to escape and have the chance for an education.

The father impetuously uproots the family to move to Oklahoma, but after a year there, though their fortunes seem somewhat improved, he reverses his decision and takes them all back to North Carolina. Throughout these travails, Belinda's lone entreaty is "Dear God, please send me some books," but no books appear, and she can rely only on her own resilience and physical strength as well as her faith that if she can get away, education will change her life.

Her portrait of rural American life in this first section is relentlessly unflattering. Not only is the work constant and wearying, making people old long before their time, but there is nothing pastoral about the community. Small-town America, as described by Jelliffe, is marked by drunkenness, scandal, violence, suicide, and murder. She is especially cynical about marriage. Many of the marital unions she recounts are established more out of desperation than love. In chapter three, a friend of hers hangs herself after marrying a stingy, controlling older man, and when the husband of Adelaide, Belinda's favorite sister, is killed in a freak accident, Jelliffe's reaction is the biting comment that though the husband may have loved

Adelaide, he has made no economic provisions for her or their infant, and she will soon be looking for a job.

Only the natural world provides a sanctuary for Belinda—here as well as in the later sections of the novel. The sense of relief and pleasure Belinda feels in the woods, whether alone or with friends, offers lyrical counterpoints to the bleakness delineated in the rest of the book. In her later life, after the period covered in the novel, Bee Jelliffe divided her time between New York City and a home on Lake George in upstate New York. Here, too, the close and affectionate observation of nature and its creatures evident in all her writing, but especially in her letters, furnishes her and her readers with one of the few respites from her evocation of mundane drudgery.

The second third of *For Dear Life* details Belinda's life after she finally leaves home at around age twelve. Sneaking off without a suitcase, nearly penniless, and wearing the only two sets of clothes she owns, she has to wait for the train. While waiting, she obtains fifty cents from an old man who plainly, though futilely, hopes for something in exchange. When her father finds her on the train, she fears he will try to make her return, but instead he gives her a dime and some typically laconic advice, "Keep your chin up." She never sees him again (she revisits North Carolina just once). Sentiment, she says, is a luxury of the rich; for the poor, it guarantees imprisonment in their circumstances, and she has too much ambition to risk entertaining it. Upon the same basis, she also rejects the normal outcome of romantic feeling. A young man, Kingland Mears, falls for her even before the family moves to Oklahoma. He waits during the Oklahoma sojourn, and on her return to North Carolina, he is still waiting. Although Belinda repeatedly admits she loves Kingsland and is tempted to marry him, especially since he agrees to wait even longer so that she can become educated, she finally rejects him. Later, he sends her a despairing letter, and on the night that he mails the letter he is killed by a train in what is termed an accident, but which Belinda suspects is a suicide.

Her eyes set on education, Belinda goes to the Pierson school where one of her sisters was formerly a student. But education, at least as available to a woman, and a poor one at that, is a disappointment. Already strong-willed and impetuous, Belinda has trouble with the strict discipline imposed in school: she fails at catechism and can't stand "Silent Hour." When the girls are taught sex education by a woman who hasn't had the informal education in it provided by living on a farm and knows nothing about her subject, Belinda parodies her to the other girls and is caught and punished.

Yet at this first school, at least, most of the teachers seem dedicated and understanding. There is a quite matter-of-fact description of one girl's three-year crush on a female teacher, an infatuation that is openly reciprocated, and of Belinda's attempt, sheerly out of mischief, to break the relationship up, an attempt at which she is briefly successful, until she decides that it is ignoble to use power for destructive ends. Earlier in her life, Belinda over-heard her mother say that she is an ugly child. Now, the headmistress, commenting on Belinda's action, tells her that she is one who will never be content in a relationship, that she is one destined, like most of the unmar-ried teachers in the school, for a different sort of love: "Love is service," Belinda is told—a sentence that, like her mother's remark, Belinda fears is an augury of her future.

During the summer, she works in a hotel—as a maid during the day and a telephone operator and bellhop during the night. There she meets Pearl, the cook, a large, intimidating black woman who, when Belinda leaves, gives her the princely sum of fifty dollars; this is one of the fortuitous encounters that, as in Alger's narratives, complement her pluck. When in the fall she goes to a university, she doesn't discover even the dedication that characterized the teachers at the Pierson school. The university is "hag-ridden with religion" and becomes yet another disappointment in her quest for education; it is also sadly typical of the schools and training programs Belinda will enter after she decides to become a nurse. Following a number of false starts at working, she finally becomes a maid for Mr. and Mrs. Fairfax, an eccentric couple who subsist on chocolate, peanuts, and sour milk, or "clabber," and whose only companion is Isiah, a parrot who tire-lessly repeats "Come to Jesus. Come to Jesus," except when the Fairfaxes aren't present, when he adds "Hahaha" to the end of his incantation.

Finally, in the novel's last section, Belinda goes north. After years of indecision about the practical outcome of her education, she chooses nurs-ing, one of the few options open to women of the time. Once more, the story is a depressing one of the incompetence, cruelty, and indifference of those in charge of both the younger nurses and the patients, told by a narrator who spares neither others nor herself in her acerbic descriptions. Her very first experience in hospital training sets the tone both in its horror and its humor. A man enters the accident ward of the hospital where Belinda works. She has been assigned that evening to the emergency ward not be-cause she is trained for it, but simply because there is no one else to cover it. In a handkerchief, the patient is carrying the tip of his nose, severed in a construction accident. While the doctor cleans the man's face in preparation for reattachment of the end of the nose, he tells Belinda to "keep it clean," an injunction which she interprets as meaning that she should put it in the sterilizer. When the doctor calls for it and she fishes it out, he whispers, "My God! You've cooked it!"

Throughout this section, Belinda continues to find herself in trouble; she cannot tolerate the petty rules, the uncleanliness, and especially the tyranny of the administrators. Only rarely can she restrain her feelings, and at one point actually slaps a head nurse. Her emotions swing wildly between anger and a bemused, protective indifference. She weeps over failures and frustrations, and then her despondent mood dissolves into assertiveness or joy. But despite her frequent despair, she always summons the courage to continue or else has a chance meeting with someone who appreciates and rewards her. In one of the longer and lighter episodes, she becomes nurse to a rich and powerful man; while everyone else kowtows to him and thereby earns his wrath, she does not and thus wins him over. As always, she paints with sure, if glancing, strokes the portrait of her unconventional employer.

Whenever she is tempted to give up, because work is in short supply, she makes one final attempt. "I'll visit one more doctor's office," she says, "make one more call." And invariably, if not always convincingly, her Alger-like persistence pays off. At the end of the novel, tired and disheartened, she nonetheless forces herself to apply for employment with one last doctor: "Stuart Ellery Jerrold," an obvious parallel to the man Bee married, Smith Ely Jelliffe. He is a famous psychiatrist, and the novel ends, quite precipitously, not with his hiring her but with her acceptance of his dinner invitation and her confidence that now all will be well: she has met someone who understands her; she has met a true friend.

Jelliffe's novel, then, is a sometimes grim, sometimes comic portrayal of the limitations confronting a woman, particularly one born poor, in America in the first third of the twentieth century and of the privations and frustrations that the protagonist (whose story is a barely fictionalized record of the life of the author herself) endures in trying to surmount those obstacles. She survives in typical Alger fashion through grit, perseverance, ingenuity, and boundless toil. But as in Alger, her pluck is supplemented by a great deal of good luck—meeting important or generous people who help her, impressed either by her tenacity or by her tears. Throughout her story, she is revealed as a paradoxical combination of victim and survivor, of fragility and strength.

Belinda Jelliffe, ca. late 1930s. *Thomas Wolfe Collection, Aldo Magi Series, North Carolina Collection, University of North Carolina Library at Chapel Hill.*

But Jelliffe leaves her story with a wit—frequently biting—and a perspicacity often absent in the traditional American success story. For example, when asked to abet a well-off benefactor, a Harvard-educated judge, in disposing of the body of a woman whom he has killed, she assists her employer without a second thought or a backward glance. Then, with dark humor, she observes that, a few months later, he turned her out of his home to accommodate his niece. Bee writes: "I had hoped Judge Reeves would help me [but] . . . I was not his child, *so why should he bother?*" Nor does she have illusions about the world she is trying so hard to enter; one of the remarkable qualities of her narrative is its revelation of her seemingly innate ability to transcend the prevailing stereotypes of the day and see through pretensions. She is befriended as often by black Americans as by whites, by the indigent as often as by the wealthy. The rich are sometimes generous, but she is equally prepared for them to be foolish or even treacherous. And once crossed, she is never forgiving.

In both her novel and her letters, Jelliffe's voice is unique. In neither case is structure her forte. Significantly, about one of her later manuscripts, her editor at Scribner's, Maxwell Perkins, remarks, "You seem to have combined three novels in it, and not finished any of them" (Sept. 2, 1938).[2] As might be predicted from her impetuous, often precipitate behavior, *For Dear Life* cascades from episode to episode with little effort at smoothing transitions; caught up in the drama of each incident, Jelliffe will often make brief and incisive asides, but she rarely is capable of enough detachment to integrate the threads into a seamless whole. Particularly disorienting to a reader is her failure to indicate how old Belinda Dan is at any given point in the book, or to provide dates or references to happenings in the larger world. With the exception of one point in chapter six, when she says that she is moving from the seventh to the eighth grade as she departs for the Pierson School, the reader is left to infer Belinda's age and exactly what the time period is. Although we now know that Bee Dobson was born in 1890, she never gives the reader even that much information about Belinda Dan (in later life Bee often professed not to know the exact year she was born), so relating the events to history becomes still more problematic. Moreover, her punctuation is idiosyncratic and sometimes distracting. As her letters reveal, Bee was never a good speller nor did she trouble herself with conventional punctuation, and although Maxwell Perkins was her editor, he seems to have preferred to leave alone Bee's rather breathless, improvisational style. Unfortunately, the correspondence between Perkins and Jelliffe about the editing of her manuscript has not been preserved. (Of course her spelling was normalized, although a few errors slip in. Twice in chapter three, her sister Sallie's name is written "Sally." And "*pot de chambre*" is allowed to stand as "*peau de chambre.*")

But Bee Jelliffe the author, like Belinda Dan her creation, is a keen observer of human behavior—warmly sympathetic when she deems sympathy merited, bitter, cynical, and doggedly self-centered when she deems it necessary to survival. And for all her dreams of city life, Jelliffe is drawn to the natural world of her roots, and her lyrical descriptive passages, fresh and often whimsical, suggest her appreciation for such infrequent moments

2. The correspondence between Belinda Jelliffe and Maxwell Perkins is located in the Scribner archives at the Princeton University Library. That between Jelliffe and Karl Menninger is in the Menninger Archives, Topeka, Kans. Jelliffe's correspondence with Thomas Wolfe is shared between the North Carolina Collection at Wilson Library, University of North Carolina, and the Houghton Library, Harvard University. All correspondence reprinted with permission. In all of the quoted correspondence, we have retained Bee's peculiar spelling and punctuation. Additionally, unless otherwise indicated by brackets, any ellipses or similar punctuation in the letters are Bee's and do not indicate omitted material.

of tranquility and her empathy for life in all its manifestations. In both the novel and the letters, she is particularly gifted at narrative vignettes, with a Dickensian capacity for evoking the defining physical and personality characteristics of those she meets. Her ear for dialogue, as well as dialect (especially the dialects of her father, Pearl, and the Orthodox Jewish mother of one of her suitors) is flawless; she is a ruthless commentator on others' motives as well as honest about her own.

From the suddenness of the last sentence of *For Dear Life,* the reader is left to infer that Belinda's troubles are in her past and the future will likely be a fulfillment of all she has desired. Horatio Alger's novels always ended, as does *For Dear Life,* with the moment of acceptance into the longed-for world, a tacit admission that the new life might not be so interesting as the life of struggle that made it possible. Jelliffe's own existence after her marriage gives the lie to that assumption, as well as contravenes the skimpy descriptions of her later life presently available.

But the ending of the novel distorts the otherwise faithful autobiographical nature of the novel. In truth, Bee Dobson went to see Smith Ely Jelliffe not looking for a job, but seeking his professional psychiatric help. He was twenty-four years older than she, a widower with five children. Although his name is little known outside the profession today, he was one of America's most distinguished pioneer psychiatrists and a vigorous early proponent of Freudian psychoanalysis. In 1917, when he and Bee were married, he was also one of the most renowned neuropsychiatrists in America. With William Alanson White, he wrote a two-volume text, *Modern Treatment of Nervous and Mental Diseases* (1st ed. 1915), which became the standard psychiatric text for the first half of the twentieth century. In 1908, the two men began the long-lived publication of *The Nervous and Mental Disease Monograph Series.* Also with White, he founded and edited the first American journal devoted solely to psychoanalysis, the *Psychoanalytic Review* in 1913. And four years earlier, he had purchased the oldest neurological periodical in America, the *Journal of Nervous and Mental Diseases.*

Jelliffe's two main contributions to psychiatry were his theory of "paleopsychology" and his elaboration of theories of psychosomatic illness. Paleopsychology, a word Jelliffe coined, suggested that individual personality development passed through evolutionary stages that could be loosely paralleled with the earth's own evolution. More influential was his insistence on psychosomatic causes for numerous physical ailments. Touchingly, in her voluminous correspondence Bee always assumed the role of Jelliffe's defender, trying to redress what she saw as an unjust neglect of his contributions. In no area was she more insistent than in her conviction that he, more than any other psychiatrist, had first understood the relationship between physical and mental illness. Among the diseases that Jelliffe was convinced had a psychological basis were such diverse conditions as psoriasis, tuberculosis, multiple sclerosis, and hypertension.

Jelliffe's success enabled him to acquire a library of twenty thousand volumes on psychiatry and related fields. After his marriage to Bee, when lack of money became a constant source of worry, selling this collection became one of Bee's preoccupations. Because of his fame, Jelliffe also treated a select clientele. Among his patients between 1923 and 1925 was Eugene O'Neill, although the treatment was, according to Arthur and Barbara Gelb, O'Neill's biographers, "sporadic" rather than systematic. The Gelbs recount details of an encounter between Bee and O'Neill as he is leaving a session with Jelliffe. They become involved in a conversation in which O'Neill chastises Bee for her casual use of the word "hate." (In *For Dear Life,* Belinda has a similar conversation with a boyfriend, Leonard P. Burke, who plans to become a minister. Disgusted with his indulgent use of the word "love," she asserts that hate is valuable, that one must hate—as long as the hate is directed toward a deserving object.) Bee agrees with O'Neill that she has been wrong in using the word so carelessly, and then repeats her belief that hate should not be suppressed but rather that one should be instructed what to hate. When she asks O'Neill what his definition of love is, he replies in the same words she heard years earlier at the Pierson School: "Love is service."[3]

Bee married Smith Ely Jelliffe December 20, 1917, when she was twenty-seven and he was fifty-one. As a widower with three daughters and two sons, the eldest daughter only five years younger than her new stepmother, Jelliffe introduced Bee into a complex emotional environment. As might have been predicted, the complications posed by the new situation, compounded by Bee's impulsive and volatile temperament, generated significant tensions, although Bee seemed to get along better with the sons than with the daughters. In his dissertation on Smith Ely Jelliffe's contribution to psychosomatic medicine, David Krasner writes that the childen had adored their mother,[4] though in a letter written after Jelliffe's death, Bee refers to

3. Arthur Gelb and Barbara Gelb, *O'Neill* (New York: Perennial, 1973), 566–67.
4. David Kassner, "Smith Ely Jelliffe and the Development of American Psychosomatic Medicine" (Ph.D. diss., Bryn Mawr, 1984), 38.

Belinda and Smith Ely Jelliffe at Lake George, New York, 1926. *Thomas Wolfe Collection, Aldo Magi Series, North Carolina Collection, University of North Carolina Library at Chapel Hill.*

the children as "nit wits" (Dec. 1943). Tragically, in early 1925, Leeming Jelliffe, the younger of the two sons, died of a self-inflicted gunshot wound, a death that was officially ruled accidental.

Despite problems within the family, Jelliffe was at the height of his professional prestige and influence. Still, his married life with Bee was quite different from the more staid life he had earlier led as a family and professional man. John Burnham, Jelliffe's biographer, writes that Bee "had little interest in close personal relations with the more dignified and powerful members of the New York medical fraternity and their wives. Theater people, whom Jelliffe also enjoyed, were more to her liking. This was an important, but subtle nonintellectual factor in Jelliffe's increasingly independent and, indeed, lonely role in the medical profession in the last decades of his life."[5] After Jelliffe's death, Bee complains bitterly in her correspondence, especially in her prolific exchanges with Topeka, Kansas, psychiatrist Karl Menninger, of the psychiatric profession's disregard of her husband's achievements and contributions, of the shabby way he is ignored. She writes Menninger, "All the yrs I knew that whole bunch [of psychiatrists] they were petty, conniving, crawling, and nasty little people [. . .] So you can imagine what I think of the whole goddam lot . . . If all their education doesn't help them to be decent whats the use? I laugh at them" (June 17, 1958). Ironically, then, Burnham accuses Bee herself of being partly responsible for Jelliffe's exile to the fringes of the medical community.

Nor did her marriage signify the end of her toil. Despite Smith Ely's earlier success and fame, the Jelliffes seem always to have had money problems, and Belinda spent an enormous amount of her time and energy trying to earn money, continuing to exhibit the same qualities of ingenuity and persistence that had distinguished her earlier life. She invented and manufactured games; she designed and marketed ties and dressing gowns, and she even made a brief venture into the shirt business. In 1935, at the same time she was working on *For Dear Life,* Bee was also extricating herself from the business of manufacturing ties and frantically trying to sell Jelliffe's medical library. In April of that year she writes Menninger,

The Tie Business is in abeyance, whatever That is . . . and i have been writing like mad . . . but tonight, everything sticks, and nothing happens . . . so dam it all i'll write you.

For instance, do you suppose that you know anyone who would buy Dr. Jelliffe's Neurological Library? You know he just about had it sold to Cornell, when the Crash, (remember?) came, and nothing has happened since. But if some son of a bitch wanted to grab a little honor which he dosn't deserve, naturally, by presenting it to some College, it would help keep the wolf from our door...and believe me if he comes in, he'll have to eat books. . . . Maybe Wolves don't eat paper? (ca. Apr. 10, 1935)

---

5. John C. Burnham, "Jelliffe: American Psychoanalyst and Physician," in *Jelliffe: His Correspondence with Freud and Jung,* ed. William McGuire (Chicago: Univ. of Chicago Press, 1983), 88.

By 1938, Bee had turned her attention to games, heading a company called Gordon Games, which manufactured Star-Ball, K-Reen-O, Tom-Tom, and Star-It. Of her newest game, Bee writes Menninger that they are selling "several hundreds a day in the biggest Drug stores and Macys" (n.d., 1938), but as Bee was prone to exaggeration and the business soon collapsed, the number was probably much fewer. Yet whatever Bee did, she did with the enthusiasm of a zealot: "I've been working from 9 am until 11 & 12 at night. I fall into my bed drunk with fatigue. With all that I made my dress for dinner out of some old window curtains. I thought I looked pretty good. It was a lovely occasion & pleased Dr. J. very much. At that it was time the bastards came through & admitted they've all taken from him—the least they can do is admit it" (n.d., 1938).

But despite Bee's frenetic commitment, none of her businesses survived for very long. Some of her labor was not much different, except in its nature, from the grueling work she had known on the farm and as a young nurse. Although the fact that the Jelliffes had residences in both New York City and on Lake George, a bucolic retreat in upstate New York, might be viewed as a sign of financial success, it can also be interpreted as an expedient that enabled the couple to lead somewhat separate lives. Bee says in a letter of 1938 to Menninger that "One of the FEW compliments Ely ever paid me was that he appreciated the fact that he never felt that I was sitting up here boiling over because he wasn't taking me out . . . that I was always occupied with my own life . . Occupied is right; I'm working days, nights, and all days sundays, making games" (n.d., 1938).

The home in New York City was indeed, as John Burnham observed, a gathering place where friends dropped in for extended stays. But the picture that Belinda Jelliffe paints, especially in her letters to Menninger, whom she seems to have regarded as one of the few psychoanalysts to appreciate her husband's work and with whom she was often unusually candid, is not one of gaiety or of an intellectual salon, but rather one of the mindless drudgery of cleaning toilets and scrubbing bathrooms, a life not much different from the semi-slavery of her early days as a nurse, as conveyed by this description of it to Maxwell Perkins: "Up to now I've not laid down a dishrag or scrubbing rag, broom or vacuum cleaner, not an hour during the long days . . . . I live in a nightmare of housework" (Aug. 1943).

Nor was Smith Ely Jelliffe the devoted prince the reader of the novel is led to expect. Bee has to share him with his family, with his work, and even with a mistress. While she is trying to work on *For Dear Life,* Bee writes Menninger, "Well, go back to last summer for a moment. I was Blessed by five extra Jelliffes, that is Helen Goldschmidt, her husband, two boys, and a nurse, were on top of me at the Lake, and I was supposed to LOVE it. I luckily, for the FIRST time in all my married life, had a room in which I could be alone. Can you imagine, never having in all my life had a room I could Lock? Well, I locked myself in, and let the God damned dirty sons of Bitches have a glorious time" (Mar. 11, 1935).

Moreover, as Jelliffe increasingly found himself displaced from a central position in his profession, he seems to have worked even harder. And, as Bee tells it, as fewer and fewer of the new generation of psychoanalysts arriving on the scene acknowledged Jelliffe's influence, he devoted even more time to helping them. In a fascinating and perceptive letter to Menninger two years after Smith Ely Jelliffe's death, Bee writes,

> Particularly I am interested in WHY he didn't have more of a following. I THINK I know WHY, but it is not an easy concept to endeavor to embody within an objective ms. I'd like to discuss this point with you when we meet up. The root of much of this was his inability to handle his homosexuality . . . . . I think that is the right word. He LOVED men, doctors, more than he loved his wives children or himself; there was no length to which he would not go to be of service to DOCTORS . . . but when he had to face up to it, he didn't know how to handle his love. As I told you more than once, he LOVED you; he really loved you BUT he HAD TO BEAT you down . . . he didn't know what to do about it . . and this was, I think, completely unconscious. I think you're wrong at the point of his not having young men come to him . . . My God, Karl, this house was FULL of them and long before I came here he had classes, for Years . . . and he worked 20 hrs a day, to do it. (Dec. 15, 1947)

Bee continues, "My God, I've had them follow us around Europe, come up to us in restaurants . . asking his advice and he gave unsparingly of his time . . . . I think that point could be improved somewhat. No, where he lost out was with his contemporaries. The old sons of bitches who hated his guts because they knew he actually knew more. [. . .] I sometimes feel that the BEST men, sensitive, loving, and lovable men, are the least able to handle their love for each other . . . Do you think it is possible that the French custom of kissing each other is a help in that field? We try to be so goddam masculine . . . . . . denying our femininity . . . . . that is, American men do . . . . . . in fact I think it is the GREAT FAULT of our men" (Dec. 15, 1947).

And, finally, in an outburst of rage and frustration, Bee responds to a Maxwell Perkins letter about the need for happiness as a justification for self-indulgent behavior. Bee explains to Perkins that while she is trying to write, running two homes, involved in the "nightmare of housework," Jelliffe has carried on a sustained affair: "Oh, if LIKING it is the point, then of course you would feel that it has been perfectly all right for my husband to live with my maid, as he has, for ten years. Some time in an off moment you might just try and visualize the life I've had to lead all these years. HE certainly 'liked' her and I have no reason, really for supposing that she did not like him. She played for high stakes, to her,—that is, marriage. Failing that, she calmly took the material advantages and made a good life for herself without the slightest thought of what it has done to me" (Dec. 1943). And then with no transition, she drops the subject and finishes the letter with a brief observation about the weather.

But if much was unfair and demanding in the marriage, if much belies the bright and confident interpretation of the ending of *For Dear Life,* still, Bee's love for her husband is undeniable. They entertained and traveled together, many times to Europe, moving both literally and figuratively a long way from her impoverished childhood roots. Their friends were among the smartest and liveliest in New York. She indefatigably nursed Jelliffe during his last years. And as we have seen, she consistently identified and passionately defended her husband's creative contributions to neurology and psychoanalysis. Between them endured a spirit of playfulness. Though every aspect of Bee's life was marked by emotional liability, despite the difficulties, Bee also managed in their union to create moments of lightness. Five years into the marriage, after the death of E. E. Southard, who had been a mentor to both Menninger and Jelliffe, Bee confides to Menninger,

In your reference to the passing of Elmer Earnest [*sic*], and your agitation over the fact that Dr. Jelliffe was suffering from the same ailment, I assure you that your uneasiness was unnecessary. You have apparently forgotten that Ely has had five years training with me, which has kept him much harder muscularly and in much better form to attack anything, than had E. E. Too bad that he hadn't had someone to keep him fit, so that he would not have succumed to that dread disease.

I have had lots of fun telling people how startled you were, when I threw the teacup and busted it over Funnies' head while we breakfasted QUIETLY. They all say, he must have thought to himself, God pity Jelliffe. Strangely enough, he loved it. He doesn't seem to desire sympathy. (Apr. 3, 1923)

Clearly, though, Jelliffe didn't inspire sympathy from everyone who knew him. Mabel Dodge, one of Jelliffe's patients, wrote about her impression of the doctor: "'A Roman Catholic priest,' I had thought at once. . . . He was commanding, quizzical, sure of himself, and not to be moved" (Gelb 565). Surely, Dodge would have been surprised by Bee's irreverent nickname for and attitude toward Jelliffe. Bee began one of her letters to the equally imposing Menninger by calling him "you boiled egg," a phrase she also gleefully applied to her husband.

The dynamics implicit in Bee's marriage to Jelliffe thus mirrored the complexities of her own psyche, revealed in the ceaseless struggles to escape the limitations of her family, her unflagging efforts to get an education, her continual attempt at writing, and her contentious marriage to a husband twenty-four years her senior. Bee's temperament reflected a volatile combination of high spirits, determination, and humor alternating with depression and uncontrolled outbursts of emotion, notably anger. Still, the shortcomings in the marriage may also have been due as much to Smith Ely Jelliffe's psychological make-up as to Bee's. After Jelliffe's funeral, Bee writes to Perkins, "I think now his harassed mind and spirit will be at rest. Surely there is peace for him some place. He was enough of a genius to be very lonely and he was shy and longed for love, but always repelled it . . . only for a short time could he allow me to love him, then he began a systematic series of continuous, persistent, everlasting efforts to destroy my love . . . he did it to others . . . almost as though he refused the thing he longed for" (Sept. 1945).

The most gratifying periods in her life certainly occurred during the course of her friendships with Maxwell Perkins and Thomas Wolfe at the time of the publication of *For Dear Life*. The acquaintance with Wolfe began in May 1933 when Bee wrote him a fan letter: "I have always wanted to tell you that I liked so much your 'Look Homeward Angel'. . . and to explain my peculiar reaction to it. When I begun it, and became completely absorbed in it, I had the most strange feeling, which I couldn't at first explain. Finally, closing the book, I let myself sort of drift, mentally, and suddenly saw the whole thing, in the most startling way. Asheville, my home town. Where I lived for years, knowing all the things that you put in your book. Knowing the actual people in the book . . . . . . it was an experience I have never had, a most profoundly disturbing experience . . . . . . I wanted to see you, and to talk to you of my own life there: of the strange and unhappy things that affected, badly, I think, my whole life. It has disturbed me psychologically ever since. It is a grand book . . . I cannot tell you how fine I think it is" (May 18, 1933).

In November, she wrote him again after reading three of his stories: " . . . there is something to me so fine, so magnificent about your writing that I cannot discuss it. I feel that it is foolish for me to try to tell you what I think. I only feel that it tears me to little bits" (Nov. 17, 1933).

Wolfe replied immediately: "You say I may not care what you or the world thinks of me and my work, but you would be wrong in thinking so. I assure you I am by no means immune to what you and the world may think . . .

"Perhaps some people who have been unwise, furious and bewildered, ruinously wasteful of their own and other people's lives, and tormented and pursued by all sorts of demons, phantoms, monsters and delusions of their own creation, may get out of the work they do the certitude and truth that has escaped them elsewhere. This may be true of me. At any rate, when I work I am happiest" (Nov. 21, 1933).

Bee's own attitude toward work was more ambivalent, as suggested by a remark she made in a letter to Perkins, "Some devil makes me work, if not at writing, then I must garden, or carry stone and build walls, anything . . . I don't think it matters, just so we are busy" (Sept. 1938).

During the next year, 1934, there seems to have been no communication between Jelliffe and Wolfe; but on New Year's Day 1935, Wolfe telephoned "Mrs. Jelliffe," as he always called her,[6] inviting her to meet him the next Monday so that he could introduce her to his editor, Maxwell Perkins. Impatient as ever, Bee asked Wolfe to come to dinner before that event; when he tried to cancel because his mother was in town, Bee insisted on meeting his mother, too. It was not a harmonious encounter. Some time later, Wolfe's mother wrote to her son Fred, "I hope Tom will spend most of his time writing this new book, & spend no more time with those two

6. Aldo P. Magi and Richard Walser, *Wolfe and Belinda Jelliffe* (N.p.: Thomas Wolfe Society, 1987), 14. This monograph provides a full and indispensable description of Wolfe's friendship with Bee.

married women. The Jew woman [Aline Bernstein] is to be preferred to the other one. I did not take to her at all. She married an old man for his money" (Magi 17).

On the appointed Monday, Perkins, Wolfe, and Bee met. According to Bee, Perkins said immediately, "Mrs. Jelliffe, you should write." Bee reports the conversation in a letter to Karl Meninnger: "I said, 'Mr. Perkins, I have been [told] that for fifteen years at least, and I have an answer, which I give to every one. I will now give it to you. I am the ONLY living White Woman left alive who READS. If I start to write, WHO is going to READ?'" (Mar. 11, 1935).

But despite her comeback, write she did. Bee continues her account in her letter to Menninger:

> One day says I to meself, all my life I've been told I Should write, so By God, I'll write. I did. About forty sheets . . . unnumbered . . . mixed up. I had never read them back. Now move down to the Wolfe Perkins point. One day, dazed, driven by my life, so much to do, I went out, and almost not realizing what I was doing, I picked up these pages, put a rubber band around them, and left them over at Scribners for Mr. P. Then I got frightfully nervous. You see I thot there was no name, and they would never know who wrote them, and that by some circutuous route, I would hear if anyone ever did read them . . . . . Three days went by, and I came in late one Sat. evening. There were two phone calls, Mr. W. and Mr. P. I figured they had phoned to say that it wasn't very nice of me to leave such a nondescript bunch of stuff for Mr. Perkins. [. . .] About two, I was still up reading, I phoned T. W. He said, with great sarcasm, "Well, Mrs. J. I see you are going to come right out into the open and face the world as a writer." I said, "Why, I don't know what you are talking about." He said, "I saw that batch of vari-colored, un-numbered sheets you left for Mr. P." I laughed and said, lightly, "Oh, Those. Those were written by a very dumb woman who visited me last summer. I know they are no good." "Is that so?" says he. "Well, Mr. Perkins has read them twice, and I read some of it, and its simply grand. Mr. P. says it's the best he has seen for a long time." . . . I simply broke down and wept, and said I had written it, and that he shouldn't say such things as I knew that it was rotten. (Mar. 11, 1935)

Here is the letter that Perkins wrote as Bee quotes it to Menninger:

Dear Mrs. Jelliffe:

I would like to keep your material a day or two longer and read it again, and then if possible talk to you. I read it almost with amazement at the ability, conscious or unconscious, with which it is done. In the first place it discloses most unusual sensibilities and equally unusual ability to express them. There are certain paragraphs that could not be beaten. One is about that girl patient dying, and the beauty of her body. Another is that about the way the mother acted when the sons had gone to the Spanish War. Another is that of lying awake and seeing the horse pass the window, and hearing everything. Another, and perhaps the best, or at any rate the most popular kind of effective paragraph is that about the return of the father after seeing Bryan, telling his wife that she was right, and he was wrong. Anyone who can write those paragraphs can certainly *write*. Certainly if you have time and inclination to work, it would be most interesting to me to go into the question with you, and I shall try to see if it would be possible to talk to you about it after a day or two. (Mar. 11, 1935)

Belinda writes that, by contrast, all Smith Ely said of her first serious attempt at writing was, "Well, that's very nice, my dear."

Thus began an incredibly stimulating and fulfilling period in Bee's life. Not only was she working on her novel, but she, Wolfe, and Perkins become a devoted threesome. According to Bee, Wolfe even asked her to divorce her husband and marry him. She wrote Elizabeth Nowell, "I brought him home. Dr. J. got up and we sat in his cold office. I got socks & pants and made TW put them on [he and Bee had gotten wet in a snowy Central Park]. And Dr. J. discussed the whole thing with him: WHY he THOUGHT he wanted to marry me. Ely said, 'I am pleased, Mr. Wolfe, because I think she's pretty wonderful too, but I have such great admiration and affection for you, I want YOU to know YOURSELF why you THINK you wanna do this.' Ended up that TW was more in love with SEJ than me, and he was smart as hell about the psychic angle" (Magi 19).

Although rumors at the time suggested Bee and Wolfe were having an affair, unsurprisingly given Wolfe's reputation for womanizing with married women, a sexual relation seems unlikely. Bee frequently says in her correspondence that she has invited Wolfe to come to Lake George where he can write in peace, but that Wolfe declines because he cannot believe that her husband understands the nature of their friendship and is not jealous.

The friendship among the three remained intense for over a year, but eventually a cooling occurred, especially between Wolfe and Jelliffe. Wolfe was traveling and writing; his mother and his ex-mistress, Aline Bernstein, with whom he was trying to reconcile as friends, both disliked Bee; and Wolfe grew irritated over some of Bee's oddities. After she had helped him find an apartment in New York, move his furniture, and buy some supplies for it, she presented him with a bill for eight dollars and some cents. When Wolfe did not come through with the money, Bee brought it up again, a demand that Wolfe saw as petty. By the middle of 1936, Wolfe called Bee "a meddlesome female" and told her not to "bother" him again (Magi 43).

During a trial involving some manuscripts Wolfe had entrusted to a man named Muredach Dooher, who then attempted to sell them as his own possessions, Bee, who had been present at the exchange, offered to testify for Wolfe. Wolfe wrote his lawyer, Ralph Lum, that Bee was "a very impulsive woman, pretty high-geared emotionally, but very quick and intelligent. I do not know what kind of witness she would make, or whether it would be advisable to use her" (Jan. 29, 1938). Two days later, he continues, "Since you already know her and recognized the familiar marks of her personality in her letter there is no need of my saying anything further. I am never quite sure just when and where and in what direction Mrs. J. is going to explode, but I do think she is a whole-souled kind of person, who will go the whole hog, as we say in the South, for anything she believes in" (Feb. 1, 1938).

Bee did eventually testify and was evidently a compelling witness. She was especially proud of being able to demolish the implication by Dooher's lawyer that she and Wolfe were lovers: "The lawyer tried his damndest to sound like I MUST be sleeping with Tom. Well, I polished him off right well" (Magi 38).

Wolfe and Perkins also had a falling out when Wolfe decided in 1936 to break with Scribner's and hence with Perkins, his editor there. One reason was financial: Wolfe wanted larger royalty payments and resented the costs assessed him for galley corrections. He and Perkins also had quite different temperaments and ideologies. But Bee diagnosed the split in psychological terms, suggesting that Scribner's had become too much like a family for Wolfe, with Perkins playing the father role. Not only did that interaction revive for Wolfe, Bee thought, the family dynamics of his youth, but it was simply too constricting: the son needed to break away from the paternal figure and establish his own identity, a need that was compounded by critics who often suggested that much of Wolfe's success was due to Perkins' editing.

Bee, however, remained attached to both men, and she was devastated by Wolfe's death in 1938. The exciting and glorious interlude had lasted but a brief time. After the publication of *For Dear Life* and Wolfe's death two years later, Perkins and Bee remain friends and continue to meet, sometimes for lunch, but more often for drinks or tea, in New York, but much of their correspondence is taken up with matters relating to Bee's failed attempts to write a second book: Perkins always encouraging her, but also rejecting her subsequent manuscripts; Bee frustrated, complaining, hectoring, despairing.

For Dear Life seems to have been written in a sustained wave of emotion. Indeed, its rough edges suggest how quickly it was composed (and how closely its design, like the tempestuous currents within her marriage, replicates Bee's own temperament). The verve, candor, and brashness of the writing, its very spontaneous quality, are perhaps part of what makes it such a compelling read. Thus, at the same time Bee was finding relief in the company of Perkins and Wolfe from the drudgery of caring for a household or running a business, she was also in the midst of a most productive creative period. Locked away in her room at Lake George, allowing her memories to resurface, and putting them on paper for her receptive audience of Wolfe and Perkins, Bee had never been happier. If her husband was somewhat condescending about her work, or at least too preoccupied to pay much heed, she had two other encouraging opinions. By late 1936, the manuscript nearing completion, the matter of a title arose. Perkins referred to the novel as "Chin Up," deriving the phrase from the advice Belinda Dan's father had given her. Bee liked such titles as "Solidaire," "More Geese than Swan," "Heart's Desire," "Non Disputandum" (these last two from Eleanor Wylie's poems), or the more suggestive "Our Bed is Green." But finally, the title that stuck, which had been considered all along, was agreed to. On August 28, 1936, *For Dear Life* was published, and Bee's happiness reached its zenith.

It never reached that peak again. The congenial trio was split apart by Wolfe's rift with Perkins, by his distancing himself from Jelliffe, and, in 1938, irreparably by his death. Although Bee and Perkins continue as friends and correspondents, a different tone characterizes their friendship, especially as Bee attempts a second novel and short stories—all of which Perkins gently rejects. Her letters to Perkins describe her frustration over not finding the time to write, over the need to please Perkins, and over the necessity to cater to a public and to reviewers who preferred works avoiding the harsh truths of the world.

The pattern originates as early as January 1938 after Bee has sent Perkins a draft of a second novel. Perkins responds, "There is very much to praise in your novel, but I am afraid you have taken it apart and put it together too often. . . . I do not think, in spite of a great deal of talent shown in this manuscript, that it could be successfully published as it is . . . " (Jan. 31, 1938). In April, after Bee persists, he writes, "What I am afraid of is that having written this book as you have done, you could not extricate yourself from the present scheme. . . . It would almost have to be done afresh, it seems to me. . . . " (Apr. 15, 1938).

Bee answers in evident bafflement: "The point is that I can't tell exactly whether you really want me to work on the story or not. Sometimes I think you're too polite maybe to say straight out that you don't think its so hot; then sometimes I think you think me a scatterbrained nit wit who can't concentrate . . . Well, where am I? How can I tell? Believe me, what I did get done, I did against a thousand duties pushing and pulling me . . . . " (ca. Apr. 1938).

Her volatility surfaces two months later when, having reworked the book, she is faced again with Perkins' rejection: "Having read this book, I can't understand why you didn't throw the whole thing away! Your patience is overwhelming and wonderful. At the moment it nauseates me; it is banal and fatuous and stinks. Oh, you should have slapped me. What I'm going to do, I do not know. I can see so clearly what you meant. Whether or not I can salvage it, I don't know; I'll let it soak for a few days . . . . maybe in the Lake" (June 1938).

At one point, Perkins suggests that Bee, still drawing on her own experiences, though this time her professional ones, might abandon fiction and write a handbook for nurses. Bee responds, "What on earth d'you mean, handbooks? What should I tell them [nursing students], except where they can get the best lethal weapons, machine guns, pistols, knives, bombs, and poison gas? Thats all they need, plus the nerve to kick the whole business, imposed by MEN, right into the garbage can where it all belongs" (Dec. 1938).

And so the letters continue over the years, Perkins making tactful suggestions but ultimately rejecting all of Bee's manuscripts; Bee trying to please Perkins but unable to change her headlong writing style. As her own writing goes nowhere, she becomes more and more angry about those writers who do succeed: "I'm a nasty sour puss old hag. When I read this story about M[arcia] Davenport I hate her guts . . . So she works ten hours a day, huh? God I'm really glad Some writer has time to write but at the same time I think, I wish the bitch had to run a rooming house in town and do a mans job in the country, take care of the toilets, etc., and see the hell goddam how much she got written" (Feb. 1943).

By this time Smith Ely Jelliffe's age and ailments were beginning to tell, and for the next two years much of Bee's time was devoted to caring for her invalid husband. He had long suffered from cardiac arrhythmia with auricular flutter and fibrillations, from hearing loss, and from Paget's disease, and on September 25, 1945, he died of prostate cancer and the ensuing uremia at the Jelliffes' home on Lake George. Two years later, Maxwell Perkins died of pneumonia.

In 1953, Bee sold the home on West 56th Street in New York. The same year the Lake George home burned. She moved to the aptly named "Crossway Smoke Rise," outside of Butler, New Jersey with Elizabeth, her loyal housekeeper and friend. After ten restless years there (she wrote: "it is such a BEAUTIFUL place, but the % of jerks is too high" [Magi 95, fn. 19]), Bee was faced with the loss of Elizabeth, who became ill and returned to her birthplace in Wales; Jelliffe moved to Bronxville, New York to be near Laurie Grimm Sutton, the child of old friends who had also become something of the daughter she had never had.

Though she continued through all these years to try to write, in utter frustration at one point she burned most of what had she had written but which had never been accepted for publication. Only two of these stories—"My Mother-in-Law" and "Agnes Island"—appear to have escaped the two conflagrations: the fire that burned her Lake George home and the fire that Bee herself set to her manuscripts. They are published here for the first time.

"My Mother-in-Law," the slighter of the two, is an affectionate reminiscence about Smith Ely Jelliffe's mother, Susan E. Kitchell Jelliffe, as she discusses her life with her daughter-in-law. Smith Ely's name has been changed to Robert and Bee's to Deborah, but the names of the two other children who had survived childbirth remain unchanged: those of Smith Ely's older sister Sarah and his younger brother Arthur. The main thrust of the story is positive; the narrator praises her mother-in-law's energy, open-mindedness, and spirit of adventure. She also admires her mother-in-law's honesty in admitting that she loves her neglectful child more than she loves any of her more considerate children. That admission suggests an undercurrent of sadness as well in the tone of the story, both as the mother-in-law reflects on her age ("We think we're cheating time, but all the same, time is cheating us") and especially from the pain she feels after her youngest son, Arthur, has left home and for eighteen years failed to write: "For eighteen years," says the mother-in-law, "I never went to sleep at night without weeping and wondering where he was, if he was well, or sick. Oh! The anguish of the awful not knowing!"

Much more subtle and more carefully constructed is "Agnes Island." Although it is marred by several clichéd metaphors, especially near the beginning, it is certainly Bee's quietest and most delicate work. The motion of the story is supplied by the arrival at the lake home of Bee and her psychiatrist husband, Dr. Jerrold (the same name she has given Jelliffe in *For Dear Life*), of a woman whose husband and another man had just drowned while the three of them were swimming.[7] What startles and perplexes the narrator is the widow's seeming composure: she eats voraciously, shows little emotion, and even drops hints about a plaque that she admires. Near the end, she goes off with a friend, an older man who has arrived, and in whom the widow places complete confidence: "Mrs. Randolph looked back, laughing happily, confusedly, and said, 'Oh, goodbye!'"

But it is the narrator's own reaction which holds the reader's interest. It is not just her inability to understand Mrs. Randolph's apparent calm, for she knows that shock and grief take many forms. The narrator also seems disturbed at her perception that her own husband would react with the same efficiency and composure as Mrs. Randolph should the narrator die—a vague sentiment that leads to her own melancholy in the face of her continuing life. When Mrs. Randolph first arrives and comments on the beauty of the place, the narrator says, "Yes. At first I couldn't bear it." Soon she repeats the phrase, wondering this time "what it was she could not bear." So, too, the confidence that Mrs. Randolph has in the friend who comes to take charge baffles the narrator, for she has no such faith: "it is a mirage." The something that she cannot bear "constantly eluded her." And so she goes to bed, lying between cool sheets, wishing that she too could lie down and sleep in the water, as the two drowned men have done. Only then, she feels, will she escape the elusive search for what it is she cannot bear. The story ends beautifully: Mrs. Randolph's "face again came before her closed eyes, and her last struggle for the right word to describe it was, As though God has come. . . . Unable to further pursue intangibles, she slept."

7. One possible origin of this story in factual details is related by Bee Jelliffe in a letter to Karl Menninger (Sept. 1934): Smith Ely Jelliffe accidentally killed a man when his boat hit another boat, tossing an old man into the lake where he drowned.

Jelliffe's only other published work is a privately printed book, *The Story of a Lady* (1957), about Suzie, Bee's cat that lived with her for twenty-three years. She placed advertisements for it in national cat magazines ("Have you ever been owned by a cat?" was the tag line) and sent complimentary copies to a number of celebrities (one copy sent to Jimmy Stewart turned up at his estate sale in the late 1990s). She informs various friends that it has sold 350 copies, then 500, and then in typical Bee fashion 5,000 and even 8,000—surely rather extreme exaggerations.

Throughout this period she maintained her voluminous correspondence. Although Magi writes that these were "the quiet years" (79), her letters become increasingly hostile and eccentric. Always a sharp observer of politics and society and never one to moderate her opinions, Bee fulminates against the direction American politics is moving, and she herself moves further and further to the right. She writes Menninger, for example, "To me it is like all of life around us now, from the President [John F. Kennedy] down to the smallest creature trying to cheat his neighbor. We are a nation of phonies and that dark you May Have Noticed in our sky is the wings of the Chickens Coming Home to Roost. . . . I have fought in politics for 40 yrs and find it fascinating to observe a whole nation driven by unconscious compulsive suicide, and it sure likes [*sic*] we are going to get our wish. . . . I don't let any of this affect my kidneys . . . but I am aware. Recently I got 2 laughs . . . one trying to induce the Prs. [Kennedy] to build a New West Berlin; cheaper than a War . . . the drawback it introduces a faint humor, verboten in ANY Govt . . . the faces of the darling Communists—who we have fed, bred AND financed during the past 30 yrs—arriving one bright morning to find a To Let sign on Berlin. WE DIVIDED Germany, Korea and Viet Nam; I hope to live long enough to see someone divide the USA" (Oct. 25, 1961).

Only one last time, in 1976, after a nineteen-year hiatus, did Bee send a manuscript to Scribner's. Before she heard from them, Bee suffered a stroke. She spent the last two years and nine months of her life partially paralyzed and unable to speak, before dying on July 28, 1979 at the age of eighty-nine (Magi 80).

Bee's disposition, as she recognized and accepted, reflected wildly fluctuating emotions and moods—severe and lingering depressions, exultant and manic highs. In many ways, she did indeed enact the Horatio Alger model: a very poor girl from the most backward part of America who leaves to pursue an apparently successful life, marries a famous doctor, travels in Europe, socializes with rich, famous, and creative friends, and publishes a briefly acclaimed novel. Yet clearly the story is not the linear one that Alger repetitively described. Bee's own life is marbled with the complex interplay of triumph and failure, joy and frustration, love and betrayal that constitutes art. She clung tenaciously to her beliefs, as to those whom she loved. She hung on to them all "for dear life," dear in both senses—cherished but costly, for as she writes in *For Dear Life*, "[w]ith human beings one had constantly to be on the alert lest they annihilate you" (152).

Her life and her single successful work should not be, as the reviewer for the London *Observer* wrote, "the shooting star of a publishing season." Belinda Jelliffe and *For Dear Life* deserve to be rediscovered. Her novel—like her life—is a remarkable work, which merits a second look and a new appreciation for what it tells us about the myths by which we live and of how they resonate in our own time.

For Dear Life

Chapter 1

I've often read books about people who grew up in the country, and have been amazed to find that they all seemed to have been great philosophers. They saw, and felt, a great deal more than I had time to see or think or feel. They seem to have responded poetically to clouds floating in a blue sky, and rhapsodized on the music of summer rain. I often wonder if they had to go two miles in musical summer rain to milk, and to carry the full pail carefully home without getting rain mixed with it, and then walk three miles through stiff clinging mud, to school. I know that often in the heat of noonday, leaning on a hoe, looking across valleys at the mountains, so blue, so close, my only conscious thought was, "*How* can I ever get away from here? How can I get to where they have books, where I can be educated?" I worked hard, always waiting for something to happen to change things. There came a time when I knew I must make them happen; that no one would do anything about it for me. And I did.

I was born in a barn. A very big barn that had been built for the curing of tobacco, with a great deal of space in the top for hanging the frames for tobacco leaves. Of course there was no tobacco in it at that time, because, as I was told, the horses were in one side of it, and the family in the other. My father had moved from Marion County, North Carolina, to this place, called Leicester, and apparently the addition to the family was taken as a matter of course. My mother had had ten children, so I suppose it was nothing to get excited about, and no one did.

My father had started to build a little house but it was not finished enough to live in, so the family lived in the barn. I can't imagine how they all slept, for there were eight children and my father and mother; they must have slept on the floor on the hay. The horses lived right in the barn, which made a good beginning for me, for all my first five years were spent with all the animals common to a farm in North Carolina.

One of the most bitter tragedies of my first five years was the death of my black cat named Job, that I loved more than anything in the world. To see the head of my strong lithe shining black cat mowed clean off by a mowing machine was not to be borne, and I tried to sew it back with a needle and thread, weeping bitterly. For days I could not possibly believe that Job would not come back. He had always slept with me. Even though my mother went from one child to another, at night, making us put the animals out, I had always managed to hide Job. When I pulled out my trundle bed that night, I felt that all the world had fallen to bits, and I cried myself to sleep.

Finally the house was finished, and how it covered us all has never been clear in my mind. There were two rooms downstairs, one of which had a fireplace, and perhaps two upstairs; there was a lean-to kitchen. I remember very well that my sister Anne and I slept in a trundle bed that was pulled out at night and rolled back under the high bed during the day.

There was a fence of palings all along the front, extending past the barn, across the brook and reaching clear to the big stables. This fence was, in many places, completely covered by honeysuckle vines that smelled sweet. Inside the fence were many kinds of roses, lilacs, and jonquils, which we always called March Flowers. This little house, the first home I ever knew, was on the highroad about twenty miles west of Carleton. The nearest village was four miles away, and was only a small group of houses and a post office. We rarely got that far away from the farm, and to go to Carleton was an adventure that occurred only twice a year. The road was a narrow country road, dry and dusty in summer; in winter a river of red sticky clay that clung to the wagon wheels and horses hooves like glue. When the wagons settled deep in this clay, the horses would pull and strain and sweat; then my father would hitch his two strong mules to the wagon and pull it out.

My ancestors had apparently always been there in North Carolina. At least I have never heard of any one who ever knew any one in the family that ever heard of living in any other land. We seemed to just belong to this soil, always in the past, now and forever.

Pictures of my father show that he had been quite a handsome young man, very tall and straight, with reddish-brown hair that curled all over his head, and light brown eyes. What dreams he may have had, and what realizations! To have married so young, to have been so poor, and to have had so many children! When I first knew him he seemed an old man, although his hair was still brown and still curled, but he was getting bald. A tornado sort of man he was, with his enormous energy; always full of great plans, for improving the farm, for raising better crops. He was always buying new tools and machinery that were never used, but left to sit and rust. I know this worried my mother.

His impetuosity was always getting him into trouble. Once, in the night, he heard a sound in the cellar and got up impatiently to investigate. Seeing what he thought was a black and white cat, he gave it a blow with a piece of a slat. It defended itself right well. We had to bury his long drawers far away from the house, and we were sick from the odor for weeks. Wagons passing would drive as far away from the house as possible, the occupants holding their noses. What he said about that animal, "that spawn from Hell, that emissary of Satan; that living example of all that is bad on earth"! Never did he display such flexibility of profanity, such blasting, helpless rage. The odor lasted for months and his rage blazed continuously, only smouldering at times when he could forget it. One strong whiff was sufficient to start him off again.

Sometimes his zeal for perfection worked to his disadvantage. Once he raised the largest potatoes any of his neighbors had ever seen, and he was proud of them. He hitched his mules to a wagon and took them into Carleton to sell. My sister Lucille and I went with him, they sitting on the seat, I on the potatoes. He showed the buyer the potatoes with great pride, and when he saw the man scratch his head in perplexity my father just stared at him. "What's the matter with them potatoes?" he asked. "Too big," the buyer answered laconically. Father's jaw dropped; he looked stunned. "Too big?" he shouted, unbelievingly. The man explained that he sold them by the quart, and as one potato would more than fill a quart measure the women wouldn't buy them. When my father realized that the man really meant it, his face crumpled up like a baby ready to cry, and his lips worked. I saw the temper flash in his eyes for a moment, as he swore a couple of oaths. Then he turned away, crushed, and we began the long ride home. His back looked discouraged, pitiful. It made my heart ache for him, and at the same time I hated him for his helplessness. I suffered less when he flew into rages. I wept for his sense of futility and his incapacity to cope with things.

Once my father bought a cow; a very old and poor cow. We could, and did count every rib. He said, "Wait till she gets proper food and you'll see.

5

She's a nice cow." That night we put her in a pasture of rich grass and clover. Next morning she was dead, her body all swollen, her feet sticking up in a grotesque manner. I can see my father's face as he returned from the field, the muscles working, tears streaming from his eyes. I wondered if he wept for her suffering, or for her loss.

My brothers were grown-up men, and I cannot recall ever having actually seen the oldest one, Joseph. I did not know them at all, except as feet, or at most, knees. At first there seemed a great many grown-ups around, vague indefinite personalities with whom I had no communion. Edward, the second son, was very handsome and seemed the favored one, since he always went to school while Winfield, the youngest son, remained at home to do the hard work. I liked him the best of my brothers, although I never talked to him, nor knew him really.

My oldest sister, Sallie, was small. They said it was because being the oldest she had to carry the baby, and as there always was a baby, she never had time to grow up. Then there was Adelaide, blonde and handsome, and my favorite. Next came Lucille the beautiful one, Mary the modest, and Anne the spitfire, and me, Belinda. I remember my mother, a dour woman with whom I never talked, the day four of her children left home. Two brothers went to the Spanish war, Adelaide went to Boston and Lucille to Carleton. I remember thinking it was all very exciting, but I thought it odd that my mother didn't say good-by to any of them. She wasn't around at the time they left. Later I saw that she had gone down to the far pigpen and that her face was as white as chalk. It tore my heart so to see her, that I felt hatred of her. I couldn't bear that she should suffer and I disliked her for it. Why, I don't know.

My mother was a very silent woman. I think it was because she had been told long ago that she didn't know what she was talking about. One of the first clear memories of my father was his bitter denunciation of "Petticoat Government." Everything he didn't like about the government, he called petticoat government. I think that was his way of putting my mother in her place. So she got tired probably, and only one thing would stimulate her to argument, and that was politics. For years and years a bitter fight went on between a Republican mother and a Democrat father. Frequently it continued far into the night, with swearing and breaking of furniture. Whenever it started, it was going full force at the time I can first recall. The older ones had become accustomed to it and were not scared any more. If the argument got too violent and an unusual number of chairs or dishes were broken, we hustled off to bed to be out of the way. Finally it was settled by Mr. Bryan.

On a beautiful sunny day my father went with about a dozen other men into the village of Leicester, to hear Mr. Bryan speak. They rode off proudly and gayly; my mother said nothing, but I think she was disgusted. What happened I never knew, but along late in the afternoon they rode back, dirty and tired, raising clouds of dust. Father waved good-by to the men, rode into the yard and got down, calling to my mother, "Woman, come out!" My mother came to the door, stood looking at him, calm and expressionless. He took off his wide-brimmed black hat and said, "Woman, you're right and I'm wrong! I'll never vote a Democratic ticket again as long as I live." My mother just smiled. They never fought about politics again.

My father's father had owned a large farm and many slaves, but I think they were all opposed to slavery. I know my father was, and I remember hearing him say that he was glad the South had lost. My mother never talked much about the war, but I remember her saying once that her brother and two cousins were marched into a river and shot down before her own and her mother's eyes. There were many tales of friends hiding silver and valuables from the Yankees, and of how every animal was shot, leaving them destitute. When my father and mother got married, they didn't have one cent, and how they ever lived I don't know. Their first two babies died, and once she spoke of returning from burying the second, but she made no complaint. It was as though it was too deeply painful for ordinary words, and it tore my heart to think of such desolation and poverty, and they so young.

My father wore mutton-chop whiskers, shaving only a small part of his face. He rarely bathed, but all the children got thoroughly washed every Saturday night and as we went bare-foot we washed our feet every night. When my father bathed, a large tub of water was brought into the kitchen where he would splash about, making an enormous amount of noise and disorder. The floor would be more wet than he, and the entire household was disrupted for the whole day. So no one ever suggested that he take a bath. No one wished for such a calamity.

Besides being a farmer my father was a blacksmith, and all the children envied us the chance to blow the bellows which made a strong swishing sound as the air came through the coals. He kept shoes on all his own horses and mules, and most of the neighbors brought theirs to him. I loved intensely the life that went on around the forge,—the old farmers chewing and spitting tobacco juice; the jokes and the talk of all that went on in the county. But most of all I loved the forge after dusk, when the sparks flew up against the black night, the figures moving between, making huge shadows. I loved all the odors; the shavings from the horses hooves, coal smoke, rusty iron, negro sweat, the red-hot iron hammered into different shapes, and the peculiar acrid odor of the cooling iron as my father thrust it into a tub of water. He would put me on the back of a horse being shod, and I felt proud and more important than the children who had no father who was a blacksmith.

My father also made coffins for people who could not afford a store one. It was always exciting when he and mother worked on them at night, and we were allowed to help. He was very deft about it, bending the wood to fit the arms, nailing it securely. When finished, mother tacked white or black calico all around inside, making fancy pleats around the head. They looked very neat and comfortable. Sometimes they brought the body and we all helped to put it in, fixing the hands properly. My father would curse and swear, damning everything and everybody if he misplaced a tool. As he worked he would tell with great glee how the rats had gnawed the knuckles of old man Winters, and how frightened the women were when they saw something moving around under the sheet.

Once he made one for Old Joe Pomeroy, who was well over ninety-eight years old. Old Joe boasted that he would see a hundred, but when his mule which he had driven in an old buggy for time out of mind got frisky, throwing Old Joe out against a stone wall, every one thought he was done for, so his son, a boy of seventy odd, asked my father to go ahead and have the coffin ready. He worked late in the night, and mother made the inside all nice for him, and we all went to bed. But Old Joe fooled everybody, for next day he was feeling fine, and got up, showing no obvious ill effects from the accident. Indeed he lived for well over a year, and failed to make the hundred mark by a small margin. In the meantime the coffin was pushed under a bed, and served as a place for my cat to have her kittens. After several months mother got tired of having it under the bed, and had it carried out to the barn. Anne and I put straw in it, and we had three hens setting on eggs; they were just due to hatch when Old Joe had immediate use for it. We argued and pled for our hens, but were forced to remove them to other nests. They said Old Joe died from a mess of turnip greens. My father said, "Nonsense! Hell, no turnip greens that ever growed could kill Old Joe Pomeroy!"

My mother was quiet. She had black hair in loose waves around her face.

Her eyes were very blue. When I first knew her she was quite pleasant, though not a great talker. I never had a conversation with her in all the time I knew her and I have no idea what went on inside her. She worked hard, and had all her life. I heard her say once that she always had a baby at each end of the corn row; one she was nursing, and to one she gave a bacon rind to chew. She just laid them down and left them while she hoed corn. And the snakes didn't bite them.

She got up about five o'clock every day, made a fire in the stove, cooked breakfast for a crowd—for in addition to the family there were usually a number of men helping with the farm work—and after breakfast, she went to the fields with the family. At noon she carried the children home, cooked dinner and after resting for an hour, went back to the field. When it was quite dark, they came home, and she got supper for them all. After putting the children to bed and washing the dishes, she knitted or carded wool, for light diversion. She made all the cloth that was used for suits for my father and three tall sons. She wove all the cotton cloth that was used for sheets and bed ticks, and wove coverlets of intricate designs for the beds. For all these she first made the thread from raw materials, dyeing it to suit her taste. They were woven on a large loom. She would sit on a bench with her foot on a pedal, sending and returning a sort of bobbin to and fro with her hands. She was a very healthy woman, handsome with her blue eyes and black hair, and I think quite happy. I think she loved my father deeply, and loved working for her children. I know that they were married for at least forty years, and in all that time there was absolutely no other outside interest for either of them. Although I never saw the slightest display of affection either in actions or words, I know as I live, that they would not have understood any intimation that there might be any one else of importance to them in their personal lives. There was something irrevocable in their union;—it would be impossible for me to imagine one without the other.

My mother's sister May was married to a man named Lafayette Brooks, and my father hated him like poison. I don't know why, and no one ever said, but I think it was because Joseph, my oldest brother, spent too much time with Uncle Fate, and my father was jealous. Their house was on a hill, with tall pine trees in front which gave it a remote, cold, dignified look. It was painted white and looked spruce and well kept, while ours never had a coat of paint in all the years we lived in it. Our house looked poor and dingy, but probably that was because there were so many children. Aunt May didn't have any at all.

We always knew when the field next to Uncle Fate's was going to be plowed and planted, because the night before my father would get down his shotgun and spend hours cleaning it; taking it all apart and oiling it, whistling happily and licking his lips. This created tension in my mother and Aunt May. As a final disposal of Uncle Fate, my father would say scornfully, "The son of a bird dog! He's so stingy he gets out of bed to turn over to keep from wearin' out the sheets."

I never liked Aunt May, but we went to her house a lot because she gave us wonderful food. Everything grew so big and plentiful for them! My mother had the same trees, bushes and plants, but we never had such quantities as Aunt May. Even wild things like chestnuts, persimmons, and wild grapes, grew bigger for them.

We never had family reunions, with all the grown-ups at table, and the children under foot as other families seem to have had. Only Aunt May and Uncle Fate lived near us, and as my father hated Uncle Fate, they never visited us. The only two relations I ever did see were Uncle Dink, who came once a year, whose real name was Benajah, and Aunt Matilda.

Uncle Dink was my mother's youngest brother. I didn't know then, and I don't know now, why he was called Dink, when he had the beautiful name of Benajah. He was a tramp,—he lived nowhere for certain, and was never known to have worked. He walked hundreds of miles, visiting relatives, and I imagine, remaining until forced to move on either by hints or more forceful persuasion. He rarely remained long with us, because, I think, he was afraid of my father, although I never heard an unkind word between them. Still, Uncle Dink seemed uneasy.

Anne and I were delighted when he came, for he knew all sorts of games, and made toys for us. He told exciting stories, to none of which my father gave the slightest credence, showing his scorn of such talk by a snort, and spitting with great vigor dangerously near Uncle Dink.

Uncle Dink was slight and blond, with a reddish mustache. His city clothes, different from the home-made ones of my father and brothers, were worn threadbare, and there was something pathetic about him,—a forced jauntiness that made me want to cry. He probably was lazy, as my father said, but he made wonderful new games for us from the crudest material. My father's scorn, though wordless, was nonetheless scathing. My mother said nothing with great eloquence, but I loved it when Uncle Dink came.

The last time he came he did something that made my father so mad, so exasperated, that he yelled and swore at him, and I think poor Uncle Dink was too frightened ever to come again. What happened was that when we went to the field to transplant small cabbage plants, father told Uncle Dink to come too. He came, reluctantly. It was tedious, backbreaking work, and the sun was hot. A hole was made in the loose earth, with the finger, then water was poured into it; then the plant, carefully removed from hundreds on a flat basket, was placed in the hole, the dirt patted around it, and more water was poured around it. Then, one straightened one's back, took a breath, and the process was repeated interminably. Uncle Dink began bravely, but I thought to myself he would not be with us long. It made me very sad. Presently I saw him disappear into the bushes, but no one spoke, for we took it for granted he had gone on a perfectly natural errand, as we all did.

When he hadn't returned after a long time, father straightened his back, spit, and said, "Wonder what the Hell that lop-eared coon dog is doin' in the bushes so long?" We continued our work, and father went on, "Guess the lazy lout has left us; never thought he'd last long, the damned lazy son of a gun."

But at that moment Uncle Dink returned, and we all stared, for he came bearing a long branch, from which he had trimmed all the small twigs, leaving a fork at one end. We wondered what he was going to do with it, but silently he went to the basket for a plant, walked to the spot to plant it, and with the smooth end of the stick he made a hole, waited for me to pour water in, and quickly reversing the stick, daintily lifted the plant, and with the forked end, pushed it into the hole, patting the dirt around it so deftly that we were amazed. He worked all the morning that way, never bending his back once, while we continued our old-fashioned way, my father muttering audibly. After his dinner he went away. We never saw him again.

I have only one remembrance of Aunt Til, but that picture is clear. She sat on a keg of nails, in the store my father had at one time. Thin and white-faced, her gray hair smoothed back from her temples, she sat quiet in her flowered gray calico dress, her gnarled work-worn hands lying relaxed in her lap. She talked to me, and in her voice was something that made me feel that nothing could ever hurt her again,—she was apart, removed entirely from pain. She said, "You see, my child, I lost all my children, my seven sons, in the war, and my only daughter afterwards. My husband too was killed in the war, and I was left with my daughter and youngest son, who was too young to go, and I thought I would at least have him." She smiled at me gently, with no bitterness. "My daughter, she was not much bigger than you; died of starvation, for I had no food she could eat; her stomach was tender. Yes, her stomach was tender." She looked past me, moving her hands jerkily, in her lap. Pain held my heart, and I said, "What happened then?"

She slowly smoothed her hair back from her white forehead and said, "Well, you see child, after my husband and seven sons were killed, as I told you, I had my youngest. His name was Daniel,—he was a handsome boy, a lively one, and full of fun. He was always ready to laugh, but he was a good boy." Wishing to see him for myself, my cousin Daniel, I said, "Did he have brown or blue eyes, Aunt Til?" She smiled and said, "Why, Belinda, his eyes were a deep dark blue, and his hair a lovely brown, and he had beautiful white teeth. Yes, he was a handsome boy,—a nice boy." Her detachment exasperated me, for I wanted to weep, while she was as unconcerned as though she spoke of a stranger. But I wanted to know more of my cousin Dan. "Then did he go to War too?" I asked. Like a child, she rubbed the end of her nose and said, "Well, yes, he went. He wanted to go, and they took him when he was only seventeen. Seemed a pity, but he was wild to go." I was absorbed in her words, and her face, trying to understand how she could sit calmly, how she could bear to speak of it. I wanted for her to go on, and suddenly her small white face crumpled up, her lips twitched and she whimpered like a sick animal, and she put her hand out blindly toward nothing, and said, "His own officer shot him! He wasn't even killed in battle!" Fear and pain held me speechless,—there was no way I could say what was in my heart, and I went closer to her, laid my hands on hers, and looked straight into her faded blue eyes. "Why?" I asked. She raised her head and moved it hopelessly from side to side, smiled again and said, "Just a prank. His captain came home drunk one night, and just showing off, he shot Daniel. One of his comrades told me about it, later. So he didn't even die in battle!"

I laid my head in her lap and wept.

Of all the incidents of my childhood that I recall, the most far-reaching was of a conversation overheard. A neighbor had come to visit, and while she and my mother talked, I played on the floor, unnoticed. My mother was carding wool, and their words made a pleasant sound, until suddenly I became aware of what they were saying, and pretending to play, I listened. I heard my mother say, waving the card toward me, "I never take this one out; it's such an ugly child."

I can feel yet the tightening of something inside me, something that made breathing difficult,—the feeling of darkness and pain, almost of physically being torn. I was aware of a faint nausea, and feared I might be sick at my stomach. Sitting perfectly still, my only thought was that I must not let them know that I had heard, and that I must get away, quickly. Playing for a few moments, I couldn't bear it, and slipped out. Without reasoning, wanting to be alone, I went to a privy that stood near the barn, the door of which could be hooked on the inside.

Once inside, I let myself be sick. After that I sat still for a long time, and gradually out of a chaos of my mind, the words returned to me clearly, definitely. I heard them now with less nausea, and by repetition they became less painful. I could breathe more easily, even speak them aloud. I wanted to cry, but thought that I had no time,—that later I might. Just now I must take this apart, look at it and know what it meant. I had no hatred of my mother for saying it, but somewhere in me, not clearly defined, was a feeling of overwhelming sorrow that it should be so,—that she should have had a child so ugly.

After a long time I came out, and I went unnoticed to a room where the bureau was, and looking steadily in the mirror, I examined my face carefully. I had not thought about it before. I decided that my mother was right, and it became possible to accept the fact. But it has not been possible to forget the pain of the first realization. After that, saying nothing to anyone, I looked at my sisters, and it became increasingly plain to me that they were all the kind that my mother could easily take out, happily. The pain went away for long, long periods of time, but even now, if suddenly I feel that some one is looking at me, it is with difficulty that I do not turn to remove my face from their view, and always that sick feeling of nausea comes over me.

One of my first duties was to carry a great stone jug of water to the men working in the fields. The spring, which was near the kitchen, was always cold, and if I hurried, the stone jug kept it so. The men would wipe the sweat from their faces, and with a sort of toss with one hand lift the jug to their lips, and I could hear the water gurgle down their hot dry throats. I remember once my father and brothers were cutting wheat with scythes,—I can see their broad shoulders, and the muscles under their wet shirts. It was the tallest, heaviest wheat in the country, and farmers came to see it. I can see the work-hardened hands of my father, as he takes the pie my mother had sent out to them; the whiskers on his chin; the taut brown cords in his neck, as he tilts the water jug to his mouth, letting some of the water run carelessly down his chin, which he wipes hurriedly with the back of his hand.

I remember working in the tobacco fields. First came the careful plant-ing of tiny helpless plants from the hotbed. We watered them every evening after the sun went down, and when they began to grow, we hoed them. Over and over we hoed them, taking out all the weeds, turning the dirt over in the sun. Later still we wormed the tobacco. That was a trying job. The worms were green, with beautiful markings, and the real big ones had horns that at times were frightening. It was a question whether to pick them off and throw them against the ground, making a nauseating thud, bursting them open, or to crush them under one's bare feet. If you did that, they were likely to squish up between the toes, which was not pleasant. We probably got sick of both methods, and put them in small buckets. When the pail was full, we carried them to the end of the row and burned them. But they were hard to burn. If we buried them they crawled out again, unless they were put quite deep. Sometimes we drowned them, but I didn't care for any of this, really.

While we wormed the tobacco, we took off green shoots called suckers, that came out above the leaves, lessening their value. When the leaves reached a certain growth, they were pulled off, strung on a thread with a large needle, and swung on frames. Thousands of these were strung, and hung in the top of a curing barn, of which we had two. Standing under them, one could look up into the endless green leaves, heads down, with a conquered look. It made me sad, for I had seen them waving bravely, like banners, in the field.

There were long furnaces under the barns, and when the tobacco was hung, fires were lighted. These had to be watched all night, until the tobacco was cured, otherwise it might easily become too hot, or too cool, and all our work go for naught. It was exciting to see the fires at night, and to be allowed to go into the barn with my father, to read the thermometer. I can smell the peculiar odor of the tobacco as it changed from green leaves into soft, tough, yellow-brown tobacco. When finished, the frames were taken down and carried into the barn in which I had been born—a cider press now sat in the exact spot—and there the sorting was done. We sat at long tables, sorting the leaves according to size, color, and texture. These in turn were tied into bunches called hands. Finally they were laid in a large hogshead, in a circle, like the petals of a daisy. Anne and I tramped them down with our bare feet. These hogsheads were hauled into Carleton and sold. I think my father made some money on tobacco, but he spent it for machinery that was never used. He never drank, or smoked, and never looked upon any woman other than my mother in all his life. He just didn't have the money sense.

On rainy days my father would bring all his harness, which was called 'gears,' into the kitchen, spread them out on the floor, and proceed to mend them. With needle and waxed thread and leather thongs he sewed and whipped and patched the leather gears, collars, and saddles. When the mending was finished, he rubbed them with tallow, and the odor before the fire was horrible. Everyone who could left the house, but my mother had to walk around them while she cooked, and dared not speak, for at a word my father would start a tirade about how "a man hadn't any liberty under his own roof, by his own fireside! What in Hell is this goddamned world comin' to anways, when a man cain't do his own work in his own house?" (Spitting right and left the while.) "Why dang my skin, a decent god-fearin' man is bein' crushed by petticoat government!" This went on for hours.

One season of the year I remember happily. That was when we made molasses. After we had hoed the cane until it was grown, it was cut down, the stalks stripped of their leaves, and ground between two large stone cylinders. The juice ran out in pails, slightly green in color and almost tasteless. This was poured into boat-like vats under which fires were built. As the juice boiled it was stirred constantly until it reached a certain color and sweetness, which was molasses.

We always had a candy pull the last night of the run, and we were allowed to lick the vats until we were often ill from it. The grown-up young people cooked molasses in small pans until it became candy, which they pulled. Couples paired off, and with butter-greased hands, would take great gobs of this candy and pull it between them until it changed from almost black to a light gold. I didn't know then and I don't know now, where the black went nor where the gold came from.

We worked very hard, yet there was a definite freedom in our house. We never felt cramped or afraid. In spite of my father's swearing and hot temper, and my mother's silence, we were never afraid of them. I cannot explain this; I only know that it was so,—that we laughed a lot and were healthy and happy. I wanted always to go away, to live somewhere else, in a different world, but I was not unhappy about it all the time. We had heavenly times picking blueberries and we went on picnics in the fall, gathering great baskets of chestnuts and chinquapins. The chinquapins we cooked and strung on a thread, making necklaces of them, which we ate one at a time, for weeks.

Another joy was in long summer evenings when the negroes brought their banjoes and joined my father who played a violin. They played and sang together, and it was beautiful, but sad. For hours I lay on the grass watching the fireflies, looking up at the stars, aware of the odor of honey-suckles, and negroes; feeling the soft breeze of a Southern summer night. I wept to myself, not knowing why.

The most clear memory of these first years has returned to me often, and always at times of great distress and fear. On a clear moonlight night I lay with Anne in our trundle bed. Two older sisters were in the high bed a step above us, and my two older brothers were in the other big bed,—all of us in this small room. I lay awake, listening to them breathe; the breathing of each one was different, distinct. That of my older brother was somehow more definite, and it hurt me like a pain from afar. Through a window I could see the head of a young horse that was free to wander around at night; he passed and repassed the window, and frequently would throw up his head, tossing his mane, and would neigh, or make a bubbling sound as he blew his breath through his nostrils. The stillness of suspended death was with me, and a great sadness filled me. Since that night I have seen it all again and again; so clear, so vivid. I hear again the breathing of young people, and it seemed as though I were an old, old spirit then, and aware of more than I have ever been since. Was it an awareness in a child so small, of the transitoriness of all things, all strivings, all emotions, all loves and hates, and desires? Many times since then, sunk into despair, I have seen that horse's head, heard those deep-drawn breaths of youth, and sadness fills my heart. I do not know why.

There is much that I recall clearly of these first years, but mostly it is a mixture of odors, animals, vegetables, dirt, honeysuckles, pigs, apples, wheat, sweat, sun, clear cold water, smoke, and the soft breezes of a Southern night. All these are so closely knit that to separate them is impossible.

Chapter 2

There was one thing that happened on the farm that I could not bear. That was pig-killing time. Oh! The shrill frightened squeals they made! A sound accusing, asking for help, full of consummate awareness of annihilation! The completely unbearable fact was that every pig was a member of the family. But every fall it happened, and when it did, I went far away from the house, not to hear their squeals. Later I returned to help clean up and take care of the meat. After it was killed, the pig was scalded in a vat of boiling water to make the hair come off; then it was scraped with heavy knives, leaving the body white and smooth.

All the different parts of the pigs were used except the hair. I wonder why we didn't use that for something? There were smoked hams, salt pork, lean and fat slabs of bacon stored in the smokehouse for winter. We never bought any meat at all. The heads and feet were used for one kind of meatloaf, the liver and heart for another. The entrails were turned inside out and washed and used for making soap. Odd bits of fat were fried until crisp and mixed in batter for bread. This was delicious, and we loved it with fresh milk. It was called Chitling Bread.

We ate a great deal of corn bread, baked in an iron pan that sat upon three legs over a bed of hot coals. Coals also were piled on the lid, which was removed as necessary, by a long iron hook. Once my father returned from Greenville where he had sold his tobacco, with a loaf of "store bread." All the neighbors came to see it, for no one had ever seen bread bought in a store. No one liked it.

My mother canned blueberries, blackberries, strawberries and peaches, as well as many kinds of vegetables. Her cellar was well stocked with hundreds of cans, and many glass jars of jellies of all sorts, for the winter. Bags of dried apples and peaches sat along the wall, and strung from poles, yards of dried string beans, which we called Leather Britches, hung with red and yellow peppers. Sweet potatoes and white ones, and enormous yellow pumpkins were also kept in the cellar, while cabbages and turnips were holed up right in the garden. From hard dry corn we made hominy, by soaking it overnight in lye, removing the outer covering, then boiling it for a long time, then frying it in bacon fat. It was very tasty.

The preparation of the thread for weaving absorbed a great deal of time. Anne and I had to clean the wool, fresh clipped from sheep. This we did by many washings, made difficult by the fat in the wool, and the sickening odor. Burrs stuck so tight it was necessary to remove them hair-by-hair. Eventually it was clean, a soft creamy white, and my mother carded it into fluffy rolls. When she'd made hundreds of these rolls, she would spin them into thread. This work was saved for rainy days when she could not work in the fields or garden; in winter it was a continuous work, interspersed with the daily tasks. She spun these rolls on a high, large-wheeled spinning wheel, which made a most beautiful sound as the wheel went madly around, while she stepped forward, running the thread onto a bobbin, holding one tiny fluffy bit at the end, to which she attached the next roll. With her right hand she twirled the wheel, let the roll run through her left hand, stepping backwards all the time until the wool was drawn out into a long, long thread. Again she stepped forward, letting the thread wind on the spindle, endlessly. Eventually she had enormous balls of wool for knitting socks and stockings and for weaving cloth, called Linsey Woolsy. Gracefully, rhythmically, she spun her thread.

All our bed covers we made from scraps, fashioned into quite beautiful designs,—Kentucky Rose, The Tulip, Horn of Plenty, and Sunburst. All were named, and each quilt was referred to by name and their exact location was always known. When the top was finished, it was quilted. This was done on a frame, consisting of four long narrow pieces of wood, with a great many holes in them, for wooden pegs. This frame was let down from the ceiling on four ropes, one at each corner, by which it was drawn up at night. When the frame was adjusted, white material was stretched taut, and fastened to the frame. This was covered with smoothly spread cotton batting. Then the top with the gay design was spread over it, the entire thing being whipped firmly to the frame. Now it was ready to be quilted.

The frame was let down to a height comfortable for a person sitting in a plain wooden chair, and the person quilting reached the left hand under and the right hand over, as far as possible, then sewed in a fanlike direction, toward the outer edge. Many quilted in very intricate designs, but there was no time for that in our family, so all ours were done in the simple way. The rows of sewing were one inch apart.

When neighbors came to visit, they brought their own needle and thimble, and they quilted while they visited. They also dipped their snuff. Most of them did this with a small stick with a chewed end, like a brush, of a tree called black gum, or a root called Beggar Louse. They took the stick from their mouth, swabbed it around in a small round tin box until as much snuff as possible adhered to the chewed end, then placed it in their mouth. Others preferred a method which consisted of catching the lower lip firmly between thumb and finger, pulling it out from the teeth, deftly pouring directly from the round box all the lip would hold, then firmly closing the lips. This gave them a grotesque expression. As soon as the snuff became wet, they could continue their conversation, albeit with some impediment. When they wished to spit, they left the frame and went either to the fireplace or to the front door,—all but Granny Cole. She was so old, she was allowed a small pail, but as her eyesight was not good, she frequently missed it. She was over ninety, but very spry, and quick to take offense. She was part Indian, and was treated with great deference by every one. Her rows of quilting often got mixed and ran crisscross, but no one spoke of it, and whenever we noticed a particularly crooked place, we laughed and said, "There's Granny Cole's patch." Her face was brown, and wrinkled like a persimmon; she had no hair, a fact she concealed by wearing a shawl over her head.

Threshing time was exciting. The threshing machine went from farm to farm, and the neighbors with it, helping each other so that they might all get their grain in when it was just ripe, and before the rain came. The loud whirring it made could be heard at a great distance, and clouds of chaff and dust rose up around it. The golden straw was made into stacks, and the wheat put into bags. At threshing time we carried all the straw ticks from the beds into the field, to empty and refill with new golden straw. They were rough at first, especially if we carelessly left a few briars, but they smelled wonderful. They were not uncomfortable, but the grown-ups had feather beds on top of the straw ticks. We lay on the straw, without sheets, with quilts over us, but everything was always clean in our house.

Once a family moved into a house across the road from our stable. I cannot recall their faces, yet two things connected with them have always remained clear in my mind. One was that the first day they moved in, some one fastened a ribbon to the top of a window; a blue ribbon, that fluttered in the wind. I wondered who put it there, and why? How could any one be so careless about a ribbon? I had never had one, and I thought that if I ever did I could never leave it out in the wind and rain. I have always seen that blue ribbon fluttering in the wind.

The other was my agony when we were told that the oldest girl was blind. I had never seen or heard of a person being blind and I set out to discover how a blind person would feel. I shut my eyes, forcing myself to imagine that I was blind, until I felt sick and faint, but it seemed that I could never really know how it was to be blind. Always, since that time, I can feel again that inability really to know, of myself, what it would be to be blind, or beautiful, or black, or lame; that feeling of helplessness at not being able actually to know things that belong to another.

One of our neighbors was an old negro with a white wife called Auntie Prim. If this sounds unlike the South, I can only say that is the way it was, and that they had been married so long no one alive remembered when any other state of affairs had obtained. They lived mostly off their vegetable garden, and odd jobs Uncle Ikie got to do. I loved them, especially Uncle Ikie. He would carry me easily, and sing negro songs to me, and I sat on his lap hours on end, while he told me stories. He had a ring of snow-white hair around his bald head, and was as black as tar. Their poor shanty always had flowers, and they had chickens, and cats. They were happy.

Once a month was a big wash day, when almost every movable object was scrubbed with the liquid soap my mother made. A big black iron pot on a crane was used for boiling the clothes, and the smoke curled up, blowing in one's eyes. There was a big wooden block on which the clothes were beaten with a wooden paddle, after they had been wet, and soaped. That removed the dirt. Every line was filled and all open spaces covered with clothes laid in the sun to bleach; sheets were spread over the lilac bushes and the rose vines. I loved sitting under the lilac bushes, under the sheets; it was not shade, nor sun. A heavenly light.

While I was still very small, my sister Adelaide had packed her few clothes, and walked the twenty-five miles into Carleton, where she had got a job, and very soon managed to enter a boarding school known as the Pierson School. I was too young to know her at this time, but subsequent events led me to feel that she was ambitious to better herself, and made this break to achieve her aims. She remained in school for two years, but an unhappy incident made it necessary for her to leave, giving up her hard-won place to Lucille. This is what happened.

My father was away, and my mother also went to visit and spend the night; a most unusual occurrence. Lucille, being the oldest girl, was left in charge of us all. But for some reason she herself decided to spend the night with a friend. Nothing happened to disturb us, but when mother returned and found what Lucille had done, she became very angry. Although she had never beaten any of us with a stick, we were afraid of what she might do to Lucille, and felt in our bones that no good would come of it all. When Lucille returned mother was prepared, and with a heavy stick she struck Lucille over the head and shoulders, horribly. Lucille howled with terror, running through the house like a desperate animal. Anne and I hid, for we didn't want to get beaten too. It was ghastly, and made me sick with fear and hate. Even nature seemed revolted, for just as the sun was going down, the sky became violent in color, like in Bible pictures I had seen. I heard Lucille screaming in fear and pain, and I stood tight up against the chimney outside, watching the wild colors in the sky, and the dark clouds hurrying before a wind. Suddenly it became quite dark, and huge rain-drops came hurtling down; I crept into my trundle bed and hid under the quilt, weeping with shame and sorrow for us all. There were ominous re-verberations of thunder, and sharp flashes of lightning. After a while the house became quiet and Anne crept in with me. For some unknown reason I could not speak to her, and I hated Lucille for having brought it all about, and my mother for striking her. We lay quiet, and slept.

Later in the night we were awakened by loud voices and excited argu-ment. We listened, and knew from what we heard that Lucille had run away, and that mother was worried. She sent Winfield to Aunt May's, and he had returned to say that she had not been there at all. I heard him say, "You had no business to strike her like that. If any harm comes to her, it is your fault." Although I am unable to recall the proper sequence of events, I know that Lucille came back, for I remember the exciting stories she told us; of how she had walked ten miles in the dark, through deep woods, and when she was tired, knocked at the door of a house near the road, and they had fed her and put her to bed. She made us believe that she had enjoyed it, but I felt it was a brave thing to walk all that distance in the dark. The result was that Adelaide left school, and Lucille was put in her place. Adelaide got a job as nurse to a woman who was ill, and went to Boston with her.

Soon we moved to another town, called Weaverton, where everything changed, and nothing changed. There was in me already a definite desire to · get away, to some place where there were books, and time to read them, though I told no one what I hoped. I planned to wait until I was at least ten years old; then I, too, would run away, and not come back, as Lucille had.

Chapter 3

My oldest sister, Sallie, went to visit a friend in another county, and the friend, knowing how poor we were, figured that it would be a good thing if she could find a husband for her. There happened to be an old man in the neighborhood, whose wife had died, and the friend, if she was a friend, had them meet. Right away in no time at all, he asked Sallie to marry him, and she did. He was old, with whiskers, and not many teeth, and he walked with a limp,—probably a memento of the Battle of Bull Run, or maybe the War of 1812. But he was a Deacon in the Church and had a home, a pig, a cow, and a horse, so I suppose Sallie thought it was a wonderful thing to marry him. So there you are. With her youth, her humor, and her warm heart, she married him, and was, at least at first, grateful for a home. She made him a good wife for twenty years, and in all that time called him Mr. Bonham. His first name was John, but he was Mister Bonham to her. I think it would have been better if she'd died, but probably I'm wrong. She drove to church with him every Sunday in a buggy on high wheels, behind an old brown horse, and sang doleful Methodist hymns; she knelt on the bare wooden floor in their kitchen, every night for all those years, while he offered up the evening prayer. This prayer never varied by jot nor tittle, in all the years he said it. What power stayed her hand? What kept her from recourse to a sharp hatchet, or perchance a carving knife? Or even an herb . . . there were some that grew wild around, that could have brewed a strange potion. Perhaps her senses were dulled through the years, but I doubt it, for Adelaide told me many years later, how Sallie came into Carleton after Mr. Bonham had died, and had her hair washed and waved and her nails manicured for the first time in all her life. She was then forty-five, and when she bought herself a gray dress and hat and shoes, Adelaide said that she looked lovely. That was her first day of freedom in twenty years, for Mr. Bonham would never let her leave home. Hearing all this made my heart ache, that a life so grim could have been lived by one with such a gift for laughter, and warmth and a great capacity for happiness within her. But after all, who finds the high white flame of living, and carries it? We all begin it with a divine assurance that all will be beautiful and good, and end in compromises of all kinds. How to save our souls at all, to prevent a gray drabness of apathy from submerging us; to fight for the satisfying light, and the glory that should be ours!

She gave all of her youth, her bright light, her unbound energy and her absolute trust to that old man for twenty years, and he tried to crush her spirit. I don't believe he did, because of the gray dress and the manicure. He left her his farm, with the proviso that she did not marry again; she got around that neatly with the help of a lawyer, and she did marry again. Perhaps a slave misses the chains. But all this was much later, and I was, in the meantime, involved in fighting my own private battles against the grim spectre of mediocrity and stupidity.

Mr. Bonham assumed a fatherly attitude when he first came to our house, tossed me to his shoulder, and skipped about, like an old goat! Had he suspected my thoughts at that moment, he would have dropped me like a viper. He kissed me, with his awful whiskers—and he chewed tobacco— but I neatly avoided that after the first encounter. All my thoughts concerning that old man I kept to myself, even then, for I sensed that there was nothing to be done about it. Besides, no one asked me.

Mr. Bonham lived about twenty miles from us, and it was following a visit my father paid them that he began talking of a new place. The next thing I recall was that he had sold the farm, and bought one from a man named Zeb Hall, who sold it because he was taking his family west, to Oklahoma. This farm was near to Sallie, and on the adjoining farm, Zeb Hall left his father, Lamson Hall, and his wife Lydia, whom we came to know very well. They were a nice old couple, although there was a coolness toward Lydia, who was a second wife, because she and Mr. Hall had lived in sin thirty years before. This was a religious community and such things are not readily forgotten.

The farm father bought had a big water mill on it, so he became a miller. Farmers brought their grain to be ground into meal or flour, for which they gave a percentage for the grinding. I loved the smell of the mill and the two huge flat stones that revolved, one upon the other, crushing the grain, and the way the flour was sent along through sieve after sieve, until all the bran was sifted out. The whole building vibrated when it was running, for the machinery made a loud whirring sound. Fine white dust from the flour filled the air. It settled on the wide black hat my father wore, giving him an odd look.

The mill was engrossing, and Anne and I spent weeks exploring every nook and cranny inside and out. We waded clear to the head of the mill-race, a wooden trough green with moss, that deflected sufficient water from the main brook, carried it swiftly down, emptying it into the great wooden buckets in the wheel, to turn it. This huge wheel went round by reason of the water poured into the buckets, which pulled the wheel down by their weight; as the buckets at the bottom emptied, the ones at the top were filled, so that it turned constantly, ponderously, rhythmically. The water splashed out, making a cool sound, and forming a deep dark pool. Willows dipped into it along one side, and the other was covered with rhododen-drons and small shrubs which, a few yards from the edge, became quite tall trees. On hot days we spent hours with most of our clothes on the bank, wading up and down this brook and as far into the pool as we dared to go. The mill was the most exciting thing that had ever happened to us.

All around the mill were thousands of rhododendrons, pink and white and purple ones, in great masses, like clouds that had fallen right down on the pool, and dogwood, white as snow, and azaleas, yellow, red, and pink, in great profusion everywhere. Along the millrace, in cool damp places we found great beds of dainty yellow lady slippers, and heavier, larger purple ones, that had a more pungent odor. There were great spaces covered with violets and small yellow flowers called sink field; and many tiny grasses, all bearing delicate beautiful blooms. In spite of this close association with such richness of color and form, I did not learn then—I have not learned since—to look upon such phenomena casually. The beauty they gave so proudly induced in me a sadness so poignant that I hid myself and wept. Perhaps it is a too keen memory of those years with great beauty that makes it impossible for me to speak at all when confronted by the complete thing of beauty, either in a flower, animal, or tree. "Aren't they charming?" is an icy wind to me; I look and listen, too stunned by the aplomb, to answer.

The house we lived in on this farm was very well made, partly of hand-hewn logs, partly of wood added in small rooms at one side. It had a good chimney and generous fireplace. Only the living room had any upstairs, but the family was much smaller now, and we had left the trundle bed behind us, for now Anne and I had a real bed. Adelaide sent us a most amazing article, a folding bed,—one that could be pulled down at night, and when closed, looked like a wardrobe. No one had ever heard of such a thing, and every one came to see it. The bed placed us socially,—that and my mother's chickens, called Cochin China, were our only claims to superiority.

The nicest thing about the place was that it had two tall trees at the side, called aspens. The bodies were silvery gray and the branches a green-gray; the leaves were small, and trembled in the most delicate manner in the breeze. One day, with no discussion whatever, my father and Winfield cut them down. We were aghast, angry, but there was nothing to say. It was done before I knew it, or I would have fought to the death for them. They cut them off about fourteen feet above the ground, using them to support a woodshed. As long as we lived in that house I hated thinking of those trees, and the way the leaves trembled, making a sound almost of water. I hated my father for it, and could not speak.

Our house was a mile from the mill, and the pasture where we kept the cows was further on past the mill, across the brook and up a steep hill through deep dark woods. At the gate we had salt boxes, and we brought meal, to induce the cows to come at milking time. Often they would not come, and we spent hours hunting them; this we hated, for we had so far to walk to school. In the summer we had time to stop at the mill, and visit Lydia Hall, who usually gave us cookies. But when summer was over, it was more difficult for us. Then we had to hurry; no dawdling. We hurried because we were driven by a lust for education. What matter that with all our struggles, and strivings and clutchings we achieved nothing of our aims? We didn't know then that it was futile, and our ambition drove us on.

We had no books in our house, and no one we knew had any. In all the accounts I have since read of the youth of country people, they seem to have had a most remarkable list of books to read. Usually they were the property of some ancestor, or failing that source, they were left by stray mysterious visitors. We had no books except the Bible and no one read that but my mother. Once I did borrow a book from a girl who lived near us; a book of bloodcurdling romance called *A Mad Love*. Unfortunately it had a millrace, not unlike ours, and the hero, in a fit of mad love one moonlight night, drowned his true love in the race. This disturbed me, and for a few nights I was afraid to come home by the millrace, but soon I forgot all about it. Once Anne and I got a sufficient number of subscribers to a local paper, to get a book. They were big-hearted, and even allowed us to choose from a list of twenty. We considered the titles carefully, compromising on the one Anne wanted, a cheerful little classic entitled *He Fell in Love with His Wife*. I never read enough of it to find out why he should have done anything so naïve.

In those days I believed in God, picturing Him as a tall, emaciated old gentleman with a flowing white beard, who thought up an astounding number of rules and sat up nights to catch us breaking them, for which we burned in Hell Fire forever. I believed that if one prayed, believing, one's prayers would be answered. My prayer was simple, easy to remember, and should have proved easy to answer. It was, "Please God, send me some books." If I'd had the slightest idea that my prayers were to be answered so completely, so generously, albeit a little late, I would have scanned my lines more carefully, and given more thought to my request. It would not have been for books. But that's what I wanted then, above all things; books and time to read them. At that time, I thought there were not many books in the world, and I knew that I could soon read them all if I could only get at them. That was my firm intention; to read all the books in the world, and to know everything in them. How one's desires change with the passing of the years!

We worked on the farm all summer, and milked the cows, and explored the country, getting to know every one for miles around. There was a family near us named Rogers. There were five children, all of whom were addicted to fits except Annie, a tall blond girl. People had become accustomed to their ailment, for one could never know when one of them would fall down in a fit and foam at the mouth. One could only straighten them out and place something in their mouth to prevent them biting their tongue.

Annie and my sister Adelaide had been good friends, but now their lives lay far apart. Annie married a tall, thin, precise, ministerial-looking old man named Professor Jamieson. Every one thought it very kind of him to marry Annie, on account of the fits; they thought she had done very well for herself.

Annie and the Professor lived in a dismal little wooden house on the main road into the village of Weaverton. It had a few straggling flowers, mostly plants my mother gave Annie, but it never looked cheerful. Annie was quiet, always smiling in a dreamy, detached way; a little sad-looking. I liked her and talked to her about how much I wanted to go to school. She was truly sympathetic and encouraged me, saying that if I went to the village school for a few years, perhaps I could get to Pierson School, where Adelaide had gone. She told me once that the Professor didn't allow her enough to eat, and that he was very strict with her. He was a cold-looking man with a sour expression, and I was afraid of him. I loved being with Annie, for she understood my longing to get away, but with the farm work, and the cows, I didn't have much time for talk. Just before school started I hurried over to see her, to gather hope from her.

It was a lovely sunny afternoon, and I felt as I hurried along that perhaps things would work out for me. The house was curiously quiet, and when I called to her, I got no answer. The silence was inimical, and I was afraid of I knew not what. Going in, I called again, and receiving no answer, I went through to the kitchen. There was Annie, dangling from a rope over the rafter. She had hanged herself. Terrified, I ran to the nearest house for help, and some one got a doctor from Weaverton; but Annie had been dead for hours. I felt sick, horrified, and thought that maybe Annie hadn't done so well for herself, in marrying the Professor. She was buried, and I felt that my only friend was dead.

Another family living near us was named Renno. There were three daughters and a son. Like us, they were poor farmers, and the oldest daughter, Ella, was getting to be an old maid. My father thought it a pity, and taking a fancy to Ella, he sent for a rich farmer living near Leicester. His name was Bassett; he was a widower with four daughters. He came, at my father's suggestion, and proposed, and he and Ella were married before you could say scat. Ella showed her appreciation by presenting Mr. Bassett with four sons, in quick succession.

The second daughter was strikingly good-looking, in a healthy country-girl way. She married the richest bachelor in the county, and was considered to have made a wonderful catch. He was a stout florid man with a black mustache who wore city clothes. There were whispers that I didn't quite understand; something about his health, and the life he had led, which made him not such a bargain in spite of his big farm and prancing horses. A year later Lina had a baby girl, who was weak and not expected to live. I heard people say, as they nodded with a sly satisfaction, "Well, what do you expect?" When I went to see the baby, I could hardly recognize Lina. She was drawn and yellow, old-looking. She had been such a glowing, vibrant girl. The baby died. I thought to myself that she hadn't done so well in marrying, either.

The third daughter, named Doris, was slender and of a pale, delicate loveliness, with gentle manners, blue eyes and brown hair. She had a sweet young laugh, and I thought her the most beautiful girl I had ever seen, except my sister Lucille. I don't know how Doris ever met the man she married, as he was the depot agent in Weaverton, and Doris had never been on a train in her life. But meet and marry him she did. He was an Englishman, named William St. George Cartwright. Whatever misgivings Doris may have had concerning the fact that he was a widower already blessed with six children, were no doubt amply offset by his handsome appearance, charming manners, and obvious superiority to the farmers she knew.

Through visiting Doris I came to know the Cartwright children, and soon to realize that they were important to me and my own struggles. There were two sons, Sidney and Maurice, and four daughters, Maud, Charlotte, Diana, and Etienne. Maud became my best friend. The boys I never knew, for they were much too grown up to waste time on children my age, and the two youngest I knew only as babies. Maud and Charlotte were near and dear to me for a long time.

They lived in quite a large white house in the village, furnished with what to me then seemed wonderful things. Maud told me that everything they had came from their mother, whose family was very wealthy; that her mother had been disowned for marrying Mr. Cartwright, who was the black sheep of a family beneath her mother's family. All this thrilled me, as did all the descriptions of her mother, whose portrait hung by a casual nail in the living room. Maud knew England only from her mother, as they had never been back after her mother had eloped with her father.

The Cartwright household was a continual turmoil. There was always an emotional crisis because they were passionate in their hates and their loves. The furniture, which had at one time been beautiful, was broken; silver of great age was bent, broken, and some lost altogether. In their battles they threw anything they could lift; if things were broken, they did not care. At first their ways astonished me, but later I understood, or at least loved them no matter what they did. They had a grand piano, the first I had ever seen, and Maud played beautifully, Charlotte not so well.

Maurice, the oldest boy, was morose, taciturn and bitterly scornful of us. But Maud adored him, and even though they fought, they also spent hours playing together, he on a violin, she at the piano. If I came in when they were playing, they displayed no awareness of me, and I sat still as a mouse, because I loved hearing them and seeing them,—he with a scowling, unhappy face, angry and pained, she with her black hair over her shoulders. They were people from another world, a world I could only imagine and I clutched at everything they said or did, joyously, eagerly.

They were possessed of an amazing unawareness of their environment;

as though they were so immersed with their personal thoughts and feelings as to preclude that of the material or practical that passed around them, unnoticed. They never remembered or recalled past fights; they never sulked. As soon as they had exploded and expended their wrath, it was finished. Immediately they were passionately interested together. Into this bedlam came Doris, a quiet country girl, and considering that they were, if possible, more strange to her than to me, she adjusted herself remarkably. Mr. Cartwright treated her with charming courtesy; the children accepted her with the same unawareness of environment, as part of the family. When within the year she had a little girl, they took it as a matter of course, and were lovely to her.

Their mother had died when Etienne was six months old, and since that time, Charlotte had assumed entire care of her. Maud looked after Diana. Many battles were due to the scarcity of clothes for the babies, and the one who got there first naturally got the choice of clothes. In their rage they would throw things right over the heads of the babies, and I was afraid they might strike them, but they never did. No matter how mad they were, or what they said, they were always kind and sweet to those two babies. The fights ended as quickly as begun and they would each sit quietly putting stockings, petticoats, and dresses on the babies, talking to them with all the mother love in the world. Maud would stand her Diana up and say, "Look, Darling! I'm finished first, and my baby is the most beautiful in the world!" Charlotte, finishing the last safety pin would squint speculatively at Diana and back to Etienne, and say, "No, love. Not so beautiful as my Etienne," and the fight would begin again. The little girls seemed accustomed to it, and rarely cried.

Through this pandemonium which was his home, serene, detached and suave, strode William St. George Cartwright. His attitude toward his children was one of deference and humorous kindness tinged with incredulity. If the battle became too noisy when he was playing the piano, which he did often and well, he would stop and say in his English way, "I say, darlings! By Jove, you *are* a noisy lot! Couldn't you manage to conduct your slight disagreements with more regard for my shattered nerves?" The whole affair would end in shouts of laughter, and peace reign for hours. The children adored their father.

The work on the farm kept Anne and me busy, now that Winfield was away part of the time. Father had only us to help him, and we hoed and gathered in the crops, anxiously awaiting the day when we could start to school. We were excited and frightened about it, because we had never been to school in a village, and were afraid we might be laughed at. We put on shoes and stockings for the first time; before that we'd worn them only to church, and even then we had carried them until nearly there, and took them off as soon as we got well away, carrying them home again.

My father must have known that we felt shy, although he said nothing about it until we were ready to go. Then he said, "I'm goin' with you." We'd got up early before daylight to milk the cows, and hurried home, eaten a bite of breakfast and put on our best clothes. We were ready by half past seven, and as we went across the fields, to save about a mile from the main road, everything was damp with dew, and still. Fall flowers were in bloom all over the fields, and along our path. Blue asters and yellow goldenrod were in great clusters everywhere, and a few leaves were already turned. We saw the rays of the sun stretched out ahead of us, while we were still in the cool damp shade of the pines. There was something inexpressibly sad in the morning light; the whole scene was imprinted on my mind complete, but I can't recall any conversation except my father saying, "No matter what happens, children, just keep your chin up!" He went with us right up to the schoolhouse, and left us to face it alone. I don't remember a single thing about that day except the walk through the new morning light, the twittering of birds and the cawing of a crow in the distance.

Anne and I went all that fall and winter to school, working on the farm in the evenings after milking the cows, and on Saturdays and Sundays. We hurried so in the morning that we had no time for breakfast, and as no one fixed a lunch for us, we just went without any, and often were very hungry. We lived on wild grapes and chinquapins and apples, that grew along the road; the tall persimmon trees were a blessing, for after the frost came, the fruit fell on the ground, all wrinkled, and was delicious. I can see their peculiar color and savor their individual flavor; not a bit like the large golden persimmons shown in the markets of New York. Drawn by the fact that they were called persimmons, I bought one once, and their entire lack of similarity carried me back to those days when we ate so many of them, and the biting sweet taste made perfect by the frost. Maybe people are like that; not so good until they have been bitten by the frost of adversity.

In spite of the fruit which we ate hurriedly, I was often hungry, and when the other children opened their lunch boxes, we pretended that we did not bring lunch because we didn't care for it, preferring to wait until our supper at night. There was a grocery store in the village that had great barrels of brown sugar standing open. I often stole fistfuls and devoured it as quickly as possible; also small bits of cheese or anything lying around loose. Anne was of more noble fibre, and would have died before doing anything like that.

A number of girls lived on the road toward our farm,—Missouri Wells, Carrie Pittman, Jane Wilcox,—and we usually left school together; but as they liked to linger and giggle and talk to the boys, and we had to hurry home, we soon parted. As soon as we got home, we took off our good clothes, and put on some old dress, making haste toward the pasture. The first pint of milk I always drank, and it was heavenly, after being hungry all day; and in the morning too I drank all I could manage, so that with the fruit and nuts, I think we had a well-balanced diet at that. When we got home with the milk and strained it into stone crocks, washed the pails and ate our supper, we studied our lessons. This we did in the kitchen which was the general sitting room where mother and father sat; usually my mother carded wool or knitted, and my father read or argued. As we had only one oil lamp, it was difficult to concentrate on our lessons. And my father would remove his shoes, and walk up and down, and around, on the rough wooden floor in his woollen socks. This made a soundless sound, like a husky whisper, a delicate, sickening sound, that made me grow cold with a nauseating hate for him.

We gave all our spare time to the farm, but at that, there were some days when we had to remain at home. Oh! Those horrible mornings when we had to go to the fields instead of school! How we hated it! But looking back now, it wouldn't have mattered much, as we learned nothing that in any way touched the reality of our lives. I was especially good in Latin, and loved the sonority of the words, but any benefit from that has been completely concealed from me.

Anne was difficult to live with, and we fought like cat and dog, whenever we had time. If we'd had more time, we'd have had more fights. Often I longed to take one afternoon off and to have one grand fight. She had developed into a slender girl with a most alluring figure, which was thoroughly appreciated by the boys; she had beautiful hands and feet, large white teeth, and hair of a peculiar crinkly kind; a nasty disposition and an extraordinary mastery of mathematics. That was one reason why I hated her, for the simple statement that two and two made four completely stunned me. I couldn't understand why it might not make five. She and I never discussed personal plans or hopes; we kept our thoughts to ourselves.

It was in this school that I had my first boyfriend. All the girls had boy-friends, but Anne and I were much too busy for such amusements, but this boy chose me, and was serious and consistent in his devotion. His name was Kingsland Mears, but every one called him King. His father was one of the important men in the village, and had many trades. He was a minister, a dentist, a lawyer, an insurance agent, a real estate agent and a justice of the peace. From these occupations he had acquired a good bit of property, and held himself above the common herd, considering himself a leader in the village. In the matter of reproduction he was completely justified in his assumption. He held to the theory that every man should plant every seed which God gave him, and in practicing what he preached, he had, with the aid of two wives, presented to the community twenty-two children. He served his God well.

Kingsland was the fourteenth, and was thirteen when we met. He was a handsome boy with dark red hair in thick waves, dark brown eyes and white teeth. His skin was brown and healthy and he was large for his age, well built even then. His father was not pleased to have his son calling on a farmer's daughter but we were children and no one paid attention to us. King's oldest sister, Sophrina, was the principal of the school. She was about forty, tall, dark and slender, with beautiful features. She was dignified, ex-pected and received respect from both pupils and teachers and from every one in the village as well. I didn't see much of her as she taught only the seniors, but I admired her tremendously and hoped some day to know as much as she.

I was teased about Kingsland, but after a few months every one forgot all about it except his father. He was aware of it, and frequently pointed out to King the foolishness of wasting his time on a stupid country girl, when he should be studying for a future life. But King came every Saturday after-noon and, if he could sneak away, on Sunday as well. He helped us with the work on the farm, and learned to milk. While he milked for me I sat near and we talked about Life, and Love, and Death, and History, and Geogra-phy,—little things like that we discussed. He was not very ambitious, but had a healthy curiosity, and we had good times together. I loved him madly. He was so colorful, and vibrant; so alive and full of fun, that I just loved him. I did not know any of his family, but at church we saw his mother, a huge, placid blonde woman, who had presented her pompous husband with an heir every year since their marriage.

Kingsland told me enthusiastically about a new suit his father had bought him, and I looked forward eagerly to seeing it. When he came on Saturday, wearing it, I was overwhelmed with his magnificence. It was the most beautiful suit I'd ever seen. It was of an odd shade of blue, not dark, and not light, but rich; it had long trousers, and the coat had brass buttons! With his red hair and brown face, it looked wonderful! The coat fitted him neatly, defining his slender waist, and giving him a military look. I was so proud of him I wanted to cry. It was much too beautiful for him to do any work in, so after that he wore it only on Sunday.

Autumn passed and winter came, making the roads almost impassable, but we trudged along to school. Now the cows were brought home and kept in the barn, which gave us more time for studying. But there were always burrs to be picked from wool and beans to be shelled from their hard dry husks, and our lessons came last.

During that winter my father began talking about going to a bigger place; some country where a man could have a chance to really do something. Low mutterings went on about how useless it was to try to farm in a one-horsed way. A man had to have more room to get anywhere. Old Mr. Hall had been telling him of what their son Zeb was doing in Oklahoma; the size of the farms and richness of the soil, and the great opportunities waiting for a man of intelligence and energy. All this had been working like yeast in him, and now he began to argue in a loud voice, with much profanity. I could see ahead, and told King of it. He didn't want us to go West, for he wanted me there with him. He was shy and troubled when he said, "Some day you must marry me, Belinda. Don't let your father take you away." He didn't know my father. He thought life was as simple as that. How little he knew, that beautiful boy!

Chapter 4

My father loved the mill at first; it was a new kind of machinery, therefore interesting and exciting. But he knew all about it now, and after Lydia and Lamson Hall read him letters from their son Zeb, his foot began to itch again. His grumbling continued, breaking out into open argument frequently, all that spring and summer, and by fall he was in open revolt. He couldn't see any reason why he should remain in such a small place, when there was a wonderful chance for a man in the West. Mother thought he should let well enough alone. "Who the Hell says it's well enough?" he yelled. "Cain't do anything with a passel of women; always holdin' a man down! Damned petticoat government." Suddenly mother said, "All right, let us go. I've always wanted to go to a new country. I'm tired too of all this." My father's jaw dropped, and he stood silent, for once unable to speak. Her agreement left him stunned. I think he was disappointed, because he thought he had something to argue about for years and years. Now he almost had to go and he faced it out. It was a brave thing for them to do, for they were not young, and were so poor.

Father sold the farm and the mill, which made me sad. I loved the mill. We had an auction, selling all the furniture, even the folding bed. Mother hated most parting with her chickens. We kept only bedding, a few dishes, pots and pans, and what few clothes we had. It was a cold bleak morning, with powdery snow whipped by a sharp wind, the morning we left. We all spent the last night with friends, arranging to meet at the station. Father and mother came with the barrels and boxes, in a big wagon; the rest of us walked. The country looked sad and desolate, but the curiosity and excitement kept me from weeping. Getting on the train was sufficient to dull all other interests.

I spent the last night with Maud, and we talked until late, pledging our everlasting friendship, promising to write, and to always tell each other everything. They all came out to the road with me, and as I turned the bend, the last thing I saw was Mr. Cartwright waving his hat. My tears blinded me. King came to the station, but he was so quiet, and looked at me so solemnly that I couldn't bear it. He had never kissed me, but now I wanted terribly to hold him close and kiss him. Shyness, and the fact that no one we knew did that sort of thing, kept me from it, and we just clasped hands, both tense and frightened, and he walked away. We promised to write.

We sat up in the day coach for six days, changing trains three times. We didn't know there was such a thing as a sleeper, and no one told us. But everything was new and strange, and the time passed quickly. Only a few incidents remain in my mind about that trip. The most numbing, horrible, unbelievable one happened in Newport, Tennessee.

My brother Winfield, from the back of the train, fired a few shots at some rocks in the bed of a stream we crossed. The conductor phoned ahead, and we knew nothing of it until the officers were on the train. We were all looking out of the windows, thrilled at the great number of people in the huge station, and didn't know what was really happening until we heard some one say, "That's him," and we saw the conductor pointing toward Winfield. Staring, we all stood up, terrified. This was an alien world, and we were alert for unknown dangers. My father bravely said, "What do you mean? What do you want?" By this time the officers had grabbed Winfield as though he were a criminal trying to escape, had jerked him around and started toward the end of the train. Winfield was looking back with a scared young face with a pleading expression to us all.

Father hurried along behind them, demanding an explanation, but the officers ignored him, pushing Winfield before them, beyond the sight of our staring eyes. My father went with them, not to be put off until he found out what it was all about. We hadn't known that Winfield had a gun. Winfield had always been a good boy; he worked hard and had never worried my father; he had never been drunk in his life, nor done any wild things. I think he bought the gun when we started West, because he wanted to appear grown up and brave.

As my father followed the men out, he looked back, still frightened but determined to go as far as he could with Winfield, and half sobbing, he called out to mother, "Stay with the children!" In a few minutes we could see them outside, the officers holding Winfield as though he was a thug, and my father still excitedly talking and pleading with them, right up to the door of a dismal red-brick building. We saw them enter, and could see no more. Terror gripped our hearts, but we sat down and said nothing. We heard the whistle blow, and heard the man say, "All aboard," but father didn't come back. Then the terror of being left quite alone held us. But just as the train started, father ran out of the big dismal red building and jumped on the last step. We had each secretly been afraid that if father lost his head and swore they would arrest him too; we were relieved to see him get on, and anxious to know what had happened.

Father was out of breath and his face pale. Signs of tears were on his weather-beaten cheeks, as he sat down. He talked to mother quietly for a few minutes, explaining why they had arrested Winfield. Mother sat perfectly still, saying nothing, with a gray deathly color in her face. None of her children had ever been arrested. It was a new and horrible experience. We didn't have much appetite the remainder of the trip. I don't know what father had to do, but after we'd been in Oklahoma a few days, he sent some money back, and Winfield was allowed to come on to us. I heard him telling father how sorry he was, and that he would make up for the money by working extra hard. Which he did.

We reached Guthrie in the night, in the midst of a bad windstorm. The train moved slowly, at times actually stopping. Sometimes it rocked perilously, and we were told not to move about; advice utterly superfluous as we were much too frightened to move. It seemed too bad father met this wind the very first night, for he hated wind, and I imagine that he dallied with the idea of turning right around and going back to North Carolina. The small breezes he used to swear at back home were remote from the generous, all-embracing, ruthless hurricanes he was to encounter in Oklahoma.

We spent the night in a cheap hotel near the station, and we were glad indeed to stretch our bodies out on a bed; to be able to sleep. We were very tired, but excitement had made us unaware of it for all those days. The next morning when we came downstairs, famished because we had eaten sparingly all the way, and saw a big dining room, we were afraid to go in, for fear it would cost too much. But our hunger got the better of us, and we somehow found ourselves around a table. The waitress gave us a menu, the first we had ever seen. But we could read and unfortunately were very knowledgable about figures. The printed words made our mouths water. The waitress realized by this time how dumb we were, for she said, "You got it comin' to you. It all goes with the price of your room." Our spirits rose, and we ordered everything in sight, and when it came in separate little dishes we were amazed. Father looked disgusted and said angrily, "What in Hell are these dinky soap dishes for?" and proceeded to empty several of them onto his plate. I think he was frightened, inside, and didn't want us to know it. Mother took everything calmly, which gave us all courage.

Zeb Hall and a friend of his, a Mr. Burton, came to meet us and when we were through breakfast they had our things piled into a big wagon, and we climbed into another, and started the long drive to Mr. Burton's farm, forty miles away. We drove all day, not stopping at all—just drove on across flat country, clouds of dust rising up around us, settling in our eyes, ears, noses and mouths until one felt a part of the general landscape. The only trees we saw were a few cottonwoods growing in bayous. It was very hot and so unlike our dear mountains, I felt that never could I learn to like this country.

When we reached the Burton farm, it was quite dark, and we all went to bed as quickly as possible. The family had stayed up to welcome us, and the house loomed up enormous in the light of lanterns carried to and fro. It was wonderful to get into a nice clean bed again, and we were all so exhausted I think we slept instantly.

Next morning I awoke in a room flooded with sunshine, and outside I saw green trees, and heard the twittering of birds, the clucking of chickens, and the bark of a dog. All the familiar sounds of home, so beautiful to hear! I jumped up and pounded Anne, calling to her to hurry and wake up; that we must see everything at once! When we got down, the men of the Burton family, and my father, had eaten hours before, and Mrs. Burton, a large, gray-haired, motherly woman, and her daughter Bessie, and a younger daughter Helen, joined us in a marvellous breakfast. We had sausages with hot biscuits, piles of pancakes made of real buckwheat flour, almost black, and golden honey, eggs and bacon with large cups of fragrant coffee. There were several kinds of jelly, sweet potatoes fried, and a great earthenware bowl of fresh sweet butter! Never in all my life had I seen so much food, or so good. They didn't seem to mind how much we ate, urging us to eat more and more.

After breakfast we helped Bessie and Helen with all the things they had to do, and later we climbed ladders into great cherry trees, gathering huge baskets of large luscious cherries. We went all over the farm, saw the cows and chickens and turkeys; gathered eggs from nests in a great barn, bigger than we had imagined barns could be, clean and sweet smelling, filled with hay and oats and straw. The stalls for the horses were cleaned every day and fresh straw laid down; the cows were washed before milking. Such things we had never seen before.

The Burton farmhouse was large and rambling, for they had added many rooms onto the original square two-storied structure built of logs, when Mr. Burton first came there. He and his wife had been among those who camped on a line, waiting for the Government to open the country. They raced to the spot they had chosen to stake out their claim. The farm lay along the Cimarron River, which was perhaps the reason that it seemed more rich and luxuriant than those further back in the Strip. His orchards stretched as far as the eye could see, like an ocean of green that moved to the breeze in softly undulating waves. Their vegetable gardens were of such richness and variety as to astound us, and everything grew so much bigger, and tasted better than on our farm back home. Great fields there were of cultivated strawberries, almost as large as small eggs, which we ate to our heart's content. There was so much of everything that no matter how much one ate or gathered, it made no appreciable effect on the supply.

There had been a large family, but many of them were married, leaving three still at home; Bessie, nineteen, Frank, seventeen, and Helen, twelve. Bessie was homely with protruding teeth and a receding chin. She was in love with the schoolmaster, Mr. Capper, who lived with them. This made me sad, for I saw at once that she would never get him, just because her face was not pretty. She was a good girl, sweet and kind, and an excellent house-keeper; she had the figure of a mother already, but with all her excellent qualities, I thought, he would not fall in love with her. My observations of her, and his attitude, led me to the conclusion that men are stupid, and prefer surface values to deep fundamental worth. She walked in the moon-light with him, among sweet scents and caressing breezes; I prayed that he might somehow see her as beautiful, at least in the moonlight. But nothing of that sort happened.

While Anne and I had been running wild all over the farm with Helen, mother had been busy washing and ironing all the clothes we had worn on the journey, getting ready to move as soon as she had a house to move into. Meanwhile father had been looking at various farms, with Mr. Burton, and after three weeks he found one, four miles north of Burton Farm. When the arrangements had been made, we gathered up our things, the barrels and boxes were again loaded into a wagon, and we went to Bennet Farm. Subsequently we were told that the last occupant, a queer sort of man living alone, who had made an unsuccessful attempt at farming, had hanged himself from a beam in the house. That did not make us more cheerful, but on the other hand it did not daunt us. We moved right in, speculating on the exact spot in which he had been found.

We had our bedding, so all we had to buy was bedsteads; we had the necessary pots and pans, dishes and knives and forks. With these few things we established a home. While mother was busy inside, father was buying farm horses, two ponies, a wagon and harness, and plows and hoes. Food was bought in a village fourteen miles away.

The house was a two-storeyed one, built of logs. It had been built by a squatter in the days of the Rush, when the country was opened. Two rooms, with a lean-to kitchen was all it was, but it proved sufficient. Anne and I slept on the floor in the attic, the others in the big room downstairs. This house was in what was called the Strip, which we discovered referred to a strip of wooded land perhaps ten miles wide and thirty long. All the farms were called Sections, consisting of one hundred and sixty acres. It was strange to us to hear directions being given as, "two miles west, three south and one east." We were accustomed to giving directions in this way. "Go to the top of the hill and bear right, past a tall sycamore; go down the road until you come to a spring, and turn left by the haystack to the fork in the road."

Soon we were all busy on the farm. My father planted fifty acres in cotton and seventy in corn. When the cotton was two inches high, there came a terrific hailstorm, with enormous stones, which killed every plant, making it necessary to plant it all over again. We all worked in the fields except mother, who worked in the garden, and cooked for us. Mary got a job with a rich woman rancher about thirty miles away, leaving only Winfield, Anne and me to help father. It was very hard work, for the rows were so long, and the sun so hot. We hoed the cotton and corn many times, as we had always done back home, and as the land was rich, loose black soil, the crops grew beautifully. The corn stood row upon row, like soldiers, green, strong and fruitful. But the cotton was the most beautiful and astonishing plant to me. It grew up like small trees, with rich green leaves, soft, wide and light, moving with a gentle rustling sound in the wind. Then the flowers came, flung with a generous hand over all the field, white at first, then turning purple in a day. They reminded me of Roses of Sharon, back in North Carolina. The plants were so tall I could walk under them, with an arch of feathery green over my head, through which the hot sun poured in checkered patterns. We planted melon seeds at intervals in the cotton, and these vines grew luxuriantly, their bright orange blossoms gleaming between the thick green leaves.

My father bought a cow,—such a peculiar old cow, of a dark red with great continent-like patches of white splashed carelessly over her. She had wide vicious horns, a large bony frame which showed her ribs, and no matter how much we fed her she never gained weight nor improved in appearance. I believe to this day that she was animated by an evil spirit. She never would come to the barn at milking time, and it was my job to go and drive her home. This was a difficult thing to do, because of her diabolic habits, and as she had a wide area in which to practise her ingenious methods, it became necessary to develop my tactics. A great deal of the pasture was covered by strange trees called black jack, perhaps a type of oak. Each tiny twig on those trees had the strength of iron, and catching onto my dress, would hold me in a vice-like grip, unbelievable and terrifying.

That old cow would stand still in the black jack trees until I came quite near. Sometimes I believed that she made herself invisible, for although she was large and spotted, I could never see her. How she moved so swiftly through those iron twigs, with her wide horns, I could never fathom. When she felt, or smelt me she would move her head so gently, making a seductive tinkle of the bell, quite in a friendly mood, as if to say, "See, I stand quite still, waiting for you! I am, after all, a nice cow and am perfectly willing to go to the barn." And I would relax and feel that it was simple after all. But when I had wriggled through the iron-fingered black jack to the exact spot from which the bewitching tinkle had come, she would be gone. Standing quiet, listening, I could hear from quite another direction, that maddening tinkle, and rubbing my scratched and bleeding arms, would creep again toward her. This pursuit would often last for hours, until panting and sweating, sometimes weeping hysterically from rage and exhaustion, I gave up. I never really won out, for when she had kept up the torture as long as she pleased, she would flick her long tail with boredom and quite of herself walk out of the woods.

On many nights she would escape from the barn and wander around in the garden or corn. Large and bony, clumsy in appearance, she was agile, deft, and dainty in all her movements. Whoever heard her in her nocturnal prowls naturally got up to drive her back, but it fell more frequently to me than to the others, for many reasons. Oh the nights that I matched my feeble wits against her! She used the same tactics by night, but it was more terrifying in the moonlight than under the sun. Slipping through the damp green corn, in my nightdress, my feet bare, the blades would clutch and cling to my bare shoulders and legs, with almost a human touch. Round and round she led me, tinkling her bell to lead me on, only to disappear completely, while I used what capacity I possessed for pretending with her, while my heart was sick within me with terror of snakes and centipedes. When she grew tired of the game, she would walk out of the corn and stand in the moonlight looking at me, and I swear that she would grin. The most diabolical grin, drooping the lid of one eye in a knowing leer; and me standing breathless from running, weeping with rage and fright. I shall never forget that cow.

The wonder of the moon, in Oklahoma! It gave a whiter, clearer light than in any place I have known. The stars seemed so close, and the whole arched sky so near, as if it might easily close down on one. Standing before that old cow, with a leer on her face, I could see every little hair on her nostrils. The trees still, every blade of corn picked out, and the old house looming up white in the clear moonlight. There was a lonely, old feeling about it; the vast plain had been like this for eons and eons. Here the mammoths used to stride about; there would be room, on those vast silent plains. Wrapped in silence that at times was somehow menacing, lay this wide land, drenched in white moonlight. The ponies would move about, snort, or kick against their stalls, every sound accentuated by the stillness and the moonlight.

Having always lived where the hills rose suddenly, and as quickly became hollows, with brooks rushing like mad down through laurel and dogwood and coltsfoot, it was startling to see large flat meadows, with tall, tall trees going straight up, making cathedral-like places. Silent! No flowers; just flat spaces covered with a wiry grass, and tall trees rising menacingly. It seemed unnatural, and somehow painful to me.

We went to school for only one week, that year in Oklahoma. We rode the two ponies, without saddles, hitching them to posts along with dozens of others, near the schoolhouse. The teacher was a tall man with large bony hands and wrists protruding from too short sleeves, and his pants halfway up his shinbones; white socks rolled around his ankles. He was, I think, a very nervous man, for if a pupil asked a question he would answer angrily, "What in Hell do you mean by such a stupid question? By God, I'll thrash you for that! God damned idiot!" It was grim, and as he didn't seem to like teaching school, and we didn't like going, it arranged itself satisfactorily. We didn't go. No one noticed particularly, and father said, "I'll bet a nickel

I know more swear words than that lop-eared, cross-eyed Methodist!" So with all the work, there didn't seem time to go to school anyway.

The farm adjoining ours on the east was owned by a German family named Weissendoncker. There was a blond, motherly woman, a widow, and two handsome blond sons, the oldest having only recently married, but not without a certain amount of persuasion. It was a 'shot-gun' wedding; she had apparently sinned, as she immediately had a baby, a lovely blond boy. Pretty as a picture, she was in no way troubled by her method of marriage, nor was any one. Every one liked them, and thought that he had been frightfully stupid not to marry her as quickly as possible, as women were scarce, and beautiful ones practically nonexistent. She was all gold and brown and blue, as lovely as a flower.

Anne and I often went to parties with them, riding ponies twenty or thirty miles, just as the sun went down, to other farms, where fifty or sixty people would gather, with banjoes, which they played wonderfully. There would be a barbecue, with loads of food and native wine, and dancing until quite late at night. The cowboys were wonderful, and none of them ever got drunk. It was grand to sit around a fire with them, singing lustily many jolly songs, and sentimental ones, and sad, wailing ones. Always at the end they sang pitifully, heartbreakingly, "The Dying Cowboy." Their plaintive voices carried in the night, "Oh! Bury me not on the lone prairie." These words came low and mournfully . . . We knew all the words, and sang with them, and I didn't know why I wept all to myself. Another one they loved was even sadder, and the words,

> You can tell the day I'm gone,
> You can tell the train I'm on,
> You can hear the whistle blow
> A thousand miles away,

seemed unendurably sad. They held the last word mournfully, and it was gay, and at the same time sad. I don't know why.

We raced home, Weissendoncker and I, on our swift ponies on the long flat road, unswerving, straight ahead in the moonlight. There was a trick the ponies had which might easily prove dangerous to the uninitiated. The roads were very wide, defined on either side by barbed-wire fence. The wagons wore deep ruts, leaving a high ridge between, which was concealed by grass. If your pony was in one rut, and decided to try the other, with no warning whatsoever, you found yourself sitting calmly on the ground behind him. After one experience, one rode prepared for such vagaries, and managed to accompany the pony, no matter how many times he changed ruts.

The fruit grew to enormous size. Apples were so big that I wouldn't dare give their dimensions. The Grays, who lived near us, had acres of vineyards full of the most delicious grapes, which they sold by the ton to dealers in the city, picked and packed at the vines. Mrs. Gray was a daughter of Mr. and Mrs. Burton, and her oldest daughter Nellie and I became good friends. We played under the vines, covered by an almost solid canopy of grapes in perfectly formed bunches, heavy with juice. Green ones, clear and almost seedless; large purplish ones, and round, dark blue ones. All ripening and giving off the most intoxicating odor! The bees buzzed around them, and thousands of butterflies fluttered over the vineyard. They gave us all that we could use, both for eating and canning. We had no grapes on our farm.

Once when I was visiting Nellie Gray, a cyclone came. It was the first one I had seen, and I was enormously curious. The sky became suddenly overcast, dull and dark, and there was an ominous stillness. Mrs. Gray quickly sent me to bring all the children in to the dugout. Their dugout was large and comfortably furnished, so that if necessary they could remain underground for days. Mrs. Gray did not go down, so I remained with her, watching the color of the sky change constantly, as well as atmospheric conditions.

Mrs. Gray was a small woman with very few teeth; her hair was thin and straggly, but while we watched, I saw her hair begin to rise slowly, slowly, until every hair stood in a wavering thin plume above her head, giving her a most grotesque appearance. Oblivious to that, she scanned the sky with a speculative eye. Now it had grown darker, the quietness obtained; a bright yellow border around the entire horizon was well defined, and when I asked her what it was, she shook her head, but did not answer. The deadly quiet made me tense and fearful. Not a leaf moved. It was the most disturbing silence I had ever experienced. After a while she pointed to the southwest and said calmly, "There it is!" I looked, and saw something that looked to me like an enormous waterspout, upside down, only it was dark, not the color one would expect water to be. It was fascinating to watch. We saw it directly over us, and she said, "I think it will miss us." It did, and as we watched it pass by, bringing with it a strong gale of restless wind, bending the trees in its ferocity, I remember saying to her, "Don't you think we should go down?" and her reply, "No, it won't come down here." We found later that it had come down ten miles to the south of us, striking in a lake, leaving it practically dry land, throwing the fish over the surrounding land. They told us any one who wished could go and gather the fish, and many did, keeping them in water until consumed. Erratic and unpredictable phenomena, there was no way of knowing where they would descend or rise, so every one had their dugouts ready.

We had no dugout on our farm, and after observing the cyclone, I wanted one terribly. No one seemed interested, so I began one all by myself, and after digging all my spare time for weeks, I got one deep enough to put a cover on, which my father did. Flush with the ground, covered with boards, then grass, with dirt on top of that, leaving a small hole for entrance. It was fairly practical, but we went into it only once. I was the only coward in the family, when it came to cyclones.

We had sufficient rainfall that summer for our crops in the Strip, but great areas within fifty miles of us were devastated by the Hot Winds. Every one lived in dread of them, and we were anxious to know what they were like. August Weissendoncker took Anne and me to see the result, and it was a pitiful sight. Hundreds of acres of corn, come almost to maturity, burned within two hours, into dry, dead stalks. Miles we rode past, and it was like a continuous graveyard, with the wind making the queerest deathly sound, as it blew through the dry blades. A true death rattle, heartrending to hear; a whisper rising at times to a weird low chuckle . . . horrible.

On the section south of us lived a nice couple named Miller. He was a handsome man with brown eyes, a jolly laugh and a brave mustache. She was slender, gay, and friendly. After I came to know them, I asked if I might come and live with them, and they said I might. With my toothbrush and comb, I moved in. I slept on a pallet laid down behind the stove in the living room, for the only extra room they had was occupied by their negro overseer. They were happy and it was pleasanter there than at home. They worked very hard, were very much in love, and had a good time living. I was embarrassed when I first saw Mr. Miller kiss his wife, for I had never seen any man kiss his wife. She would run to meet him when he'd been away, laughing happily, and throw her arms around him, hugging him tight, yelling at the top of her voice, "What have you brought me, you big egg? Didn't you bring me anything nice? I'll cut your heart out if you haven't, you low bastard!" But he always had something nice for her, and when I'd been with them a few weeks, he brought me something too.

The negro overseer was very fine-looking, and well educated. He slept in the attic, and ate with us. I can see the dining room now, with the white tablecloth, shining silver gleaming in the sun; yellow pancakes and golden syrup, and this black man who seemed to give color to the whole scene. He was a graduate of a Southern college, and had travelled all over the country, engaging in many types of labor. He said he was going to write about labor, and negroes, some day; of the problems of poor people all over the land. His name was William Henry Howard. He told us that his parents had been slaves belonging to a wonderful man named Howard, whose son had given him a chance to improve himself. At night, when the work was done, he read to us, as we sat around the table in the living room, on rainy nights; when it was fair, we sat around a chopping block, supporting the lamp, in the back yard under the trees. His voice was beautiful, and we all loved hearing him. For me, I thought it the most wonderful thing I had ever heard. He read all sorts of things, his own books, but mostly he read Whitman. He loved Whitman, and read us often, "O Magnet-South." He spoke the words as though he loved them, both as words and places. The Roanoke, the Savannah, the Altamahow.

I was very happy there, and sorry when cotton-picking time came, and I had to go back and help father and Anne and Winfield. Mr. and Mrs. Miller wanted to adopt me, and went so far as to speak to my father about it. I think he dallied with the idea, as they had no children, but Mrs. Miller spoiled everything when she said to him, in a bantering tone, "Why, you wouldn't miss her, Mr. Dan; you've so many others!" He flew into a rage, and said, "You ignorant woman, leave my house! Wouldn't miss her, eh? Well, let me tell you I'd miss any of my children and you get the hell outa here, before I throw you out." She was nervous, and dropped the whole idea, but continued to be a good friend to us, showing it by sending wonderful food to us in the field. Their field joined ours, and whatever she sent out was shared by us all. She would send great rich cakes, and enormous cans of ice cream, which was too heavenly to bear, when your throat felt like burning tin, and sweat was rolling down your back and legs. To hold it on the tongue, letting it melt and run down inside, cooling, soothing, delicious!

We had to pick our own cotton, but Mr. Miller was a rich rancher and had professional pickers. A group of twenty-five men, managed by a big blond man, who started them down in Texas, and picked their way North, as the cotton ripened, was now on the Miller Farm. This young man was charming; healthy and tanned a dark brown, his blond hair burned to various shades, his teeth were strong and clean. His name was Felix Worth. He was very friendly to us, coming over to help me drag my sack when it was full of cotton, and very heavy. Often we sat down on the sack, and extracting from his pockets a knife, and spoons, and salt, we would eat cantaloupes. They lay close to the earth down under the green leaves of the vines and the tall cotton plants, and so delicious were they we ate many.

We had many arguments, for soon I told him of my ambitions to go to school, and he thought it rather unnecessary. I told him how hopeless it seemed, and he was sympathetic, but could not really see how important it was to me, for he had no such yearnings. He had his own plans, which included eventual great wealth, to be arrived at somehow through cotton. He had other strange ideas, I discovered, when he came to call one Sunday morning toward the end of his contract with Mr. Miller.

Mother and I were sitting on the cool shady side of the house, Mother reading her Bible, and I sewing on a blue silk bag, lined with yellow. He said good morning to us, and as there was no chair, he sat cross-legged on the ground, when Mother said to him, "Make yourself at home." He seemed embarrassed, and fumbled his words, tousling his hair nervously. After a time he managed to make it clear that he wanted me to marry him, and was making a formal request to my mother. When she got the idea, she removed her spectacles, looked at him almost with indifference, and said, "Well, it's her business, young man; but I think you're foolish. You're buying a pig in a poke; she's only a child, and no knowin' what sort of woman she'll turn out to be." Speaking up bravely, he said, "I'm not afraid, Mrs. Dan. I'm more than willin' if she will take a chance with me."

I said nothing, but my heart was full of gratitude to him for wanting me, in my dirty calico dress, and barefooted too, with freckles on my face as big as dimes. Turning to me shyly, he said, "Well, Belinda, what do you say?" I couldn't bear it, and I wanted to cry. He looked so strong, and fine, I had to be honest with him. There was no coquetry in me, and I said, "No, Felix," and burst into tears. He was terribly unhappy, and came to me and put his arms around me, patting me, and said, "There, don't cry. It's all right; I shouldn't have ast you maybe." I stood like a gawk, unable to think what to say, fumbling with the silk bag I had been working on. After a few minutes, he said, "Will you give me that thing you're makin'?" I hated to part with it, for we had few bits of silk to make a bag, but he was so sweet, and good, and I felt so mean I could not refuse him, and handed it to him. He took it without looking, and put it in his pocket, saying, "Don't bother. I'll see you tomorrow in the field," and was gone.

We had a long talk next day, sitting on a pile of cotton, eating cantaloupes.

He said I might yet change my mind, and told me where I could always write to him. When I said that I would never give up my ambition to go to school, he said, "Well, if that's what you want most, why I'll help you. I'll send you to school for two years, three, if you like, if you'll say now that you'll marry me then." That made me cry again, for it seemed so easy, and the only way I could get to school. But I could not honestly promise, so I said, "What if you did that, and then I wouldn't, or couldn't marry you? What would you do?" He pondered that for a long time, and took my hand in his, saying, "Well, in that case, honey, you'd just have to keep your bargain, for I don't aim to be made a fool of by no woman, leastwise, not by a kid like you." So it was all over. We parted friends, and I never forgot him.

Our cotton ripened so fast it seemed impossible to get it all picked. It was an amazing thing to me that a tall green plant with beautiful flowers could later have pure white cotton bursting from green boles! It seemed unnatural, to me. We dragged a long sack behind us, with a strap around our neck and over one arm, into which we put the cotton. By the time we had picked a long row across the field and back again, we saw the row we had just picked all white again. It was maddening, for it was always ahead of us; we could never catch up. On moonlight nights we went back to the field and picked, hoping to catch up, but we never did. We picked for weeks; it seemed years. Finally father got tired of the whole business, and told Anne and me that we could have for ourselves all that we picked after that. How we picked! We gathered every small shred we could, and worked from dawn to dark and after, for weeks. When our cotton was weighed in, we got thirteen dollars each! And I had imagined I'd have enough to go away to school!

In my hopelessness and despair, I wrote to my sister Lucille, begging her to help me get away. I spoke of how my hands were bleeding from the sharp points on the cotton boles, and ended by saying, "Your answer will be my death warrant, or my reprieve." She was apparently amused, and either sent the letter, or wrote it, to others in the family, and I was laughed at and teased for years. It made me sick with shame that I had exposed my soul to any one, to be shamed. I never did that again.

All this year of hard work, with the driving passionate desire to get away, to go to school, to be educated! The moonlight nights spent in trying to outwit a clever cow; the hot endless days in the corn and cotton fields! And the hopelessness of it! There was no light, no ray of hope.

As soon as the crops were sold, father got the itching foot again. He spoke of going farther West. We had heard of a place in Colorado, where a man would have a chance to really do something. The low muttering began, which preceded as always a louder more vigorous argument. One day mother said to him, "Haven't you done right well in this place? With your cotton and corn? What do you hope to do in one year? What's the matter with this place?" In a rage father rushed around the room, swearing and kicking at chairs, yelling, "Thar you go again! Will you *tell* me how a man can do anything, agin a passel of women? This god damned petticoat government, allus a hinderin' a man!" But for once she insisted that he give her an answer to her question, without meandering off the subject. "What's the matter with this place?" she asked again. "What's the matter with this god damned country, you ast me? You *dare* to ast me that? You got the blastedest nerve to ast me that!" Mother quietly said, "Yes, that's what I asked you. What is the matter with this country? I like it here." That was the last straw,—that she would dare to say that she had an opinion about anything! "Well," he shouted, "I'll tell you what's the matter with this god damned wind-swept country! It's got too damned much *weather*! Too much wind, too much hail, too much rain, too much heat! Too much of every known and unknown sort of weather! No damned sense to it! No rhyme or reason to it! Cain't count on nothin', and *that's* what's the matter with this blasted flat, dismal, hot, cold, quiet, loud, weak, strong, wild, tame, goddamned country and *I don't like it!*"

This went on for several weeks, and although I don't know how it all came about, we found ourselves packing our barrels and boxes of bedding and pots and pans, to return to North Carolina. We had gone West with nothing and we returned with less.

Chapter 5

All that has gone completely from my mind, but I remember that we lived with my sister Sallie and Mr. Bonham, until my father found a place for us to live. Soon he bought a farm near Sallie, and built a small wooden house not unlike the one we had lived in near Leicester, and we moved in. Winfield had remained in Oklahoma, so the family now consisted of mother and father and Mary, Anne and me. The land on this farm had not been culti- vated for many years, so it was necessary to clear it of a heavy growth of small trees and shrubs. After the trees had been cut down and removed, we dug up the smaller ones by the roots, with a mattock or grubbing hoe. This was particularly hard work as the roots had become so intertwined that it was necessary to go over every inch of the ground, and even so it was im- possible to remove them all, and in a few weeks, strong green shoots came up in spots all over the fields. Again my father bought furniture, and horses and cows, and farm tools, and there we were, just as we'd been before, only now we didn't have the mill, which I had loved. On the other hand we didn't have to go so far to milk the cows. All spring we worked, and when fall came we started to school in the village. The Cartwrights had gone; they had moved to a suburb of Carleton, where he was the depot agent. I missed them very much.

King Mears was glad that we had returned, and again came to the farm often; I was glad of his friendship, for it gave color and life to an infinitely discouraging existence. He helped with the work as he had before, and in the evening we walked about. As there was nowhere to go, no comfortable place to sit, we returned and sat in the end of a long room in which my father slept, and I sat frozen in nauseating agony, waiting for the telltale sound. Frequently my father would break wind; Kingsland pretended that he did not hear it, while I sat too shamed to speak. The oil lamp burned, almost obscured by gnats and moths, and outside the tree frogs kept up a continuous sound, while King quoted the Scriptures to me. Although his father was a preacher, King was not very religious, but I think he loved the sound of the lines. He was accustomed to them, and while he half-whispered these to me, "Tell me, O thou whom my soul loveth, where thou feedest; where thou makest thy flock to rest at noon; for why should I be as one that turneth aside by the flocks of thy companions? Until the day break, and the shadows flee away, I will get me to the mountains of myrrh, and to the hill of frankincense," I would listen for the terrible sounds my father made, and my soul was sad within me. He would take my hand, and say, "Don't you think those lines are lovely?" I could not answer him, for I wanted to scream and fight; I wanted to get away, anywhere, from this tiny house, from a father who cruelly destroyed every feeling of restraint. I was unable to respond to King's courtship. When I could bear it no longer, I would say, "Let us go for a walk." But when we'd walked up to the road, to the church, and the graveyard, we had only to return. Sometimes on Sunday we went to the woods, and walked under the trees, and I loved that; when we were tired, we returned to a playhouse Anne and I had built of the limbs of spruce cut down in the clearing of the farm. The branches were set up around, and over the top we laid them almost thick enough to keep out the rain, and ferns, and green moss grew in it. There in the shade we sat, and King would say these lines, "Behold thou art fair, my beloved, yes, pleasant; also our bed is green. The beams of our house are cedar, and our rafters fir." With his beautiful passionate face, and his religious training, and my passionate desire to be educated, we had little to say to each other. He wanted me to marry him, but we avoided bringing it to a point, but I knew that sooner or later it must come. Next to my desire for education, I loved him more than all the world.

When school began, we went, and it was nice to see all the boys and girls again. They questioned us about all that had happened to us in Oklahoma, and we made enquiries about every one in the village. Nothing had changed. The Morrisons still lived in the large white house just out of the village, but no one knew anything more about them. The son, Francis, came to school, but he was aloof, and cruel, his beautiful face at times sinister, and we didn't know how to be friends with him. Sometimes he was charming, and we all felt drawn to him, but instantly it was gone. He told us once that his little sister, a fragile, white-faced child, ate dirt, and rags, and string, and hair; that frequently it was necessary to operate to remove them. That was an amazing thing to us. No one knew the Morrisons.

Just across the road lived old Miss Lydia Kendall. She was rich, fat, and jolly, and we loved stopping to see her; she gave us cakes. Mr. Paxton, a lawyer in the village, had been courting her for forty years, and just before we went West, they got married. They had a wonderful wedding, and it seemed a good idea, for they had been courting a long time. Upon our return we found that they had been divorced. When we reported this at home, my father said, "Hell, what can you expect? A man cain't know a woman in only forty years!"

One of my girl friends, Nancy Hyatt, had a beau. Charlie Pennell, the son of old Dick Pennell, the richest man in the village. Old Dick had long complained of cold feet, and it was said that he would pay any sum of money to any one who could warm his feet. The old men sitting around in the grocery store used to speculate on how they were "going to warm old Dick's feet," but whatever method they considered, they always dropped the subject if any women or girls came in the store, but I did hear a young farmer say that it would be "Plenty." I wondered what he meant.

The father of another girl, Tennessee Maloney, kept a blacksmith shop; I know that fact attracted me to her home. They had a very nice house in the village, and her mother was an invalid, who for twelve years had directed the household from her bed. She looked the picture of health, talked incessantly, and ate heartily. I often wondered what ailed her. Once when Tennessee and I had been playing at housekeeping, in a shed back of the kitchen, we became interested in something else, and left the small toy stove burning. Presently from the blacksmith shop we heard loud screams, and saw clouds of smoke coming from the kitchen. Then we saw Mrs. Maloney, in her flannelette nightdress, her feet bare, running wildly toward us. Mr. Maloney got help, and the fire was quickly extinguished, but Mrs. Maloney never took to her bed again. She turned her home into a boarding house, and cooked for dozens of people for years after that. Tennessee, years later, became a painter of bad pictures, and even later, was confined in an institution for the insane.

We were fairly happy in school; when the time came to harvest the crop, we had to stay home and help father. We hated that, but the last straw was when we had to stay home to help in clearing a new field. The large trees had been cut and removed; the smaller ones left on the ground to dry out, had been burned off, leaving the field covered with stark, skeletal branches.

These charred, blackened branches we had to cut and pile for further burning. The black ash stuck to one's hands and clothes, and as they slithered and rolled upon one another, they made a sickening sound. We worked for many days, and during that time I knew that I was through; that I could no longer exist as a farmer's daughter. I frantically sought a way out, and decided that at least I would get a job in the village and work for my room and board, while I went to school.

Through my friend Nancy Hyatt, I did get a place with her sister, whose husband was one of the teachers. Mrs. Morton, Nancy's sister, had two baby boys, and as a friend of Nancy, I was allowed to come and wash dishes and diapers, to sweep and clean and cook, for my room and board. This left me no time to study, but it was better than walking three miles through the sticky mud, and working on the farm too.

While I worked there, I saw King only at school, for I was somehow afraid for them to know that I had a beau. But he wrote letters to me, and let me know that he was always my friend. I was depressed because I had no time to study, but when I overheard Mrs. Morton say to her husband, "I don't know what's the matter with her, but if she can't be more cheerful, I'll have to let her go," I was frightened, and began to whistle and sing happily, pretending, because I wanted to stay. But it all came to naught, for Mr. Morton got mixed up in some way with Allie, a daughter of the village policeman, and Mrs. Morton moved back to her mother, taking her husband away from the danger of Allie, so I was out of a job.

The next place I went was to a minister and his wife who had a neat little house in another part of the village. After a few weeks, the wife, who was a thin, sour little woman, said to me, "We'll have to let you go." Shocked, I asked what was wrong with me. She was kinder than she looked, and said, "There's nothing wrong with you child, but you cook things too good, and we eat too much, and we can't afford it." In vain I suggested that I might cook things badly, so they wouldn't eat so much, but she said dismally, "No, it's the Lord's will that you go!" Enraged, I said, "Well, if the Lord made it possible for you to eat a little more, he'd be at better business!" She lifted a thin admonishing hand, and said, "Hush, don't blaspheme!" Well, there was nothing to do but look for another place.

My pride gone by now, I went from house to house, begging to be allowed to come and work, but no one could have me. Some because they didn't need me, but many because they couldn't afford to feed me,—and I didn't eat much; I had been trained to live on very little. I went into the post office, and stood at the shelf where horrible pens and filthy ink bottles were, and laid my arms down on it, dropped my head in defeat, and cried. When I heard some one come in, I stopped, dried my eyes, and tried to look unconcerned. It was Judge Reeves, and giving me a keen look, he said, "What's the matter, Belinda?" I told him all, and he said, "Now don't worry. You come along with me, and we'll speak to the Boss about it." Happy, I went along, wondering just who the Boss was. He was, I discovered, referring to his wife, Mrs. Reeves. She was a lovely young woman whom I had seen in church, and his second wife. Her father and mother had been among the few educated people in the village, and when they had died, she became a schoolteacher. Judge Reeves' wife had died, leaving him with four children, three girls and a boy. He had known her parents and so they were married.

When we reached his house, he took me into the living room, and said, "Here's Belinda Dan, darling; I'll let her tell you what she wants," and he left me with her. At first I was afraid, but she was friendly and I told her what I wanted to do. She was sweet, and said I could live with them, and took me upstairs to a small room at the end of the hall, saying, "You can sleep here. Leave your things, and come down. I'll tell you what I want you to do." When she left me, I thought how nice she was, and that I could love her with no trouble at all.

I remained with that family for several months, and learned a great many things that I did not understand,—things I never told any one. Only years later, looking back, did they clarify themselves. I knew thoroughly that I adored Mrs. Reeves, and also the Judge. They were fine people. He was a handsome man, and had been to Harvard, which set him apart from all the people in the town. I didn't actually know what Harvard was, but my father must have known, for he told me with awe and respect in his voice, "Judge Reeves is a mighty larned man; a man who has bin to Harvard, and don't you forget it!" He practised law, and had inherited money from his mother. Mrs. Reeves was twenty-five years old; her hair, which she wore in curls around her head, was the color of ripe wheat; her eyes were a merry brown, and her teeth small and white. In my bed at night, I thought how wonderful they were, and that I would give my life for them, if need be. The daughters went to school, but I saw little of them. They rarely spoke to me, but I didn't mind because Mrs. Reeves helped me with the dishes, and we had lots of fun together.

Judge Reeves was quiet, and sometimes cynical, but he was always kind. He usually sat late in his study at night, after the household was in bed. His son Daniel, who was then about seventeen, and like his father in looks, was a little wild, and often came in late. The Judge would open his study door and say, "Hello, Daniel! Come in for a chat, won't you?" Sometimes he went in, but often I heard him say, "Not tonight, dad," and go up to bed. I knew his father was worried about Daniel, and I had heard that he was running around with the bad girls in nearby villages.

Mrs. Reeves was always cheerful and friendly to me, and I told her of my ambitions to go to school, and she listened, but I often caught a strained, apprehensive look on her face. I grew more worried, for I could see that Judge Reeves was tense and unhappy, and often came down in the morning with a tired white face. Sometimes I couldn't go to sleep, listening for I knew not what.

There was a large dark girl in the village, named Lolita Carmel. I had often seen her, and had once been to the house in which she lived. She was beautiful in a dark, laughing way. It was said that she had colored blood in her, and the respectable people had no use for her. I don't know where she came from, but I loved to see her, for she was different from other women in the village,—more jolly, and free.

One night I was up late doing my washing, and at twelve, I saw the back door which gave onto a small porch, slowly opening, and I stopped on the stairs and watched, frightened. Slowly it opened, and Lolita Carmel came soundlessly in, closing it quietly behind her. Next morning Judge Reeves looked white and drawn when he came down to breakfast. I couldn't wait to serve him, and I said, "I'm sorry Judge Reeves, but I'll be late for school." He smiled sadly and said, "That's all right, child. Run along." I wanted to cry, he looked so sunk in despair. Many nights he was out late, and Mrs. Reeves always had an explanation, but he became more and more troubled, and I was sure that Lolita was coming more often, late at night. I was afraid some one would gossip about him, and that made me sick with anxiety. I wanted to go to him and ask him what it was, and if I could do anything, but I couldn't. He was a kind, wonderful man, but austere and proud. Often at night I heard him in his study, having tense, high words with Daniel, and I had seen the boy fling himself out angrily, and grab his hat from the rack in the hall, and rush out of the house.

One Saturday morning, as I was cleaning the silver, Judge Reeves came down, beautifully dressed, charming; I thought he looked more rested, more alive than he had for weeks. He watched me for a few moments, and picking up a glass, he said, "You make the glasses shine so! What do you use that makes them so clear?" I said, "Only soap and water and elbow grease!" He laughed, and then quietly said, "I wish that could be used on a lot of things in life, with the same beneficent result!" His son came in, and instantly the atmosphere of the dining room became tense, portentous. I gathered my cleaning things and hurriedly left the room, frightened. I heard them talking loudly, and later Mrs. Reeves was sobbing in her room. All this went on secretly; even his daughters knew nothing of it. No one in the village knew, but I felt that something terrible might happen one day, and it did.

It was a very hot, sticky night in the late fall, and I was in my bed in the tiny room at the head of the stairs. I had been asleep, but was awakened by some sudden sound that struck terror to my soul. I got up and crept into the hall, and listened; I could see down the stairs, where a low nightlight burned. I couldn't hear a sound, but something made me creep down the stairs, slowly, step by step, listening all the time, terrified. Just as I reached the bottom, the study door began to open, very slowly. I stood still, in my cotton nightdress, my feet bare, my hair in pigtails. The freckles on my nose must have looked queer; they always did when I was scared.

Quietly, in the door, stood Judge Reeves. He looked at me so straight, thoughtfully, for a long moment, and I felt my heard pounding against my ribs. He said, in a whisper, "Come in here." I slipped past him into his study, and he carefully turned the key in the lock. There on the floor lay Lolita, with a knife sticking right up out of her breast. Looking beautiful, but quiet. I went near Judge Reeves, and whispered, "What shall we do now?" He hadn't spoken a word. He looked at me searchingly, and said, "Will you do something for me?" I came closer to him and said, "Yes, of course! What shall I do?" He slipped his arm around my shoulders, absent-mindedly, and said, "Go to your room and get dressed and come back." I said, "Yes, Judge Reeves," and he cautiously opened the door and I slipped out.

When I came back, he had removed the knife and put some sort of bandage around her to cover the wound. He told me that I would have to help him carry her. I did. He took the head, and I carried her feet, carefully out on the small back porch, down the steps, out into the hot sticky night, down the brick walk and into a long alley that ran behind some livery stables. She was heavy, and if I hadn't been a strong girl, and anxious to show Judge Reeves that I had courage, I think I would have dropped from exhaustion. We didn't see a soul. He told me to watch carefully, and I did. Several times I felt that I could go no farther, but he went on, somehow stepping backwards, or sidewise, like a crab. Suddenly we stumbled on a wheelbarrow, and I whispered, "Let's put her in here." He didn't answer, but slid her down, with a sigh of relief. Then we rolled her along for quite a distance, took her out and laid her on the ground. Judge Reeves straightened her out nicely, there on the dry, dusty ground, behind the livery stables. We went back, not speaking at all. Once inside, I thought I'd go right on up to bed, but he said, "Come in here a moment." I went into his study, and very quietly he told me how this had all happened, but I felt very sleepy, and remember only that it was about Lolita having been the child of his own father, or his brother, and that she had been making him pay her to keep it a secret, for a long time; how he hadn't minded that, but that recently she had been leading Daniel astray, and when he had remonstrated with her, she had laughed at him. He told me a lot, but I was too sleepy rightly to take it in, and I wasn't particularly interested. I just didn't want him or Mrs. Reeves to be worried. When I got into my bed, I was happy, thinking that he had not considered it necessary to ask me not to tell. And how he had said I polished the goblets beautifully, and had trusted me. I went to sleep as the thunder began, and the rain pelted on the roof over my head. Lolita was found, but no one ever knew who killed her. Various men friends were suspected, but no one convicted. I loved Judge Reeves.

I was happy at Judge Reeves' home, because I had great respect for them, and they were kind to me, but after a few more months, a niece of his first wife wanted to come and live with them, and go to school, so they had to let me go. She was an ugly girl with a pimply face and stringy hair, but no doubt I was prejudiced. I was out again, and this time I gave up hope, and went home to the country. I had hoped that Judge Reeves would help me, but he didn't. After all, I was not his child, so why should he bother?

Kingsland still came to see me, but it was dismal, for I couldn't make him understand my yearning to go to school, and we wrangled about it. On Saturday afternoon, I would walk to the village, and as I stood beside the railroad tracks, while the train went by, I wept. It was a symbol of what I wanted; travel, education, to see and know. Following the tracks, I came to the depot, where King would meet me, and we would sit in the dirty waiting room, emblem of all that is arid, in a small town, and then walk home again. After a few months the pressure of my longing for a new life, and my unhappiness and loss of hope, forced me to develop a plan; it seemed simple of execution, and I determined to carry it out.

There was an old man in the village, who had a general store, and a big white house behind trees, surrounded by a nice lawn. He was a Deacon in the church, and a pillar of society, I suppose, but he had looked at me in a way that made me think he liked me, so I determined to ask him to help me. I had no intention of telling him what I planned to do, but from all the people in the village, I chose him, and I knew them all. I held a peculiar sort of position in the village. Every one seemed to trust me, and told me secret things, and I knew all that went on in their lives behind the front. Not belonging to the village, and having no visible home, I think I was like a ghost to them, some one of no importance, unreal, in a sense.

I made up my mind to ask this man for fifty cents, to pay my way to Carleton. One day after school I went in his store and talked to him, smiling sweetly, and he asked me to come to the back of the store. I was wary, but determined to get the fifty cents, at all costs. I followed him, and he showed me some new shoes he had just got in, for schoolgirls, and asked me if I liked them. I said that I thought they were wonderful shoes. Then I said laughingly, as though it were a lark, "Mr. Blalock, will you give me fifty cents?" He smiled and looked at me a little as though he might eat me, and said, "Why certainly, Belinda." He took it from his pocket and handed it to me. It seemed a simple thing. I took it and thanked him, but for a long time afterwards I wondered if I had been a good sport, or if I had taken money, giving nothing in return. On my way home, I decided that on the following Sunday I would leave. I would run away.

On Saturday I washed and ironed all my clothes, and with six bananas my father had bought, I made a banana layer cake. I remember the cake, because later I had a badly written letter from my mother in which she said, "I tried to eat some of your banana cake, but it stuck in my throat," and I recall even now, with pain, the constriction of my throat, and the scalding tears that sprang to my eyes.

All day Saturday while I worked, I had felt tense, and frightened. I looked at my father and mother and suddenly it seemed that I had never seen them before, that we were not related, but strangers, who had never even touched each other, who knew nothing of the inner life of each other. In spite of this strangeness, pain twisted my heart when I looked at them, and realized that they were old; that I might never see them again, and that my going would hurt them. I wanted so to put my arms around them and to say, "I'm sorry. Please forgive me, and understand that I have got to go," but a barrier not of words, or stone, came between me and them. As I could not talk to them, nor speak truly with them, I wanted to get away, where I would not see them. Something in their aging, work-worn bodies hurt me more than I could bear, and the chasm I was unable to bridge between them and me, drove me as much as my desire for education, to get away.

Sunday came, a warm sunny spring day. Nothing was green, but the consciousness of green was in the air. Some of the family went to church; my father went to see a Mr. Henderson about some pigs. The house was still, and I was alone. Hurriedly I dressed in all the clothes I owned,—two suits of underwear, two Ferris waists, two pairs of drawers with ruffles of embroidery at the bottoms, two petticoats, and one cotton dress, with a wool one over that. On top of all these I wore my coat, which fortunately was not heavy.

I carried only six school books, my toothbrush and comb. The books were an Algebra, a book I could not understand, an ancient history, by Myers—I remember and can feel the texture of the binding yet—a Latin grammar, and a small book of the Declaration of Independence, which we had been studying in school. But more clearly than any of these, I remember my *Alice in Wonderland* which my sister Adelaide had sent me, and which meant so much more to me.

Unobserved, I set off across the mountains, a distance of eight miles, instead of going to the village. The sun was hot, but in the shade it was cool, and lovely walking through the woods; silent, without a sound of human life to be heard. Later it became hot, as the climb was highest through a pasture, where the sun beat down. After crossing the highest point, and starting down the other side, I came to a brook, and sat down to rest. I removed my coat and hat, laid my books on the ground, and bathed my face in the clear cold water. The mountains rose all around me, their peaks shining in the sun; silent, not a sound except that of birds, or the crackling of a twig as a rabbit scampered away. I felt so alone, so sad, that I lay on the ground and wept, but realizing that I had a long way to go, I gathered some trailing arbutus, which lay pink and fresh under the leaves, their odor penetratingly sweet, and started again. My books had grown heavy, and I thought I'd leave one, but being unable to choose, I finally took them all, and went on.

It was well after noon when I came to the railroad; there was no station, but I thought it was what was called a flag station, and quite near the track there was a shack in which lived a poor family with many children. At the door, a slattern woman asked me to come in, and brushing a lot of old rags, and a pot with a smoke-blackened bottom from a chair, she asked me to sit down. The stovepipe did not go all the way to the roof, which allowed the smoke to pour out into the cabin. Two children, incredibly dirty, were playing on the floor; several were playing on the hard dirt yard in front, and the mother, who was about thirty, but so disfigured by poverty and childbearing that, with all her teeth out, she looked about fifty, carried a baby on her lap, in a nonchalant manner. The baby was nursing at her breast all the time, pulling her around in a grotesque way. I eased down on the chair, and asked what time the train came by. The man, who had been cleaning a gun, stopped, and spat in the general direction of an open fireplace, full of dead ashes and dirty rags, chewed his tobacco and squinted one eye at me, and said, "Wall, miss, ye cain't be shore. She mought come at two, and she mought come at three, but ye'll hear her blow at the junction, and' I'll flag her fur ye." I thanked him, and as it had become unbearably warm, and the smoke made my eyes smart, I said that I would wait outside. Time passed slowly, and I let my mind go back home, trying to imagine what they were doing, and if they had missed me. I felt sure that my father would go to the village, and when he did not find me there, he would get on the train, for he would figure out that I would do just what I had done. In this case, I was prepared to fight; I would not go back.

Finally the train did blow, and the gaunt, shambling dirty man flagged it and I climbed on. I tried to appear casual and at ease, although I was shaking inside. In a few minutes my father came through, looking for me. He smiled in an embarrassed way, and sat down beside me. I looked at him in fear and hate, waiting for him to speak. After a long silence, he said, "And whar d'you think you're goin'?" I quickly thought that I had better say something that would make him easy about me, so that he wouldn't try to make me go home, so I said, "To Pierson School." He didn't answer, and we sat in uncomfortable silence. My own mind was a mixture of sadness, fear, and hatred, and a determination to go on. Father sat looking out of the window, and as we passed a bend in a brook, where the willows grew thickly, with that young painful red they have in the spring, so beautiful it always made a lump in my throat, he turned to me and said, "The red in them willows is purty, ain't it?" I thought that I would die. I could not bear the way he said it.

When we reached Carleton, we got out, and walked through the station, and stood waiting for a trolley, he in his country clothes with no tie on, and me with freckles all over my face; we must have looked an odd pair. The trolley wound through the shanties of negroes and poor whites, and up a long hill to the square, in the middle of the city, where one changed cars for all parts of town. We got off, and stood together for a few minutes, saying nothing. I wanted him to go, to let me be alone, and I was afraid he might insist upon going on with me. I had a need to go on alone. Looking straight into his brown eyes, I said, "I must go on alone from here." He grinned, spat, and said, "All right. That's all right," and he put his hand in his pocket, took out a dime and held it out to me and said, "No matter what happens, keep your chin up!" I took the dime and he turned and walked toward a car that would take him back to the station, and I to one that would take me to Oakdale. He never looked back, and I saw the back of him only once, and looked no more. I never saw my father again. Since that day, I have travelled alone. In spite of having friends, and a certain amount of what is recognized as success in life, I have always travelled alone. At the core of me I am alone, alone, alone. There is a part of me that no one and nothing, has ever touched; I am alone and will be till I die.

The trolley went down a long incline, past stores and hotels and livery stables, and out across a flat valley, between scattered shabby houses, and up another long rise, which it climbed slowly. I knew where to get off, although I had been there only once, when my sister Adelaide was there. Father had hitched up the mules to a big wagon, and brought Anne and me, and my mother, to a festival at the school. I remembered being lifted down, and my father carrying me up the long drive between tall fir trees; it was like an approach to a castle, or so I remembered it. It was to us a magnificent place, and I had never forgotten it. I had not known that I was coming here, until I suddenly told my father that I was, and then it seemed that all the time I had known that this was my destination.

Now, alone, I got off the trolley and walked up the stone steps, in fear and agony, watching the car disappear around a turn. It was Sunday afternoon. I turned and walked slowly up the remembered drive, through the tall dark fir trees. The wind made a sad, light, sighing sound through the feathery tops of the tall graceful trees; a relinquishing, renunciatory sound. At one place they were so thick as to give a twilight, and somehow frightening feeling. I went on, and all at once the large building was before me, and I walked up two low steps onto a long veranda, that seemed familiar. At the end was a door, and instinctively I felt that it was the one I had been coming to for a long time. I went to it and knocked.

Chapter 6

I was ready to run, in sheer terror, when the door was quietly opened by a small dark-eyed woman with snow-white hair, dressed in dark blue silk, with cream lace at her neck and wrists. Looking at me questioningly, she said, "Won't you come in?" I walked tremblingly past her, into a dark hall, and stood while she softly closed the door.

Inside I saw a beautiful room, magnificent to my country eyes. Lighted dimly by the slanting rays of sun, leaving it half in shadow, I had a feeling of beauty around me; beauty and peace. I saw the polished wood, books, and an open fire. She smiled at me, showing white, even teeth, and a bright, warm friendly feeling seemed to come from her. She was so tiny, and so alive and healthy, and her eyes were two luminous parts of a whole shining being. Like a very young girl, she whispered to me, "We must be quiet; it is the Silent Hour."

Not knowing what the silent hour was, I kept quiet mostly because I was completely stunned by her, and the place. She took me by the hand and led me through a short passage, and motioned for me to go, but quietly, up a rather narrow stairs. We went into her sitting room, which was cosy, beautiful, and quiet. Three big windows across the back admitted the last of the sinking sunlight, filling the room with a golden glow. There were flowers in stone bowls, and a small fire burning. She sat down in a small rocker, and asked me to sit near her, after she had taken my books and asked me to remove my coat. Quietly she said, "What is your name?"

For some reason that I could not define then, nor since, I did not want to tell her my name. She urged me, and finally said, "But you must tell me your name." I twisted my hands, and felt so much shyness and fear I could not speak. Then she said, "Why have you come here?" I could answer that, and said, "Because my sister was here once." She smiled and said, "Your sister?" Nervous, I said, "Yes, my sister. And I was here once, when I was small, and I have waited all these years to come back again." Talking quietly, calmly, she overcame my tension, and when she casually said, "What was your sister's name?" I said, "Adelaide Dan." She was excited and pleased. "Why, Adelaide Dan was one of our finest girls; I am very happy to know her sister. What is your name?" and I told her. She continued, "Miss Bond will be delighted; she was very fond of your sister." Then she asked me what I wanted to do, and I told her how hard I had tried to go to a good school, and how discouraged I was, and how I had run away from home, and that I would never go back; that I must go to school, somewhere, somehow. She listened, and said, "I don't believe I'll be able to take you in just now, as all our classes are full, and the house also."

At that moment something seemed to burst, to dissolve in me. All my restraint, all the tension under which I had lived and moved about for the whole of my life, was lifted. I felt that every atom of my body would fly apart; that I could no longer keep all of me inside my skin; that this was indeed the end. I could go no further, could make no further effort. In abandonment I fell on my knees, and laid my head in her lap and screamed as with pain; I sobbed as though all my life I had waited for this one moment at last to weep. Hysterically I wept, and it was a great release, a pleasure, a keen joy, which I had long wanted, and had not had, and at last to have given in, to admit my defeat, I who had thought that if I were strong, and fought hard, nothing could defeat me. She let me cry for a long, long time, saying nothing, just holding me. When my sobs had become less tearing, she had gathered me up in her lap, my head was on her breast, and she was giving me gentle pats on my shoulder, but saying nothing. When I had finally exhausted my well of sorrow, and came back to an awareness of time and place, the room had become quite dark, lighted only by the flickering flames of the fire. I got up, feeling weak, but no longer ashamed or afraid. I saw that I had drenched the front of her waist with my tears, and I touched it and said, "I'm so sorry. Do you think it will ruin it?" She gave me a puzzled look, and said, "No, I don't think it will ruin it; it may do it good." She lighted a lamp, and I said, "How can you think that it might do it good?" She looked full at me with shining eyes, and said, "You're too young to understand," smiling at me.

When she had lighted the lamp, she said that she would leave me now, and go to her supper. Showing me the bathroom, she said, "Now you must bathe your face and hands, and remain here. I will send you a tray, so that you may have your supper alone tonight. After supper, I will bring Miss Bond, for I know she will be happy to meet a sister of Adelaide Dan." She went away, and when I'd washed my hands, and combed my hair, I felt much better. I crept quietly around the room, reading the titles of many books, and I wondered if ever I would have a lovely room like that, with books of my own. There seemed to be many kinds of books in the room, and a full shelf of poetry, but I was happy when I saw that her copy of *Alice* looked pretty well worn.

I heard footsteps, the door opened, and the dark-eyed white-haired woman, whose name I knew to be Florence Hamilton, came in, followed by Miss Bond, a blonde, effervescent much younger woman. Miss Hamilton said, "This is Adelaide Dan's sister, Belinda." Miss Bond came quickly to me, her dress making a rustling sound, and in an impulsive, friendly way put out her hand, saying, "I'm glad to meet a sister of Adelaide Dan; I am devoted to her. She was one of our finest girls." Miss Hamilton sat down in her small rocker, while Miss Bond began examining my books which lay on the table. Her face was enigmatical until she came to *Alice*. She held it up to Miss Hamilton, laughing heartily; a young, giggling laugh that made me love her. I said nothing, for I was so anxious to know what they would do with me.

Miss Bond sat down, and motioned for me to sit, and in a casual, conversational way she said to Miss Hamilton, "Well, what are we going to do with her? You know we are full . . ." Miss Hamilton rocked, her small foot moving up and down, and thoughtfully she said, "We might send Jane to her Aunt, and she could come as a day pupil." Miss Bond laughed again, and said, "Don't pretend, Florence! You know very well that neither of us would think of not taking Adelaide Dan's sister, whether Jane goes to her Aunt or not." Miss Hamilton said, "Yes, that's true; we must take her," and to me she said, "Come along, Belinda. I'll show you where you will sleep tonight; it is not permanent, but it will do nicely." I took my coat and followed her, saying good night to Miss Bond, and we left the room.

Across a long dark veranda I followed her short quick steps. At the end, she opened a door, and we entered a long hall, from which doors led to different rooms. We passed several doors, and at the fourth she knocked, and immediately it was opened by a thin girl wearing thick-lensed glasses. The girls stood up very straight when they saw that Miss Hamilton had come, and as her quick glance went over them, I saw that they had great respect for her. To a tall dark girl she said, "Gladys, there is an extra bed here, isn't there?" The sombre Gladys said, "Yes, Miss Hamilton." Making an inclusive movement with her thin small hand, Miss Hamilton said, "Girls, this is Belinda Dan. Her older sister is one of our old girls. Will you look after her? I leave her in your care," and to me she said, "Good night, Belinda. I'll see you in the morning," and quickly left us.

They girls were friendly and voluble, curious as to why I was coming in mid-term. I answered them with care, for I had no wish to explain my entire life to them. Soon the gong sounded, a warning to prepare for bed, and when the fifteen minutes allowed for undressing had passed, we were each in our own narrow cot. Almost instantly I slept, knowing surely that I was among friends.

This school had been a harbor for hundreds of girls who would never have had a chance to improve their lives or minds. I think that there must be thousands of girls, women now, who look back on that school as the finest, best thing in their lives. It must be so, although I have no way of knowing. For me it was the realization of my dream. We worked hard, were severely disciplined, but always with fairness, and often love. I am too inept to express my profound appreciation of the drive that made it possible for women like Miss Hamilton and Miss Bond to give up all that so many consider Life, and to give their strength, generously, to that school, for years and years on end. And I have wished that instead of erecting so many statues to generals, who have made of killing a science and a profession, we might erect to women like these, wonderful statues, and carve these words, "These women were more than mothers."

The school had been established many years before by a minister and his wife, for the education of the daughters of ministers, but as the years passed, they had taken others whose fathers had not been ministers, for which I was extremely grateful. My father did preach sermons, but not the kind heard in pulpits.

There were spacious grounds around the school, which consisted of three large buildings, with a vegetable garden and stables. The lawns were well kept, and flowers grew in profusion. The school was supported by contributions, I think, for very few of the girls paid anything. We did all the work of the school, and we were taught every type of housework, thoroughly.

Every six weeks we gathered in the large study hall to hear the work list read. By this method of rotation, we learned every type of housework. My first six weeks I was on Teachers' Linen, which meant that with another girl,

I washed and ironed all the linen from the teachers' dining room. If, upon inspection, it was not absolutely perfect, we were asked to do it all over again. In my second six weeks, I was on Bread, which meant that another girl and I made all the bread consumed by the entire school. The bread was made with yeast, and set to rise in enormous iron pans. Every morning at five o'clock we had to be down in the bread room, to knead and mold the rolls, and bake them for each day. We had wonderful fresh bread. We worked hard, and happily. We were taught every type of sewing, and before passing from the seventh to the eighth grade, it was necessary to make a sample of varied stitches. These samples were placed in a big book, on the right-hand page, and on the left was written a description of that particular stitch. I was proud and happy when Miss Bond complimented me on my book of samples, and asked me to leave it at the school, to show to visitors; perhaps it is still there.

We were in bed and lights out at nine, and at six we were awakened by the rising bell. Dressing rapidly we sleepily gathered in Chapel for morning prayers, conducted by Miss Hamilton. After prayers we returned to our rooms to tidy and make our beds. Our rooms were carefully inspected every day, and they had to be clean and orderly. The next bell was for breakfast, and after that we went to the large study hall for a general talk. A chapter from the Bible was read, one song sung, and a poem read. We learned many poems by heart, and recited them in unison; one I remember well, we always recited when it snowed. I can see the large room, and recall dozens of faces of the girls sitting in rows, and the windows through which we could see trees and shrubs covered with feathery flakes, as we repeated this:

> The snow had begun in the gloaming,
> And busily all the night,
> Had been heaping fields and highways
> With a silence deep and white.
> Every pine and fir and hemlock
> Wore ermine too dear for an earl,
> And the poorest twig on the elm tree
> Was edged inch deep with pearl.

Another test necessary for passing from the seventh to the eighth grade was the recitation of the Catechism. When I learned that many girls had remained as long as three years in the seventh, because they could not pass the Catechism, I thought that I would get that over with at once, so when I had been there one month I asked permission to recite it. There were one hundred and seven questions, with their answers, the first one being, "What is the chief end of man?" and the answer was, "Man's chief end is to glorify God and enjoy him forever." It was compulsory to have every "an" and "the" absolutely correct, and Miss Hamilton expressed doubt of my ability to do this. I assured her that I was prepared, so with several others, we went to the home of the minister, and one at a time, recited it to him. I passed all right, but a few days later I discovered that I remembered hardly any of them; they had gone from me. Perhaps I should have remembered them. All those who passed were presented with beautiful Bibles, but I sent mine to my mother, and never saw it again.

Every Sunday, from two until five, we were supposed to remain quietly in our rooms, learning Bible verses, which we recited to our teachers. This was Silent Hour. I found it difficult to do this, and as I could memorize the verses very quickly, I frequently sneaked out of my room and spent the time in the Library. After having been caught out of my room several times, I was sent to Miss Hamilton. I was frightened, and when she asked me why I had broken the Silent Hour, I explained that I had learned my verses, and wanted to read something else. She said to me, "You do not appreciate this now, but later you will pray for the opportunity of being alone, and quiet, for two hours. Take them now; hold them as precious jewels; store up within your soul some inner quietness on which to draw when life becomes too hectic, too rushing; when circumstances will be such as to prevent your having even one moment alone and quiet. You particularly of all the girls, Belinda, should take this counsel to heart, because you are bound to have an unhappy life. You are too impetuous, too demanding of life; you will never find the perfection you seek, never be able to encompass the gener-osities of your nature. Learn now to sit quietly, and let the waters of life roll over you; learn to bend in the storm, for you will be broken if you meet it with defiance." All the time she was speaking, she looked straight at me with shining dark eyes. She spoke passionately, earnestly, and once her voice trembled. Suddenly she stopped and turned away, saying, "There, that will do. You may go."

I left her so torn and touched by her insight, that I wanted to be alone, to think over all that she had said. I sat in a small music room and tried to remember every word, to accept her advice with as much courage as it had been given. And I have known so often since, how right she was.

When school closed that spring, and the girls were planning for their summer, I wondered what I could do, for I was determined not to go home. Miss Hamilton sent for me and said, "Well, Belinda, have you chosen a girl to take home with you?" I knew that girls who had homes were expected to take with them one who had none, but I said, "Miss Hamilton, I'm not going home." Coolly she said, "Where are you going?" My fear overcame me for a moment, but boldly I said, "May I stay here, Miss Hamilton?" She tapped her pencil on her desk, and said, "You should go home; you could take some girl with you, and give her a lovely summer in the country. Won't you?" I felt mean and ungrateful, but I could not help it, and said, "No, Miss Hamilton, I can't. If you don't want me here, I will find some work, but I will not go home."

In the end they let me stay, and it was the happiest summer I had ever had. I had not hoped for anything so perfect as that summer! To awaken in the morning with the sun pouring in, and the birds singing like mad! To have no classes, but lots of time to read! The days were too short for such joy. Long evenings in the dusk, with no one to see that rules were obeyed! Just quiet and peace! To lie in my little bed, alone in the big room, with rows of white cots showing so clearly in the moonlight!

There were two other girls, much older than I, who remained also, and we had certain work to do, such as mending all the linen, and window curtains, canning vegetables from the garden, and toward the end, cleaning the entire house before the pupils returned. Ladies from Carleton sometimes came to take us out to picnics, or to church, but I managed to avoid going. I couldn't bear to lose one hour of the peace and quiet of the house, the silence and beauty of twilight. I was afraid to leave it; it might not be there when I came back.

Having been, as it were, in residence, all summer, I felt a proprietary air when the girls began pouring in, and I welcomed them as to my own home. There were shrieks of laughter, and joyful reunions, and the halls were filled with sound. It was nice to see the old girls, and exciting to meet new ones. Almost at once the familiar routine began, and our lives were regulated, classes arranged, rooms settled, and presently it was as though the summer had never been.

Discipline in Pierson School was severe, but just. Careless infringement of rules was punished, perhaps lightly, but surely. We knew to a nicety the gravity of the offense by the degree of punishment inflicted. For the most grave, the most severe punishment was to be whipped, with a slender strong cane-like stick, before the entire school. That was a solemn affair, and usually given for something too serious for discussion. The next punishment for slightly less grave reasons, was to be taken to Miss Hamilton's room and soundly spanked with her bedroom slipper. That I experienced, and for this reason.

A teacher named Miss Grove, whom I could not like, was our instructress in Domestic Science. That seemed to be a wide subject, for one of her duties was to give us information concerning reproduction. Poor woman! She was so unattractive that it was difficult to imagine her having ever had to cope with the impetuosities of man. Her teeth protruded, and her chin receded; she wore nose glasses suspended on a thin gold chain. When she haltingly tried to tell us about babies she was so embarrassed that I felt sorry for her, and wished that I might tell her just how it all came about. Having lived on a farm with animals, I knew from practical experiences all that was to be known about the way in which life was created. Finally, desperately, she said, "And the little baby lies close up to the mother's heart (here she placed her hand dramatically on her left side), where it is carried, rocking, rocking, until God is ready to allow another little life to come into the world." Unable to explain this, her words implied a wafting of wings, a painless, beautiful transformation; it was somehow horrible.

That evening I was visiting Janet Ball, and standing up before a group of girls, I mocked Miss Grove, repeating her words in an angry, satirical voice. The girls laughed, and in desperation I said "But girls, don't you *know* that that is *not* the way life is created? How can you sit like idiots swallowing such lies? Didn't you ever live on a farm? You know darn well it's sloppy sentimentality!" I was halted in my loud denunciation by a peremptory knock on the door. One of the girls sprang to open it, sensing danger. Framed in the doorway stood Miss Hamilton, dignified, dominating, queenly. "Will you come with me, Belinda?" she asked, and I followed her, too frightened to think. We knew by her expression that I was in for something this time.

Silently we crossed the veranda and in a daze I found myself facing her in her sitting room; the same room in which she had let me weep upon our first meeting. She pointed to a drawer at the bottom of a bookcase, and said quietly, "Belinda, open that drawer, and bring me a slipper you'll find there." I obeyed her. The slipper was of black leather, with a smooth, worn sole, and when I handed it to her, she took it firmly in her hand and sat down on a straight-backed chair. "Bend across my knees," she said. I did, and she lifted my skirts and spanked me with the slipper. Briskly, firmly, she applied the leather sole to my rear, and it was exceedingly painful, but I made no sound. Ten times she struck me, and then said, "Stand up." I stood up, pulling my skirts down. She handed me the slipper, and said, "Return this to the drawer." When I had done as she asked, she said, "Now, tell me why you found it necessary to discuss unkindly any teacher in my school?" I told her, honestly, why it sounded so awful to me. I repeated the 'rocking, rocking' line and said, "Miss Hamilton, you *know* that's not true. Babies are not carried nestled under the mother's heart. It's nauseating!" She was fair about it, and admitted that it was not scientific, that personally she thought it might be presented with more reality, but that she had whipped me because it was dishonorable to make fun of a teacher behind her back, and said that if at any time I had a criticism to make, I must make it to her.

A girl named Jean Parker was whipped before the school, and although we did not know exactly the reason, we knew that it involved in some way the son of the housekeeper, a little boy of seven. There were no hard feelings after punishment, and no one laughed or sneered, because one never knew when she herself might occupy the same position. When it was over, every one forgot about it.

During my second year something happened, or developed, difficult to explain, which forced me to decide that I must go to a co-educational school. Kingsland Mears had written me,—had been once in Carleton, and we had seen each other. When he said, "When are you coming back to Weaverton?" I had answered, "When I can find no other place to go." Now, at the close of my second year, I knew that I must find some place to go. I will try to explain what this was, but it was an intangible fear, something dark from which I knew I must run away. Something that made me want to be with boys.

Many girls in the lower grades had "crushes" on either an older girl, or a teacher; it was a natural thing, and accepted as such. But there was a girl in my class, named Nina Blythe, who had a "crush" on one of the teachers, a delicate, frail young woman named Miss Nankeville, who was the head of the Music Department. This crush was different from others, in that it had continued over a period of three years, and the pupils accepted it with respect.

Nina Blythe was a love child, or what is euphemistically termed by our respectable society, a bastard. Her half-sister, born in holy wedlock, was also in our class. When their father came he saw them separately, and there was a certain curiosity concerning them. Nina was more attractive and brilliant than Kitty, the legitimate, and I felt a desire to protect Nina, to fight for her, but the environment afforded me no outlet for these emotions; there was nothing from which to protect her, and no one to fight. There was nothing held for her but the greatest admiration and affection, both by the pupils and teachers. She was the best musician in the school, playing the piano extraordinarily well, and in a warm, rich contralto, she sang beautifully. She was not exactly beautiful, but she was happy, and vivid, so that she seemed lovely. She was short, rather stocky, with small feet and the wide, supple hands of a pianist; her eyes were wide blue-gray, her mouth wide, and her hair fine soft silvery blond. The shape of her forehead gave her a little-girl look, which will never change, I think.

I do not know why, but the idea came to me to break up her alliance with Miss Nankeville. I think I wanted to show that I was stronger than she, or in some way to make myself important . . . in any case, I decided to do it. My first move to that end was made in reading hour in Miss Hamilton's office, to which on Sunday evening the seniors were invited. Only those who were invited could come, and it was one of the few honors ever given, and greatly prized. At one of these occasions I made a point of sitting near Nina, and during a discussion, I casually caught her hand and held it in mine for a few minutes, and as casually released it. But there was something passed between us, some awareness of each other, which surprised me very much. When we left the room she slipped her arm through mine, and we went across the dark veranda to my door, and as I said good night, I stooped and kissed her lightly. Her face was radiant as she smiled and turned away. After that she made every possible effort to be with me, managing to change her seat at table to sit near me. When we passed in the halls, there was something tender, personal, and secret in our smile. I had only to smile, and Nina would do anything I asked. But I made no requests. She came to my room at night, after lights were out, to tell me some little happenings of the day, and for an extra good night kiss.

I had wanted simply to take Nina away from Miss Nankeville, but when I had accomplished this, completely, I didn't know what to do next. The girls had talked about it, and even made bets as to who would win, and when I had won, their interest languished and died. But I was disturbed and overwrought; now I was frightened, for Nina was a passionate, impulsive brilliant girl, and she demanded much more of me than I could give, displaying jealousy of every interest I showed in others. Also, I knew deep inside me that I cared much more for her than I could openly admit. In my perplexity, I decided to go to Miss Hamilton and tell her the whole truth, and ask her advice, but before I had obeyed the impulse, I was told to report to Miss Bond's room that night at eight o'clock. The hour signified Serious Deportment lack, liable to severe discipline.

At her "Come in," I entered, nervously, and found her busily sewing fine white lace on what was called a "dickey," a bodice of net and lace. All Miss Bond's clothes were lace liable to rustle as she walked, and she always smelled sweet. She asked me to sit down, and for a few minutes talked of her sewing and incidents of slight importance, and all the time I was tensely waiting for her to get to the subject she had on her mind. I knew vaguely what it might be, and was anxious for her to speak. Laying aside her sewing, she settled herself in her chair and said, "Belinda, it is necessary for me to speak to you about your conduct, your personal development, and I have asked God to guide me, for I feel my inadequacy keenly. If I fail to bring you the help you need, then indeed I will feel that I will suffer; I must speak to you of your relationship with Nina, and of your power over her." She paused, but I was unable to speak.

She began again, and although some of her words I do not recall, the essence of them I feel as keenly as then. She, who had been brought up in a religious Southern home, a narrow environment perhaps, told me more of the Facts of Life than the most learned people I have since met. She knew what had happened between Nina and me, and she told me that I had done one of the most ignoble things that could be done by one person to another,—to use one's power to destructive ends. She told me this without humiliating me, yet showing me plainly the lack of dignity and intelligence in my actions. She got up and walked restlessly around the room, and coming close to me she said, "You have not the excuse that you love Nina, for you know that you do not. You have probably destroyed a fine, constructive friendship between Miss Nankeville and Nina, an honorable relationship, which yours is not. You will have to learn about what love is, my child, and perhaps I can help you now." She stopped at a table, and laid her hand on a book, running her finger along the groove in the binding. Turning to me suddenly, passionately, almost angrily, she said, "You think perhaps that I have never known love; or what you think of as love. You are mistaken. I have had all the love one can have, more than my share. The fact that my lover died before I experienced fully the joy of physical love, with him, makes only this difference: I have been willing to forego the chance of that joy with any one else, because I always have had the certainty of what it would have been with him. Don't think that I have not walked in the moonlight,—that I have not known a lover's embrace, and the kisses of passionate love. If I choose of my own free will to give up my life to this school, that is between my own soul and me, but do not think that I am ignorant of what different kinds of love we are all capable." She was walking around the room again, and angrily stood over me to say, "Have you any idea what Love is, you gawky young thing?" *Have* you?" She waited for my answer, insistently. "No," I stammered. "Will you tell me?" She frowned, and said, "No, for if I did, you would not believe or accept it, and you won't for many years, if ever. It is too simple, and youth cannot understand that it is simple. Love is Service." She stood looking at me, raising her two hands before her, palms up, as if offering me something I could not see. "There, you see! The words mean nothing to you, and I have not the power to make you see what they mean,—if only I could, and save you many heartaches."

She came and sat down near me and went on, quietly, "I've watched you since you came to us, and I know more of your troubles, and your ideals than you think I do. I think I am right when I say that you are one of us, one of the old maids who take care of the children other women give birth to, and you must not feel discouraged. There is a need for many of us, or God knows what would happen to the children! I don't know, Belinda Dan, but it seems to me that a certain type must bear them, physically, biologically, but another type must bear them spiritually and mentally. I have had so many children I could never count them, and I have loved every child I have borne, and if physical pain in delivery is more tearing, more agonizing than the pain I am experiencing right now, in trying to give birth to you, then I am mistaken in my whole scheme of life. Don't let your heart be troubled. If you give all that you have, and you have much to give, for you are a loving girl, do not expect love in return. You will always be alone, inside you, as I am,—because every child that you bear will leave you, must leave you, as you will leave me. I will be here when you and hundreds who follow you, will be gone, for I am healthy and will live to be a very old woman, likely. All my children leave me, but new ones come, and from what suffering, what lack of love from their physical parents! Don't weaken, whatever happens; be strong and clean in your contacts. Try to think things out for yourself, and face whatever life brings you in a sporting way. God knows, child, I have wearied you,—you must forgive me. Now go to bed, and sleep; tomorrow begin a new life. Every morning you are new, the past is done, you are new, new, new!"

I could only say, "Thank you, Miss Bond; you have helped me, good night." I lay awake a long time, remembering every word she had said. I was filled with admiration for her, and felt a warm affection and humble gratitude to her. She was a wonderful woman.

When spring came again, Miss Hamilton sent for me and again asked me if I had chosen a girl to take home with me for the summer, and again I replied that I was not going home. "Then you must work," she said. I told her that I wanted to work, and asked her if she would help me get a job for the summer, and she said, "I will think about it." Later, she told me that I could go to the home of Mrs. Pierson, the wonderful little old lady who had founded the school. Every one stood in awe of her, and when she visited the school, great deference was shown her, and I knew that to be sent to her was a great compliment. Her home was in a lovely park, not far from school, and her household was large, but I thought that if I worked very hard, surely I could please Miss Beecher, who was one of Mrs. Pierson's adopted daughters, and the head of the house. When school closed, and all the girls had gone, the day came for me to leave also,—to go to my new home, with Mrs. Pierson.

Chapter 7

The day I left school to go to Mrs. Pierson's, I wore my new dress, which I had made from natural-colored linen Adelaide had sent me. The skirt was pleated, and made beautiful ripples as I walked; the waist was of white linen, with a soft ruffle around the neck, and on the short puffed sleeves. It was beautifully made, for I had profited from my sewing lessons, and I remember it so clearly, as it was the only new dress I had had for years. All my other clothes I had obtained from the clothes room. This is the way that was arranged.

On a slip of paper one wrote the size and description of whatever one hoped to get, and placed it in a box marked "Clothes." Every Friday afternoon at three, the clothes room was opened, and we stood in line; whoever got there first had the best chance at the clothes, all of which were sent down from the North by rich people who were interested in the school. Sometimes there were lovely things, and once I got the most heavenly blue dress with a little jacket, that I wore for years. We worked for the clothes, at two cents an hour. That was extra work, having no connection with our regular allotment.

So I walked on this lovely spring day, across our grounds, and through woods, in my beautiful poem of a dress! I don't remember my hat at all, but I probably had one from the clothes room. Through a beautiful iron gate, I entered the park, and up to the front of an imposing house of red bricks, with pale cream-colored steps, and veranda and door. I rang the bell, and the door was opened by a girl about my own age, and I gazed in wonder, for she was almost as beautiful as my own sister Lucille. Dark hair curled around a small dark face; her eyes were large, brown and shining, her teeth like pearls. She asked me whom I wished to see, and I stammered that I didn't know,—that I was the new maid from school. At that she burst into peals of laughter, and continued laughing, after she said, "Come in." I was puzzled and embarrassed, for I didn't know what amused her, and when we were inside, I said, "If you can control yourself, I'd like to see Mrs. Pierson." She became serious, and said, "Now don't be sore. I'm laughing because I thought you were a guest, and when you said you were the new maid, it just struck me as funny. You'll know why when you've been here a while. I'm awfully glad our new maid is you; come along and I'll show you your room, and then I'll take you to Mrs. Pierson."

We went up the broad hall stairs, which were polished so that you could almost see your face in them, and I thought, "That's the way I'll have to keep them, probably." We went to the third floor, where she showed me a small room next to hers, saying, "This is your room; I'm glad you're next to me. Now I'll introduce myself. My name is Faith Charron. My mother and sister Hermione live in Oakdale, and I live here because my grandmother was a great friend of Mrs. Pierson. I'm not adopted, as the others are, but Mrs. Pierson wants to bring me up to be a beautiful society belle, and marry me to some important young man in Carleton. Isn't that funny? She doesn't think my mother is the right kind of a person to bring me up. Now tell me your name." I told her and she seemed to like it, but now she said, "Come, I'll take you down to Mrs. Pierson."

We went down to the second floor, and into a large light room, in which sat a little old lady so tiny as to be startling. Faith said, "Mrs. Pierson, this is Belinda Dan, the new maid from school." The dear little old lady put out her thin dry hand and said, "How do you do, Belinda?" I was fascinated by her small, wrinkled face, her sharp intelligent eyes, and could only stammer, "Very well, thank you." She smiled and said, "I hope you will be happy with us, Belinda," and to Faith, "My daughter, you must make her feel that she is one of us; when Sara returns, let her know that Belinda has come." Faith leaned over her and kissed her lightly, gayly, and said, "Yes, Mrs. Pierson," and we left the room.

Sara Beecher was one of Mrs. Pierson's adopted daughters, of whom she had an even dozen; she was the housekeeper, and gave me my orders. In a few days I knew my duties, and although every one was kind to me, I never did feel comfortable in that house. I was right about the stairs; I could never make them shine to please Miss Beecher. She made me do them over and over until my tears would fall on them, and spoil the polish. The more she scolded the more I wept, until finally she gave up and allowed me to do them the best I could.

My mornings were spent in cleaning the rooms and making the beds of the various occupants, which included three of Mrs. Pierson's daughters. They were mature women, and they each had a job, leaving the house every morning. One was a teacher and one a secretary, and one did church work. After the rooms, I arranged flowers on the dining-room table, and laid it for lunch, gathered and prepared vegetables for dinner. When there were visitors, I served tea, in a smart cap and apron. In my spare time, I mended the linen and polished silver. Once in a long while I read a book at night, but usually I was too tired.

Faith had beautiful clothes, and Mrs. Pierson invited important people who had sons, hoping, I think that she would marry well, but I soon saw that she was going to be disappointed in that, for Faith confided to me that she was in love with George Cameron, the son of a carpenter who had a shop in a shabby part of Carleton. She managed to have me meet him, and with a radiant face she said, "Don't you think he's wonderful?" As a matter of fact, I didn't. How could I tell her that to me he looked a very ordinary sort of young man? She met him secretly at night, after the family were in bed, sneaking down to a summerhouse on the lawn, and that worried me, but I didn't know what to do.

On hot summer afternoons, Mrs. Pierson would have Celia, a lovely, gentle girl who was the cook, make a tall pitcher of lemonade, and fresh cookies, and we would go through the flower garden, through a gate, into a lane of negro cottages. Mrs. Pierson carried the cookies, and I the lemonade, and we went from house to house, dividing it between them. They all loved her, and those were happy afternoons for me.

One afternoon Faith took me to visit her mother. On the way she told me that her father, who was dead, had been a Frenchman; her mother had married again, and was now divorced. When we got to her house, and Faith fell on her knees beside her mother, who was lying in a swing on the veranda, and clasped her in her arms, murmuring the most passionate words of love, I was frightfully embarrassed. "Oh! Mummy Darling, how are you? Have you missed me? Do you still love me? What have you been doing? You must tell everything! Mummy, I love you so," Faith said, asking questions rapidly, and when her mother laughed a low, gurgling sort of laugh, I felt revolted, and hated myself for such a feeling, but I had never heard such words between a mother and daughter. She lay there laughing quietly in her throat, complacent, relaxed, sensual, and answered Faith lazily, "Why of course I always miss my beautiful daughter; I've been doing nothing,—it's too hot." I did not like her. Faith's sister Hermione came in. She was a thin intelligent-look-ing child of nine. They called her Hermi, and I discovered later that she knew a lot more about her witty, temperamental, lazy, good-looking mother, and the many men who visited her, than Faith.

On the way home I asked Faith why, if she loved her mother so much, she didn't live with her, and she said, "I don't really know, but I think it's because Mrs. Pierson doesn't like my mother, and thinks it better for me socially, to live with her. When she gets me married, she plans to take Hermi, but if she does she'll find she has more than she can handle; she doesn't know Hermi."

The summer passed, and I often begged Faith to stop meeting George secretly, to face it out, to tell Mrs. Pierson everything, but she wept hysteri-cally, and begged me to be her friend, to not turn against her too. She was so appealing, childish and sweet, that I couldn't hurt her, but my common sense told me that I should tell Mrs. Pierson. I could never find a way of knowing whether to tell all, or keep my mouth closed, concerning situa-tions which might so easily lead to tragedies. It is still a closed book to me.

When the summer ended, and I left for school, Faith cried, and kissed me, begging me to come back and see her, and I promised that I would, but before I saw her again, I heard that she had eloped with George Cameron, and that Mrs. Pierson would not allow her to return, not even to visit. I went to the hospital to see Faith, after she had her baby, a lovely little boy, and later, she was allowed to return to Mrs. Pierson's, but her husband was not permitted to come. When I saw her there, she told me that she still sneaked out at night to meet him, but she had changed. Now she was quiet, laughed seldom, and was more serious than ever in her devotion to George Cameron.

The last year in Pierson passed quickly. Nina and I were casual friends, and I knew that she had spent the summer in Canada, with Miss Nankeville, and I was glad that their friendship had resumed its old status, for I knew that we could never be real friends, though I didn't understand why this was. There were new pupils, and two new teachers, but our lives pursued their customary channels. Toward spring, I asked Miss Bond for an ap-pointment, and she told me to come to her room at nine. I went, and asked her advice, and when I said that I wanted to go to a co-educational school, she said, "Why?" her keen eyes searching my face. Hesitating, I said, "Be-cause I'm going to live in a world run by men, and I want to know more about them. I must learn by what they live, what they are like, really, for

I've never known any men." I told her of my brothers, so much older than I, and of my father, and Kingsland Mears, who wanted me to return to Weaverton and marry him; that I did not know him very well either, had never kissed him.

She listened thoughtfully, and said, "I think you're right; you should go to school with boys, but how can you do it? Where can you go, where get the money?" I said that I thought of getting a job as waitress in some big hotel in Carleton, and with my salary, and perhaps tips, I might be able to manage. She thought it not a bad idea to try, and that is what I did. I got a job as waitress and night bellhop, in a hotel called Maple Inn. In the meantime I had written to a college in Tennessee, called Gray University, because at some time in her career, my sister Lucille had gone there for a few months. She had, apparently, made her presence known in no uncertain way, and although she had done nothing bad, she had undoubtedly outraged their Methodist conceptions. The contrast between my reception as the sister of Lucille Dan, and that at Pierson, as the sister of Adelaide Dan, was vivid, unmistakable. Much later, I discovered to my regret, that it was a very religious school.

When I went to the Hotel to ask for a job, the proprietor, a stocky man with a blond mustache, asked me where I came from, and I said Pierson School. He came around from behind his desk, and looked me over carefully, saying, "Anybody is lucky to get a girl from Pierson. You can have as many jobs as you like." Taking him up on that, I said, "What other jobs can I have, besides being a waitress?" Surprised, he said, "You don't want two jobs; you'll find one will keep you busy." But I explained to him what I was doing, and why I was so anxious to make enough money to go to college, and he was very kind, allowing me to have the night job as well, so I got two salaries; with tips, I thought happily, I'll make enough.

Chapter 8

Happy that I had a good job, I returned to school, packed my clothes, said good-by to Miss Hamilton and Miss Bond, and a few girls who had not yet gone, and returned to Maple Inn. The clerk showed me to my room, which I was to share with Pearl, the cook. It was directly over the kitchen, and the heat of the stove, and the broiling sun on the tin roof, raised the temperature to an appalling degree. The clerk asked me to report to him as soon as I had changed my clothes.

Alone, I surveyed my surroundings with misgivings. The room was square, the walls covered with paper on which had been at one time enormous cabbage-like roses, now faded to a dismal blur, and in spots gone entirely. I dallied with the idea of tearing it all off, and painting the walls a cool green, but hastily continued my inspection, while I changed my clothes, hanging my beautiful linen dress on a hook under a wooden shelf, and putting on a plain clean gingham work dress. The bureau had lost a leg and teetered uncertainly; the mirror broken across the top gave only a wavering distorted image of some entirely unknown person.

Discouraged I certainly was, but I thought, "It is only for the summer, and then I'll be in college." That thought made any discomfort unimportant, and very soon I went down to the office, where the proprietor, whose name was Joseph Henning, showed me the dining room, pantries, and explained my duties to me. In a few days I had my schedule worked out, and felt sure that I could manage quite well. As for my room, I was not in it enough to bother about it.

At six o'clock every morning the eight maids, including myself, met in the supply room, where we got our brooms and dustpans and dusters, and separating, began on the halls and stairs. These were carpeted in a design of red and green, rather bilious in effect. I remember it clearly, for I swept it every day for three months. First, we put down wet newspapers, torn into small pieces; in sweeping them along the hall, they collected the dust. When we'd done all the halls and stairs, we hurriedly washed our hands, put on clean aprons, and served the breakfasts; the doors opened at eight sharp for the guests. And what guests! Shall I live long enough to erase from memory those horrible guests! Fat old women, obscene in their gluttony; children quarrelling around the tables; miserly old maids who had saved for years in order to have a few months in the mountains, in the Big City. Every type of pest known to summer hotels was there, with all the known and unknown complaints accompanying them.

We had to be clever and quick to manage four tables, and the food was served in separate dishes, like the ones my father had called soap dishes. The greedy guests moved and shifted the little dishes about in different formation, determined to get their money's worth. It was difficult for me to remember my orders, for a normal order in the dining room became something wholly different when screamed over the long table in the kitchen. Cryptic combination of words, bearing no relation to the things desired, such as Adam and Eve on a raft, for ham and eggs on toast, were recognized by Pearl, who weighing well over two hundred pounds and as black as tar, had big white teeth which gleamed as she rolled her eyes and filled our orders. Standing in line, sliding our trays along on a wooden bar, we took our turn in getting orders. As the menu was generous and varied, it was confusing and painful at first. Pearl would move up and down in front of a huge black range, waving a sharp shining carving knife before us, and if she became annoyed, would bring this knife down on the serving table with force and precision, right by your hand. She had good aim, and never touched you, but it was nerve-racking just the same. Her huge bulk swimming before us in the heat, her white teeth shining from black ebony dripping sweat, she would howl at us, "Git along dar, white gal! Who de hell does yuh think yuh are? Make it snappy, you puny bastard; what yuh holdin' up de lin' fo', yuh cross-eyed whore? *Give yuh order*, slow poke, move along an' git outa mah way, befo' I trows yuh out!" At first I was scared but I soon discovered that Pearl was the salt of the earth, and would not hurt a fly unless it lighted on her nose. I watched my step.

The confusion, the noise and the heat were exhausting at first, but I learned to stand and take it. I kept my head and prayed for tips. From a few men I got quite good ones, sometimes a dollar if they remained a week, and two if longer. Once in a while a woman would get big-hearted and part with a quarter, but usually it was a thin dime. It became known to the regular ones, those who remained for the whole summer, that I was working to go to college, so they were more generous than they would otherwise have been. I froze to every nickel.

I had one job that I loved, which was to gather and fix a vase of flowers for every table. Early in the morning, before the other maids came down, I left my switchboard where I had dozed with my head on my arms, and went to the back yard to gather nasturtiums and sweet peas and marigolds. How pungent their odor wet with dew, before the hot sun dried them! How bravely they grew with little encouragement from soil, around the cindery yard behind the kitchen. The riotous color in the early dawn was breathtaking.

When the guests had all breakfasted, we were allowed time to eat our own, and we were free to eat as much as we wished. The food was good, and it was the first time in my life I had ever had access to all the food I could eat, continuously. I began to get fat, and by the end of the summer I was certainly a sight, weighing one hundred and sixty pounds, and suddenly, too, I was a grown-up woman.

After our breakfast, we went to our different jobs. Mine was to clean and set up all the tables for lunch, after which I went to help with the rooms. This occupied us until half past eleven, when we were allowed to go to our rooms to wash up and get ready to serve lunch. Again we went through the deafening din of ordering; again Pearl stood or moved slowly behind the serving table, waving her carving knife. Pearl served all meats, her assistant, a slim yellow boy, the vegetables. Sometimes the heat in the kitchen and pantry was almost unbearable, but it was always cool in the dining room. Cool breezes came through the shaded windows, wafted down the long cool dark halls, and the wide veranda with gay awnings were always cool and comfortable. For the guests.

When the guests waddled out and we had ours, and had set up the tables for dinner, some of us had time off. We divided the time, half remaining on duty to answer bells and make salads for dinner, the other half going to their rooms to bathe and change, and perchance lie down for a few minutes. Many of the guests ambled their full stomachs to chairs under gay umbrellas on the lawn, where during the afternoon they ordered cool drinks. I managed to serve as many of those orders as possible, for they gave a five-cent tip.

After dinner, when all the guests had stuffed themselves to repletion, they streamed from the dining room, belching and picking their teeth. The men bit off large black cigars, the women waddled their broad beams out onto the veranda where they eased their unattractive bodies down in rockers. We saw their backs with pleasure.

Hastily we ate our dinner, tidied and set up the tables for breakfast, and the others got away as fast as possible. It was usually half past ten, and the maids went to bed, too tired to think of going anywhere. This group of women was a painful study for me. Two of them were girls of good family, who through misfortune had been forced to earn a living, and having no training had drifted into this work. Several of them drank just enough to keep comfortable, but not enough to interfere noticeably with the performance of their duties; one or two were old maids who had failed in that quest of all women, a man. Dry, scrawny, they moved like automatons, performing their routine, oblivious to all that happened outside their immediate environment; just going on and on and on. There was no life, no hope, no laughter in them. They were all much older than I, and we had little conversation, but they were fair and honest and, on the whole, a group of decent women. But somehow sad, depressing, puzzling.

When the other maids went off duty I became another person with a new job, that of night telephone girl and bell hop. I attended the switchboard, delivered telegrams and packages, and answered all bells. Usually the older guests were in bed and snoring by eleven; a few in which glimmered still a spark of life, stayed up until twelve, while the straggling, pimply faced, long-legged boys, flirting with equally gangling girls, giggled and shrieked on the dark ends of the veranda until one. There was always one old maid who was desperately trying to ensnare a man. We watched her progress with relentless eyes, and it was too pathetic to bear continued scrutiny; I was glad when she remained in a basket chair on the lawn; it was less exhausting to one's sympathies. God help women who have reached a certain age and cannot give up; those who still talk baby talk, and act kittenish, dated and damned. We have all seen them, and have been torn in our sympathies, unable to laugh at, or weep with them.

Two afternoons each week I had two hours off, when I went to the top of the house where the other maids slept, and had a bath and a nap. The hot room with Pearl was too noisy for sleep, but I explained it to Pearl, for I wanted her to understand that I in no way minded rooming with her. She was a grand person, and proved her friendship for me.

In the evenings, when the air was soft and cool through the trees, I could hear music far off, coming from homes and other hotels both far and near.

My heart would contract with pain and loneliness, with longing for the beautiful scenes I pictured in my imagination. Shaded porches where beautiful young girls in fresh summer dresses sat on swings, with handsome young men who wore clean shirts and quoted poetry; cool rooms with shiny floors where beautiful young people danced gracefully, held tenderly in the strong arms of desire. Sometimes I wept as I sat on the veranda for a few quiet moments after the giggling group had gone; but not for long. I reminded myself that I was lucky to have a job, and that I was going to college, that some day I would meet much more wonderful people than those now having a good time. God save the mark! It didn't turn out that way at all.

There was one guest who gave me some qualms, until I came to understand her. She was about thirty-four, pretending to be twenty-two. She had grown up believing that a woman should be gentle, clinging, willowy and sweeping. She managed to sweep when sitting. She told me that she had come to the mountains for her health, and as this inn did not take tubercular people, she chose it, but she looked suspiciously tubercular herself. She was determined to catch herself a man, and made valiant, though misdirected efforts to that end.

One night when she had rung a great many times, for no good reason, I became exasperated, and told her that I couldn't leave the switchboard so often without a good reason; that I had to hold on to my job. She apologized, and I felt sorry for her, for I suspected her real trouble. Suddenly she burst into sobs, and when I said, "Don't cry, Miss Kerr; tell me if there is anything I can do to help you," she told me, between tearing painful sobs that she simply had to get married; that she had taken all the money that her mother and brother could scrape together, to come to the mountains, on the chance of getting a husband, and she felt that it was her duty to succeed. She simply couldn't go home without a husband; she said, and meant it, that she would kill herself first.

I let her get it all out, and when she was quiet, I told her not to worry, that I would go down and plot some way to help her get a husband, and would come back later and tell her. She seemed to believe that I could, and was grateful. I returned to my board, and wrote down all the possibilities among the guests, and checked them over carefully, and finally chose an elderly man who had frequently talked to me in the evenings, and seemed lonely. He had been coming to the Inn for many years, and I'd been told that he had lots of money, and was a bachelor. After all, I didn't see why he shouldn't have some trouble in life. His name was Garret Johnstone. When

I worked out my plan, I went up to her and said, "Now listen, Miss Kerr. I'll help you if you promise to do exactly as I say. Will you?" She was so glad of help she would have promised anything. I told her my plan. At first she was against Mr. Johnstone, because he was too old, but I persuaded her. I felt like saying, "Well, you're no spring chicken yourself," but didn't. There was an instant's fleeting thought of consideration for Mr. Johnstone, but I brushed it aside. Hadn't he said to me, leaning on my desk one night, that he wished he had some one to love him? And wasn't I getting her for him? I had thought of saying, "If you'll help me go to college, I'll love you," but I didn't, for he knew darn well I was working to go to college, and if he had been so big-hearted as he represented himself, he could have given me a quarter tip instead of a dime. My conscience troubled me not at all.

I had pictured him to Mary Kerr as a very distinguished man of excellent family, and said that in my opinion the woman who got him would be lucky. That evening while he rocked and smoked, I went out and sat with him, and after a little while I said, "Poor Miss Kerr! Up there in a sweltering hot room." As a matter of fact she had a lovely cool room. He said nothing, and I rocked, then said, "I think I'll ask her to come down for a breath of air." She was ready and waiting, and came down trailing yards of tulle in her wake. Languishing, willowy sweeping, she joined us. I stayed until they were at ease with each other, and left them.

Almost every evening we sat on the veranda, and I left them alone a great deal, with the result that before the summer was over she actually landed him, and he was as proud as punch. I could foresee a long life ahead of him, a great deal of which would be spent in adjusting her scarf, picking up her bag, her gloves, fan, smelling salts, and handkerchiefs. She fluttered and flapped around, pretending to me that she had fallen in love with him at first sight. She had honestly forgotten that I had spent hours selling his stock to her a bare six weeks ago. But I think she appreciated my help, because the day they left to return to her home for the wedding, she left a note for me. I was taking my nap of the month and did not witness their departure. It was a flowery little note, with ten dollars enclosed; perhaps she figured that out on a percentage basis.

One night during the summer Kingsland came in to see me. He hated the fact that I was working as a waitress, and his father, who was a snob, had made cutting remarks to him about it. I asked him to come at twelve, as after that I was not so busy, and we sat out on the veranda, with cool drinks. We talked over old times and friends, of his life, and mine. I told him that I thought I would have enough to go to Gray University in the fall. He was not enthusiastic, but grudgingly admitted that he admired my courage; when he said, "Then I'm to go on waiting until you prove to yourself that you cannot do what you think you can? When you have, then will you marry me?" The same old pain and conflict between us. I said to him, "King, you deserve the best, not second. Forget me, let me go on alone; I cannot help wanting to be educated." He laughed and said, "No, you poor dumb girl, I'll wait. I love you, and no one else seems the same." We parted friends, but he looked sad.

Although Pearl had been particularly kind to me, often saving special food for me, and sometimes yelling at the other waitresses not to crowd, to give me a chance, I had not realized the deep affection she had for me until the day I left. I went to the kitchen to say good-by to the steward, and the girls, and Pearl. I found her sitting out behind the kitchen fanning herself, as she wiped sweat from her ebony face. I offered her my hand, and said, "Good-by, Pearl, thank you for all your kindness to me; I'll never forget it." She raised her enormous bulk, and from the cavernous folds of her voluminous skirt she brought forth a tiny parcel, a tightly folded piece of newspaper, which she put into my hand. "Good-by, wite gal," she said, grinning. "I gives yuh dis lil present, an' I wishes yuh good luck. Wen yuh gits high up wid de gran' folks, jist rem'ber Pearl wasn't a bad skate!" To my astonishment I saw tears in her big black eyes, and I said, "But, Pearl, what is it?" She waved a fat black hand in dismissal, and said, "Doan yuh ast no questions an' I'll tell yuh no lies!" I felt great love for Pearl, and I put my arms around her enormous sweaty shoulders, and said, "Thank you, Pearl! I'll not forget." When I opened the package I found fifty dollars! Nearly two months of heat and sweat and life of black Pearl in my hand! I could not bear it; my heart seemed near to bursting. I kept it, and wrote to her many times, for that was the most wonderful thing that had ever happened to me. Dear black Pearl!

I went to my sister Adelaide and spent a day getting my clothes in order, and the next morning I left Carleton for Troy, and college. Alone on the early emptiness of a hot morning, carrying my new straw suitcase, I got on the trolley that would take me to the station, where I bought my ticket. I was actually and truly on my way to be educated.

In Troy I inquired the direction of the University, secretly pleased to use the word, it had such an elegant sound. I wanted to run quickly to it, to be at once inside, where all would be quiet and peaceful, where I could study and learn, and I made haste, my suitcase bumping against my shins. It was a short walk, and I needn't have hurried. In fact, I might better have walked in an entirely different direction, perhaps, in which case, however, I would have missed an interval of fantastic stupidity quite beyond imagination; an experience to be realized only by active participation. No doubt it was worth it.

It was not a long walk, and when I reached the grounds I saw, instead of spacious old green velvet, shaded by great plumed trees, as I had seen them in my imagination, a thinly grassed plot enclosed by a low wooden fence. The first building I reached was a large red wooden affair, to which a new wing was being added. Going up the narrow walk to a huge door standing ajar, I rested my suitcase on the steps, and rang the bell. Presently the door was opened and I beheld before me a fantastic apparition. It was, I presumed, a woman, but a woman with the most terrible gargoyle face, such an old witch that I could not speak. It opened its awful mouth and said, "Are you a student?" I said, "Yes," and it moved back, mouthing an irritable "Come in." And as I followed her, she said, "You are a day early; we are not ready yet."

Once inside, she pushed the door to and said, "I'm Mrs. Lacey." This was the head of Holden Hall! A voice inside me counselled me to turn and run, but I had worked so hard to get here, and had dreamed of such grandeur, I could not quit now. There this awful thing stood, stooped, bent and wrinkled, dressed in the most astounding collection of rags I had ever seen. On her feet were old felt slippers with run-down heels, that made the same sound that my father's woollen socks used to make on the rough wooden floor, a dry, hissing, reptilian sound; above them cotton stockings of a dirty gray rolled in careless abandon. A flannel petticoat followed, and at the top a gray woollen bed jacket, over strange ancient underwear. Around her shoulders she held with claw-like hands, a knitted shawl, called in those days, for some occult reason, a "fascinator." The ensemble did fascinate, but also repelled. The fascinator flopped around, except when held under her arms, an adjustment she was constantly performing. That lifting of the elbows, the flicking of that fascinator!

She was perhaps a woman of sixty, but a driving, dominating, mean, passionately spiteful, hagridden sixty. A few strands of gray hair which had been unsuccessfully dyed, meandered over her repulsive dome. Great bald patches showed through, and those spots were scaly with dandruff. Her loose mouth enclosed a few old teeth scattered at irregular intervals; her watery old eyes looked keenly out from pouches of decayed-looking skin. All this I saw, and this was college.

Tucking her fascinator under her arms, she told me that she would show me a room, although it was not yet prepared. I followed her up a flight of stairs to the second floor, and down a long hall, into the new part. Showing me where the mattresses and sheets were kept, she left me to make up my bed.

In my haste to get to college I had not stopped to eat, and I began to feel hungry. I wandered around the halls, and only the echoes of my own footsteps returned to me. I was thirsty and could find no water. Along in the afternoon, having explored the entire house, I put on my hat and went into the village for food and water. When I had eaten heartily and drunk an enormous amount of water, I returned to the University by another route, wishing to see the town. This required at most twenty minutes.

When I returned, and started down the hall, the old gargoyle shuffled out of a room, half dressed, with pins in her cavernous mouth. She asked me where I had been, and I told her. She listened vaguely and said that she was going to a meeting at the Church, and if I cared to do so, I might accompany her. Since I was alone, and the lights not on, and the water wouldn't run, I said I would be glad to go. Besides, I wanted to see what she looked like, once all the pieces were assembled, with a hat on top.

I saw, to my horror. At the top she put on a basque, with below a very full skirt of ancient vintage. She changed the gray cotton stockings for black ones, and the felt slippers for black leather shoes that laced a long way up her ankle. She attached to her sparse gray hair, great gobs of grayish blond curls. On top of these she perched a hat on which bits of birds and fruit and flowers were sewn at unpremeditated intervals. Although the heat was intense, she drew on her gnarled old hands tight black kid gloves; she carried carefully a prayer book and Bible.

The meeting was held in a side chapel of the Church, and I do not recall its purport, but on the way there and back, she kept up a flow of irrelevant conversation, from which I picked a few stray bits of information I thought might be of use to me if I were to remain in this awful place. One was that a friend of hers had died, leaving the University enough money for Holden, with the provision that Mrs. Lacey remained as its head as long as she lived. When we returned she took me to my room by the light of a candle, which she carried away with her, but I had sufficient light from the moon to undress by, and inexpressibly sad, I lay down and went to sleep. Even the gargoyle didn't appear to haunt me.

Next morning I got up early and tried to find her and food. I was successful in the first, but not in the second. I don't know what she ate, but she told me to go to a restaurant not far away for my breakfast, and to return, as she wanted me to arrange the furniture, and prepare the rooms for the pupils who would begin to arrive the next day.

When I returned, she was arrayed in the same costume in which she had first appeared, and continually wiping a drop from her nose with the back of her hand, she showed me how she wanted the beds and bureaus placed. I had come with the understanding that I was to wash pots for my room and board, but as the pots hadn't been used yet, I moved furniture. I pulled and hauled and got five or six rooms quite nicely arranged, when she changed her mind, and asked me to move it around again. This continued until late afternoon, with no lunch, and several girls arrived. I showed them to their rooms, explaining nothing. I had made my own discoveries, and didn't wish to deny them that pleasure.

One of the girls, Medora Cortez, came from Texas. She was very dark, and charming, so I asked her to have supper with me. We went to the restaurant, but the food was very bad, and we ate little. When we returned I went to bed, not feeling so good. During the night I had terrible nightmares, and awoke with an overpowering thirst. I tried to find water, as the gargoyle had said it would be turned on during the day. I could find none, and in desperation I went down and knocked on her door. Through the pale dawn I could see her face, and it was revolting. "Water!" I gasped. Hitching her fascinator over her shoulders, she said, "Come." We went through the kitchen and pantry out into the back yard where there was an iron faucet. She showed it to me and shuffled away. Putting my mouth under the pipe, I drank and drank. My thirst at first concealed the brackish taste so different from that of our clear mountain water, but it was wet. I returned to bed, but when the time to get up came, I didn't. I was delirious, and one of the girls found me raving. She was frightened, and told the gargoyle that she must get a doctor.

That day is gone completely. I knew nothing until the following morning, when I came back from a hell of nightmarish imaginings to find a doctor and the gargoyle in my room. I lay still, trying to recall what had happened. As the doctor left I heard him say, "Now Mrs. Lacey, remember what I say; this girl must have quiet and rest. No more moving furniture for her." Gradually things cleared up and I began to feel better. Many of the girls had been lovely to me, and in spite of everything, I was in college, and that fact still thrilled me. In a week I was up, and found that things had assumed a reasonable amount of order; that the pots and pans were waiting for my attentions. Three times a day I washed pots. This required time, strength, and the application of strong soaps, and even iron-meshed pieces for the removal of food burned tightly to the bottoms. Study was over long before I was finished. As I had not enough money to buy textbooks, I borrowed them from other girls, and as we were not allowed to study in our rooms, I sat on a toilet near my room after lights were out, but after a few hours this position became cramping. The teachers were nice human beings, and I liked them. The girls in Holden were grand, and many of them paid, doing no work at all. There was never at any time any evidence of snobbery among them. I always wondered why any girl whose parents could pay should come to such a place.

This University was hagridden with religion. Raised up as I had been on "Washed in the blood of the Lamb," a horrible song that sent me to bed with visions of little lambs all dripping with blood, and a nauseating revulsion toward anything so unnatural as washing in their blood, I had heard songs at Pierson School that made God attractive, such as "Now the day is ending, Night is drawing near," and others, insidious but less horrible than those I had known before. And now, inadvertently, I found myself again deeply involved in the Washed in the Blood of the Lamb.

On the very first Sunday we all marched two by two behind that old witch to church, and they sang "Stand up, Stand up for Jesus!" I didn't sing, and when we returned, Mrs. Lacey sent for me; angrily she asked me, "Why didn't you sing this morning? Such a noble, inspiring song, 'Stand up, Stand up for Jesus!' and you didn't open your mouth! Why not?" I feared her, but I told her the truth. "For many years I have sung that song, Mrs. Lacey, but I've found that Jesus doesn't stand up for me, so I will not sing it any more." She was furious, and said, "You'll sing the songs we sing, and I don't want to have to speak to you about it again!"

I was not a very bright student, and having no books handicapped me somewhat, and the pots interfered, but I always managed to pass the examinations. I hated Mathematics with a deep hate; in English I wasn't so bad, and better in Latin. Ancient History was anathema, but it was given by a darling old Professor Henderson, and I tried hard for his sake. I never could care desperately whether the Phœnicians attacked with two hundred and ten foot soldiers, or two hundred and eight . . . of whatever kind; dates left me cold, and whether it was 411 B.C. or 412, I found myself watching the rhythmic movement of a peculiar growth situated just in front of his left ear, which moved up and down as he talked, his lips rarely meeting over protruding yellow teeth. Yet he was a dear old man.

When I discovered that the class in Botany went on long walks across the fields, boys and girls together, I displayed an enormous amount of interest in plant life. On our very first walk I managed to get into conversation with a very nice-looking boy, who talked to me of specimens, about which I told him I knew absolutely nothing. I might easily have gone further and admitted that the only specimen I was interested in at the moment, was man. He told me his name was Leonard P. Burke, and I never did find out what the P. stood for; that he came from Kingsville. He was very tall, had very pink cheeks, and very black hair. Everything about him seemed very commonplace, but he was my first boyfriend since I arrived, and I treasured him. On the way home he asked me to go to prayer meeting with him on Wednesday evening. I liked Botany.

Holden Hall also had Silent Hour on Sunday, but unlike Pierson, we did not learn Bible verses. We were not allowed to lie down, at least not on the beds. If we wished to take a nap, we lay on the floor, as the old gargoyle said we mustn't "muss up" the beds, and she sneaked around in her old felt slippers to catch us out. Sunday evening we went to prayer meeting. I did wish I might stay home, as that was the one night of the week when I could have studied without sitting in the toilet, but prayer was compulsory. I lived in terror for fear they would call on me to lead in prayer, for there was something indecent about praying and confessing in public,—it seemed a personal matter.

The dining room of Holden was in the new building, and had a floor of tiles. Every Saturday morning I was supposed to scrub this floor, after I had done the pots and pans. Even Mrs. Lacey relented, and sent two girls to help me. On our knees, with soap and brush, we scrubbed. It was a very large room, and the floor seemed endless, because every speck of dirt seemed to embed itself into it. Nothing could clean that damned floor! One morning when we three were down scrubbing, we heard the voice of the gargoyle, showing a visitor around, heard her bragging voice as she said, "And this is our lovely new dining room! Isn't it beautiful, with all the windows? I'm hoping to have some decorative pieces at intervals around the room." When I saw that the visitor was Leonard P. Burke, I almost fell into my pail, thinking, That's the end of that romance! In my dirtiest dress, our rumps sticking up, and the old witch speaking of "Decorative Pieces." I could have died of shame, and was sure he would never speak to me again. However, all he said was, "I think it's a shame you have to do such work." We remained friends.

Morning prayers occurred in the dining room, after breakfast. On that hard tile floor we kneeled until paralyzed, while that old hag used the occasion for a general release of all stored-up hatreds. This is the manner of her petition to God:

"We come before you this morning, dear Lord, to render thanks to thee for all thy many mercies to us. Help us to appreciate all the blessings of the modern improvements of the new building; the running water, and the lovely tile floor in the handsome new dining room. Teach the girls, Blessed Savior, to appreciate the new Singer Sewing Machines, on which they can make their clothes, and the beautiful Grand Piano, of the finest mahogany, which I am sorry to tell you, dear Jesus, some careless girl has already marred with a scratch, which was so kindly presented to us by the Ladies' Guild for the Improvement of the Characters of College Girls. We know dear Father, that they come from homes that are not blessed with these beautiful and useful articles" (looking around to her left, "Janet, stop that twiddling with your pencil; it disturbs my train of thought"). "And, dear Lord, don't, I beg, I beseech you, *don't* let any of our girls be tempted by Satan, and led into the iniquities of the Flesh! Don't let them even *think* of wearing short sleeves! Show them the way, I beg, I entreat, show them the way, dear Father, to be Ladies!" ("Mary, will you stop that whispering when I'm praying?")

"Help us each and every one to deserve the manifold blessings thou hast bestowed upon us. The nice new beds, with excellent mattresses; and the new sheets of fine goods! And" (sinking her voice to a whispering confidential supplication), "dear, dear Lord, see to it that none of our girls use that instrument of sin, face powder! You know, Father, that this is co-educational, and realize full well that I must display extreme agility of both mind and body, to properly circumvent the very appearances of Evil." (Stopping, straightening up on her knees, and looking full at the room full of girls, whose gaze has been directed toward her, due to her sudden pause, "*Who*, I say to you, *who* was the girl standing under the fourth maple from the Library last night at eight o'clock, engaged in frivolous conversation with a young man? I cannot call him a gentleman, who so flagrantly breaks the rules of this noble institution. I ask you who it was? Speak up! Let your sins be as scarlet, I will make them white as snow! I beg you to admit your sin, here before us all." Silence, profound silence. "So, the girl who has the boldness to break a rule has not the courage to confess? Well, I'll find out, rest assured of that, then God and

I will both know.") Resuming a pious position on her knees, her prayer continues. By this time our knees were absolutely numb, past pain.

"And now, dear Lord, as we bring our morning offering to a close, let me make just one more request. It is this, dear God. I beg, I plead, I humbly ask that you save my girls from that most heinous crime, talking to boys in class, or on the campus. Give them strength, (*will* someone go out and get that pail that is blowing around? Makes such a din I can't hear myself speak!) to avoid the weakness of yielding to the male. Especially watch over one of our pupils who suffers from the sin of pride; teach her to be humble before her God. I refer, as you probably know, dear Lord, to Belinda Dan. And with these few words, I leave us in thy hands. Look after us in the future as you have in the past, comfort us, (Lucy Watts, I can conduct my communications with the Lord without your help, so if you will stop moving your lips you will oblige me, and no doubt simplify things for God; besides, it makes me awfully nervous). So until tomorrow, kind heavenly Father, I leave us in thy care, trusting in thy understanding heart. Amen."

Rising stiffly on her poor old knees, brushing her skirt, looking swiftly around the group, she waved us aside, with an admonishing, "Go to your work, girls," and she scuttled off. Every morning we went through just that, only sometimes it was worse.

The winter wore away and lovely spring came, making the most grim surroundings hopeful. The maple trees became covered with tender green, and flowers bloomed, so that even the drab little town had an air of beauty. We brought great bunches from our botanizing walks, and now my beau walked with me. He was not very interesting, but he was a man. Kingsland Mears wrote to me regularly, and sent me his photograph, which I showed to the girls, and I was surprised when they raved about his good looks . . . I had known him so long that I never remembered that he was handsome. He still urged me to give up my fight for an education, to return to Weaverton and marry him, and sometimes I was almost persuaded, for certainly college had turned out a frost,—so different from what I had imagined.

When school closed, I said good-by to all the girls, and Leonard carried my suitcase to the train. Down the same street that I had walked so joyously in the fall, I now walked in the spring, without the joy. The year had somehow left me with a sense of defeat . . . maybe I had built my hopes too high. In any case, I must find work, and if I meant to return to college, I knew of no way to make the money except as a waitress. I thought it might be nice to marry King and live in Weaverton, after all.

In Carleton, I told my sister Adelaide all about the school and how disappointing the whole thing had been, and with her usual optimism, she said, "Forget it,—make a new life." I told her that I would go home, and perhaps marry King,—that if I did not, I would be back. At Weaverton I got down at the dismal, dirty station and began the long walk home, carrying my suitcase. Climbing the long hot dirt road from the village, I met John Hyatt, Nancy's brother, who took my suitcase and walked with me. We came upon two thin, white, dirty little boys playing in the red dust of the road, and I said, "Whose children are they? They look so thin and unhealthy." John looked embarrassed, and said, "They're Nancy's. She lives just up the road here." When we reached the small wooden house, drab and dismal, set back behind broken palings, with never a flower nor tree near it, he said, "This is where Nancy lives." He called and we waited at the gate. When Nancy came out, down the hard dirt yard, I felt my heart would stop. She was so changed; her front teeth were out, her hair uncombed, and her calico wrapper hung shapelessly around her. She was perfectly at ease, unaware of any astonishment in my face, and that was the most painful thing of all. She laughed happily and I promised to come down and see her before I left.

As I went on alone, for John remained with Nancy, my thoughts were troubled. I couldn't forget Nancy,—it was as though I had seen her dead, had gazed upon a shell from which all life had gone, leaving no semblance of the healthy, happy, beautiful child I had known and loved. Where had her youth and beauty gone? And Why? For What? And would my complacency equal hers? Was this all that life held for me? Something in me revolted. I knew at once that I could not marry King. I resolved that I would fight on, for something braver and better than that. I didn't know what, exactly, but something containing more of life, more of beauty. If I failed, I would go down with a struggle, to the end, to nothing.

It depressed me to see my mother older, no longer pink-cheeked, more bent, more gray. Sallie looked different too, but perhaps I was in a state of mind, or emotion, which precluded the possibility of seeing things with a sound perspective. My father was away on a surveying trip, and I remained but one night. I never saw my mother or Sallie again. I could not go back,— it hurt too much. There is no turning back, when one is poor. Only the rich may vacillate; the poor must fight on against every hindrance. Families part, and never have enough money to return, even for a visit. Money is necessary to the continuation of feeling, among families or friends. I had no money, therefore I eliminated family feeling as much as possible, as a luxury I could not afford. The poor must fight against even emotional hindrances, or they are lost forever.

I returned to Carleton, to Adelaide, and after a few days started out to look for a job, all desire for an education at least temporarily crushed. I went to see Doctor Mears, King's uncle, who was a dentist. He had been nice to me when I had seen him, with King, and I asked him if I could come in his office and learn to be a dentist. He said I could, and so I started there with him.

Chapter 9

While all these things had been happening to me, my sister Adelaide had not been overlooked by bad luck. She had, three years previously, married a very fine man,—a widower with two little boys,—named James Wesley Meriam. He was very well off, materially, and they were in love and happy. One day, meaning to go for a ride in the car, they walked around their house to the garage. My sister stood by the car, while he ran upstairs for something; he spoke to her, and she looked up to answer him. As he turned away, his foot slipped and his body came hurtling down almost at her feet, breaking his neck. She was left with a six-months-old baby girl, and no money. He had loved her, but made no provision for her, and when I heard that his brother, a minister, was administrator of the estate, I thought, "She'll be looking for a job soon." She was.

At this time she was in Carleton, while she looked for work which would allow her to keep her baby with her. Soon she found it, and left for Gremont to become housekeeper for an old couple, and I was left alone. Stunned with grief, she was trying to steer her own bark, with an added passenger, through the uncertain and perilous seas of life. I was sad when she left, for I didn't feel so brave and bold as I did when I was fourteen, but at least I had a job.

Doctor Mears was a tall, stooped, taciturn, putty-colored man of fifty. He was, probably, a good dentist, but his office, which was up a flight of dirty wooden steps in an old red-brick building, was grimy with the dust of years. An odor of iodine and old teeth overlay a permanent permeating odor of old rotting wood, musty overstuffed chairs, and a faint, persistent odor of bad plumbing. But I was extremely anxious to learn a lot about practically anything, and thought that if I were to be an assistant to a dentist, I would do it thoroughly. I sent to a number of Dental schools for their prospectuses, but as I had no money, nothing came of that. They were interesting reading.

In a few weeks, when I had learned the names and uses of the various instruments, Doctor Mears said, "Now you must learn to clean teeth." I tried, on one patient, but I knew instantly that never in my whole life, would I be a dentist. I told Doctor Mears, and he said, "Well, Belinda, I guess you're just not cut out to be a dentist," and I agreed with him. We parted amicably.

While I worked for him I lived with the Culpeppers, the remnants of a fine old family, struggling, with indifferent success, to keep alive. The mother, a young-looking, vivacious woman, was tubercular. She made beautiful clothes for the rich women of Carleton. The father, a fine, healthy-looking man of forty, was a drunkard. When sober, which was seldom, he built houses. Their one daughter, Katharine, was fourteen, and a levelheaded child she was. She wanted to be a dancer, but her father's habits made finances uncertain. In her room she had a ballet-bar, a strong gymnastic bar for limbering, which her father had installed for her. I was enthralled when I first saw her dancing on her toes, and with her encouragement, I soon found myself doing all her exercises with her. She was not pretty, but her body was beautiful.

Katharine and her father were great friends. She could tell by the way he opened the door whether he was drunk or not. She tried to protect both him and her mother from each other. Her mother would scream imprecations at him, and weep hysterically when Mr. Culpepper came home drunk, so Katharine concealed it as well as she could. But every one knew, and his many cronies were loyal. After a few days she allowed me to help her with him.

One night when we had all gone to bed and Katharine and I were almost asleep, we heard the front door opening very carefully. Quickly she got up and put on her dressing gown and mules and I did the same. When we got downstairs, we found that her father had brought a friend home with him, and they were both drunk. They were both very dignified and careful in their speech. We left them in the dining room, quiet, seemingly peaceful and friendly.

We went to bed, and a long while later, we heard a sound of things falling down. We ran quickly and quietly down the stairs, and Katharine tried to open the dining room door. It was locked, and she called to her father quietly, hoping that her mother had not heard. When Mr. Culpepper opened the door, we saw that he had blood on his clothes and hands, but remained upright with a swaying movement. Katharine put her arms around him and said, "Father, what's the matter? What was that noise?" He focused his eyes for a moment, trying to adjust his features, apparently found it impossible, and began to weep; then he smiled slyly, happily and said, "Nothing, dear. Bob and I just had a little argument, but it's all over; nothing to worry about." Katharine began to lead him toward the stairs, urging him to go to bed. In the hall she motioned for me to remain there, and when she had put him to bed, she returned.

We went to the dining room to see what had happened. The other man lay on his side, relaxed, apparently asleep. Katharine went to the phone in the hall, and quietly called a number, asking them to send an ambulance. I heard her say, "Bob Hilton is drunk on my dining room floor, and will you take him away quietly, as I don't want my mother to know." She was a very efficient child. Very soon they came and removed him, quietly. They knew what to expect in this house.

When they had gone we put out the hall light and went to the kitchen to make some coffee. It was now four o'clock. When the coffee was bubbling, I got out cups and saucers, and Katharine went to the dining room for spoons. Suddenly I heard her gasp, hysterically. I turned to see what had frightened her, as she came through the door, holding a curious object between thumb and finger, her arm stiffly in front, staring at me in horror. "What is it?" I whispered. To me it had the appearance of a skinned mouse. Without a word, she dropped it on a plate on the table, and as it settled wetly down, she slid down to the floor.

I rubbed her face with a wet dishtowel, speaking to her, trying to bring her back. After a moment she opened her eyes and great tears began to roll down her cheeks. Her face was perfectly calm, and she looked so odd, with tears welling up and pouring down, yet she was not weeping. "Katharine," I said crossly, "what is it? What frightened you? Tell me!" Her tears still falling, she waved her hand weakly toward the table and said, "The eye! The eye!" Annoyed, I said, "Now, Katharine, don't be silly! Pull yourself together. Whose eye? Where?" She pointed in a childish way to the table, and said, "On the plate! Look! It was on the knob of the silver drawer!"

I got up from my crouching position by her side, and cautiously approached the object, and I saw that it was an eye. Now I was scared too, when I saw that it was not a mouse, and whispered to her, "Get up, Katharine, for pity sakes! Let us go upstairs." She got up, and as we went into the hall, we heard some one at the door. Katharine opened it, and we saw that it was the young man on the ambulance. They too had discovered that the man was shy one eye.

I liked the Culpeppers very much, especially Katharine and her father. I didn't care for Mrs. Culpepper, and presently I discovered why. While we sat sewing in the evenings, many of her women friends came in and helped, and while they sewed, they talked. I listened to their conversation, which frequently concerned itself with tuberculosis, and the different cures advocated by various doctors. The most popular one with them was that which advised the having of many children, thereby passing it on, and becoming well themselves. Doctors had told them that the babies would take the disease from the mother, and they mentioned many of their friends, who had become entirely cured by pursuing that method. Mrs. Culpepper spoke gloatingly of the fact that she had had six children, younger than Katharine, all of whom had died, and she in consequence was very much better; in fact practically cured.

At first I couldn't believe my ears, but upon constant repetition I was forced to realize that they were in deadly earnest. One day, revolted beyond discretion, I told them that I thought they were nothing but graveyard ghouls, murderers of little children. By that I achieved nothing except the necessity of finding other sleeping accommodations, which I did. Through an acquaintance of Katharine's, I heard of a German woman who gave music lessons, and I went to see her, offering to work for her, if she would give me lessons. She was a kind soul, and we came to an agreement that for working all day in her boarding house—for, plus musical activities, she also took boarders—she would give me one lesson a week. So I went there.

Her name was Mrs. Amos Foote, and her husband, a meek little man about half her size and weight, had a cigar store and news stand near their home. She gave piano lessons, and singing lessons, and was the soloist in the First Baptist Church, in Carleton. She had no time for the house, so I cleaned and dusted and made beds, helped the cook and waited at table. The first week went rapidly, and so did the second. During the third week I asked her when she was going to give me a lesson. She said, "Vell, I vill tell you, Mees Dan, I haf been zo beezy I coultn't fin' time, but you vait. I vill gif you a fine lesson soon. Gif me time, gif me time." Well, I gave her time. One month passed and she had not yet achieved it, so I wrote to my sister Adelaide that I must do something, and she wrote inviting me to come to her on a visit. I took my straw suitcase and left. All I had learned was a wonderful way to cook rice, but nothing of music.

No matter how discouraged I became, nor how bad things were, getting on a train was always thrilling. It was adventure, and might lead to any-thing,—to new lands, fine people, golden opportunities and happiness. The train ran through beautiful mountainous country, brilliant with the color of azaleas, dogwoods and rhododendrons, which reminded me of the old Mill. Also it sped past poor mean shanties, hanging onto the steep hillsides, and I knew the poverty of those lives; the utter hopelessness of thousands of American mountaineers, like me and my family. There was nothing ahead for me, but I looked forward with hope and joy to seeing my sister, to a new place, where something beautiful might easily happen.

When the train stopped at Gremont, I climbed down, glad to see my sister waiting for me, her hair shining like gold in the sun. She laughed at me and my suitcase, and said that she had walked from the Fairfax home, where she worked, and that we would walk back. As we went along, she told me about the town, and of the two old people for whom she worked; that Mr. Fairfax was a retired Presbyterian minister, and that they got their money from a sand bank, somewhere in the north. She said, "They are an amazing couple; don't be surprised when you see them. You'll understand later. But I must warn you about Isiah." The sun was hot, and I said pee-vishly, "Who is he?" She laughed and said, "An old parrot." Presently she said, "Isiah is the most important person in the house, and whatever he says or does, don't laugh; at least not before them." Troubled, I said, "Is he funny?" Thoughtfully she said, "In a way; they love him more than any one in the world, so look sharp." She was so serious that I rested my suitcase on the ground, and sat on its upturned end. "All this sounds ridiculous to me! After all, what's an old parrot?" I asked her.

She walked on, and picking up my suitcase I followed. "You'll find out, when you know Isiah. Remember what I say, and treat him with respect, for your visit depends upon his reaction to you. If he takes a dislike to you, you'll have to go." That made me mad, and I angrily said, "Well, if they allow an old bird to select their guests, to the devil with them; I'll leave." She didn't answer, and we turned in through a big iron gate of a lovely looking place, with tall trees, green lawn, and flowers.

As we approached the house, I saw to the left of the imposing entrance, a heavenly rose garden, a riot of color, the odor delicious. We entered, and in the front hall my sister whispered to me to wait a moment. She went into a room at the right, and in a moment came out and said, "Come and meet Mr. and Mrs. Fairfax."

Frightened, I walked stumblingly behind her, across an expanse of polished floor and down a long high-ceilinged, white-walled room to where they sat. I stared stupidly at what seemed to me apparitions,—characters from a book I had imagined but never read. They sat in high-backed chairs, with open books in their laps, the sunlight from windows behind making a golden glow over and around them, turning their silvery white hair a golden color. From their two faces four beautiful dark, intelligent, friendly eyes looked at me. My sister said, "This is my little sister Belinda," and Mrs. Fairfax said, "How do you do, Belinda? I hope you will enjoy your visit," and Mr. Fairfax unfolded himself and stood up and walked carefully toward me, put out a long white hand and said, "I'm glad to meet you, Belinda; you're a big girl to be a little sister," and he laughed at his little joke.

Mr. Fairfax was very tall with a flowing snow-white beard. He wore a black coat, tightly buttoned at the waist, giving him the look of an elongated beetle. On the top of his snow-white hair he wore a small black velvet skullcap. His cuffs and collar were white, and his tie wide, black and flowing. His face looked exactly as I had always imagined God, in His kinder moments,—when He was not creating, or destroying in His anger. I had never seen or expected to see anything like that, and I was speechless.

Mrs. Fairfax was equally marvellous. Her white hair hung in ringlets, and a bang on her forehead curled in a little-girl way. Her large dark eyes were softly beautiful. Her dress was of white material that fell softly around her. I learned that she always wore white except for travelling. My sister exchanged a few words with Mrs. Fairfax, and we left the room. I had been so tense, so excited that I felt I had behaved stupidly, and as soon as we were safely away, I burst into tears. My sister said, "Never mind, I felt the same at first,—you'll become accustomed to them." At our supper that evening, we decided that they weren't real at all, that we had imagined them,—that when they came down to supper, they wouldn't be there at all. Imaginary people we called them, and after that, just IP's.

Their diet as well as the entire atmosphere of the house contributed greatly to this feeling. They had, apparently, been trying different diets for many years, and my sister had arrived during the goat-milk period. This had continued until they began to have boils, and their doctor had advised them to change their diet. An old woman named Hattie, whose efficiency was somewhat impaired by a slight touch of idiocy, had charge of the goats.

How they chose the diet on which they subsisted at this time, I never learned. It consisted of three items; first, candy,—all kinds of chocolate candy. Second, peanuts,—just plain peanuts, in their shells. For liquid, they drank sour milk, called clabber, which they ate with spoons. It was too awful to see them descend the beautiful stairway, he so straight and tall, she with her white robes trailing in queenly fashion, enter the high-ceilinged dining room, sit in high-backed carved chairs, talking across a bowl of beautiful roses, cracking peanuts in their long white old fingers. I saw them, but was unable to believe them. But there they were, and we proceeded with our life as though they were everyday mortals.

Isiah was brought into the dining room every time they ate, and they talked to him in a familiar, loving way. He behaved beautifully when with them. His vocabulary was extremely limited, consisting of one single phrase, but it was extraordinary the many intonations, the varied expressions he could encompass in those few words. When he was with the Fairfaxes, he spoke in a low, sweet gentle tone, persuasive, pleading, "Come to Jesus," startlingly reminiscent of the voices of ministers I had heard in revival meetings,—so human in quality that it was with great difficulty that I could believe the words issued from that evil old face.

When they left the dining room he became quite another bird. Cocking his old head on one side, he would listen until he was sure they were out of hearing; and he always knew, for he never made a mistake. When they had gone either upstairs, or out into the rose garden, he would stalk across his cage, carefully placing his feet with the caution of an inebriate, darting the most vindictive looks at us, and would scream in a raucous diabolical voice, "Come to Jesus! Ha, Ha, Ha, Haaa." At first it was uncanny but, like my sister, I adjusted myself to it.

Again, he would cock his wise old head on one side, walk in a swaying, helpless, pathetic stagger, and query in a plaintive way, "Come to Jesus?" If we didn't give him the attention he craved, he would become very military, and march around his cage strutting like an old General, his breast covered with medals, and with a great agility, march, turn, march, march, turn, yelling at the top of his lungs, "Come, Come, Come to Jesus!" giving the order, demanding obedience. My sister would glare at him defiantly, daring him to make her obey, then we'd laugh at our own seriousness.

Sometimes he would squat on his bandy old legs and glare at us with old evil eyes, apparently thinking things over, listening intently to our conversation. At amazingly suitable moments he would shake his head, make a series of short, stuttering sounds like "tut, tut, tut," shaming us for our words. We were healthy, and laughed until we ached, but many times I thought that for a nervous person, Isiah would not be so good. After a few days Adelaide said, "Now we're safe; Isiah likes you." I had yet to learn his reaction when presented to some one whom he did not like.

Isiah had a virulent hatred of poor half-witted Hattie. If she came within his vision, he went mad with rage. He threw himself against the bars of his cage, flapping his wings in a futile endeavor to get at her, shrieking so rapidly one could hardly distinguish the words, "Cometojesus, cometojesus," in demonic fury, until he exhausted himself. Now I understood my sister's warning. Those whom he did not like were not allowed near him. It is a solemn thought to me that at that particular turning point in my life, my direction depended upon the uncertain, unpredictable reactions of an old, evil, mangy-looking parrot named Isiah, who could only say, "Come to Jesus." If he had turned his gray, iron-like toes down, where would my life have led?

But that old bird could reason,—for one time I happened to wear a blue dress, and when he saw me, he displayed all the fury he usually reserved for Hattie. I went near him, yelling above his own voice, "I'm *not* Hattie, I'm Belinda!" He eyed me doubtfully for a moment, came across his cage and studied my face speculatively, and apparently deciding that he had made a mistake, he shook his head and said, "tut, tut, tut," and quieted at once. At first we couldn't figure it out, but we recalled that Hattie usually wore blue, and he had become confused and reacted to the color hastily. Oh! That old bird! And I was to spend months with him! But never to be real friends, for of affection he had none.

Isiah had a carefully arranged diet, differing however from that of Mr. and Mrs. Fairfax. His consisted mainly of a preparation which came in a can, composed of equal parts of meat and nuts, but whether it was for birds only, or not, I do not know. I do know that I was to become so hungry that many times I ate part of his food. It was delicious fried in butter. He had exactly so much water every day, so many grains of barley or wheat, and once a week a lettuce leaf, but we contributed variety to his diet by way of old stray bits of chocolates left in the dining room, and a few peanuts, all of which he ate with relish and was none the worse for it. Indeed it was our private opinion that he could and would have eaten anything on earth with equanimity,—that nothing could possibly have killed him.

He had a beautiful cage, which had to be kept immaculate. Any one who has associated at all intimately with the feathered species knows well the efficiency of their metabolism. It was no slight task to keep him ready for instant inspection. He had a beautiful silk cover, his name embroidered in bright scarlet thread across one corner, which was thrown over him at night, and also in the afternoon, from three to five, when he took his siesta. We were expected to have quiet, to see that Ruth, my sister's baby, did not disturb him. Luckily she was a wee baby and slept also in the afternoon, and when they were both safely tucked in, my sister and I sat out back under the trees, and sewed and talked. I was enjoying my visit in spite of the incredible atmosphere of a household completely regulated by an old bird. But I was glad to read *Alice* before going to bed at night,—it was so balancing.

Mrs. Fairfax was a painter. Several rooms on the third floor were packed with literally hundreds of paintings. Pictures of Biblical nature, or allegorical, or sickly sentimental,—to me they were horrible. Every year she added to the collection. She was also a musician, and every evening she would play after their walk in the rose garden. For hours, her soft white robes flowing around her, her lovely old face framed by her white curls, her long bony hands over the keyboard, she played,—Mr. Fairfax sitting silently listening, his hands making a church steeple before him.

They were kind to me in their austere way, and sometimes Mr. Fairfax would ask me to go for a walk with him around the grounds. Once he said to me, as to a child bent on mischief, "And what do you want to do with your life, Belinda?" He looked frail, but I answered him with decision, "I want to go to school, to be educated. I want to know about everything, so that I may help other girls like me!" He smiled tolerantly and said, "Spiritual knowledge is more important than what you think of as education,—the memorizing of dates, solving mathematical problems, and such." Defensively I said, "Yes, Mr. Fairfax, but I have no time just now for spiritual education,—my time is getting short, and I must find some way to go to school!" He paced the gravelled walk, following his snow-white beard and patiently he said, "If you believe in God, read your Bible and pray, all will be well, my child." Ready to cry with impatience I boldly answered, "Oh! Mr. Fairfax, can't you *see* that I've got to go to school? Weren't you *ever* young? Didn't you go to school? Why doesn't God help me? You say that if I pray . . . well, I *have* prayed, and nothing happens. Do you think that for some deep, dark purpose God doesn't want me to be educated? *Why? Why?*"

Now tears were streaming down my freckled face, and he was disturbed at my lack of control. Patting me awkwardly on the back, he said, "There, there, my child, don't cry. Everything will be all right; be humble,—you must learn to walk humbly before God. It is a test of your character; by bearing your burdens you will be strengthened, and God will trust you with larger ones." I dried my tears, for I had no answer to all that. At least none that I dared give to such a kind old man. I knew that it was useless to talk to him, that no one would help me, and I knew not how to help myself.

Every morning my sister and I came upstairs to a high white and gold drawing room for prayers. The furniture was fragile, gilded, brocaded, the floor polished like glass. In a large armchair, Mr. Fairfax sat before a stand on which lay an enormous Bible with a wide purple ribbon marker with fringed ends and gold scrolls. He read a chapter, sitting very straight, turning the pages slowly, solemnly with his long white fingers. After certain passages, he would pause, gaze benignly at us over gold-rimmed spectacles, to emphasize the importance of the words. When he closed the big Bible Mrs. Fairfax swept in her trailing white robes to a tiny gilt piano and played a hymn, and we all sang. Then we knelt on the polished floor, while Mr. Fairfax, on his bent old knees, carried on a long discussion with God. At least it gave the impression of a discussion, although only one voice was heard. I could rarely follow what he said, but his voice was melodious, inducing a state half somnolent, half fantasy. He always ended by asking God to forgive us all our sins and to help us to be good. It was a simple request, and perhaps for him and Mrs. Fairfax and my sister, it was so, but in my case and that of Isiah, I had an idea it was much more complicated.

I tried often to imagine them as little children, then as long-legged school kids, later as grown-ups. The children I could see: prim, proper, always doing the correct thing,—never loud nor rude. But I found it impossible to imagine them as ever having gone through an awkward age; of having ever been puzzled; tremulous or tempted. Mrs. Fairfax had told my sister that she and her husband had been children together, and they had always loved each other; that they had been married very young, and had always been happy together. They had never had a child. How peaceful their lives seemed to have been, she painting her terrible pictures, he writing little tracts. Their only problem had been finding different diets to follow. Perhaps that was why they were so calmly beautiful.

When I first came, Adelaide told me that Celia Butler, the sweet blond girl who had been cook at Mrs. Pierson's, was also in Gremont,—that she was companion to a nice old lady, and very happy. I was so glad, for Celia was good, and deserved something more agreeable than cooking. One afternoon we went to visit her, a distance of about two miles, taking turns in carrying Ruth.

Beyond the Fairfax home, there were two or three others, and after that, the road wound through beautiful forests of oak and pine. Flowers grew along the road, and in places filled the air with their sweet scent. When we came near the house, a different Celia than I had known met us. Her cheeks were rosy and she laughed happily,—it was joyous to see her again. She brought a rug and spread it on the ground under the tall pines, and brought out to us homemade bread and butter, and jam, and lemonade. Ruth was a healthy, happy child, and played near us. The food was delicious after the long walk, and besides, we were always hungry. Mrs. Fairfax told my sister to get anything she wished for herself, but somehow made one feel that it was gross, and perhaps a little vulgar to eat bread and butter, and pork chops, so we confined ourselves to bacon and eggs.

That afternoon has never left my memory. I can see the flowers and tiny twigs and leaves,—hear the wind sighing through the tops of the trees, a sad, yet happy sound. I can see Celia, her cheeks pink, her straight blond hair and her gold-rimmed spectacles; my sister, handsome and gay, and her lovely brown-eyed child, all of us there on the rug. For those few hours we were isolated, entirely cut off from the fantastic world, and everything made sense, there on our small island of rug under the tall pines.

Celia asked me if I had seen Faith Charron while I was in Carleton, and I said, "No, I didn't. I was too busy getting and keeping a job; I didn't want to see old friends until I had accomplished something." Celia looked hurt and said, "You mustn't feel that way, Belinda! Friends do not depend upon success." Dear Celia,—with her that was true.

I told her of my extensive college course, and said that I had almost given up hope of ever going to school again. "How I wish I could help," she said. "Stay here with us,—we'll get you a job, won't we?" She turned to my sister who said, "If she wants to try it." I asked Celia what she wanted most in life, and she looked away through the trees and back to us, and answered firmly, "I know exactly what I want most!" Gentle Celia spoke with such finality that we were surprised. "Tell us," we said. Her cheeks grew pinker as she hesitated; finally she said, "I want a big old house with lots of ground, with trees and grass, all for my own, where I can have hundreds and hundreds of sick babies, and nurse them back to health. For the whole of my life, I want just that!" I could have wept, that it was not hers instantly. I said, "Oh, I hope to God you get it, Celia! I hope you do!" She did.

When I had been there a week, my sister told me that she wanted to leave, and that Mrs. Fairfax would take me in her place. I did not like to do it, for I remembered how she had given up her place in Pierson to Lucille, but she assured me she had other plans. So she and Mrs. Fairfax settled that I should stay and eventually go North with them,—my salary being ten dollars a month, my railroad fare to be worked out on that basis.

Kingsland Mears wrote me that he was coming down to see me, and my sister advised me to tell Mrs. Fairfax about him. I did, and she was mildly interested, saying, "Are you in love with this boy?" Embarrassed, I hesitated, and she opened her brown eyes in wide astonishment, shaking her gray curls impatiently. "Come, come, my child,—you must know whether or not you love this young man?" she said. I felt an awful fool, and desperately said, "I don't know. He wants me to marry him and live in his little house in Weaverton for all my life, and I know that I don't want that. I want to go to New York with you." With a graceful wave of her hand she dismissed the entire problem. "Let him come, and I will talk to him. I will tell you whether or not you should marry him." So, it's as easy as that, thought I to myself!

I was afraid that when he came she would not like him, and I did want her to know that he was a very fine boy; on the other hand, I was afraid that if she did like him, and told me to marry him, I would never have the courage to stand up and refuse. She was a woman with a "whim of iron."

When Kingsland jumped from the train almost before it stopped, and ran to me, I was proud of him, he looked so handsome in a new gray suit and a nice blue tie. He looked happy, and much more assured than when I had last seen him. "Gosh, it's good to see you again," he said, and he kissed me in a way that I liked. "I've certainly missed you! Where do you live?" he asked, as we walked from the station. I told him and we started up the road to the Fairfax home. On the way I told him about how amazing they were, and about Isiah. He told me all the news of Weaverton. We were happy.

My sister took King in and introduced him to Mr. and Mrs. Fairfax, when they came down to supper. He saw what they were eating, and appeared incredulous; we explained and he laughed in a puzzled way. We had a happy supper, though meagre, with Ruth in her high chair, and Isiah marching in his best military manner, eyes peering at the newcomer questioningly, occasionally interrupting our conversation with his admonishing "tut, tut, tut." After supper I knew that King would want to be alone with me, so in a carefully casual way I said, "Let us go for a walk," and he quickly joined me. As soon as we were out of sight and sound of the house, in a far corner of the rose garden, he put his arms around me and held me close, kissing me rapidly, passionately, and I let all thought of education go, and kissed him in return. He sobbingly said, "Oh! Darling, don't ever leave me again! I've missed you too much, too much! Let me love you tonight, and for always!" Touched and torn by his love, and my own for him, I felt deep in me the need, the hunger for his love, for the touch of human arms, some shield against the aloneness I had felt without him. In the moonlight in the seductive odors of a warm Southern night, the tall trees making dark shadows around us, I loved him. For one evening I stifled my driving desire for education, for distant places and new opportunities, for adventure, I loved him, and he gave me that which is too beautiful to last; all the time a leering devil laughed over my shoulder.

Next morning Adelaide asked us to go to the village for some things, and we ran like mad to the gate, where we stopped for breath, laughing with joy, just to be alive on such a heavenly day. When we'd done the shopping we went into a drug store where we sat on stools and had chocolate sodas. We laughed at nothing, happy, each determined not to be serious. King held my hand, opening my fingers, and kissing my palm, folding my fingers back over the spot, and said, "There, now you can never remove it. You'll always have a kiss in your hand, and it will scare away all the boogaboos." We laughed, but I knew with something deep inside me that all this was for only a day.

Before supper that evening, we saw Mrs. Fairfax and King walking up and down in the rose garden, and we felt sorry for him. She was speaking graciously, he listening with a scowling, puzzled frown, his red hair rumpled. I never knew of what they spoke, but I sensed her implacability, and his passionate young protest. He was silent at supper, and asked me to come for a walk. I went reluctantly, for I knew what was coming. I wished that we could have had just the memories of the beautiful evening before, without soiling it by arguments and dissension.

We walked a long way, the road a pale sandy gray in the shadows of tall trees, and all the while he against my ambitions, begging me to settle once and for all: would I or would I not marry him and come back to Weaverton and live in the little house he had built for us "Oh! Linda, give up this senseless search, this foolish battle. We are poor, and you will never have money for education. That is only possible for those who have money. I love you with all my heart, and I have a good job. Why can't you give in, and be happy with me? Don't you want children? I do, and I want yours, and mine! Please, I ask you to torture me no more!" His dear beautiful face was twisted with anguish and desire for his life and happiness, and his sincerity made me wish that I were dead. I could not answer him, and he raised his voice, screaming at me, "What sort of person are you? Have you no heart at all?"

Emotions of opposing content were tearing me to pieces, but his suffering I could not bear. I put my arms around him, holding him quiet, talking to calm him, and finally I got him to sit with me on the grass, under a tall tree. Then I said to him, "Listen, King. You have told me of your desires, may I not tell you of mine?" He said nothing and I went on, "First, I want above all things to go to school; next to that I want to make you happy. If I marry you with this other thing in my heart, you will never be happy, nor will I,—but if you will give me two more years, and if in that time I have made no progress, and you still want me, I will marry you." At that he jumped and strode angrily up and down the road. "So, I'm to be second choice? You will marry me after you have failed in something else! Oh, no you won't!" He spoke in anger, and stung to a bitter response I said, "You speak of love! If you loved me at all, you would understand, and sympathize with me. You want children! Good God, how can you wish to bring life into this heartless world. I will not, ever, have a child unless I can give it at least a chance to live! That is not love, but selfishness. You are too absorbed in your own desires to give anything to me, and I will fight you to the end." Oh! how we hurt each other, cruelly, stupidly. My whole physical being cried out for him, but something else could not give in. We parted in anger, and when the household was quiet, I sat alone in the back yard, my heart torn with sadness too deep, too sharp to be borne.

Suddenly I smelled smoke, and looking around I saw a blaze in the ridge-pole of the kitchen roof. Running madly, I awakened my sister, who immediately carried her sleeping baby out of danger, while I wakened Mr. and Mrs. Fairfax. We gathered pails of water, and handing them up to King, who was immediately on the roof, we quickly extinguished the blaze. When it was out, we stood about in the kitchen, speculating on its possible origin. It was my secret opinion that Kingsland Mears, in his blind, helpless rage, had started it, intending to display remarkable heroism in saving us all!

King was dirty and blackened by smoke, my sister and I dishevelled, but Mr. and Mrs. Fairfax looked just the same, in perfect order,—he in his long nightshirt, his clerical coat neatly buttoned at the waist, his velvet skull-cap on his snow-white hair. She wore a nightdress not appreciably different from the one she wore during the day, but on her soft gray curls she wore a sweet lace nightcap, and on her tiny feet, small slippers with white fur. Pictures from a fairy story they were. Calmly they thanked us for putting out the fire, and said good night.

Kingsland left next morning. I walked to the station with him, still anxious to be friends, but he was hurt, and angry. He was silent, and said good-by in bitterness. Later I wrote and told him that I was leaving with Mrs. Fairfax, and his answer, saying that I had ruined his life, and that if I did go, he would end it, only made me hate him. I did not answer it.

In a few days my sister left, with her baby, and I was alone with the Fairfaxes, and Isiah. At first the big house was too quiet, too lonely, but the preparations for departure began and I was too busy to be lonely. Mrs. Fairfax told me to get anything I wanted to eat, but like my sister, I ate mostly bacon and eggs, until overcome by a desire for green that drove me to buy cabbages for five cents each and eat them leaf-by-leaf, including the stalk, in the woods. Every morning that dear old man would creep down, and sneaking quietly to the kitchen, looking like God except that his nose twitched at the odor of bacon, and say to me, "May I have just one tiny slice of your bacon, Belinda?" and I would give him two or three. Eating it ravenously, he would say, "You won't let Mrs. Fairfax know, will you, Belinda?" and I assured him I would never tell. He had been married for over fifty years, and I think in all those years he had few square meals. He loved his wife and followed her diets, but he also loved the small slices of bacon I gave him.

When King had gone, Mrs. Fairfax spoke to me about him, saying, "You must not marry that boy, Belinda; he is too hot-tempered, too impetuous, and has not the proper respect for God, even though his father is a minister," and I loathed myself for a filthy traitor to him, wanting to say that he was the salt of the earth, and I loved him madly, instead of which I said, "No, Mrs. Fairfax, I won't."

Chapter 10

The day before we were to leave Gremont was a busy one for me. All morning I packed away blankets from moths and mice, and covered furniture with slips; the piano was buttoned into a canvas cover, which gave it the appearance of a prehistoric monster, ready to leap. Trunks were packed and sent to the station, leaving only small bags to be carried.

In the afternoon I hurried to the Warner home to say good-by to Celia. We cried because I think that we both realized how helpless we were; how insignificant in the scheme of things, and inwardly aware of the fact that we were being tossed about rather carelessly; each hoping that by sheer persistence we could in time force things to come right for us. With a warm embrace and a kiss hastily bestowed, I hurried back to serve the chocolate candy and peanuts and clabber milk, and to take care of Isiah.

That last night I lay in my bed, alone in that big house but for two old people who seemed not to belong to my world. They were serene, safe in a bay of calm sunlit water; I out on a troubled sea, with no guidance, no one who cared where my ship sailed or what port I might make. The soft Southern breeze came in at my window, sweet with the odor of roses, and it made me unbearably sad. Lying in the dark I tried to reason things out, feeling almost a physical need to have a number of phenomena explained before I could go on as a reasonable human being. But there was no answer, and weeping with sympathy for me and all the girls in the same state, I slept, weary in body and mind.

Isiah slept in the room next to mine, with windows looking on the rose garden. Mrs. Fairfax explained to me her selection of that room, saying that she wanted Isiah to have fresh sweet air and a lovely view. That old bird! He looked with an evil eye, no matter where he looked! Strangely I never heard her express similar desires for either my sister, or Ruth, or me.

Next morning I woke early and lay quiet, listening to the small twitterings of birds just awakening; listening to the silence of the enormous house, a stillness that held all the sounds of day pregnant, latent, waiting. Everything seemed immense, illimitable. The little town lay asleep. Dr. Dalziel, Miss Purdy, fat old Mrs. Erskine, the depot agent, the clerk in the drug store, quiet gentle Celia, and I could feel them all, lying helpless in the new dawn. An awareness of all these I knew, or had spoken to, and the millions all over the earth whom I had not and would never know; their driving ambitions, their secret desires, all for a few hours halted, beaten, submerged; for these few hours helpless as little children. With the light, they would each rise and begin their routine of evasions, sly plannings, circuitous methods, each in their own way hoping to achieve their heart's desire, at the moment all-powerful and felt to be necessary and final. A great sadness weighed me down, an overwhelming loneliness engulfed me; a doubt of the validity of my own driving ambitions and their final importance. Fear of some devastating fate if I persisted in fighting for something obviously not intended to be, held me for the moment suspended. For the space of a second I felt myself give in. The ominous silence of the house frightened me more than the difficulties to be met in the light. But at the moment of submission something deep at the pit of me refused. The knowledge that I would never give in was so strong that I felt it in all my body. I knew that come what might, to the end of my days I would fight the deadening but seductive thought that it was futile, stupid; that the cards were stacked against me from the beginning. Against the whispering voice that said, "How stupid you are! Why not marry and be happy in a small way? What do you think you'll gain in the end?" I heard another, and stronger voice that said, "Stop whining! Get up and fight!"

I jumped up and quietly bathed and dressed. I finished packing my suitcase, put away the blankets from my bed and covered it for the summer. With my hands full, my hat on one ear, I stopped at the door and looked back, taking it all in at once,—the large ugly wooden bed, the dresser, the shadowy corners and the faded flowered rug. It was all the rooms everywhere made to be left; fit only for transient occupancy; rooms in which no love is or can be; rooms for the restless, driven mass of those who question. Empty, dead, unhappy rooms. I had a feeling that all my life I would be leaving rooms like that; that there was no room inhabited with content or happiness for me.

Carrying Isiah in my free hand, I crept down the beautiful curving stairs, ghostly in the pale morning light. In the kitchen I gave Isiah a lettuce leaf and other stray bits of food to finish. While he picked with his iron beak, chuckling in his throat, which was his most benign expression, I ate my last slice of bacon and drank a cup of black coffee. I collected all the odds and ends including half a jar of jam, some old cheese and a few small potatoes, for old Hattie, whose diet was as meagre as mine, and she would appreciate anything. In a small box I placed sufficient food for Isiah, and as a precaution, put in two hard-boiled eggs for myself.

When everything was ready, I went into the rose garden. The first rays of sun were touching the top of the goat house, and the shadows under the tall pines were dark and cool. Everything was damp, and cool, and still. The beauty of the roses, glistening with dew, was painful. My heart was bursting with excitement, with joy and fear at actually getting away. Mr. and Mrs. Fairfax came down and I gave them their breakfast, and while they cracked their peanuts, I went up and closed their rooms, bringing their bags down to the front steps. They were so calm, I had to remind myself that this was not an adventure to them, as it was to me.

I locked the back door and gave old Hattie the key, and with Isiah, waited at the front door. Mrs. Fairfax looked somehow young, ageless, in her neat gray dress, with snowy bands of organdie at neck and wrists. Her gray curls fell softly below her tiny gray bonnet-like hat, with its bow of blue ribbon matching the band at her small waist; across her forehead her bangs curled childishly. Mr. Fairfax, hands clasped behind him, walked up and down in the rose garden, singing happily to himself. He wore his usual black clothes, but for a wide-brimmed, black, clerical-looking hat, instead of his velvet skull-cap.

The sun was well up by this time and the whole scene was clear and beautiful. Long shadows of pines lay across the house, making dark islands in the brilliant light. A dampness of dew still lay on the grass and flowers, the pine needles gave off a pungent earthly odor. It seemed extraordinary, my having been there at all, and my going away with them more unreal. Isiah alone possessed for me a reality, and I assumed a calmness I did not feel, for fear they might not, even now, take me.

My fears were stilled by a firm conviction that just as soon as I got up North, some wonderful person, either a beautiful woman or a handsome, kind man, would see me and at once recognize my unusual character. I knew that this wonderful person would smile at me, understanding all my longings and ambitions, and say, "Why, I've been looking everywhere for a girl like you! I will give you the opportunity you so desire, and all the books you can read; you may pursue any form of study you choose. In the end you may become a great leader of women, showing them how they may achieve knowledge and greatness. You will encourage them and hold them up when they are in danger of becoming embittered by the stupid cruelties of life. And with all this, you will have a great love,—a man who will see you and know you instantly, and will help you in all your undertakings; who will love you and hold you precious for all your life!" I *knew* that this would happen as soon as I got up North, and therefore, could hardly wait. That this had not happened down South was because every one knew me,— it could happen only in quite a new place, where I was unknown. Why some doubt of this occurring failed to take hold upon my mind, seeing that the Fairfaxes, and even Miss Purdy, were from the North, and they had shown no awareness of anything extraordinary about me, I do not know, but it didn't. I *knew* that once I got up North, it would not be any time at all until I met the understanding person who would trust me and help me, and life would be too beautiful to be borne.

A two-seated carriage came from the village to take us to the depot. The driver made the circular sweep to the front door, and stopping with a flourish, jumped down and quickly placed the bags in front, assisted Mr. and Mrs. Fairfax into the back seat, while I climbed up with Isiah in my lap. We waved good-by to old Hattie, and she waved stiffly back, a foolish grin on her vacant face, and we rolled away. The sound of the horses' hooves as they trotted down the drive and out of the big gate, was clear in the morning air. A cool breeze stirred the silk fringe that hung down around the top of the carriage, and out on the highroad, the sun was hot in the clouds of dust that rose around the wheels.

At the station the driver carried the bags in, and almost at once the train started, and I knew then that I was actually on my way to the North, and the time passed quickly. Isiah was not troubled, as he was accustomed to trains, and Mr. and Mrs. Fairfax were as happy in their stateroom, with their religious tracts, as at home.

When the train stopped in Washington, I wished that I might get out and see the Capitol, and all the wonderful places, but realized that it was impossible. As soon as we left Washington, Mrs. Fairfax came to me and said, "Belinda, we're going to spend the night in Baltimore with a girlfriend of mine, Mrs. de Saussere. We have been friends since childhood, although she has lived abroad a great deal. When a young girl, she married an Italian Count, who died, leaving her a widow with one son. Now she is married to a Frenchman who is, I believe, in Europe. She is living in her father's old home in Baltimore, where I spent many happy months with her when we were children. And now we are going to spend the night with her."

This was a surprise to me, for she had never mentioned it, and the phrase, "girlfriend" stuck in my mind, for I could not ever imagine her as a young girl. "What shall I do?" I asked her, and she smiled in a friendly way and said, "Just what you have been doing. Take care of Isiah and do little things for us. You have been a good girl, Belinda, and a great comfort to us." That was the first time she had ever said anything like that to me and I was glad that I had pleased them.

I took Isiah into the ladies' room and fed him, and changed his paper, got all our bags ready, and waited for Baltimore. When the train stopped, the porter took our bags out, and I gave him a quarter, for he had been very nice to us; I was afraid Mrs. Fairfax wouldn't give him anything, for although they were very religious, they were not careless about money. A man in livery was waiting for us, and quickly gathered the bags, and said, "The carriage is just out here, Madame," and we followed him out. I carried Isiah, whose cage kept bumping against my shins, in my excitement.

Presently there was a beautiful carriage, with another man holding the reins of two fine sleek horses, whose harnesses shone with silver buckles. At their heads were gayly colored plum-like decorations that moved gracefully as they pranced out of the station. We drove at a smart pace for what seemed quite a distance, turned into a curving pebbled drive between tall old trees and flowering shrubs. The carriage stopped in front of a very large redbrick house with a big white door and wide white steps. One of the men carried our bags through a side door, while an elderly maid came down the steps and courteously welcomed us.

We walked up the wide white steps and into a cool high hall, across which long glass windows extended, and through the glass I could see masses of flowers. It seemed like fairyland to me. The maid said she would take us to our rooms and we could rest,—that Madame de Saussere was resting and would see us at four. We followed the maid up stairs so clean that I wondered what they used to make them shine so, and yet look so deep and dark.

The maid showed Mr. and Mrs. Fairfax into a large sitting room gay with flowers,—a cheerful room connected with a bedroom by an enormous bathroom. The tub was like nothing I had ever imagined, being of what looked like rose-colored stone. I asked the maid about it later, and she said that it had been brought from France,—that some famous woman had used it before that.

We left them there, and the maid took me to a room on the other side of the house, the loveliest room I had ever slept in, even for a night. The walls were pale yellow, as were the curtains through which the sun was pouring, and on the big bed with a high painted headboard, was a yellow silk cover, embroidered in fascinating colors. The chairs were covered with a yellow silk material that had small blue flowers scattered over it. I was almost afraid to touch anything, for I was sure it would vanish if I did.

The maid showed me a closet for my coat and hat, and the bathroom, talking cheerfully, and then said she would have to leave me. Left alone, I sat in the window seat with Isiah, and just looked at the beautiful room, and out on the flowers in the garden. Later I hung up my coat, and examined carefully everything in the room,—the little china figures on the mantel, of a charming girl with curls, holding up her skirts on each side, as she danced toward the gentleman in tight short pants, in the act of sweeping his plumed hat before her. That reminded me of a doll I had once, that had a head of china, to which one sewed a body,—I loved it very much because I could wash her face and it didn't fade nor melt nor come apart.

After a while Mrs. Fairfax came in, saying that they had rested, and now we were to see Mrs. de Saussere. She talked to Isiah, and he gurgled and chuckled. To me she said, "Come along, we'll go down to Millie." The little pet name sounded odd, from a stately old lady; it was more odd, when I saw Millie.

We went down a wide hall to the front of the house, and approached a large double door painted all over with flowers and angels, like a Christmas card. Mrs. Fairfax opened it, and we walked into the largest room I had ever seen in a private home. It extended across the entire front of the house, and away in the distance I saw a couch on which sat a large blond woman, who called out to us, "You'll have to come to me, Madge; I won't get up, as I'm much too fat." I saw an enormously fat woman sitting among dozens of pillows, her tiny feet on a little stool, their brilliant buckles scintillating as she moved. She lifted her face to be kissed, and Mrs. Fairfax bent over her. I was busy trying to think of them as Millie and Madge.

Turning to me, the fat one said, "Who is this?" Mrs. Fairfax said, "Belinda." Squirming around among her pillows, she persisted impatiently,

"Belinda what?" I stepped nearer to her and said, "I'm Belinda Dan." She held out a fat little hand loaded with rings to me, and I gave her mine. "Don't be shy with me, Belinda Dan; I'm fat, but harmless, a simple soul I am, and I like every one around me to be happy." To Mrs. Fairfax she said, with a giggle, "That's why I left François in France."

Mr. Fairfax came in, and I thought he looked a bit more like Moses, perhaps, than God, as he kissed her hand charmingly. He said, "And how are you, Millie?" She laughed like a fat child, and said, "Fat, Hal, fat! Can't you *see* I'm fat, and getting fatter? Whatever shall I do? I love good food so much!" I wondered if she knew, and if so, what she thought of the IP's diet.

They talked about mutual friends, recalling past episodes in which they had been involved, Millie laughing heartily, Madge more serious. Mrs. Fairfax said to me, "Belinda, bring Isiah for Mrs. de Saussere to see," and as I started to go, Millie said, "Who's Isiah? Oh yes, I remember! Does he still say, 'Come to Jesus'?" and looked bored. I brought him in, and she spoke to him, pretending interest, but I could see that her heart was not in it. She asked me to make him speak, but I told her that I couldn't,—that he spoke only when he chose. Just as I was leaving the room, he yelled in his mean voice, "Come to Jesus," and I heard Mrs. de Saussere laugh, and say, "Good for you, Isiah!" but I was sorry, for I had never heard him speak in that tone before Mr. and Mrs. Fairfax. They said nothing, but I saw Mrs. Fairfax raise her big brown eyes and say, "It would be well for you to heed Isiah this time, Millie. Some day it will be too late,—you will have to face your Maker, and I fear you are not prepared."

Mrs. de Saussere's childish face broke into pathetic wrinkles, and she whimpered as though she might cry, as she answered. "Now, Madge! Don't begin on me again, as you always do. I'm not nearly as wicked as you think, and my Maker knows all about me! And I'm not going to be gloomy, no matter what you say." The happiness of the room was shattered, and as I went out, Mrs. de Saussere called to me, "Come back and have a cup of tea with us."

When I returned, the maid had brought in a silver tray on which a silver teakettle swung over a flame, and a great silver teapot, with beautiful cups and saucers. Mrs. de Saussere poured the tea, asking Mr. and Mrs. Fairfax if they still liked it weak with sugar. I watched to see if they really drank it, for never since I'd known them had they drunk a cup of tea. When she asked me how I liked mine, I didn't know, for the only tea I had ever had was birch tea, of which we drank a great deal when I was a child on the farm. It was made from the bark of birch trees and sweetened with molasses. This tea was different, so I took a chance and said, "Sugar please." I liked it very much.

Mrs. de Saussere laughed a lot, her old face wrinkling up in all directions, sometimes entirely concealing her eyes. Her blond curls were obviously false, which troubled her not at all, for she said, "How do you like the color I have my hair now, Madge?" Mrs Fairfax considered it seriously and said, "You know that I don't like false hair." Turning to Mr. Fairfax, she said, "Well, Hal, how do you like it?" Seriously, politely, he replied, "I think that if you tip it slightly more to the right, it will be more becoming,—the color is a little too bright for you, Millie; a more natural color would be even more becoming." All this fantastic situation was completely absorbing to me. Since they were considering the color of her wig, I did the same. "Well, Belinda, what do you think? I suppose you think an old lady like me should have gray hair, like Madge! Gray hair depresses me, and makes me bad tempered; then I'm nasty to the maids, which is bad. Blond hair makes me happy and kind, therefore, I choose to wear blond hair. Don't you think that's better?" I honestly liked her false curls and her, very much, regardless of what Mrs. Fairfax might say, I answered, "I do indeed, Mrs. de Saussere."

When we'd drunk our tea, and settled the wig problem, Mrs. de Saussere put out her fat little hand to me and said, "Give me a hand, Belinda! I'm going to my room; you may amuse yourselves as you wish, but for me, I'm much too fat to move about much. If you want to walk in the garden, Millie, do so. I'll see you at dinner, which is at seven."

She held my hands, and I pulled, while she gathered herself together, and between us we hoisted her from her nest of pillows. I was surprised to see, when she stood up, that she was quite tall, and really enormous. Billows of pink chiffon fell around her, covering layers and layers of fat. Her fat chins shook as she moved, grotesque below a childish little mouth with strong white teeth. Moving across the polished floor, she resembled a large pink cloud, wallowing across a sky. At the door she turned to Mrs. Fairfax and said, "What do you and Hal eat now, Madge? Is it hay, carrots or goat's milk? I can't see how you do it! Me, I like good food. Won't you, just for tonight, forget your diet and have one good dinner with me? Please?" I waited for the answer with curiosity. Mr. Fairfax's face was twitching at the mere thought of a good dinner, but he waited for his wife to answer. "Thank you, Millie. Of course we will have dinner with you, but don't expect us to eat as much as you do, for we simply couldn't! Besides, I have no desire to be fat." Mrs. de Saussere said, "That's fine. I'll see you at seven."

She turned toward the end of the room, and waving her fat hand, said to me, "That, my dear Belinda, is me. Gaze upon it and weep with me!" She held my arm, and we looked up at a portrait of a young girl in a pale blue velvet dress, the lips parted in an eager childish smile. Moving her ponderous bulk toward the door, she sighed, "Heigh ho, life is sad!"

Mr. and Mrs. Fairfax walked on old moss-grown red bricks laid in diagonal pattern through a beautiful garden. I went alone to explore, and away in the back I found a nice old gardener busily transplanting small vegetable plants from the hotbed. I watched him, and timidly said, "Hello." He straightened his back, eyed me speculatively from under an old straw hat, spit, and said "Hello." I asked if I could help him, and he grudgingly assented, but when he saw that I really knew how to do it, he became very friendly. When we had done a great many, he took me around the garden, showing me many different kinds, one of which I had never heard of, called asparagus.

The gardener told me that his name was Henry. We were so busy and I so happy that before we realized it the sun was almost down, and Henry stopped and said, "You'd better hurry, miss; you'll be late for supper, and the Madame loves her food and can hardly wait to eat it. She hates folks that keep her waitin'. Nice woman so long as she has her nose in the old feed bag, but let her git hungry, and land sakes, she'll raise cain!" chuckling reminiscently. I hated to leave Henry and the plants,—they were so simple. I could understand them, while everything about those three old people was fantastic. I could, to a certain degree, understand that seed will grow, properly watered and warmed by the sun; it offered no unsurmountable obstacle to my power of reasoning to believe it natural for a plant to grow, in the rain and the sun and the dirt. But my reasoning stopped short of the three human beings with whom, for the time being, I was in close proximity,—not to mention Isiah. There was no need for being on one's guard with a young beet, or an onion, or, for the matter of that, the strange one called asparagus, with its feathery top, but with human beings one had constantly to be on the alert lest they annihilate you.

I hurried to my room and tidied myself for dinner, and gave Isiah his. The nice maid came and I told her what a good time I had had with Henry. She was pleasant, and told me that I'd better hurry down, as dinner would be served soon, and Madame de Saussere hated to be kept waiting. She said her name was Peters,—I didn't know whether she meant first or last, but hesitated to ask her; it seemed a personal matter.

She took me to the dining room and showed me where I was to sit, and left me. While I was alone I hastily examined the room. The walls looked like very old oak, dark and polished, and carved in beautiful folds, like linen. One end was filled by a large window made of colored pieces of glass, arranged in a thousand figures,—some of those in the front being quite large. Ladies in elaborate costumes leading little children and sheep; men in plumed hats, astride fat white horses. It was all intricate, and I wished I could know what it meant, but now Mrs. de Saussere's tapping heels were heard, and she came in, a dazzling sight.

She was dressed in white, her neck and arms bare,—her skirt trailed behind her for about a yard, and I watched to see how she managed it when she sat down. Peters followed her in and pulled out a high-backed chair at the head of the table, and into it she eased her great bulk. Smiling at me she said, "I hope our friends will come soon,—I am starved and I hate waiting for my dinner." But almost at once Mr. and Mrs. Fairfax came in, and Peters and another maid began at once to serve the dinner.

I noticed that Mrs. de Saussere's hair was a different wig from the one she had worn in the afternoon, and I learned later that she had many wigs, suitable for all occasions. This was her dinner wig, much higher, fluffier, and decorated with two shining stars, one on each side. She had jewels applied to every crevice, and where they could not be worn around, or pinned on, they were hung around her neck. Great ropes of pearls swung to and fro across her enormous breasts and stomach, the value of which I had no idea.

The maid poured wine into thin-stemmed glasses, and Mrs. de Saussere said, "For this once, drink a toast to me!" And Mr. Fairfax rose, tall and thin in his black clothes, and holding his glass high he said, "To Millie!" and we all drank happily. I had drunk wine my mother made, in Oklahoma, so I felt familiar with it, but it had not given me the feeling of abandon that I felt creeping over me now. The maid filled my glass a second time, and I vaguely hoped I would do nothing silly . . .

There were many courses, some of which I did not recognize at all, but I watched the others, and as Mrs. Fairfax was occupied with her own dinner, I ate enormously and enjoyed it. The maid filled my glass again, and I knew that I'd better be careful, for things began to take on a casual significance. When the dessert was served, it gave me to pause. It did not stop me, but it did give me to pause, and was, in the end, my undoing.

Peters brought in a large silver tray on which sat a gayly colored rooster, made entirely of ice cream! And around him were small hens, and eggs, also of ice cream! The arrangement was magnificent, the rooster held his head in a gallant poise, his brilliant comb proud! I could no longer remain on my chair, but jumping up, I raced around and around the table, waving my napkin wildly, shouting, "It's beautiful, marvellous! It's the most wonderful thing I have ever seen!" laughing loudly, while part of me looked on, fearful of the result of my exuberance. I suddenly realized where I was and blackness covered me,—now I had ruined everything, and they would put me out. Mr. and Mrs. Fairfax would not take me any further,—this was the end. Weakly I sat down, looking at my plate, waiting for them to speak. They were laughing, not angry at all; Mrs. de Saussere, her fat body undulating with mirth called out to me, "Good for you, Belinda! I wish I could dance and sing with you as I used to do! But come now, let us eat the rooster!" Oh! the shame to destroy him in all his proud arrogance, so male above the hens! "No, no," I cried in agony. "Let us eat the hens and the eggs, but leave him whole!" At which Mrs. de Saussere glared at me in mock rage, dramatically speaking, "Traitor, thou traitor to thy sex! Off with his head, and at once!" as she brought the knife down on his neck, his head toppled over. I wanted to weep for the havoc,—to see so much complacent superiority brought ignominiously low! But I also wished to help eat him, and forgot to be sad.

The Fairfaxes forgot their food fancies for the evening, and ate sparingly of everything, and drank wine. Their stomachs must have had a shock when rich, delicious food descended into them. We sat a long time at dinner, for Mrs. de Saussere said, "Don't hurry! I have few pleasures left in life, and eating is the main one,—so I like plenty of time to savor every bite, to feel the warmth of the wine as it goes down my throat! So dawdle, my friends, dawdle! Dawdling is an art, perfected by so few; let us revive the ancient and honorable art of dawdling! Let us be happy tonight!" By this time her wig was on the right ear.

Tiny cups of black coffee were served, and we dawdled over them. The two old ladies talked again of their childhood, and as I listened, I learned that Millie had always been rich, that her father had died leaving a great deal of money to her mother and her. I learned that Madge was a minister's daughter, very poor always, until she married Mr. Fairfax. They had met in some school and had retained their sincere affection for each other through all the changes life had brought them, although they were so unlike.

When we had sat over the coffee for a long time, Mrs. de Saussere again asked me to give her a hand. I grasped her hand firmly and pulled, while she drew herself slowly to her feet; I pushed her wig back in place, and she said, "Thank you, my dear! You are very kind to a fat old lady!" My heart was full of compassion for her,—of pity for her loneliness. Some warmth, some human quality which she possessed, touched me deeply.

We walked slowly through tall arched doors into a spacious, delicately furnished drawing room. Still holding my arm, she billowed to stand in front of another painting of herself, of a later period than the one upstairs. This was the portrait of a slender, beautiful young woman, proud, sure and humorous. A smile lifted the corners of the lips, and a laugh was in the eyes. She stood looking at it for a long time, silently, then shaking her wig sadly, she eased her bulk into a throne-like chair, asking me to place a small embroidered footstool under her small feet, on which were tight cream-colored satin slippers, pointed delicately, their brilliant buckles shining in the light. She leaned her head against the chair back, her wig again askew, her tiny hands jewel laden, clasped over her expansive stomach; closing her eyes, she said, "Play for me, Madge! Play as you used to long ago."

I was full of food and dizzy from the wine, and I sat down quickly. Mr. Fairfax had been strolling around the room, looking at the paintings, his dignity unimpaired. He sat down, crossed his long legs comfortably, and Mrs. Fairfax began to play, at first carelessly, indifferently. Soon there was a change, and I heard her playing as so often I had heard her at home in Gremont. In memory I could see her white robes spread around her, her thin ghostly fingers over the keys, and only her dark eyes alive, gleaming. Now she played as though she had forgotten our presence, giving herself to something we could not know. I felt my heart beating and my breathing quickened,—an overwhelming desire to weep, and yet not to weep, assailed me. The music she made carried me into a place I had rarely been, a place where I could not remember the ambitions that had driven me all my life, on a fruitless quest; a place where everything was at once more trivial and more important. As she continued, my tension grew; I became more clearly aware of the futility of trying to impress my ego on life, of the unimportance of any human achievement I might desire to secure for myself. I felt that if she continued I would scream aloud, and yet I dared not move; Mrs. de Saussere sat as though asleep, removed entirely from reality, and Mr. Fairfax remained immobile. My knees felt stiff and my hands enormous, and I began to see people walking ghostlike around the room, when suddenly she stopped.

Mrs. de Saussere opened her eyes and said, "Thank you, Madge. How completely you take me back to so much that has been, and is gone! Wonderful to hear you again, just as I did years ago,—as I have heard you in my dreams so often!" She held out her fat little hands and said, "Help me up, Belinda!" When she steadied herself and kicked the footstool impatiently from her, she said, bitterly, "It's too easy to think of the past! I will not! As I have no future, and will not think of the past, the present is all I have." She straightened her wig and said to Mrs. Fairfax, "Madge darling, you're probably tired, but you and Hal do whatever you like,—I'm going to bed with a new novel. Belinda will help me up, so I'll say good night," and they kissed. Mr. Fairfax, tall and straight, offered his arm, and she so dainty and lovely looking, put her hand on it, and they went up the stairs. Unbelievable.

We moved slowly across the floor, her high heels somehow tapping in spite of her weight, and started up the stairs. At the first landing, she stopped, looked at me and said, "Whatever are you doing with three old dodos like us? Have you no life of your own? Have you no beaus? Don't let them lead you in their way . . . too much religion! Still, I wouldn't advise you to go my way either." I said nothing, for I didn't know which question she wanted answered. She went up a few more steps, and said, "I've had a good time, Belinda. I've done all the things I shouldn't have done, and I don't regret it! What do you want to do with your life? Be gay, or a missionary like Madge?" Tense, afraid, I thought, "Maybe this is the person who will understand and help me!" I saw her wig slipping, and my heart misgave me,—but I couldn't let a possibility pass; she *might* be the one, so I took a chance and said, "I want to go to school!"

Her mouth dropped open in absolute astonishment. Staring at me incredulously, she eased her bulk down on the steps, pulling me down with her, and she said, "Whatever for?" At my serious face she burst into peals of laughter. I did not laugh. Controlling her mirth, she looked at me curiously and said, "Don't you see how ridiculous it is? No, I suppose you can't. You're too young to, and it's a pity. Forgive me for laughing, but you look so serious, and it's difficult for me to tell you why I laughed; you wouldn't understand." Again she laughed, more quietly. Puzzled, and angry, I said calmly, "Why is it ridiculous for me to want to go to school? You went to school, didn't you? Mr. and Mrs. Fairfax went to school; everybody in the world goes to school but me! Why is it funny? Tell me that!" She thought a long time, and then slowly said, "Because nothing you learn in school ever fits any situation, when you're out in the world. I know. My mother sent me to more finishing schools than you have fingers,—I finished them instead. All that silly rot they teach you!" I had no good answer to that, so I said nothing. "Napoleon advanced with six hundred and fifty-eight men," she said in a mincing, satirical voice. "Hell, maybe he had six hundred and fifty-nine; wouldn't that just spoil everything?" she asked bitterly. "And what good did that do me? I gave up grammar when we got to some strange, peculiar stage called Infinitives! And split, too, if you please! Never shall I forget what that word did to my imagination! Split or not, I quit. None of that is any use to you, my girl." Angry, I burst out, "But I've been out in the world! Where do you think I've been all my life, but in the world? And I want to know what an infinitive is, and *why* it is split, and who split it, and with what! It would help me a great deal to know these things." She shifted her wig to the other ear and squirming her huge pile around to me, she began again, "Listen, you ignorant girl! It would *not* help you to know these things! Tell me, how would it help you?" Excited now, for I had an answer for that one, I said, "It would help me to meet charming people,— distinguished people,—kind, cultivated, wise people!" She looked at me as if she suspected me of having lost my senses, shaking her jowls ponder- ously, pursing her childish lips. "I hate to tell you, but you're on the wrong track. All the things you are searching for will never be cornered by an infinitive, split or otherwise. The attributes you are looking for are not governed by dates, nor parts of speech! It's something quite different; some- thing you'll find in no school book . . . it's something you've got yourself, if only you had sense enough to know it, or I the words to make you see it."

I wanted to scream at her, and pull her wig, instead of which I said quietly, "If you know where I will *not* find the things I seek, then you must know where I *will* find them, so tell me. Tell me, if you are so wise! What then, shall I do with my life? How shall I earn my living? It is easy for you, who have always had money, to talk, and now that your life is ending, you laugh at me! Why do you laugh at me? Why don't you help me? You cannot discourage me, no matter what you say! I will go to school, and I will learn what an infinitive is, yes, and even participles! You'll see! I'll show you!" My words tumbled over each other, and I was weeping with rage. At the word participle, she threw up her hands dramatically and said, "Stop! God for- bid! Not participles, I beg of you!" She put her enormous arms around me, patting me, and said, "There now, don't cry! I'm a stupid old woman,—let us go to bed. Tomorrow we'll feel better, and we'll talk about it again. I'm sorry I've made you miserable,—forgive me!" I said no more, but helped her up, and took her to her room, then went to mine.

I threw myself on the bed and cried until I was worn out. Then I got up and took a hot bath and went to bed, to lie awake for hours thinking over all that she had said, and of how queer they all were, finally falling asleep to dream a long-continued argument with her, in which I offered the most incontestable proofs of my beliefs, an argument in which I was completely successful. How different our dreams from reality!

Next morning I awoke in that beautiful room to the sound of rain dripping from the trees, and Isiah sputtering for his breakfast. I sat with him on the window seat while he ate, and listened to the friendly rain, remembering how sad I had been when I went to bed. But the drenched trees, from which silvery drops fell softly, the fragrance that came in the window, of earth, and growing things, lifted my heart with joy. I could not be sad on such a heavenly morning. I could almost see the grass growing, and the leaves waved and wriggled in the rain, with delight. I thought that if I hurried I might be able to see Henry and our plants that must already be growing.

In the dining room Mr. and Mrs. Fairfax sat eating peanuts, apparently none the worse for their dissipation. They said "Good morning, Belinda," pleasantly and enquired after Isiah. I assured them that I had left him in the pink. The maid brought me real food, with a knowing look, and I made the most of ham and eggs and pancakes, real manna from Heaven, for I knew what I'd have from now on. Mrs. Fairfax said that Mrs. de Saussere never came down to breakfast, and that we were to go to her room to say good-by.

I hurried through my breakfast and asked Peters if she would lend me an umbrella to go down to the garden, and she said yes, adding, "Look sharp you don't get too wet!" and I called back, "No, no," as I scurried down the old brick path. Under the biggest trees it wasn't raining at all, and the birds were twittering, the sound of the rain on the leaves made a gentle musical symphony. I found old Henry in a potting shed, gay as a lark. "Fine day for our plants, miss," he said through his whiskers. "Oh yes," I said, but I wanted to lay my hands on the ground, to somehow feel the growing things. Along the side of the shed were lilies-of-the-valley, a thick bed of green leaves with creamy, white heavily scented flowers shining among them. Henry wanted to give me some, but I said, "No, Henry,—they'll only die on the train, and they are so grand right here in the rain." How I hated leaving Henry.

When I came back, our bags had been carried down and Peters told me to go to Mrs. de Saussere's room to say good-by. I found Mr. and Mrs. Fairfax there, and when Mrs. de Saussere said "Good morning, Belinda; isn't it a shame it's raining? I'm trying to persuade Madge to stay another night," I said nothing, for I loved the rain. She sat propped up in the bed by dozens of lacy pillows, against a headboard painted with angels blowing horns, intertwined with trailing sprays of flowers and fruit. The bed had no footboard, and when she saw me looking at the place it should have been she said, "What are you looking at?", I said, "I just wondered if this bed ever had a footboard, or if you had it removed?" She laughed and said, "Oh, yes, it had one, but I couldn't face a bunch of fat angels leaping about,—it depressed me, so I had it removed. Don't you like it better?" I said yes, for I did.

Mrs. Fairfax kissed her good-by, while Mr. Fairfax held her hand, and they exchanged affectionate promises to see each other more often in the future, and as they left, I said good-by, sick with disappointment that she displayed no desire to resume our conversation of the night before. She had apparently dismissed the whole thing from her mind, and only said, "Good-by, Belinda! I've enjoyed having you, and if you ever come this way again, come and see me." I thanked her, thinking bitterly that she could have so easily helped me if she had wished. But private thoughts were banished, for the carriage was at the door, and I had to go. I thanked Peters for her kindness, the carriage turned the gravel circle, the horses trotting briskly in the rain out of the big gate, and we were soon on the train, and nearing New York.

My suppressed excitement at actually seeing New York made me quite ill; my head ached horribly. The negro porter saw that I was not well, and asked me if he could do anything for me. I told him that I thought it was the excitement,—that this was my first trip North. He said, "Pardon me if I sound fresh, but I want to say something rather personal to you." I said all right, and told him how I had been with the Fairfaxes, and Isiah. He said, "Yes, I know them very well; they have gone down with me many times, and also Isiah. But if this is your first time North, I want to tell you that I'm a Southerner too, and have lived up here and gone to school here, and it's not at all the way you expect it to be." I looked puzzled, and he said, "It's hard to explain, but I don't want you to be too discouraged; if ever you're in a tight place and need a friend, go to this address. If I am away, as I usually am, my mother will be there, and she will help you,—you can trust her. Any time you need a friend, go to her. Will you remember?" and he gave me an address in Harlem. He was so serious, I thanked him and promised, although the likelihood that I would ever need it seemed remote. Which proves something, only I don't know what.

The train ran through flat country dim in the steady rain that poured, and I remembered a Sunday in church when I was very small, watching the rain come from across the mountain, then the meadow, and the cornfield, right on up to the church, and over it. Clearly have I seen a thousand times the rain coming, and recalled the astonishment I felt then, that one could actually *see* the rain like that, where it was raining, and where it was not. Before then I had supposed that it rained all over at the same time, with no edge.

We came into the station and I had no time to be appalled by its size, for we almost immediately, with the help of a porter, got into a train for White Plains. My head was bursting, and it was all I could do to conceal the fact. At White Plains we got out and piled into a rattling old carriage and trundled down a long street, to what seemed the outskirts of the town. We turned in at a gate, following a circuitous drive up to a very ugly house, which had a great many unnecessary turrets at unexpected places. The driver carried our bags in and rattled away, and there we stood in the musty smelling ugly house. I opened some windows, and gave them their supper, and Isiah his, but there was none for me. No one thought about it, and as I was not well, it didn't matter. Mrs. Fairfax asked me to keep Isiah with me for the night, and when I had made up beds for them and opened windows, I left them, going to a room she had told me to use.

After I cleaned the house it was quite comfortable, and my life fell into practically the same routine as that followed in Gremont. The only excitement was that they added cheese to their diet,—just ordinary rat cheese which they nibbled, not unlike mice. Mr. Fairfax still sneaked down in the morning for his share of my bacon, and I still bought cabbages and onions and ate them raw, under a tree near the gate.

Even after I had filled vases with flowers, the house had a cold disagreeable look. There were only five books in it, and those were dismal reports of the Episcopal Diocese, stories of missionaries, and one huge volume on bee culture, in which I was not interested. But even those I read in sheer desperation. My sister Adelaide sent me five dollars, and I went to the village and bought beautiful blue silk and made me a dress. It had simple white collar and cuffs, and I got a white sailor hat for a dollar and twenty-five cents. It was all beautiful, but I had nowhere to wear it. Although Mrs. Fairfax didn't say so, I knew that she would not allow me to go out in the evening, nor to the village at all. I felt very lonely, wondered what I should do, but in a few weeks something so horrible happened that I felt I should go really and truly mad, or kill myself.

A letter came from Kingsland, forwarded from Gremont, which frightened me and made me cold with fear of my passion for education. Maybe I was wrong, I thought, and perhaps I should give up all hopes or desires for it. This is what King wrote:

Dear Darling Linda:

I have heard that you are leaving Gremont, and going North with Mrs. Fairfax, and my heart is dead within me. Why have I no power to touch you? No words to make you see that you are being driven by false desires? I have given my life into your hands, against my own desire or will, and you are partly responsible for it; you cannot so easily avoid your charge. If you have left me forever, knowing what it will do to me, then you are indeed heartless and half of me is dead. I'd rather die completely than live half alive, for you are a part of me, and without you I cannot be whole. A man cannot live half a man. I have not wished nor planned that this be so, and I find that I have hate in my heart for you, and too late you will know that your ambitions will recoil upon you, and you will know that your desire to be of importance in the world will cause you great bitterness of soul. You are too blinded by your ambitions to know that those you think important are more lonely than you or I; that each one must build their own citadel. So I will go out alone. My little house will not know us, nor our lives continue in it. Some one else will know it, and some day you will know that you are mistaken in what you think is worth living, fighting and dying for. I would that I could make you see this in time. Aside from me, if you cannot love me and make your life with me, I tell you that your driving ambitions will come between you and every real thing in your life. I love you, foolish Linda. I would like to have seen you just once again. Good-by.

King.

I had no one to whom I could speak, and showed the letter to Mrs. Fairfax only because she had assumed a certain responsibility in the matter. She took it very lightly, merely saying, "He is young, and his pride is hurt; he will get over it." How wrong she was, as I learned to my bitter sorrow. Within a week my sister Sallie sent me a newspaper from Carleton, containing news of his death. The item stated briefly that Kingsland Mears, nineteen-year-old son of Doctor Alexis Mears, was accidentally killed by the evening train, just outside of Weaverton, on a certain date. I counted back, terror in my soul, to find that he had died on the night of the day he had written me. No one knew how it happened, as it was not known that he was anywhere near the place at the time. His body had been found after the 10:55 train had passed, badly lacerated, lying by the tracks, two miles east of Weaverton.

The words swam before my eyes, and now I knew that I must surely die,—that I could never bear this. I felt that all this had happened before; that it was a rehearsal for a play that would never be produced, or had already been. It was real, yet not real. Part of me was numbed, feelingless, and part of me was detached, and I felt hatred of him for adding to my already rotten life. One part of me said, "If he had really loved you he could never have done it," and another part said, "You have killed him,—you and your ambition. No amount of education and knowing about split infinitives can bring back that strong, wonderful body, or make new again his beautiful face; cause his good heart to beat again." All these conflicting thoughts went through and through my mind until I was completely dazed. Those two old people suddenly became repulsive to me. They were evil, old and dead, and I had allowed them to influence me against King, to aid me in this cruel thing. Yet I knew that they had not; that they had said nothing to induce me to any decision; that I had asked them to let me come with them, and had decided for myself. Thus I argued day and night, my heart sore, my head bursting, around and around to complete exhaustion.

Then I received a letter from King's father. A veiled, rather curt note, asking me if I had a good photograph of King, and if so, would I send it to him, as they had none. I sent the only one I had, a beautiful one, and as I wrapped it up, I thought I would die of pain and anguish. I sent no letter with it. I had no words.

I felt so closed in, so shut off from the world, that I wondered if I had imagined the whole thing. The world was seething around me, and I was on a tiny island, with two old unreal people and a too real old bird. All over the land there were colleges with boys and girls walking under trees, and going to classes, living, learning, and here I was, formally serving chocolate candy and peanuts to two imaginary people, and giving lettuce to an iron-beaked limb of Satan, gnawing raw cabbage leaves until I began to feel that we were all crazy. I couldn't go away, for I had only a dollar left from my five, and I had not yet worked out my fare up, so there was no way out. I sought desperately for some way to get at least in the neighborhood of books, but everything seemed closing in on me, and I often thought of suicide, and that King was better off than I. The giants I had thought to overthrow in my march to victory had become invisible, myth-like fantasies. I could not see them plainly, and could find no place to strike.

Luckily, I suppose, something happened to change the routine of my life. Mrs. Fairfax informed me that for many years she had been in the habit of giving vacations to women from the slums, twelve at a time; that they slept in a large barn-like structure in the back of the big house, and asked me to make up beds for them, as the first batch would arrive in two days. She showed me where the bedding was, and left me to prepare their quarters. While I worked, I thought that at least the affair had one bright spot,—she would have to buy food for them, and if I had to cook it, I would get some too.

Chapter 11

The arrival of the first twelve women, composed of many nationalities, was a new and fascinating experience for me. I had never been in close proximity to a foreigner, and the Polish, Hungarian, Italian, Spanish, and Irish names made me yearn to know those far countries, to speak their languages. Three were Jews from a country called Russia, a name so mysterious to me that I looked and looked at them, trying to realize that it did in fact exist; and there was a dark, sullen, unhappy woman from Spain; and an Irish woman who laughed and made amusing remarks in a brogue that endeared her to me instantly. Some were young and still possessed of energy and hope; some old with tired, driven, bitter faces,—some listless, indifferent, taking things for granted.

I cooked a big dinner, for Mrs. Fairfax had given me a generous list of supplies to purchase, including huge roasts, green vegetables and fruit. They all ate heartily, the first six having dinner at five-thirty, the second at six o'clock. I enjoyed feeding them, for they brought life into the dead old house, and I felt that it was a fine and generous thing for Mrs. Fairfax to do. My only regret was that the work entailed—the cooking and dishwashing, cleaning their quarters—prevented my getting to really know them.

When they had been there two weeks, they returned to New York, and twelve more took their places the same day. With the second batch, I tentatively suggested to Mrs. Fairfax that some of them might like to help with the work. "No," said she, "they work hard at home,—this is their rest; you should gladly serve them, for it is all for God." I made no reply, but privately I thought that God wouldn't mind if they made their own beds.

By this time I felt reckless, and didn't particularly care whether or not I remained, for in one more week I would have paid for my fare, and I would be free. One day a man called on me with a letter of introduction from my sister Adelaide. He was nice-looking, healthy, about forty, with a goatee. I was glad to see any friend of my sister, but told him that I could not talk long, as I had too much to do, and besides, Mrs. Fairfax might not like it. He asked if he might come back after dinner and take me out, and I said I'd love it.

He came that evening at nine, and I was ready, in my new blue dress and sailor hat. Oh! It was good to be out, just to walk along the street with a nice man! He asked me what I wanted to do, and I said that I had no idea,—that I had never been in the village at night, and didn't know what one did. He couldn't believe me, but I didn't care whether he did or not, I was so happy to be out. It was all I could do to walk along in a respectable way, for I wanted to shout, and yell, and run like mad! But we went decorously to a drug store and had ice cream, which brought so forcibly to my mind the last ice cream I had had in a drug store, with King. I looked in my hand where he had placed a kiss, saying that it would always be there, always with me, and I wished that I were dead.

The man, Mr. Robert Howland, said, "Let's walk along the street, and if we see a nice place to go, we will." Soon we came to a sort of beer garden, where we could see people dancing. I was afraid to go in, but he insisted, and we sat at an iron table and had beer, which I hated. He wanted to dance, but I told him I didn't know how; he offered to teach me, but I was too self-conscious, and wouldn't. All the time I felt that I was a stupid country girl, which indeed I was, and that he must be sorry that he had come to see me at all. We talked about my sister, for whom he expressed great admiration, and told me how she had asked him to come to see me, because she felt that I was not happy. I admitted that I was in no immediate danger of laughing myself to death.

Suddenly I knew that I had better go home, and when he said it was just twelve, I was in a panic. He paid his bill, and I made the poor man scuttle hastily out of the place, and kept him running behind me all the way home. It was a lovely evening for him, and as it turned out, equally enjoyable for me. I said good night hurriedly, took off my shoes and sneaked in, hoping they would not hear me. But they did.

After the slum ladies had eaten their breakfasts, I had to clear the dining room for the IP's. Their usual rich repast was on the table when Mrs. Fairfax came down next morning, and I knew from her expression that all was not well. I was prepared for the worst, but when she rose and said, "Belinda, I wish to speak to you,—will you come with me?" I felt faintly ill from nervous tension. With cruel solemnity she asked me to sit down facing her, and she began with, "Now, Belinda, I want you to tell me the truth." I could have cried. Why should I not tell her the truth? What was it? I said, "Yes, Mrs. Fairfax." In a biting, cruel voice she said, "*Who* was the man you were out with last night? *Where* did you go?" I told her his name, and said that he came from my sister Adelaide; that we had gone to a drug store and had ice cream. "Then where did you go?" she demanded. I hesitated to mention the beer, but her shrill voice forced me somehow, and I said, "We went to a beer garden and had beer."

At the word beer, her face took on a malignant expression, her eyes narrowed and she lowered her voice to an ominous quietness. "So, that's the kind of a girl you are! For all our kindness and interest in you, at the first opportunity you go with a stranger, and a man at that! To a low place, and drink beer! Blinded by the wiles of Satan! I can see that you are not the kind of girl I wish to have in my house. No doubt you did not stop at that,—what else did you do, to keep you out until a late hour at night." I felt that she wanted me to tell her something terrible, and sought vainly for something that would satisfy her, but I could think of nothing more, and said, "He brought me home." That was the end.

Maybe without the beer, things could have been smoothed over, but the beer put the lid on. Her brown eyes flashed and her lips curled scornfully, as she rose and positively hissed at me, "And this is the ambitious girl who wanted an education! I had intended, if your actions proved your sincerity, to help you, but you have shown clearly the weakness of your character, your yearning for the flesh-pots of Satan, which you obviously prefer to a life of honest endeavor and devotion to God." I just looked at her, wondering what the fleshpots were, and she went on, "I owe you three dollars; here it is, and I must ask you to leave my house by tomorrow morning. I have already sent to an agency for a cook and a maid, so if you will pack your things and go, you will greatly oblige me," and she swept her long white dress behind her. For a few minutes I sat frozen in my chair, stunned by the whole affair. My world seemed to have toppled again, and I knew not where to turn. I went to the kitchen and prepared lunch for the ladies from the slums. I had little time for self-pity during the day, for I wanted to leave everything clean.

Upstairs I took a good bath, for I didn't know when I would have the chance again, packed my suitcase and lay down. Now I could let my tears fall comfortably. I dared not dwell on the coming day, for I was really frightened, but I could look back and try to figure out why I was in my present position.

Nothing made sense, and toward morning I slept, waking early. I took Isiah down, gave him his breakfast and made myself some coffee; I didn't feel hungry. I knew Mr. Fairfax would be in for his bacon, so I had it ready when tall, benign in his skull-cap, he came in, visibly agitated, and put out his hand impulsively, saying, "Belinda, I'm so sorry! My heart aches for you; don't let this discourage you,—keep your faith in God, and pray!"

I didn't know whether to laugh at him or weep for him, he looked so pathetic, but I said, "Mr. Fairfax, you're a nice old man, and I like you, but don't you mention prayer to me. You pray, but I can't see that it makes you do anything good. I think you and Mrs. Fairfax have forgotten all about life, and are only interested in what's going to happen to you after you're dead. Unfortunately I'm alive now, and I've got to look after me; no one else wants to, neither God nor man," and I gave him his bacon which he ate ravenously in spite of his distress.

When I was ready to go, I said good-by to Isiah. He was disturbed, and ruffled his feathers, making queer sounds in his throat. I had a moment of regret at leaving him, surprisingly enough, but after all we had lived intimately together for over four months. I gave him a long look and said, "Good-by, Isiah, I hope the next maid heeds your plea," and closed the door. I thought of King, and the fact that I seemed always to be closing doors. Mr. Fairfax was in the dining room, and he got up politely, holding out his hand. I gave him mine, and he said, "Good-by, Belinda! God bless you!" Said I to myself, Small Chance, as I put on my nice straw sailor, and carrying my suitcase, went out, closing the door behind me.

I went down the walk and out of the gate to the street. The sun had been shining when I got up, but now the sky was overcast and rain began to fall. I was afraid it would ruin my new sailor, and that was what made me go into a place that had a sign on the front, "Mrs. Newell's Sanitarium and Training School for Nurses." I thought, "I'll try this." My sister Adelaide had been a trained nurse, and although I had no desire to be one, the rain and my nice sailor decided for me.

I rang the bell and a manservant opened the door. "What do you wish, Miss?" he asked, looking down his long thin nose. "May I see Mrs. Newell?" I asked. Giving me a suspicious look, taking in my cheap suitcase, he said, "Wait here," opening a door on the right of the hall. He left me, glancing at me as though warning me not to make off with anything.

The room was depressing in the extreme. A center table with a drab cover supported some very old moth-eaten magazines; tired wicker chairs were disconsolately about, and in one corner was a large glass case filled with stuffed birds, which brought Isiah to my mind. "Perhaps it's better to stuff them, less trouble," I thought. Now it was raining hard, and I hoped I might stay here, on account of my sailor hat. My thoughts wandered, and a drowsiness crept over me.

The door opened and I sat up with a start, trying to look intelligent. A very nice-looking woman came in and said, "I'm Mrs. Newell; what can I do for you?" I said, "I saw your sign, and I would like to stay here and learn to be a nurse." She smiled and said, "Perhaps, but you'll have to tell me who you are, and give me some references." I told her many facts, and when I stopped, she said, "Why have you left Mrs. Fairfax? They are famous for their good works, and their charity." So I told her about the man, and the beer. She thought for a moment and said, "I'll take you on trial for one month and by that time you will know if you want to stay, and I if I want to keep you." Which seemed fair enough.

Few memories of that interlude remain in my mind. I know that the head nurse was a beautiful blond girl, named Mrs. Claypoole, who had left her husband and was in love with a young doctor who came frequently to the Sanitarium. They were kind to me, but in a short time I decided that if I was going to be a nurse, I wanted to do it thoroughly. Mrs. Newell's was not a registered hospital, and she could not give diplomas. It was not what I had chosen to do, but I thought I could learn to like it, and it was, after all, a school.

I wrote my sister Adelaide about it, and she agreed with me, and told me that she had written to a friend of hers, Muriel Whitcomb, to communicate with me. Muriel was making her living as a nurse in Brooklyn, and in a few days I received a letter from her, asking me to come in and see her. On my next afternoon off duty I went. She was a delicate, frail blonde, very sympathetic with my efforts, and advised me to train in one of the Brooklyn hospitals. Why, I don't know. I had already chosen the Presbyterian, in New York, for I knew its reputation was of the highest, but I let her persuade me, mainly because I was dependent upon her for financial aid. Had I been able to buy my own uniforms, and to go to the hospital of my choice, how different my life could have been! I understand that adversity builds character. If this is true, and I doubt it, and it works with any balanced ratio, then I have acquired sufficient character for ten women, and to spare.

Muriel recommended the Olympia, as one of the largest and best; perhaps she was right. I didn't train in all the others. I sent for application blanks and filled, them out, lying about only one thing, my age. It was necessary for me to be older by four years, but that was a trifle. I had already added a couple in order to get the job in Maple Inn. When I told Mrs. Newell about it, she said she thought I was being very sensible; that I should train where I would be given a diploma.

On an old sewing machine in the attic, I made two checked gingham dresses, for my probationary period, and four aprons. The list required for admission was four times that number, but Muriel had very little money and I none, and we thought I could get by with that amount. As for the number of shoes and stockings, the lists of underwear required, we just laughed, and I said, "I'll just add them in my mind, as I have added to my age. Besides, I might not be accepted anyway, so why waste the money? The day came for me to go, and I said good-by to Mrs. Newell, who had been fair to me, and got on a train for New York.

When I got to the gate of the hospital in Brooklyn, I sat down on a bench before going in, and held a conference with myself. "Now, Belinda Dan," I said, "this must be your last move for a long time. Here you remain, come Hell and high water, for at least three years. That's not long, and when you get out, you can make some money and still go to school, if you aren't in a wheel chair." With determination, I picked up my suitcase and walked up the long path toward dismal red buildings.

I enquired at the main office for the Superintendent of Nurses, and was shown into a large room where I faced an elderly woman with gray hair and brown eyes, sitting behind a flat desk. I read a story once in which the heroine entered a training school for nurses. She was graciously received by the Superintendent, and given tea, while they discoursed fluently of music, literature, and kindred topics. My experience was at variance with hers. The gray-haired woman looked at me sharply and said, "What is your name?" I told her. She ran through a file and took out a card, pushed a button, and when a nurse came in she said, "Show Miss Dan to her room," and to me she said, "Report for duty on Ward 10 in half an hour." The interview was over. I was in;—for three years at hard labor.

Chapter 12

How can I write of a period in my life so beset with unsuspected dangers? I had decided that if, as it seemed, I could never go to school, I would be the best nurse that ever was, that I would learn all that I could out of books, and through practical work, and to this acquired knowledge I would add the energies of my healthy body, and whatever I possessed of humor and sympathy for human beings. It seemed simple; one need only to work intelligently, observe and listen well. But when I entered Olympia, even on my first day I discovered that it was not so simple as that; that it was more complicated than I could have imagined. Although at times I had felt that God himself had for some reason a down on me, I had never before witnessed unnecessary cruelty, coolly, deliberately planned by one human being against another. I was to learn much more than how to make a bed and give medication before my life in Olympia was finished.

There were ten girls in my class known as probationers, which name sufficiently explains itself. We wore checked gingham dresses and white aprons and collars, and cuffs, but no bibs or caps. When accepted as student nurses, we would be allowed to wear different dresses, with bibs to our aprons, and a white lawn cap. When one achieved that enviable position of Senior, a narrow black velvet ribbon was added to the cap, which gave it a most charming appearance. How I hoped to have someday a black ribbon on my cap!

It was several weeks before I knew the names of all the girls in my class, as we worked in different departments, and at night we were so tired we went right to bed. I never knew many of them at all well as the student nurses did not talk to probationers, and the Seniors spoke only to give orders. Callie MacPherson I came to know first, as I worked with her on

Ward 10, but my roommate I learned to love dearly. Her name was Yoshi Ishmoto. She was young and slender, her hair incredibly black, her teeth white, her cheeks red, and her skin dark brown! She was beautiful. She was shy and sensitive, and as the others looked upon her as strange, not quite human because she was foreign, she was lonely. We became warm friends and had lots of fun together.

Yoshi was very homesick, and alone in our room at night she would weep like a little child and say to me, "Oh! Mees Dan, I want so to see my mother!" And I would say, "Now, Yoshi, you're a big girl now—you must not cry—you will see your mother. As soon as you have finished your training you can go home, and everything will be fine." Sometimes she stopped and smiled, but in the night I heard her sobbing, and went to her, trying to comfort her.

When Yoshi had been there a few months she lost her high color, and she walked lamely. She told me that she had never worn western clothes before, and that her shoes hurt her feet. She was engaged to a charming young Japanese who was studying in New York, and they planned to be married as soon as she finished her training. She finished it, but not in the way expected.

My first head nurse was a Japanese girl named Hiro Saito: she and Yoshi were the only Japanese nurses in the school at that time. She was small and lithe. Her tiny hands, as brown as autumn leaves, fluttered about, but with such efficient results that I felt clumsy and stupid in her presence. She showed me how to make a bed, and said, "Now you make it." I began—it took me seventeen minutes, and she shook her head in despair. "You must make it in three minutes,—you must work more queek!" she said. So I made it again and again. I made that bed so often that it seemed that I had been doing it for years; tightening the under sheet, stretching the rubber sheet, then the draw sheet, next the top sheet, which had to be mitred at a perfect angle. My hands were hot and swollen, sweat rolled down my forehead, but I kept on making that bed. She was occupied with her own work, and completely ignored my efforts, yet, subtly let me know that she was aware of my progress, knew exactly how many times I had made it, and the time cut at every completion of the performance.

When she came to inspect, she noted every detail with a sharp eye, and said, "Not so bad, but you must do it in three minutes; the last took seven," and she took it apart again. Again I made the bed, and at twelve, she sent me to lunch; I ached in every muscle. After lunch she let me scrub the supply closet for a change, but the next morning I had the bed again, and for a whole week, until I got it right in the specified time with less perspiring and aching of muscles.

Probationers were assigned to different wards, under various head nurses. I had no idea how the others felt, but at no time in my life have I ever felt so completely futile, frightened and clumsy, as during those first few months. The terror, constant and all-pervading that accompanied me was eventually justified. I made the great and horrible mistake that had been hovering menacingly over me for weeks. It happened like this:

One afternoon the nurse who was on duty in the accident ward was ill, and due to a shortage of regular nurses, I was sent down to relieve her. No probationer was ever placed in so responsible a position before, and I doubt if one ever was again. When I got down, the young intern in charge saw that I was nervous and said, "Now don't worry; everything is very simple. I'll show you exactly what you have to do." I thanked him, and following his instructions I got the instruments out, and had the sterilizer boiling, bandages ready, dressings for any sort of case that might come in.

We stood talking, he telling me about Texas, and I a few things about myself. The sun came through the window making ribbons of light across the bubbling sterilizer, and I felt calm and happy. Suddenly the harsh iron-like clamor of the ambulance bell caused me to lose my so recently acquired confidence. Almost at once a tall man walked in, holding a handkerchief to his nose, and gingerly carrying something in his hand, in another handkerchief. Calmly he held out his hand and gave what he held to the doctor, saying, "A steel girder fell and cut off the end of my nose." The doctor took it, looked at it, and handed it to me, saying, "Keep it clean," and clean meant only one thing to me.

Dr. Warren carefully sponged the man's face with cleansing fluid which we had prepared, opened a package of sterile sponges, then broke a glass tube of cat gut, and threaded his needle to sew it on, turning to me he said, "Let me have the nose." With a pair of long sponge sticks I began feeling around in the sterilizer for it. Dr. Warren looked at me, and his face went white. He gasped, and almost whispered, so low were his words, "My God! You've cooked it!"

Everything swam crazily around me, and I felt peculiar; when the tables and chairs, the sterilizer, Dr. Warren and the man himself had stopped floating around, and assumed their proper positions again, I looked at the patient. He was sitting very still, looking at me thoughtfully. The room was deathly quiet, and I wished that some one would speak. Dr. Warren looked at me with a baffled, hopeless expression, and then turned to the man with a pleading, explanatory look, and as though meeting an answer in the keen blue eyes, proceeded to affix a dressing to the man's face. The man stood up, at least six feet of him, and he gave me another steady, long look, made some short remark to Dr. Warren, who answered him, and walked out. In a deadly, level voice, Dr. Warren said, "I'll have to report this," and I said, "Yes, I know," but could not move. He fussed around the table for a minute and said, "I think if you go up and report it yourself, first, it will go easier for you." I thanked him and went out, through the long dark corridor, up a flight of steps and along another hall, through which the same sun that I had seen so happily one short half-hour ago, still shone.

I stood outside Mrs. Bender's office, steadying myself, and knocked. A much too well-known voice said, "Come in." With my mind an almost complete blank, numb, I walked through that feared and hated door, and stood before that great inimical bulk, in the top of which were two bright brown button-like eyes, staring through glasses. Happy in her belief in her capacity for meeting and handling any emergency, she said, "What do you wish, Miss Dan?" In reality saying, present your problem and I will show you how to deal with difficulties,—what a pity to disturb such complacency! Some wandering wave of indifference settled over me, and coolly meeting those two beads of brown I said, "I've just boiled a man's nose."

Moving cautiously, slowly, she rose, her pudgy hands holding on to the desk in front of her, the broad bulk of hips looming up portentously behind. She seemed to grow bigger with the increase in her astonishment and rage, horror and disbelief that met and mingled on her face. All this time she had remained silent,—either from sheer surprise, or from fear of my sanity.

Gathering herself together, she stepped from behind her desk and walked toward me, destruction in her bearing. At any other time I would have automatically retreated, simply for self-preservation, but now an awareness of what I had done produced a lethargy so complete as to prohibit movement on my part. She put her face close to mine,—I noticed that she had quite a heavy black mustache. She spoke quietly, but in its quietness was the sound of death. She said, "You *what*?" I retreated an inch from her mustache, repeating myself, "I've just boiled a man's nose,—cooked it, you know."

Her inability to imagine the details of a performance at once so trivial and so horrendous made it impossible for her to sustain her position of command. She moved her squat feet with cautious haste toward the door, as though movement alone would preserve her from complete collapse. From the door she flung at me these words, "Remain here until I return, you fool!" and I was alone. I knew that she had gone to investigate the scene of the crime, and that when she returned she would be in a frightful, and more articulate rage. To pass the time I read the titles of a few books she had, examined the pictures from all angles, my ears alert for her heavy footsteps.

When she returned I saw from her expression of bewildered rage that she, even with her extraordinary capacity for subtle cruelties, was up a tree. Murder would have been a simple solution. With a malignant look she said, "Go to your room, and remain there." Leaving her office, I went down steps and across the lawn into the nurses' home. My room was a peaceful haven, a dark pool of safety. I felt very tired and sleepy and, lying down, almost instantly passed into a sleep so deep that, being awakened by a dis-agreeable sound which evolved into the voice of Mrs. Bender, I could not bring myself back for a moment. I had been as though dead, and it was infinitely pleasant. I saw her standing in the door, the light from the hall outlining her menacing bulk. My knees felt weak and wobbly, but I man-aged to stand stiffly at attention, aware of the unusualness of her presence. Her edicts were issued from the office ordinarily.

"You will go at once to isolation, on bread and water for two weeks," she spoke gently, enjoying the torture she was inflicting. "This matter will have to come before the Board of Governors,—the man, naturally, has a legal right to claim the tip of your nose, in which case it will be removed and transplanted to his. You will be notified of their decision." I weakly said, "Yes, Mrs. Bender," and she plowed her way down the hall. I was alone.

In a daze I gathered a few things together and went down the hall, turned to the right across an open space between the buildings, into one of two rooms reserved for infectious cases or punishment. At the moment they were both unoccupied, and I chose the dark one on the court. For some reason I craved dark, deep, cool dark, and silence. The bed was unmade, but on a table lay clean linen and I made my bed, removed my clothes and lay down. No one came near me for a long time, and as my watch had stopped I had no idea how long I had been there when I heard a timid voice whispering, "Mees Dan! Mees Dan!" I opened the door and there was Yoshi. Against the rules she had come, bringing me the remainder of a box of chocolate candy her young man had given her. Glad of the candy, for I was hungry, I told her she must go back at once, but she was so sad. She cried and said that she missed me and was so afraid. I laughed and said, "Now, Yoshi, don't be silly! Everything will be all right; isolation will do me good, so you get back to your room before they catch you!" She went away, still weeping and whispering "Oh! Mees Dan," and I went to bed again, and a thick curtain fell between me and all that had happened; I slept profoundly.

Next morning the maid left a dirty tray outside my door on which lay a slice of bread and a glass of lukewarm water. I ate the bread, and the candy Yoshi had brought, washing it down with the water. Nothing occurred to break the monotony until eleven, when who should appear in shining white but my old friend and well wisher, Mrs. Bender. I should have felt flattered, for she seldom paid calls on probationers, and never in the morning, but I knew that she had come to bring me glad tidings of great joy, and was prepared for the worst. Smiling blandly, she swung her hind quarters through the door and studied me with her button eyes, obviously distressed to find me calm, when by all her calculations, I should have been bathed in tears of shame and humiliation. I stood, waiting for her to speak. "I've come to tell you that the Board is meeting at eleven; it will decide what is to be done with you. You realize fully, I hope, that in the event of this patient demanding it, we shall be obliged to cut off the tip of your nose. Have you thought over that point?" Almost sweetly she spoke, and my only answer was, "Yes, Mrs. Bender."

When she had gone, I went to the shabby bureau, studying my face in the cracked mirror, which distorted my features so that the absence of a nose would hardly have been noticeable. In imagination I saw myself going through life, minus the tip of my nose, and the horror of it shook my soul. Touching the tip of my nose often during the day, I realized for the first time that it was my nose, and that I had a deep maternal feeling for it; it was a part of me, and without that small part I would not be whole. My soul was sick within me, for now at last I realized what I had done,—the insult I had inflicted upon the physical body of a living man. The only thought that helped me to face it was that I had not intended doing it, but honesty forced me to admit that the result was the same.

At four in the afternoon I received another visit from Mrs. Bender,—now in an expansive, genial mood. To a casual observer she would have appeared a kindly, motherly woman. I stood, waiting for her to break the news, which she delayed as long as possible, walking around the room, looking out of the back windows. Coming back to me, smiling benignly, she said, "Well, my girl, the Board has decided that for the time being you will not lose your nose. We will wait and see if the man sues the hospital,—if he does, it will be necessary to discuss it again."

Whether I weakened, or was merely hungry, I don't know, but becoming hysterical, I begged her wildly to save me; to prevent them from ever cutting off my nose. I made extravagant promises to do anything she asked, any menial tasks, for three whole years, if she would intercede for me! She smiled unctuously and said, "I can promise nothing. In the meantime you will remain here." Again she left me, exhausted by fear and anguish,—and hunger.

Almost as soon as she had gone, two men came with apparatus for fumigation, and were surprised to find me. At first I thought that Mrs. Bender was determined not only to isolate me, but to fumigate me. Resolved to fight to the death, I told the men to report to Doctor Schwab, who was in charge of Infectious Diseases, as I refused to be fumigated. Dr. Schwab came over, and when he saw me in the room he had ordered fumigated, he was furious. He told me that he would send dressing gown and slippers, and for me to leave all my clothes in the room for fumigation, which I did. I never heard the gory details, but it was known among the nurses that Dr. Schwab had spoken to Mrs. Bender in no uncertain terms when he found that she had put a nurse in a room from which a patient suffering from scarlet fever had been removed to the morgue the night before. I heard no more about the nose until weeks later, when Dr. Warren told me there was absolutely no danger from the man, as he had signed a paper absolving the hospital of blame, and that there had been no meeting of the Board at all.

The Assistant Superintendent of Nurses was a charming, quiet lady of forty, named Miss Russell. She conducted several of our classes, and never at any time in my training did I see or hear her do or say an unkind thing. If nurses fainted, as they often did, while standing in class, it was not her fault. Standing straight with your hands behind you for one hour was exhausting, especially when added to the order to keep our eyes upon her face. The flow of words and the rigid position combined to produce a state in which a film came between one's eyes and her face; objects seemed to swing rhythmically, making it difficult to retain an upright position. Once the line between relaxation and awareness was crossed, one was lost, and at almost every class one or more crumpled up, sliding quietly down on the floor. Two nurses were asked to remove the body and the class continued. Perhaps it was a good idea, for after a few weeks, we didn't fold up any more.

For the first three months our work consisted in the main of scrubbing, serving trays, washing bed-pans and urinals, folding linen, making beds and surgical dressings. When we had mastered these, we progressed to those which necessitated the use of a patient. Bathing in tub and bed was demonstrated by the use of a patient who was well enough to stand it. It was to me a wonderful thing to bathe a sick person without moving her,—to change the linen without lifting or causing her pain. Bandaging too was taught by using a patient. All these things were absorbing and fascinating in their detail of execution.

One revolting job we had was bathing patients of incredible dirtiness. Their ragged clothes, stiff with old malodorous filth, and often their feet were wrapped in strips of dirty rags, in lieu of stockings or socks! A nauseous stench accompanied the removal of these rags, for having been on the feet so long, the flesh had begun to grow over them. Such feet were kept in soap poultices for days, and washed many times before becoming clean. But that was Sunday in the country compared to cleaning the snags of old teeth that by searching about in cavernous, ill-smelling mouths, we discovered with cotton swabs on toothpicks. What burned me up was that often when we got them clean for the first time in their lives, the patients were dead. Perhaps the shock,—I wouldn't know. The time we spent on the dead, that could have been spent on the living!

After the nose episode I was under a cloud with the interns, and many of them would make cutting remarks concerning it, especially one vulgar little Irishman named O'Leary. He would cover his nose protectively with his hand and back away from me in simulated terror every time he saw me. At first I felt sick with embarrassment, but after a time I opened my eyes and saw the interns for what they were,—I learned very soon to watch out for them, and for almost all the doctors, for they would assume no responsibility for mistakes if they could possibly blame a nurse. One had to keep on the alert against them, which used up a great deal of energy that could have been more beneficently directed. The young interns showed too eagerly their desire to curry favor with the attending physicians by quickly attributing all mistakes or lack of foresight to the nurses, no matter how flagrantly at fault they themselves might be. Once I learned this, it became a case of matching my wits against theirs, in terms of self-preservation. But it was exhausting, nerve-racking, to be constantly on guard against those who should have been our friends.

At the end of my probationary period I was accepted as a student nurse—probably with misgivings on the part of Mrs. Bender, and on my part great doubt and fear. I borrowed enough money from my sister for the material and on the housekeeper's sewing machine made my beautiful new blue dresses. We all felt proud of our new uniforms and caps. Yoshi was so excited and happy that her cheeks got red again. The collars were tight and high and hard as iron—they cut raw red rings around our throats, but what matter? We were now regular nurses.

Very soon after that I was put on night duty, but not on the Men's Surgical, where I knew and could manage the recalcitrant patients to a degree; no, but on the Women's Medical about which I knew nothing. This ward also included the Children's and Babies' Ward, which was on a roof out toward the morgue. It is a fearful thing to be left alone in the night, responsible for the lives of fifty people,—the shadows loom up like shapes of monsters, the dark corners of the long wards hold ghostly secrets, and the hours are endless.

Night duty implies that you work at night and sleep during the day. We worked by night, but as we were not separated from those on day duty, and there was a constant coming and going, of slamming doors and conversation all day, we got little sleep. After giving a full report to the day head nurse, at exactly seven, you were off duty. You then proceeded to the dining room for breakfast, and then to bed. If you had contrived a deep sleep before the day nurses began coming off for their hours, it would frequently be shattered by a knock on the door, and wrenching yourself back to the world, you were ordered to report to the office. You got up, dashed cold water in your face, dressed in the cleanest outfit that could be collected. Arriving at the hallowed, hated door, one stood.

There was a phrase used to denote the position, which was, being on the Carpet. Against the wall one must not lean, but stand at attention, hands behind the back, eyes straight ahead, until asked to enter. This became increasingly difficult as the day wore on. Eventually one is in, and standing before those gimlet eyes waiting to hear what dire deed has been inadvertently committed. You have been careless, lazy, untidy; you have endangered the discipline and morale, even the honor of the entire school! You have forgotten to place a period at the end of a sentence on a chart! When one is made fully conscious of their offense, and with not so veiled threats as to the final disposal of one's person, should such carelessness eventuate in future, one is allowed to go back to bed. As many nurses are off duty by this time, the futility of attempting further sleep presents itself, so you remain dressed for duty at seven again. When this procedure had obtained for several days, you found yourself feeling very tired and sleepy.

Certain duties were supposed to have been performed and charted before a given hour, at night. Perhaps I might give a list of them. The first duty of a night nurse was to take the temperature, pulse and respiration of every patient under her care, and chart them before eight o'clock. This sounds a simple thing to do, but one finds that it is not so. Placing the thermometer in the patient's mouth, holding watch in hand, counting the pulse for a full minute, then the respirations, also for a minute, removing the thermometer and reading it, and writing it down on a pad, requires, as you will see by applying simple arithmetic, at least three minutes. Multiply this by forty patients, or as it might well be and often was, fifty. Well, where are you? But naturally no one did that. One counted the pulse for at most half a minute, usually a quarter, made a guess at the respirations, removed the thermometer in half a minute, and by dexterous manipulations, covered the actions in a minute and a half flat. Even then one could not finish in the allotted time. Luckily there was usually one patient who had been in so long that they knew practically everything to be done, and one could turn a great many things over to her, if one risked getting caught.

Or take the administration of medication. About fifty doses were to be given at eight, each one to be measured accurately, many of them being extremely dangerous drugs, and carried on a tray with a pitcher of water, to each patient as ordered. As I found that I could not possibly do this in conjunction with the other duties, I charted medication as given night after night, when I had not even unlocked the medicine cabinet. Some of the patients were sharp, and it was necessary to give them theirs, or they would report it, but usually only the extremely ill ones received attention.

Now add to these simple duties the fact that on this ward there were six typhoid fever patients, each ordered a fever-reducing bath also at eight. Since we had been well taught that to effect results by this treatment requires at the least three-quarters of an hour, giving six would bring you well into the night, and perhaps one or more patients into Heaven. Also fever patients were supposed to be fed a well-cooked gruel, cooked by you, every two hours. The great difficulty was successfully to pretend that one had done all these things, but when driven to it, it is remarkable the number of subterfuges one can devise, such as using the same sheets and blankets from one patient to another, in giving fever-reducing baths. Even so, it could not be done, for interspersed with these duties, there were frequent calls for bed-pans, the admitting of new patients, preparations of patients for operation, in itself a lengthy procedure, and as will annoyingly happen, even in hospitals, a death to be reckoned with.

While all this has been in progress, the babies out on the roof were howling for their food, which was expected to be given before eight, each bottle to be held while the baby took its food. Picture to yourself one person holding from seventeen to twenty babies' bottles at the same time! That was the doctor's orders, and ostensibly they were carried out. I worked as I had not known that I could, and yet by leaving off practically everything, still I could not do it. After two weeks of this life of lies and stupidities, I became desperate,—I asked to see Mrs. Bender. The last straw that threatened my balance entirely was the two black cats that fought every night on the top of the morgue. I was told, but did not verify it, that the nurse on duty just before me, had killed herself when she discovered that she had given five patients carbolic acid instead of epsom salts. The large bottles containing these two drugs stood in a row, all exactly alike, and the light was so poor that it was extremely difficult to distinguish them. I had been fully warned by the night superintendent, so perhaps it was true, although she did say that only two died after all, and she felt that the nurse had gone a bit too far in her remorse.

So I stood outside and waited to see Mrs. Bender. For hours I waited, and when I stood before her, she said, "What do you want, Miss Dan?" I told her. I told all; all the things I had not done, the lies of the charts; I told her how many times the new patients died before I had even seen them, and that I couldn't bear to have them die alone like that. I wept and begged her to tell me how I could possibly do my work honorably. Her answer was, "Don't take up my valuable time with whining; others have handled that ward efficiently, and you can if you wish. Attend to your work, and let me hear no more of this." Well, I had tried; after that I just muddled along, doing all that I could, trying not to think of it.

One night a very ill patient was admitted. She died before I could get her bathed properly, as I was expected to, so I put her in the bathtub after she was dead, and her body floated to the top. Alone in the night, with a lovely dead girl floating in a tub made me distraught for a moment. She had the most beautiful body I had ever seen, and I found myself bathing her gently, forgetting that she was not there. I can see her body still, so young, so tender, with beautiful breasts and legs and hands. Her childlike face, her lips flower petals just opening, speaking. I combed her hair, and it curled around my fingers and on her forehead, a live, golden brown. Reading her chart I learned that she was a well-known trapeze artist, and bicyclist. I made her look lovely, lying so still in the bed, but at the time I had to hurry,—patients were calling.

For the most insignificant infringement of rules we lost our uniforms; that is, we took off our blue ones and returned to the checked gingham ones, for a specified time. This happened to me while I was on night duty. One very hot night I was hurrying with my work, and perspiring, so I loosened my stiff collar, which buttoned in the back. A casual glance would not have disclosed the fact, but Mrs. Bender, whose glance was never casual, came on the ward and caught me. She was very angry and ordered me back to probationers' uniform for two weeks. This pleased me very much, as they were much cooler.

Usually we designated patients by their ailment, as "the man with the leg," or "the woman with the arm, or stomach," as the case might be. One of my first patients was a man with a back. He was an Italian laborer who had been hurt by a falling timber. He was paralyzed from the waist down, and suffered great pain constantly. His dark little wife came as often as the rules allowed, bringing one or more of their children. His face would light up at sight of them, and they chattered excitedly as she unwrapped parcels containing oranges and salami. Due to the breakdown of tissue he developed bedsores, which had to be dressed twice daily. A rubber- inflated mattress did not suffice to ease his suffering. To move him in order to change the dressing caused unbearable pain, and as his condition progressed, small bones from the vertebrae came away from his spine. His pain, mental as well as physical, was horrible to behold. A healthy peasant, wiry and strong, struck down, one-half of him dead, the other half in searing pain, to lie and wait for death. And the wait was unnecessarily long. "Oh! Mama Mia!" he cried ten thousand times. His brown eyes searched my face as he begged me to let him die, to help him out of his hell. "Please, please, nursie! Why don't you help me die?" he begged. If I had dared, I would have helped him, for to see continued, useless suffering over a long period of time is impossible to one with the love of their fellow man in their hearts. I often thought that if the doctors themselves had been constantly with him they would surely have been kind enough to help him. But he finally died.

Another one I had later was a woman "with a stomach." She was quiet, gentle, and very good-looking. Every day the doctor washed out her stomach,—a trying performance. One hot night Doctor Luther, one of the few decent interns, came on the ward to give her this treatment. I had the rubber tube in a basin, coiled around ice. She saw it, and retched with revulsion. Looking appealingly at the doctor, she said quietly, "Not again! I cannot. If I swallow that again, I will die!" Doctor Luther made a large gesture with his hand and said, "Now, Mrs. Johnson, don't be childish! You just be a good girl and swallow it; it won't take a minute." She lay so still, and repeated her words, "Very well, but I will die." She was a good girl, and swallowed it,—and died. Oh! the look of surprise on his face! I knew she was telling him the truth, but I said nothing, for he wouldn't have believed me any more than he did her,—nor any more than they believed me when I told them that Yoshi would die if they didn't give her back her uniform. People are dumb.

Yoshi lost her uniform for the horrible crime of hanging a patient's face towel on the left-hand side of the bed, instead of the right. She was crushed, and wept inconsolably. Alternately scolding and loving her, I hoped to get her to accept it and adjust herself to it. I reminded her that I had lost mine, and got it back, assuring her over and over that she would have hers back in no time at all. Nothing I could say helped,—she wept and reiterated again and again, "No, Mees Dan! I will never have my uniform again!" She couldn't sleep, nor eat, and became thin and white. Worried, I even dared face Mrs. Bender, and begged her to give Yoshi back her uniform, telling her how ill she was, and that if she didn't get it back she would die. Her button eyes flashed angrily, and she said, "Nonsense! Don't let me hear such talk from women supposed to be nurses! You will oblige me, Miss Dan, by attending to your own work, and leave the discipline of the school to me!" That was that, in a manner of speaking, but I knew no good would come of it.

After a week Yoshi was too ill to report for duty, and when I went to see her, they had moved her into a room alone, and the nurse said that she was too ill to see any one. That afternoon I was worried, wondering what they had done to Yoshi. At seven I rushed off duty, but again the nurse said no one could see her; that she was much too ill. "With what?" I asked. The nurse said, "No one seems to know," but I said to myself, I know, and went to my room. Yoshi was dying of a broken heart, a broken spirit, and I could do nothing. The inactivity drove me mad, and later in the night I heard voices and the sound of doors opening and closing. I watched, but nothing occurred until long after midnight. I heard rapid footsteps, tense low conversation, and putting on my dressing gown and slippers, I sneaked down the long dark hall, concealing myself in a corner. I watched for a long time, as the dark changed from gloom to a pale gray. Presently I saw Doctor Hutchinson, the most important attending surgeon of the hospital, come out and go away. Still I waited, and later, saw Doctor Silverstein the Internist accompanied by two house physicians, close the door and go away.

Now all was silent; I could hardly breathe, from dread of what might have happened. Then Mrs. Bender came out, looking dishevelled, walking slowly down the hall, and the stairs; I heard her door close on the floor below. After listening a long time, I crept to the door and put my eye to the keyhole, but could see nothing. When Miss Kohler opened the door I fell to my knees. I picked myself up as she said, "What are you doing here?" Whispering, I said, "I came to see how Yoshi is." She carefully closed the door,—her face the color of the morning light, and tired. "She's dead," was all she said.

For the space of a second time stood still. I felt the wall pressing against my back, but I could not speak. Fumblingly I began tying the cord of my dressing gown tighter around me, and I said aloud, "Dear God! For this once do the right thing! Give me strength!" and I walked away. Miss Kohler whispered after me, "Where are you going?" Looking back at her, I said, "I'm going to attend to a very personal obligation," and continued down the stairs until I reached the door to Mrs. Bender's room, and knocked.

She opened the door, looming large in a voluminous nightdress, her gray hair in disorder, her glasses off. Without a word I struck her, hard; I hit her anywhere I could, as fast as possible; with my bare fists I hit her, and with my open hand I slapped her. She backed away as rapidly as possible, but I followed her, and while I struck her, I kept saying, "You devil! You stupid old devil! You've killed Yoshi, and I'm going to kill you!" Over and over I said it; I heard myself saying it, and was aware of my breathing, and a part of me looked on, happy. She made no reply, fending me off, and when I had exhausted myself, she held my hands, quietly. I felt sick and faint, while for a moment we stood in silence, there in the sickly gray light of morning.

Removing my hands from hers, hating her touch, I walked with leaden steps from her room. Naturally I expected to be dismissed at once, but it was of no consequence. The world and everything in it looked nauseous to me, and I wished that I were dead. I bathed and prepared for duty. All day I made beds, changed dressings, served food, and made all the thousand movements of that nightmare day. Some part of me had died, and there was no feeling.

The next day, Yoshi, dressed in complete uniform, lay in a magnificent coffin in the living room, and at noon a minister came and read about "I am the resurrection and the life," and I hated him. I saw Yoshi's young man but his face was more than I could bear. Officials came from Washington for her cremated body, which was sent back to her mother in Japan. Yoshi was seventeen years old.

During the day I had little time to miss Yoshi, but in my room at night

I saw her dark face before me, and I could not believe that she was not there. For several weeks I was alone, and was grateful. I heard no word from Mrs. Bender, and in time I decided that for reasons of her own, she would ignore my breach of discipline, until she could strike suddenly, with deadly aim and result. She did.

All the nurses knew how to dance, and I was anxious to learn, so I looked about. I saw a sign which stated, "Dancing Lessons, twenty-five cents." To the mother and daughter who ran the place I explained my finances, and they were very kind. Starting a Victrola, the daughter gave me my first lesson. Unable to grasp the intricacies of one, two, three, I thought to abandon the whole idea, but she encouraged me, advising me to come in the evening, when the men came.

With an eleven o'clock late leave, I returned, and sat with many others, some of whom were pretty awful, hoping that some nice man from the row along the opposite wall, would ask me to dance. The muscles of my face ached, set in the mold of casual indifference, but my patience was rewarded. A tall young man rescued me from the abyss of painful pretense, and as I tried unsuccessfully to keep my feet out of his way, he informed me that he was Captain of his own boat, and would not like for anyone to know that he came to such a cheap place. By the second dance I was able to forget my feet sufficiently to become vaguely aware of him.

Another evening I sat for a long time, and was asked by a fine-looking Japanese, who danced beautifully, and from whom I learned a lot. He informed me that he was in the Legation, and would not like for any of his friends to know that he came to such a cheap place; that he came only for practice. All nationalities were represented, as were all types of labor. I never knew if all the men said the same thing to the other girls as they did to me, but when the fourth one approached and tendered me an invitation to the waltz, I said, "Now I'll tell you first. You only come here to practise, and you wouldn't want any one to know that you frequent this type of place. Well, I'll never tell, so let us proceed with our practising, for that's what I come here to do also." He didn't ask me again.

The third time I went a nice tall gawky boy from Kansas danced with me, and he was grand. His name was Bob Castleton, and he earned a meagre salary as reporter on one of the Brooklyn papers. I told him what all the others had said, and we laughed together. It was wonderful to be with a natural, healthy country boy whom I could understand. We became good friends for a short time.

I had completed the first year, said to be the hardest, of my training, when something happened that forced me to resign, losing the whole year of gruelling labor. An experience that gave me a vision of the depths to which a human being can sink and remain socially acceptable,—something that showed me completely the colossal stupidity of what might be laughingly referred to as a "sense of honor," and gave me more than a glimpse of the enormous disparity between what I had been brought up to take for granted, and the reality of the world in which, presumably, I was to make individual adjustment.

After a few weeks of solitude, another girl was moved in with me—a girl with whom I knew I could have no friendship. She was large, gawky, and untidy; her hair red in color, and crinkly. The most I could manage was a noncommittal politeness, which she met with a servile, ingratiating bid for friendship, using the loathsome word "pals."

The rule which forbade social contact between the nurses and interns had not impressed itself upon my mind, because, in the first place, none of them had attracted me sufficiently to produce a desire for their friendship, and secondly, none of them had shown the slightest desire to go out with me. I knew vaguely that many nurses circumvented this rule in different ways, one of which was to crawl in through a window on the ground floor; another method was for two nurses to leave the hospital together, one with a legitimate late leave, separate outside, and meet at a pre-arranged time at the gate. The one with the late leave entered the hospital, handed her leave to the night superintendent, who gave the key to the night watchman, who in turn accompanied the nurse to the door, where the other waited. They entered together, and all was well.

Neither of these methods had involved me as yet, so that when my stupid roommate, Jean Hickson, told me that she wanted to go out with an intern named Palmer, I was not interested. When she pursued the subject and asked me to go with her, following the method just described, I refused. Her hurt look made me feel mean, and, thinking that after all she was just a harmless dope, I consented. We arranged to meet at the gate at exactly midnight, and as I had no late leave, she would get the key.

Telephoning to Bob Castleton, I explained the plot, and he said, "Fine! We'll go to Coney Island." Jean and I left together, separated as planned, she to meet her intern, Bob and I going to Coney, where we shot at dolls, ate hot dogs, and laughed, returning early. He left me at the gate at eleven-thirty, as he had work to do, and I sat alone. Twelve came, but no Jean. I waited until one, and then I knew that she had let me down. If I had gone in at eleven-thirty, I could have blamed a trolley; at twelve I still could have concocted an alibi; but by one, all was lost, as there remained only the entrance by the window. For some reason I am completely unable to explain, I could not make the effort to save myself, but angry and full of hate for Jean Hickson, I went in to the night superintendent, a roly-poly little blond German-American woman who spoke with a lisp.

She automatically held out her hand for my pass, and still dazed by the perfidy of that dumb girl, I said, "I haven't any." She gave me a troubled look and said, "You know what this means, Miss Dan?" and I replied, "Yes." We had seen a lot of each other on night duty, and she was reluctant to let this situation pass from her hands where it possessed the possibility of adjustment, into the next stage,—that of handing the key to the watchman. Making a nervous, pleading motion with her hands, her sweet face tortured, she said, "Why don't you make it possible for me to help you? Tell me something, some reason, that will give me a chance!" She was a nice woman, but I could not speak. She knew that it meant the loss of my work for a year; I knew it, and still I could not involve her. I put out my hand, and she took it, held it firmly, and I said, "You've been good to me Miss Plaut, and I appreciate it, but I guess this is good-by." She turned away, her hands over her eyes, and I followed the imperturbable watchman out.

In my room I stood looking down at the sleeping hulk that had wrought this havoc, but I had no reaction either of hate or disgust. Once again, as at other times in my life, when full realization meant death either for me or another person, I felt the familiar sheath of indifference, detachment, settling over me, all-enveloping, shutting out further thought. I awakened to the familiar sounds of a hundred nurses dressing, talking, hurrying, making ready for the day's work. I lay still and watched Jean comb her ugly crinkly hair. She felt my eyes, and turned a cringing, ugly face to me, so meanly terrified that I felt ashamed for her. Quietly I asked, "What did you do? Why did you do it?" Like an animal, stupid, frightened, she said, "I came in at nine." I laughed and she said, still cringing, "How can you laugh?" I got out of bed and started to the bathroom; turning back, I said, "I just pictured you, in all your magnificent stupidity, and that mangy little intern! You couldn't bear each other longer than that!" and left her. Obviously the thought of going to Mrs. Bender and telling the truth, had never entered her so-called mind, nor would it.

Knowing that the axe would fall at any moment, I went on duty as

usual. The news had percolated and some of the nurses looked at me intently as if to remember how the body looked before the accident. At eleven
my head nurse asked me to report to Mrs. Bender. I stood again on the
Carpet. For hours I stood, and was at last admitted.

A stormy scene ensued, centering on the fact that Mrs. Bender knew
some nurse had been out with me, and her efforts to force me to name her.
"If you will tell me the name of the nurse involved with you, I will make
your punishment as reasonable as possible, which will probably be your
resignation, instead of summary dismissal; I'm giving you your last chance!"
She was angry, and I replied, "The nurse who was out with me knows what
this means for me; if she doesn't tell you herself, I cannot." This continued
for hours, and in the end, Mrs. Bender said, "I'm sorry, but you force me to
this; I must ask you for your resignation. It is up to you." I agreed, and
asked for the paper, which she laid before me, and I signed it. Then she said,
"Where are you going?" Outwardly calm, but inwardly quaking, I said,
"I'm going to enter another training school." In exasperation, she screamed,
"But don't you know that you can't do that without telling them why you
have left this one? And that when you do, they will not have you? Unless I
help you, you cannot enter any other school!" Defiantly, I stood straight
and said, "I will tell them, and they will take me." She was, I honestly
believe, trying to do the decent thing, but through lack of practice, she
didn't know what it was. Walking up and down her office, her broad beam
shaking with every heavy footstep, she spoke vehemently. "Stop being dramatic; you'll have to lower your stubborn chin and beg me to help you,
before any reputable hospital will take you." I assured her that I would
manage it alone. "Have you any money?" she asked. "With the large sum of
five dollars a month, minus breakage, would *you* have any?" I answered her.

This fight continued through lunch time, and well into the afternoon,
and when we were both exhausted, I had the last word,—childish, foolish,
if you wish, but infinitely satisfying to me. Drawing myself straight, and
lifting my chin, I talked back to her. "Now, Mrs. Bender, I go,—as I go, I
say to you in all kindness, you are a stupid woman; a cruel and stupid
woman, destroying all before you, in your lust for power. Didn't you ever
suspect that there is another sort of power? Perhaps you've never heard of
it; it's simple kindness. You might try it some time; you might have tried it
on Yoshi." At that I saw her face blanch, and I pressed on, wanting passionately to say everything before she put me out. "You've been rotten to me,
and I don't even hate you for it; I just ignore you. Now I'm going, and you

will keep and graduate a sly, stupid, treacherous girl who has never heard of a sense of honor; she will ably represent your school. If you had honestly wished to know who she is, you could easily have discovered by a process of elimination. You didn't want that; you only wanted to make me a squealer and you can't do it. Someday you will know what a mistake you have made. Good-by!" and I left while I had the courage, leaving her sitting behind her desk, her button eyes following me to the door.

I packed my suitcase and telephoned to Bob Castleton. We met at a small restaurant and had dinner. I told him nothing of the hole I was in, because he was only a young boy, and could do nothing. We talked and laughed, and for a while I forgot the black cloud that hovered menacingly over me. After dinner he said that he was going to take me to a theatre, and I told him I had never been in one, and had only the vaguest idea what it was like. "Then you'll see," he said. I did.

We had seats in the balcony, and the play was "The Prisoner of Zenda." As I watched the stage, following the play, I forgot completely where I was; everything had disappeared but the stage; that alone was real. When a beautiful lady came out in a long black velvet dress, and a wide black hat from which a plume drooped over her shoulder, and raising a graceful white hand, said "My King can do no wrong!" I burst into such hysterical sobs that every one around us began shushing me, while through my sobs I said, loudly God knows, "I can't bear it!" The usher came and asked us to leave unless we could be quiet, but poor Bob, taking no more chances, got me out as quickly as possible. Down in the street I continued to weep bitterly, saying to Bob, who was annoyed beyond words, and half frightened, "But it is impossible! It can't be! I can't bear it!" He shook me angrily and said, "Bear what? Have you gone completely crazy?" I tried to stop, without much success, and he said, "For God's sake stop it! People are staring at us; they'll think I've seduced you or something!" He edged me into a bar, and inside, I drank something he ordered, and felt horribly ashamed of myself. He was a nice boy, and asked me what on earth had upset me, and I tried to tell him. He couldn't believe me when I said that I'd never been in a theatre before, and he said, "And you never will again, at least with me." He took me home early, and I knew that I would never see him again.

Next morning, instead of dressing in my uniform, I put on my blue silk dress and my sailor hat, and left the hospital. No one said good-by, no one knew where I was going, least of all myself. And I had only thirty-seven cents with which to get there. Suddenly I remembered the card the negro porter had given me, and looking frantically in my bag, I found it. I had not thought of it since, but it looked beautiful to me. I set out for Harlem, and on my way, I decided that now I would let nothing prevent me from going to the Presbyterian Hospital.

My desire to train in the Presbyterian had been thwarted, and now I knew that with a black mark against me it would be more difficult than before. In the subway I thought of every possible way, and concluded that the only way I could ever do it would be to ask some one to help me. Having seen articles in magazines about the wonderful goodness and humanity of Helen Gould, I felt sure that if I could only see her, she would understand; that if she asked them to take me, they would do so.

The address the porter had given me proved to be a nice little house with a white paling fence, behind which were flowers and trees. I knocked on the door, and a small dark woman with gray hair opened it. She asked me to come in, and I at once explained why I had come, and she said, in a charming voice, that any one her son sent was welcome in her home.

Over cool drinks, which she placed on the table in her spotless kitchen, I told her a great deal of my life, and of the predicament in which I now was, and of my intense desire to enter the training school of the Presbyterian. She listened with intelligent and sympathetic understanding, and I felt that I had indeed found a friend. She agreed with me in my idea regarding Miss Gould and said, "Have you any money?" I told her I had twenty-seven cents. She went to her bedroom and returned with a worn flat black pocketbook, from which she took seven dollars and fifty cents. She handed me the seven dollars, and when I hesitated to take it she said, "I'll keep the fifty cents. As soon as my son returns I'll have more, and besides, I don't need it. With my vegetable garden I need very little money." I took it, unable to express my gratitude.

We talked awhile,—she told me of her own life, of how she had been a teacher in the South and had come, a widow with her one son, to the North many years ago. She was a cultivated woman of gracious dignity, and in her house I saw the first real library I had ever seen. She showed me her books, worn and obviously much read, and her vegetable garden, with a quiet friendliness that made me hate to leave her. "May I leave my suitcase here until I find out where I am going, Mrs. Hall?" I asked her, and she said, "My child, my house is yours," and I wanted to go down on my knees, put my head in her lap and cry. "And if I fail, may I come back to you, and stay with you?" I asked her. "You will not fail,—but come back and tell me all that happens, for I am anxious to help," she said.

Returning to the city, I got a train for Tarrytown, where I knew that Miss Gould had a home. From the station I walked along the street until I came to the gate, having asked directions from a passerby, and turning in, I walked across a long rolling meadow, smelling of new-mown hay. Near the big house I came upon a bent old gardener, who straightened up and asked, "What do you want?" I told him that I wanted to see Miss Gould. "She's in Roxbury," he replied, and my hopes fell. I walked back to the station, and with my last penny, I bought a ticket for Roxbury. After a long tiresome journey I reached it at ten o'clock that evening. It had rained hard all the way, but when I got out, the moon was shining on the still dripping trees,— the air was clean and sweet.

Not knowing where Miss Gould lived, and not wishing to ask, I walked along with other people who had got off the train, down a hill and up the road sharply to the right, where it joined what I thought must be the main street. At the corner was a country hotel and I went in and registered, saying to the clerk that I was going for a walk,—wondering how I would pay for the room.

Walking along the tree-lined street, in the air laden with the odor of wet earth and flowers, the moon making yellow light between dark masses of leaves, I thought to myself, "Something will tell me the house,—when I come to it I will know it." I passed two houses and an open space, then a church, and I knew presently that I had found it, knew so thoroughly that I turned in the gate unafraid.

Near the house a man stepped forward from the shadows and in a voice of authority said, "What do you want?" and I said, "I want to see Miss Gould." Resting what looked to me like a big rifle on the stones he said, "You can't see Miss Gould; she has gone to bed." Desperate, I said, "But I must see her! I've come all the way from New York, and I don't want money from her, but I must see her!" Perhaps I wore him down, for he said, "Wait here, and I'll find out if you can see Mrs. Shaw." I stood in the bright moonlight and waited. He returned and said, "You can go in," and opened the door. I stepped into a cheerful, quiet living room, where a motherly looking woman sat. "I'm Mrs. Shaw," she said, "what can I do for you; what is your name?"

I told her as quickly as possible, my words rushing out, I was so anxious to win her interest. She stared at me in astonishment, and when I stopped she said, "But you haven't come all the way from New York, alone at night, just for this?" I assured her that I had, and began to explain again, but she interrupted me to say, "I don't understand. I don't know what you are talking about, truly I don't. You return to the hotel and come back in the morning. I'll ask Doctor Bleeker to talk to you. He is Miss Gould's nephew, and is an attending physician at the Presbyterian Hospital." That seemed a wonderful omen for good, and thanking her I left. I slept well, for I knew that now everything would be all right. Mrs. Shaw had been bewildered, but at that, she had been kind, and it was like a cool drink from a mountain brook to me.

Next morning I awoke to a world flooded with sunshine. Over wide fields of green, and on flowers in every yard, golden sun. I had breakfast and walked down the lovely shaded street to the house I had found in the moonlight, and arrived just as Mrs. Shaw was finishing her breakfast. She asked me to wait until Doctor Bleeker came down, and when he did, she introduced me and said, "Doctor Bleeker, I don't know just what she wants, but it has to do with hospitals, so you will know." He smiled, sat down and said, "Now tell me just what you want."

He was tall and thin, about thirty, with blond hair and a sweet expression of such natural friendliness that I felt no hesitancy in telling him everything. I told him how I had wanted to train in the Presbyterian before, and had missed it; how terribly anxious I was not to be misled again. I told him that I had come to Miss Gould only to ask her to say a word for me, so they would surely take me. He listened, and when I stopped Mrs. Shaw said, "Why doesn't she go home to her mother?" I was afraid he would agree, in which case I would have to go on alone. But he said impatiently, "No, no, she doesn't want to do that,—she wants to work, and make a success of what she has begun." He understood so well, and we arranged that I would return to New York that afternoon, and come to his office the next day, as he was also returning.

They took me to a simple lovely church with them and after services, Doctor Bleeker took me for a walk in a charming park near the church, talking so interestingly of many things, making me forget all my troubles. When we parted, he promised me that he would make an appointment with the superintendent of nurses, and assured me again that my difficulties at Olympia would not count against me. At the house I said good-by to Mrs. Shaw, and when she removed her hand from mine, she left a folded bill. Realizing what it was, I started to thank her, but she blushed and said

hurriedly, "No, don't, it is a pleasure—please." My heart ached with gratitude to her, for her sweetness and kindness.

Doctor Bleeker gave me a book of commutation tickets, and when I
asked for my bill at the hotel, I was told that it had been paid. Oh! What
wonderful people there are in the world! I returned to Harlem and Mrs.
Hall. Doctor Bleeker had asked me where I was staying, and I said, "With
a wonderful friend, a Mrs. Hall." I did not speak of her color for fear he
might not understand.

That night we sat up late, while I told her every detail of my experience,
and of how kind they had been. I wanted to return her seven dollars, as the
bill Mrs. Shaw had given me was ten dollars, but she would not let me,
saying, "Wait until you're settled; you may need it again." She listened
avidly, her sweet face glowing with excitement and happiness. We made
plans for the following day, which included my return to Olympia for a
cardboard box I had left in the trunk room, which held all my uniforms
and family photographs. Then my appointment with Doctor Bleeker, and
Miss Blackwell, the superintendent of nurses.

When I reached Olympia, I found that my box had been ruthlessly opened and the contents taken. Disheartened most on account of my aprons,
which I could have used anywhere, and sad at the loss of certain pictures of
family and friends, I asked the housekeeper about it, but of course she
knew and could do nothing. When I told Doctor Bleeker, he seemed almost pleased, for he said, "Well, now we can make out a more comprehen-
sive list, beginning with a trunk to put them in." As I left for my appointment with Miss Blackwell, I asked him if I should tell her about Olympia,
and he said, "Yes, tell her everything you told me. Good luck to you," he
said, smiling.

Miss Blackwell was a gracious, intelligent woman, and received me kindly. I told her all that I had told Doctor Bleeker, and she asked me a few direct
questions, which I answered, and reiterating my desire to train under her, I
begged her to let me come. I finished, and she said nothing; I was frantic for
fear it would not come right for me, and I asked her if she held the episode at
Olympia against me. Quietly she said, "No, I do not, but I must discuss this
with Doctor Bleeker before I can say yes or no," and she ended the interview.

I left in a turmoil of apprehension, and that night I kept poor Mrs. Hall
up practically all night, going over and over the same things until tired out
we went to bed. Later in the night, unable to sleep, I got up and went to her
room, waking her to ask again, "Do you think they will take me? Oh! My

God, do you think all this will come to no good?" and she sat up in the middle of a big bed, a small dark spot with a feather bed rolling up around her intelligent face, answering me again, "No, I don't think it will be against you; they will take you,—and if they don't, then we will think of something else." How comforting she was, how kind! Sitting on the foot of her bed, I talked, unable to rest. "Do you think that Miss Blackwell will telephone Mrs. Bender? If she does, you *know* she will say awful things against me! Do you think she has already told them that I'm a bad lot? Then *what* shall I do?" And I wept. She said, "No, I don't think that Miss Blackwell has phoned; they will do nothing behind your back,—they aren't that kind of people." She got up and made coffee, and we talked while dawn came, and soon it was time for my appointment with Doctor Bleeker.

At nine I was waiting, and when he came I was afraid to ask him what had been decided. He looked somewhat evasive, and I thought, "Now he has changed,—he does not believe in me anymore." He began to make the list of what I would require, and I could bear the suspense no longer. "Require for what, Doctor Bleeker?" I asked. He tapped the desk with his pencil, but did not answer. "Where am I going? Will Miss Blackwell take me? Please tell me now." He got up and walked around the room nervously, and said, "Now, Belinda, you must be quite calm; I will explain everything. We both feel that you are too overwrought to enter a large training school in the city; you are in no condition to undertake it." Again I felt some unseen force that I could not touch, and I said, "What you mean is that you and Miss Blackwell have decided that I am not good enough for the Presbyterian,— why don't you say so plainly?"

He stood silent; I sat down at his desk, and laid my face on my arms. I could not weep,—a black chaos held me in vacuity. He came near me, laid his hand on my shoulder and spoke firmly, quietly. "It is not the way you think; I would not pretend to you. It is the simple truth,—you are too tired and nervous to begin a new and difficult training, without a vacation first." At the word "vacation" I raised my head and saw him, so calm, so sure of himself, and I said, "Vacation? Oh! Yes, I remember! That's a plant with shining green leaves; in the fall it has red berries." He didn't laugh, and I thought, "It's not so smart, at that."

He sat down and talked for a long time. He asked me if there was anywhere I could go for a few weeks. I thought of Mrs. Hall, but I was afraid that if he found out that she was a negress, he might say something deprecatory, so I said that I knew no one, no place. He told me of a farm owned by a cousin of his, three miles out of Roxbury, to which I might go if I wished. If I preferred, he said, I could go to Miss Gould's house, with Mrs. Shaw. He asked me to choose, and I said, "The farm, please." He was pleased, and made plans to that end.

The list completed, he gave me twenty-five dollars, and as I left, he said, "I know a small hospital in the country that I think you would like. The superintendent is a Presbyterian graduate, and a very good friend of mine. She would be a good friend to you." I had no answer, for now I knew that God or someone had strong convictions against me doing anything I wanted to do in the place I wanted to do it. I saw my dream disappearing again, and could not restrain my tears.

When I came to pack my things, I found that Mrs. Hall had washed and ironed all my clothes; that night we sat up late again talking, and next morning I left for Roxbury. Doctor Bleeker had been wonderful to me, but Mrs. Hall was my real friend. By the afternoon I was on my way, and at the station a farmer came up and said, "Are you for Mrs. Logan?" and I said I was. He got my trunk and put it in the back of a buggy, and we rolled along a dirt road, a dark, dry path in the moonlight. He was not loquacious, and I was too tired for questions; we went silently except for the clop-clop of the horses' hooves. The night was beautiful, the small pipings of frogs sad, but soothing. He let me out at the gate of the farmhouse, lying still and white, saying, "Go right on in, Miss," as he drove around to the barn.

A month of sun and good food, quiet companionship with the other boarders at the Farm, brought me back to sanity and health. One of the guests was a famous painter, and I spent hours against a row of dahlias while he painted a picture of me. It did not seem to be me—it was too lovely; he left out my freckles, and the dahlias were a great help—but the others loved it. From there I returned to Montrose Hospital, where I spent three difficult but absorbing years of my life, always sad that it was not the Presbyterian.

The superintendent at Montrose was a wonderful woman without whose keen sense of justice, understanding and humor, I could never have come through. Her name was Miss Helen Merryweather. She was tall and gracefully built, and strong, sure in her movements. Her ashen blond hair had always a smooth wave; her keen kind eyes were observing, but fearless. She spoke in a clipped, decisive way, and her poise gave me courage,—awakened in me instantly a great desire for her respect and friendship. Her cleanness of body and mind was such as to prohibit even the thought of sly, underhand actions near her.

After a short conversation in which she said that Doctor Bleeker had talked to her of me, she sent for a nurse to show me to my room. Her every word and action was of a simplicity and directness that caused me to think as I left her, "She's grand! I'm going to love being in her school!" During three years I in no way changed my opinion of her, except to raise it higher. Although she displayed no personal interest in me, I had always the comforting conviction that she would be fair, human, and just in every situation. In time, I think she had a certain affection for me, due to the number of times she saved me from disaster,—gave her a proprietary interest.

It was necessary for me to begin at the bottom again, as my year at Olympia was of no account in a new hospital. By the time I got out I would be too old to go to school even if I could make enough money. I learned later that the other nurses had been very curious about me, due in part to some fancied partiality shown me by Miss Merryweather. They decided that I was her illegitimate daughter—even nurses have imagination—and some credence was given this hypothesis because of a definite physical resemblance.

Doctor Bleeker had been kind, but he had given me only the bare necessities, and I arrived at Montrose with eleven cents. As every nurse was required to have in her possession a pair of bandage scissors and forceps and all her textbooks, I went to Miss Merryweather and explained that I was unable to pay for them. She allowed me to have them, their cost to be deducted from my salary which was eight dollars a month. Unfortunately a slight accident usurped my first, and indeed almost my second month's salary.

Every private room was equipped with a washstand on which sat a bowl and pitcher, soap dish, tooth mug, and two small glasses for thermometers. By the side sat a tall slop jar, and inside, a *pot de chambre*. I dropped the pitcher, breaking the bowl, the pieces of which in falling broke not only everything on top but continuing its path of destruction, broke the jar; every article was smashed. The assortment set me back eleven dollars, and my reaction was of horror and despair; then I reflected that if I could remain in debt, they would be less likely to dismiss me, so by judicious breakage I remained in debt indefinitely.

My first few months were spent on the men's Surgical ward, where there were a great many Italian patients. They were cheerful and had usually some musical instrument to which they would sing the moment their pain lessened. I loved that ward, and my head nurse often complimented me on my work there.

My fears of dismissal were in abeyance, when an incident occurred which brought back again my apprehension. But this time I said to myself, "To Hell with honor,—I'll protect myself." There was one nurse to whom anything that provided the sole requirement of belonging to someone else was irresistible. We accepted it, and every so often we gathered in her room when she was on duty, and took back our things. But outside of that one girl, stealing was not countenanced in any degree.

An apron was missed and as it was not found where all migratory articles usually were found, search was instituted. It was found in my bureau drawer. My every instinct of self-preservation was aroused; I knew the guilty one, but had no proof. I found her in her room, and smacked her; she had not time to turn the other cheek, I turned it for her, several times. By her skinny throat I held her and shook her, dropping her, a crumpled heap on the floor. Returning to my room I washed my hands of the nauseating feel of her, and went to Miss Merryweather's door and knocked. She opened it, and I said, "I'm sorry, Miss Merryweather, but I've just killed one of your nurses." Calmly, she asked, "Which one?" as though she had a selection of her own. She came out and we went to the scene of the crime.

At Miss Merryweather's appearance, the girl tried to rise, achieving it with difficulty. At the question, "Did you or did you not put the apron in Miss Dan's bureau drawer?" she stammered, "No . . . yes, no . . ." Miss Merryweather turned away in distaste and I followed her back to her room. I waited for her anger. "Sit down," she said. I sat, awaiting my dismissal. Quietly she asked, "Why did you do it?" I told her everything—of how Jean Hickson had trapped me at Olympia, and of what I had suffered for it—that if I died for it I would never again submit calmly to such a procedure.

She listened, then said, "I see your point, but you'll have to find some more intelligent method of fighting than the physical. There are better methods, and if you wish to survive you'll have to learn them." I asked her to give me one more chance, and she said, "Very well; but you must discuss this with no one; next time, see me first, will you?" I promised, and left her so filled with admiration for her that I would have done anything she asked.

One of my classmates was a Scotch girl named Cameron. Her brogue was broad, and although she was as hard as a nail, she was very amusing. We happened to have the same afternoon off one week, and we went to New York together. We went window shopping, and eventually found ourselves in Wanamakers; just looking, not buying. Presently we were in a beautiful part, carpeted in gray, pervaded by an air of quiet elegance. At intervals a beautiful hat rested on a stand. Struck by the overwhelming beauty of one particular hat, she removed it from the stand and offered it to me, saying, "It won't cost you anything to try it on, Linda." I demurred, saying, "Why bother? You know I couldn't buy it, no matter how little it cost." She insisted, so I removed my fifty-cent hat, and placing the beautiful creation carefully on my head, I saw myself in a long mirror; at least I saw someone who might or might not have been me. The freckles alone were familiar. The hat, made of soft beige velvet, adorned by a soft plume of gray shaded into rose at the center encircling the crown, dropping over the brim, almost touching my shoulder. I saw a beautiful clinging velvet gown below it, but was brought back to reality by the approach of a saleslady. I carefully removed the hat, and Cameron said, "It's a crying shame for you not to buy it, Linda,— it does so much for you." I needed to have a lot done for me but I said, "You known darn well I can't buy it; why do you argue?" Tossing her head she said, "And why not? You can pay a deposit and come back for it later."

The French saleslady said, "Yes, that is possible," and began writing out the sales check. "How much do you wish to leave as a deposit?" she asked. Feeling that I was rushing headlong toward a frightful precipice, I said hastily, "Two dollars," thinking that I'd still have my fare home. The saleslady looked faintly annoyed and said, "Does Mademoiselle know the price of the hat?" Cameron spoke up belligerently, "Yes,—it's seven-fifty." Backing a little away from us, she said, "But no! The hat is seventy-five dollars!"

When I came to, Cameron was fanning me, and through her laughter, scolding me for fainting. Ashamed, praying for a quick death, or if not that, at least a speedy departure from the locality, I begged Cameron to come away at once. I asked her not to tell of it, but she told, and the girls shrieked with laughter. It was not funny to me then,—it has never been funny to me.

Our class consisted of twenty girls,—a group of great variety of temperament, character, and looks, in which dissension flourished. The peacemaker was Martha Morgan who was my good friend. She was flamboyant in color, with red hair, clear pink and white skin, shining brown eyes, and white teeth; all the requirements of beauty, yet she was not beautiful. But her mind and spirit were. We were, and have remained friends until this day. I knew that if in an unaccountable rage I should murder some one, and tell her, she would simply say, "Shall we hide the body, or confess?" Once I asked her why she was loyal to me through all the difficulties I seemed to attract, and her reply was, "Because you do all the things that part of me wants to do and can't; you are the part of me I can't be, so I naturally have to protect you." Dear Martha!

Upon an occasion I ran from the nurses' home toward the railroad tracks, taking time in my mad departure to inform my audience of my intention to end it all. I ran wildly, heedlessly, filled with black hatred of everything, and right behind me came Martha, her red hair flying, her starched apron rattling around her. Just across the bridge she caught and held me, crying, "Now, now, Linda, don't do anything foolish,—let's have some ice cream," edging me into a tiny Italian stand, she ordered two chocolate sundaes, talking soothingly to me. I insisted that I must go away, completely; she said, "If you do, I'll go with you. You'll not be able to kill yourself unless you do me in first, and won't we look funny running around in our uniforms!" She made the most dramatic situation seem a natural everyday affair; while she removed the drama, and the pain, she added a healthy, humorous sanity that in the end made it necessary to laugh at oneself.

On Christmas day an accident case was brought in. An extraordinary case of a little Italian girl named Carlotta Favorita, who had been gathering coal on the railroad tracks, and was caught under the train, having both feet cut off just above the ankles. We all felt sick about it. She was put to bed, and from that moment her gayety infected the entire staff down to the maids and orderlies. She was life keyed at the highest; her laugh was like a bubbling brook. She dominated every one with her indifference to her tragedy. She ignored it with a supreme humor, an unawareness of its poignancy. As soon as she could be in a wheel chair, she whirled around the wards and halls like mad; she attended the very ill ones with astonishing efficiency, and knew their names, and their troubles. Her eyes opened every day on glory, her happiness never bound nor hindered. The wonder of her left us speechless and humble.

We learned that some wealthy woman was going to have the best artificial feet made for her, and as soon as she was well she was taken home to wait for them. How we missed her! The ward seemed drab and uninteresting without her.

Several weeks later Martha and I were walking up Mount Street, when we saw something that resembled a small tornado, a flying collection of arms, hands and legs; this bundle of energy flung itself upon us, hugging and kissing us extravagantly, and shrieking with joy, "Look, Nursie! See my new legs and feet! Ain't they grand? See, I can run harder than ever! I can jump and skip an' everything!" There in the respectable air of Mount Street she proceeded to show us, lying down and kicking her heels in the air. We tried to talk to her, but having satisfactorily displayed her agility, she was gone, running at incredible speed. Martha and I, astounded by the miracle, looked into each other's eyes, aware of the inadequacy of speech.

My first night duty at Montrose was on the women's medical ward, which included the men's medical, the children's and the maternity wards, and also the preparation of midnight supper for every one on night duty. These were the nurses on ward duty, specials, which means graduate nurses taking care of one single patient, the engineer and night watchman. They all enjoyed excellent appetites.

The kitchen being almost completely isolated from the wards, it was impossible to know what was happening while cooking dinner. When I heard a thud, and felt the entire wing tremble, I knew that Ippolito had fallen out of bed again. An Italian woman, weighing well over two hundred pounds, it was difficult to get her back. One night in the midst of dinner, I heard strange sounds, and following their direction, I arrived at the men's ward. Jimmie, a quiet, gentle patient, was standing in the middle of the men's ward, waving an open razor menacingly in the faces of terrified patients. I'd been told somewhere that the way to control a madman, was to look him straight in the eye. I tried it, and it worked; when I said, "Why, Jimmie, what are you doing out of bed at this time of night?" he handed me the razor and quietly went to bed. When I got back the toast was burned black.

Some nights were hectic, but always at the crucial moment, Miss Merryweather would appear on the ward, and say, "How are all the patients tonight, Miss Dan?" and suddenly everything was fine. I never knew if she realized how tense and frightened I was; I only know that she saved me over and over again. Often she would remain on the ward while I prepared supper. She taught me something about new babies I had never known. They had been crying for several nights, although I had dried them and fed them, and they were perfectly well. She listened a minute and said, "Your babies are cold." I got hot-water bottles and warm blankets, and they went to sleep instantly. I had not known how much warmth they required.

Nothing happened to scare me for several months, mainly because Miss Merryweather had kept her eye on me, I think. Then an unfortunate incident brought back all my fears. One of the attending physicians lectured to us once a week, on Anatomy. He was eminently capable; his words flowed over and around each infinitesimal bone familiarly, presenting them to us with virgin clarity. Standing before us, his slender supple body in perfect evening clothes, a white carnation in his buttonhole, his feet encased in glove-fitting, patent leather shoes, he was the answer to a maiden's prayer.

His black hair shone under the light, and his eyes sparkled with enthusiasm as he made graceful gestures with well-manicured hands. Gratitude should have bound me, but I found it hard to actively appreciate his words, after having been on duty since seven a.m. In no time at all I felt the old familiar glazed feeling creeping over my eyes, enveloping me in a delicious, dreamy haze which practically amounted to unconsciousness.

Imbued with his own eloquence and beauty, he prolonged his lecture unconscionably. When words of wisdom had poured from his finely chiselled lips until ten-thirty, he approached, by way of the metatarsal bones, the subject of shoes, of which his family were well-known manufacturers. At his words, "You girls are ruining your feet with cheap shoes; I never pay less than fourteen dollars for my shoes," I came alive sufficiently to whisper to my seatmate, "Thank God his family don't make uniforms," and he heard me. His face flushed angrily, and he said, "I'll see you later, Miss Dan."

After the lecture, I said, "Please excuse me, Doctor Mills! It was rude of me, and I'm sorry." Twas no use; he was too angry; he spoke with a fastidious hatred, "You are a low, common girl; you are not fit to associate with the girls in this school. I dismiss you!" I went as quickly as possible to Miss Merryweather, not stopping to answer him. I knocked on her door, and when she opened it I burst out, "Doctor Mills has dismissed me; he says I'm low and common," and began to weep wildly. She interrupted me by a sharp slap on my rear, saying, "Stop that noise, and unbutton my blouse!" The buttons were down the back, and when I finished, she asked me what had really happened. I told her and she laughed so hard I had to laugh too. She was a wonderful and lovely woman.

We received our training in Obstetrics in a large efficiently run hospital in New York City. We were sent there to learn about the delivery and care of mothers and babies, and we did, but thoroughly. The work was so pushed that one didn't realize one had learned until long afterwards. Six nurses left Montrose and six who had been away three months, returned. We approached the experience in fear, for there we worked with nurses from the large city hospitals. But we were rated very highly, and I myself heard one of the attending physicians say to the head nurse, "Put a Montrose on this case,—she must have the most efficient nursing possible." I told Miss Merryweather of it, and she was pleased.

New nurses were usually put first on babies,—which meant chiefly the delivery of the babies to their mothers for nursing, every two hours. This was accomplished by transporting them in a high-wheeled rubber-tired wagon, consisting virtually of two trays, on which we laid the babies, feet in, heads out, until both trays were filled. It was against the rules to lay another row lengthwise, or to run with the wagon. Both rules we broke constantly, because of the distance: it was imperative that we exercise the greatest possible speed in order to get them out in time to bring them back, in time to get them out in time to bring them back, world without end. Whirling this wagon into the ward, the process of getting the right baby to the right mother was affected by holding up a baby, reading the name on the wrist, "Dubinsky!" and mamma Dubinsky yelled wildly. When the babies were all in the nursery at one time, and all howling, they made a noble discord, not unlike animals in a zoo.

After being on babies for two weeks, I was advanced to breasts, which meant that I had entire charge of all the breasts on that floor. While this was enormously interesting and important work, it was repellent to me. If one mother had too much milk, it devolved upon me to express it, and give it to a baby whose mother had an insufficient amount. Many treatments were ordered, and all day long I handled and observed breasts until in my sleep I saw them. Large ones, small ones, dark ones, light ones, they floated before my eyes at night. I never wished to do that work again.

To the perennial question, "But weren't you afraid you'd get the babies mixed?" I usually gave the conventional answer, "No, they are marked at birth with a tape sewn firmly around the wrist." But the truth, which no one wants to know, is that my real anxiety was not that we might mix them, but that the mothers would swap them. Often they would try to swap a puny ugly little one for a nice pink pretty one; if a mother died, leaving a lovely one, several women would make a pass at it and claim it as theirs. In weariness at the constant watchfulness, I closed my eyes, and I know that upon two occasions the change was made. When one is dead tired it doesn't seem so important, and often I thought, "Oh! What's the difference! Swap if you like!"

One order I was given on night duty that I didn't understand; to watch the mothers while the babies were with them. "Watch for what?" I asked. "To see that they don't go to sleep and roll on them and smother them." It seemed superfluous and fantastic! Imagine a mother accidentally smothering her baby! Besides, the wards were nearly a block apart,—how could I watch them all? However, I kept a sharp lookout, but even so, two babies were accidentally smothered during my night duty. Poor things! You couldn't blame them,—they were poor, and many of the babies were illegitimate.

The most astounding character connected with this hospital was the night clerk, named Ignatius Butt. He was slight and dark, with a small black mustache. He was ageless in appearance; he might have been thirty, or one hundred and thirty. I think he had been there many years, else how could he have developed his eye and intuition to such an appalling degree?

When I was put on the admission ward, I was told to ask Ignatius no questions,—that when he said a patient was going to be delivered in thirty-two minutes, there was no possible benefit in arguing; she would be delivered in thirty-two minutes. A percentage of the inmates were firmly convinced that even against the woman's desire or nature's plans, if Ignatius named a specific moment for the arrival of another baby, it would appear, and at the moment chosen. I have with my own eyes, seen him take the name and address of a patient who stood panting to get in, and without the flicker of an eyelash, without having noticeably observed her, say casually, "Go out and walk around; return at eleven-fifteen." At her hesitance, I said, "Don't argue; just go out and walk, but return at exactly eleven-fifteen." His timing was uncanny, infallible.

There was a not incredible story circulated concerning Ignatius on a trolley. He observed carefully the lady opposite, lifted his dapper gray hat, and said, "Pardon me, lady, but you'd better hurry; it'll be here in twenty minutes." The indignant woman gave him freely of her mind, advising him to mind his own business. How little she knew! He retreated, chagrined, but the baby was born between Eighteenth and Nineteenth Streets.

Six weeks in the out-patient department gave me first-hand knowledge of a million lives different from any I had known or imagined. On the farm we had been poor, but there had always been animals, and trees,—not to be compared with poverty in the slums. Every day we left the hospital with our little black bag, ten cents for carfare, and our list for the day. These were in strange territory, to become familiar in time, but at first the words, "back house" puzzled me, until it became apparent that behind the houses fronting the streets was another row of dirty, dismal buildings. The words were exactly descriptive.

In many of the dark, dirty holes called homes, we found practically nothing, and in many cases, literally nothing in which to wrap the new baby. Often some member of the family would remove the dirty cover from a dilapidated overstuffed old chair, and in one case my own petticoat had to serve. But I had a limited supply of petticoats. Sometimes we delivered them in cellars, the walls of which were damp with foul-smelling ooze.

Why the babies born in these squalid, unhealthy rooms were invariably the fattest, pinkest, and cutest ones, I could never imagine.

Hester, Allen, Grand, seething with human beings, appalling, overpowering. Among all these lives in dirt and squalor, the only clean ones I came upon were Spanish. This may not hold true in general; I only know that every Spanish patient I had was clean, gracious, hospitable, no matter how poor they were. They always gave me tea, which they sweetened with chocolate candy.

Young doctors there for their obstetrical training delivered babies all over Lower Manhattan. I shall never cease to respect and admire the speed and dexterity with which they transformed a crowded kitchen, with clothes-lines crisscrossed four ways, into a clean field for delivery. Miraculously the table was cleared of rags, and pots and pans, the room of progeny, relations and neighbors, water boiling, the patient prepared and, in most cases, concluded with astonishing rapidity and efficiency. They were splendid, those young doctors.

In the neighborhood of Hester Street I found myself constantly accompanied by an unattractive Jewish girl, about twelve. She was bright, and even grasped the simpler forms of cleanliness. Her name was Rosie, and one day I brought her home with me. In my room she was enthralled by pictures I had casually collected,—copies of famous paintings, and popular stage stars. She relinquished them with obvious reluctance, so I told her she might have them. She gave me a suspicious look and said, "What'll I do with them?" Puzzled by her serious face I said, "Put them on your wall." She shook her head and said, "We ain't got no wall." Annoyed, I said, "Don't be silly; of course you've got a wall." Stubbornly she insisted that they had no wall; curious, I went to see, and she was completely truthful,— they had no wall. In a not too large room, five families lived, divided by chalk marks; Rosie's family lived in the middle. She told me with pride that one of the corner occupants had two borders. There was no aspect of living or dying with which Rosie was not familiar, in that room of five families, all of whom had several children.

Long convinced of my naïveté in thinking that some wonderful person would help me to go to school, I had to a degree, accepted my position. At times I longed for companionship, for a man friend, and still believed that some day I would find one with whom I could talk and dance, and explore the city. Many nurses went out secretly with the interns, and a few were engaged to mysterious, glamorous creatures whom we never saw. Lonely, I wanted someone to love,—I wanted passionately to have a beau. Leonard P. Burke still wrote me nice friendly letters, but I could not recall his face,— he did not suffice.

To this end I made efforts to interest one of the interns, with indifferent success. I did not care for him particularly, but he was handy, and I thought that he might prove interesting if one knew him better. He asked me, not very enthusiastically, to meet him one afternoon, and with great expectancy I dressed in my best clothes, borrowed an umbrella against the drizzle of rain, and set out to meet him. I imagined a walk, then coffee in some nice old restaurant where interesting people gathered, where we would talk, and become friends. When we met, he smiled in a friendly way and said Hello. As we walked along in the rain, under my umbrella, his face was expressionless, and I didn't know just what to say, especially now that I had seen him in street clothes, he fell far short of my ideal young man. He was stocky, freckled, and had pale gray eyes. I thought that perhaps he was thinking the same of me, and I endeavored to make up for my lack of beauty in sprightly conversation.

After a few blocks under my umbrella, he stopped at the entrance of a dismal hotel, and said, "Let's go in here; a drink wouldn't be a bad idea on a day like this. Get in out of the rain anyway." Inside, a shabby room divided into booths, almost successful in concealing the occupants, of drab, uninteresting appearance. A long bar filled one side and several men leaned upon it; there was no warmth or cheer. Determined to be friendly and cheerful, I talked about the hospital, and eliciting no response, I tried the city, its size, and wonders, with no more success. He ordered a Tom Collins, and not knowing what it was, I said I'd have the same. Hating its taste, I drank it, for I didn't want him to think me countrified.

When we finished the drinks, he said in a matter-of-fact voice, "Come on,—let's go upstairs." Fear clutched my heart,—the word "upstairs" didn't sound so good. He paid for the drinks, and got up awkwardly, and I followed him, wondering just how I could get out of it all. In the small entrance he stopped, and I stood there, seeing the ugly linoleum floor, the cheap imitation marble walls, and the first steps of the stairs. He took me by the arm, and I drew fiercely back. I had no intention of going up those, or any other stairs. His face clouded angrily, and he grasped me firmly around my waist, moving toward the stairs. Jerking loose, I struck at him, hitting his nose; furious, he shook me and I screamed. He twisted my arm and said in a low angry voice, "Stop that noise! Come out of here; I'll teach you a lesson!"

Out on the street, I could have left him, but did not. I wanted to know why it was like this,—all my hopes for friendship, all beauty imagined, remaining, was drab, gray dirt. Was all life like that? I waited for him to speak, wondering what was wrong with me, that men would not be friends with me. In stories girls were always beautiful and men enthralled with their charms,—what was it they had? If only I could find out! We walked sadly in the rain.

Presently he turned on me savagely, "What sort of a sap are you, anyway?" he asked. Carelessly, sadly, I said, "All sorts!" He walked on, saying, "What do you think any man would expect, when a girl comes out in the rain to meet him?" I had no answer for that, and he went on. "What business have you to lead me to expect the usual thing, and then spring this innocent country-girl stuff? Tell me truthfully, are you a virgin?" Wanting some solution for my loneliness, I let him fling the words at me, leaving only a feeling of physical repulsion. "Yes," I said. He stopped, and looking at me under the umbrella he said, "My God! I believe you are!" and walked on. "Is that a crime?" I asked. "Should I keep it a secret, as something not quite nice?"

Seriously, perhaps trying to be kind, he said, "Listen, I'm going to tell you something for your own good." I was all ears, for I felt that now, surely, I would learn something. "Don't do this again unless you are ready to go through with it! Just don't do it." Helplessly I said, "Do you mean that I mustn't try to have a man friend unless I live with him? Can't I have a man who would take me out, and talk to me, and dance with me? Never? Is there something wrong with me? Is it because I'm not pretty enough? Or interesting? Tell me!" Wearily he said, "Oh! For God's sakes! I'm not your granny and I'm not going to teach you the Facts of Life! I only know that you're green, and that being the case, just you stay home, or go out with the nurses,—don't go out with the interns. I'm telling you for your own good, and that's all I care to be bothered about it. I have an engagement, so goodby!" And he left me, too sad and puzzled to weep. I walked along in the rain, trying to think, but my thoughts got in the way, and I went home and took a hot bath, still wondering why things grasped were never as imagined. I determined never to try again,—as long as I lived I would not try to have a beau, nor friendship with a man. I would visit Mrs. Hall, whom I enjoyed being with, and go with the nurses, but men were out. I often had dinner with Mrs. Hall, and I had returned her seven dollars long ago.

The most ill patients were in the Solarium, where they received the same attention as that given millionaires on the private floor. Special nurses, fresh fruits, every delicacy of diet was given them. At night it was wonderful to look down on the lights of the city, to feel detached, swinging high in the sky; mornings I watched dawn come up over the river, with a yellow moon turning to silver, the dream-like city emerging from the mist, long dark shadows thrown by tall buildings growing lighter in the first faint tremulous light of day. It is just then that the breeze of death comes; a gentle, almost playful breeze, blowing idly, yet with a purpose, there just between the night and the day. For five minutes it blows, and is gone. It is then that most patients die. I know it well, that gentle, caressing breeze; it brings peace.

With a mind fairly bulging with a completely confused accumulation of facts, and equally indiscriminate emotional reactions to birth and babies, and New York, I returned to Montrose, to be instantly caught in a vastly articulate dislike of No. 24. An old man named Porter, incurably ill, a fiend from Hell, who had proved his capacity for flattening a strong healthy nurse within a week. Every nurse prayed to be spared, and Martha said to me, "Wait until you get twenty-four! We've been saving him for you, to welcome you home; we couldn't bear you to miss him,—you'll learn about nursing from him!" When I said, "But what does he *do* that is so devastating?" she shuddered, saying, "I don't want to spoil him for you,—you must meet it with fresh innocence. You'll see." I did.

A week went by, and the nurse on twenty-four was excused from duty and put to bed with cold compresses. She had spots before her eyes, heard voices. When I saw her face as she went off duty, stark terror gripped me, for my hope of life lay in the reality of graduation, and I lived in fear of its ultimate failure to materialize. But I was next. With my hand on his door, I stopped, and humbly, pleadingly asked God to help me.

Perched high on pillows I saw an emaciated little old man, whose two enormous eyes burned malevolently in a sallow, skeletal face. His hands, talons that were never still, his lips a sardonic line. He eyed me evilly and cackled, "Are you my new torturer? Seems like they change them every week, so they will be strong to bedevil me, and wreak their vengeance on me! But I'll beat you all at your own game! Same as my family, you all want me to die, and I won't!" He chuckled to himself, plucking at the bedclothes. "They think they'll kill me, but I'll show 'em! By God, if I can stand the stupid nurses here, nothing will ever kill me!"

This glimpse of what the nurses had meant cautioned me to be wary, and pleasantly I said, "Well, Mr. Porter, I'll join you, and together we'll withstand them." He cackled again, and raising his voice in old wicked humor said, "Oh! So that's your little game! You can't trap me with your sly words, you hussy! That's been tried before, but I'm on to your evil ways." Sinister evil emanating from him gave me to pause.

A nurse, in order to keep him amused, perhaps, had rigged up an arrangement whereby he could have a number of articles, such as cigars, pencils, scissors, and other small objects, near him, but sliding them along on cords. If one of his playthings escaped beyond his reach he became wild with rage, throwing things at his nurse. He was a bundle of nerves and evil temper in a dry shell that rattled. I felt sorry for him, but inwardly I felt sure that he would be greatly improved by being dead. He made very obscene remarks, intimating the most lewd fancies of his evil old brain, nauseous and shocking to hear,—some of his practices were strongly reminiscent of so-called lower animals.

Determined if possible to kill him before he did me, I laid my plans accordingly. If he wanted a fight, I sweetly agreed with him; if he wanted to snooze, I talked continually until he would scream, "For the love of God, keep still!" Innocently I would say, "Why, Mr. Porter, I thought you wanted me to talk!" and continue senseless chatter. When he wanted to talk, I remained silent and he would scream, "Answer me, you dumb girl! Don't you hear me talking to you?" and mildly I would reply, "Why, Mr. Porter, I thought you wanted me to keep quiet." With tears streaming down his cheeks he would whimper, "But that was an hour ago, when I wanted to sleep!" By blocking him, exhausting him, I wore him down, and I imagine he gave up, for within the third day he passed on. We celebrated his taking off with a party confined to his victims.

One of my classmates was a silent girl, with smoldering black eyes. She was an excellent nurse, of great efficiency and integrity, very well educated, and despite her fiery temper and taciturnity, she was liked and respected by us all. At one time she was on night duty and I on day. In a semi-private room a colored man lay suffering from incurable cancer. He was so good and patient that we ached with our sympathy for him. He lingered interminably, his pain only partly mitigated by morphine. For months this continued, and we were torn by his sufferings beyond bearing. One evening when I was going off duty, I said to this nurse, "I think that room needs airing, don't you?" She gave me a searching look, and quietly said, "Yes, I do. Leave it to me." Next morning the room was empty and turned out to air. She was a kind nurse.

When I'd been back a few weeks, I was put on the Children's ward, and

I loved it more than any work I had ever had. There were usually around twenty children, ranging from six months to six years. Nothing that I have ever done, or I think that I shall ever do, can give me the pure happiness that I experienced in bringing back puny sick babies to health. To see small bird-like bodies, frequently full of sores, limp, almost lifeless, change slowly, day by day, into beautiful, smooth-limbed babies! I rubbed their thin bodies with oil, praying that my hands could by some magic transfer my energy to those weak dangling limbs. Some of them I fed a spoonful at a time, until they were well enough to feed themselves. The response brought such joy to my heart as to make me desire no other work.

I learned how fine and sporting they were, for if a new, very ill one was admitted, I had only to look at them, and they would be quiet, assuming their share of the responsibility. They obeyed me in the most minute detail, and yet they were not afraid, but laughed with joy when I came on duty. My head nurse asked me by what method I preserved perfect discipline, achieved my results, yet allowing the children to play freely, happily. My answer would have been too simple to be readily understood. It was that I loved them. To spend one's whole life at such a task would be a full account,—sufficient to satisfy every need of a full heart and a free mind. I thought of Celia, and wondered if she had her house, and her children.

My children did not cry or fret. If they had pain, they bore it bravely, with courage. It was here that I saw demonstrations of mother love that left me white with rage and hate. Mothers who through ignorance or necessity had allowed the life in their charge to be drawn out until only a thin thread held it, who had in many instances been forced to bring their child to the hospital, would visit them. Taking them up, handling them with a too-possessive familiarity, totally lacking in respect, they would fuss and talk and feed them until, at the end of their visit, the babies were ill. Temperatures shot up, their arms and legs twitched from nervous exhaustion. No matter how often I begged them not to, those loving mothers would give them indigestible food that completely destroyed the balance I had so painstakingly built up. They were blood sisters to the old woman who boasted, "I've buried seven,—I guess I ought to know how to raise children!" Oh! I had evidence enough of mother love! Some of them got well enough to bear it, for I saw them afterwards; the stronger ones.

Miss Merryweather was proud and pleased with my children's ward, and brought all the doctors and visitors to see it and my lovely children. For once I was perfectly happy.

After months of happiness with the children I was again put on night duty, and although familiarity with the dark corners had lessened my tension, still the nights were fearful. An incident occurred which might have proved extremely painful, but for the help of God.

One of the most strict rules of the hospital was that all clothing belonging to patients must be carefully listed and locked in a room for the purpose. This list was written in the Clothes Book, with the date and signature of the nurse in charge. Nurses were absolutely responsible for clothes listed above her signature. During hectic nights I had admitted many patients, and would cheerfully have sworn that I had followed the rules meticulously, but one morning when I had fallen into a sound sleep, I was awakened and told to report to the office.

On the desk before Miss Merryweather lay the Clothes Book, and my heart stood still. She picked it up and said, "A patient named Chestnut is dismissed, but they are unable to locate his clothes; have you any explanation, Miss Dan?" She gave me a quick look and I opened my mouth like a fish, but before I made a sound, she said, "Excuse me a minute," and left the office. Desperately I demanded, "God, where *are* you? Tell me quick what to do! I can't bear any more punishment!" and a voice as clear as day said to me, "*Eat it!*"

When God answers as quick as that, I obey. Tearing a page from the book, I stuffed it in my mouth, chewing rapidly. The paper was stiff and not very clean,—my mouth dry from nervousness, so that it didn't moisten easily, but I chewed feverishly, swallowing great gobs as quickly as possible fearing she would return and catch me. As the last morsel went down, I gulped as she entered, and resuming her remarks in a curt, formal manner, "Now about this list, Miss Dan," looking at the book. I said not a word. She looked faintly surprised, and said, "There is a page missing here," and still I was silent. "If a page is gone, naturally we can't be sure you failed to list them; you may go." I managed to say, "Yes, Miss Merryweather," and got out, puzzled as to whether or not she had deliberately given me an opportunity to save myself. I imagined her saying to herself, "I'll leave her alone with the book, and if she has any brains at all, she'll think of some way out of this," for I think she was tired of punishing me. With her keen eyes, I know that she knew that leaf was not gone when she left the office. She was a wonderful woman.

The next thing that might have had catastrophic results, but didn't, was amusing. One of the attending physicians was a fat, jolly doctor named Harper. All the nurses liked him, for he was always kind, but further than that, he was a bachelor. Some one always invited him to our dances, but he had never come; as he and I were on call for the delivery room, I invited him, and when he accepted I was thrilled, for I was so tired of always being a wallflower. To stand or sit against a wall, pretending indifference, as though this were among the more trivial of our social engagements, was horrible pain. My heart goes out to all the wallflowers all over the world. Past, present, and future wallflowers that are being born every minute. Death can offer nothing comparable to that keen sense of isolation, when the natural flow of girl energy is toward the dance floor! When you are in the arms of a man, no matter how inferior in looks and mentality, for the moment he is romance; you are wanted, and the blood flows again, warming the body, flushing the cheeks and tingling the fingertips.

One of my classmates, a comical, not very good-looking girl named Sarah Dunne, had a heart of gold, and hid her beautiful dreams of romance deep in her soul. We were old wall cronies, having stood for more consecutive hours than any two nurses in the school. Some of the pole sitters could learn a lot from wall standers. One evening when we had stood until our knees felt wobbly, and our shoes were full of feet, she whispered to me, "Let's move over to the other wall, Linda, it's softer." She met the pain with humor; I met it with hate. Hating the stupidity that made me come. When the music played, I had to come, knowing well that not a soul would ask me to dance. There weren't enough doctors to go around, and those who did come danced only with the prettiest girls. As I was not one of those, I stood against the wall, squeezing back my tears. Of all the rot that is taught about virtue and goodness winning! Maybe. But from my observations, it's the prettiest girls, no matter how brainless they are, who get the men. There were three lovely looking girls in our class, and they danced continually, their faces flushed with happy laughter. As I watched them I thought for my future that I would not look for romance, nor expect it; I would stand alone, independent of men; never would I let this horrible feeling of embarrassment crush me.

With Doctor Harper's acceptance, I had a man for at least one evening who would certainly have to dance with me a few times, and I was glad. We hoped that no patient would choose those few hours in which to increase the already overcrowded population, but in the midst of a dreamy waltz, at which I rather fancied myself, we had to rush to the hospital. We hastily put sterile gowns on over our evening clothes, hoping to expedite matters and return to the party. Mrs. Klein was reasonably co-operative, demonstrating a modicum of neatness and dispatch in giving birth to a baby girl.

Doctor Harper always had his little joke, but when he said, in sepulchral tones, "Oh! Mrs. Klein, your baby has no penis!" and poor Mrs. Klein wailed, "Oi, oi, oi, Mein Gott!" I thought he was crowding it a bit. He relieved her anxiety, saying calmly, "It's a girl."

We attended to all details, saw Mrs. Klein rolled back to the ward, then looked around for the baby. We couldn't find her. Believing that naturally she was there under our noses, we laughed a good deal, but presently it was not funny at all. We looked high and low, and faced each other with astonished fear; Doctor Harper mopped a perspiring brow and said, "Hell, we *did* have a baby here tonight, didn't we? Didn't you *see* it?" I said that I not only had seen it, but I distinctly recalled his not very funny remarks concerning its sex. Panic held us, when I remembered the large can for soiled linen that sat just outside the door. Lifting the lid, and removing a few pieces of soiled linen, I found Miss Klein, cosy as you please, none the worse for wear. Presenting her in all her pristine splendor to the night nurse, we returned to the party.

Everybody on the Maternity ward was excited and interested when Jessie Anderson was admitted. For one thing, she was old to be having a baby, and when the young doctor took her history, and she calmly said Miss Anderson, he looked at her in surprise, but went on with his questions. Mother and father, sisters and brothers; where born, when? White, single, fifty-three. Later he said to Miss Harmon, "Fifty-three! And having her first baby! It's a shame!"

Miss Harmon strode in, sceptical of the young intern's facts. "Are you Miss or Mrs?" she asked Jessie, in her high and mighty manner. Jessie, pink-cheeked, white-haired, looked at her and laughed. "Miss. Single; and my first baby! What do you think of that?" and laughed heartily again. Ruffled, Miss Harmon adjusted her glasses and snapped, "I think you ought to know better, at your age!" Jessie stopped laughing, and her answer carried in it her surprise. "Gosh, I thought at my age it wouldn't matter!" Not to be outwitted, Miss Harmon continued, "But how did you happen to be such an idiot?" Jessie thought for a moment, then said, "Well, I'll tell you, Miss. It was at the fireman's ball; I went, thinking for once to have a good time." Her gaze was out now, seeing two interns knocking a tennis ball idly. "I met a nice carpenter there, and after the ball I had a drink with him,— my first drink. He wanted to spend the night with me and I let him. I didn't want to die without knowing what it was that people make so much of. Well, I never thought it would come to this."

Miss Harmon stood stiffly, slight disgust showing on her face, schooled in tolerance. She had seen and heard a lot, in her years as head-nurse of a maternity ward. Looking down at Jessie she said, "It seems a pity you couldn't have curbed your curiosity a little longer," as she left Jessie to her own cogitations.

Jessie was a cleaning woman; she went out by the hour, and she told us that many of her people were grand society folks who often gave her presents of old clothes, or picture frames, or odd pieces of furniture they didn't want any longer. She was jolly and brisk, helping with the trays, deftly for all her bulk. We had to stop her carrying bedpans, or she'd have been busy at that all day; but she helped with the dusting, talking and laughing all day. She even laughed at Mrs. Briggs who referred pointedly to "my husband," giving Jessie a nasty look the while.

When the doctor on duty examined her, he looked grave; later we saw by her chart that her heart was none too good. We felt then that she had a good chance of not coming through this that was expected of her, and we were troubled. We were all extra nice to her because she was so cheerful, so unconcerned about it, and because we had become fond of her. Her difficulties and problems had become ours.

When her pains began, Miss Harmon told her to keep walking. She walked up and down the ward, in her old felt slippers, her hospital gown flapping around her legs, her gray hair in curls on her damp forehead, her cheeks pale now. When she went into the delivery room, we all continued our work in a sort of daze, listening, apprehensive. One of the women said, "I'll bet she'll have a hard time; her so old and all, and her heart not so good." Miss Groef spoke angrily, "Don't make such senseless remarks; of course she'll be all right. She's a perfectly healthy woman and her heart is all right too." But we noticed that even Miss Harmon, veteran of a thousand births, whom we had long suspected of having a Frigidaire where hearts are usually found, looked white, and was short with even her favorite, Miss Lowell. We served the supper trays, brought the babies to be nursed, all the time wondering what was happening in the D.R. At half past six when the door opened, four heads turned as though attached to the door by a string, and our hands were still, waiting.

They rolled Jessie out and put her in the end bed. She lay very still, and when Miss Harmon bent over her she smiled wanly and said, "Kind of a tight squeeze, wasn't it? Guess I'll just lie still awhile." She slept, and catty Mrs. Briggs kept quiet; every one moved gently around the ward. We asked Miss Harmon how it was, and she said, "Everything went all right; she's fine, and the baby is a boy." We were all relieved, and went about our work more comfortably.

When Jessie woke the day nurses had gone, and only Miss Hayes, the night nurse, was there. When Miss Hayes spoke to her, she smiled and said she was hungry. Miss Hayes brought her a glass of milk, which she drank eagerly. "Could I see him?" she asked timidly. Miss Hayes was young, and liked Jessie. "Sure; I'll bring him in," she said. She went to the nursery and returned carrying the newest of all the babies. First she held him up so Jessie could see him, turning him around to display his nice head. Jessie stared unbelievingly. "He's a very handsome child, Miss Anderson, and has excellent manners; howled only a few minutes upon arrival,—probably didn't like us very much, but he'll learn to," Miss Hayes said. Jessie said nothing, just looked. When Miss Hayes moved to lay him down by her side, Jessie blushed with embarrassment. "What'll I do with him? I've never held a baby." Adroit Miss Hayes said, "Never mind, you'll learn to; I'm going to leave him for a while so you'll get acquainted."

When she went away, Jessie looked down at this strange baby, trying to feel that it was her child; nothing happened, and she held him awkwardly until her arm went to sleep. She tried to remove her arm, jostling him a bit, and he opened his eyes, staring seriously into hers. She slipped her arm around him and held him close, her feeling of strangeness gone. When Miss Hayes came to take him, Jessie laughed and said, "I think I'm goin' to like that boy fine."

There was a deal of speculation going on about Jessie and the baby, practically every one feeling that it was a personal problem. He was a beautifully built child, without scar or blemish, and as the days passed he grew better looking, changing from a bright pink to a soft reddish brown, with a smooth, rounded little body, wide-awake blue eyes. Jessie learned all the things to be done for him, her brown eyes shining with pride.

There was talk of adoption, we heard, and we all took sides for or against that. Of all this Jessie was utterly oblivious, she was so busy learning exactly how to take care of him herself. One day Doctor Miller spoke to her seriously, asking her what she was going to do when she left the hospital. "Why, go back to work of course," she answered. He looked embarrassed, saying casually, "Don't you think we ought to have your baby adopted if we can find the proper parents for him?" He felt the tenseness that overcame Jessie. When he could meet her eyes, he saw that her face was white as she smilingly asked, "Don't you think I'm a proper parent for him? No, Doctor, get that right out of your head. I'm not going to give up my baby after waiting fifty-three years for him." Doctor Miller was a dear, and liked Jessie as we all did. "Well, Jessie, if you weren't so stubborn about telling us the father's name, so we could get him to help you raise this baby . . ." Jessie laughed happily and said, "Why, Doctor, I wouldn't know the man if he walked in, and as for marrying him, I'd as soon marry a Chinaman. I never saw him but the once, and besides, I don't know where he is. He don't know anything about this, and it wouldn't be fair to spring it on him now. He didn't mean to cause me any trouble and I don't blame him at all. No, I couldn't do that, Doctor Miller. I'll manage; you'll see." Doctor Miller gave up.

But Miss Harmon went to Jessie with determination in her eye. "Now, Jessie. No more foolishness. What is the man's name?" she asked, but Jessie stubbornly refused to say. Miss Harmon tried cajoling, praising the baby, saying that it would be a crime to take him to a little room. In the end, she played her last card. "Well, if you won't, you know Doctor Miller can take him away from you, legally, if he proves that it is best for the baby." Frightened, trapped, Jessie said, "All right, Miss Harmon. I'll tell you his name. It's Henry Halliday, but I don't know where he is. He won't want to be forced in a case like this, and I won't let him do anything for my baby unless he asks to do it." Miss Harmon secretly triumphant, left her. She told Doctor Miller, and he suggested the Unions, which she did, and found that he was in Detroit, working. We got together and made up a letter, which Miss Harmon wrote:

Dear Mr. Halliday:

No doubt you will be surprised to know that you are the father of a fine son. He was born on Oct. 16th, and weighed seven pounds. His mother, Jessie Anderson, refused until now, to give us your name, but we persuaded her, because we feel that you should help Jessie raise this baby, he is such a handsome boy. Will you let me know what you are willing to do in this matter?

Sincerely yours,
M. Harmon.

We waited anxiously to see what Henry would do, and wondered if he was the right sort for a father. Jessie's baby was much the best looking baby in the nursery; in fact the best we'd had for a long time. He was extraordinarily bright, cried only for legitimate reasons, and otherwise conducted himself in a most philosophical manner, ready to smile at a gentle poke in the ribs. Miss Harmon spoke severely to us about spoiling him, but we noticed that she spent more time than necessary around his crib.

As the days passed and no word came from Henry, we all got more and more worried. We hated to think about Jessie and the baby leaving, not knowing where she could take him. About two days before she was to go, at eleven in the morning when Doctor Miller was making rounds, accompanied by Miss Harmon in her stiff white uniform, while all the patients on their best behavior waited their turn, we heard a great commotion from the front hall. Doctor Miller paused, every one listened, wondering. There was obviously an argument between a man and little Miss Davis in the front office. We heard him say, "Where's my baby? I had a letter tellin' me I had a baby here, an' I want to see it." By this time he was up to the door of the ward, poor Miss Davis trying vainly to intercept him as he towered above her, telling him that of course he could see his baby, but that he mustn't be so noisy about it.

Doctor Miller walked to him and said, mildly, "What is your name?" When his voice boomed out, "I'm Henry Halliday," our hearts stood still. Miss Lowell dropped a tray from useless fingers, and Miss Wilson left the ward hurriedly; we knew where she was going,—to the pantry where Jessie was fixing the trays. When she told her that Henry Halliday had come, Jessie just stared, then said, "For pity's sakes! What'll I do? How does he look?" Miss Wilson reassured her, "You needn't feel ashamed of him; he's not bad-looking at all."

While Miss Wilson was warning Jessie, Doctor Miller and Miss Harmon had calmed Henry down, and the three of them moved off toward the nursery, they telling him what a fine boy he had. They told him to be quiet, and pointed out the crib, and Henry went slowly to it, looking down where the baby lay sleeping. Henry held on the iron rail of the crib, the knuckles of his hands showing white through the brown. In a dazed way he rubbed his eyes with a work- worn hand, and turned to Miss Harmon saying huskily, "He's a nice little feller, ain't he?" She said, "Yes," and asked him if he wished to see Jessie. He hadn't remembered her for the moment, but he said, "Yes, I would," so she told him to wait in the reception room outside, she would send Jessie in to him.

When Miss Harmon came back to the ward, we were all chattering about

Henry, but when she told Jessie that he was waiting to see her, Jessie looked stubborn. Miss Harmon said, "Now, Jessie, don't be mean; go and talk to the poor man." Jessie put down her tray and reluctantly went out.

Henry was looking out of a window when Jessie came in, and didn't hear her at first. She went up to him, feeling, as she told us later, a perfect fool. They looked at each other, each trying to remember how the other had looked and they both suddenly laughed. Jessie said, "Listen, Henry Halliday; I didn't want to send for you, but they talked me into it. I never would have given in, but Miss Harmon said they might take my baby if I didn't. I wouldn't let them have him adopted." At the word "adopted," Henry stiffened belligerently, and growled, "Adopt *my* baby? Why, Hell, *who* thinks they'll adopt my baby?" And Jessie said, "*Your* baby, Henry Halliday?" His face flushed, and he said, "Well, it *is* my baby, ain't it?" Jessie said, "Well, that depends. I know nobody's going to adopt my son but me. I don't know what you're going to do, Henry Halliday, but I'm going to keep my baby."

Henry walked around nervously, then said, "Will you let me help raise him, Jessie? Will you marry me and we'll both raise him?" Jessie tried to look stubborn but couldn't quite manage it. She laughed and said, "Well, Henry, seeing that we're both responsible for him, I guess it's up to us to raise him. If we can do a better job together, I'm willing." After further talk, they decided to get married the next day, just before she left the hospital. She returned to the ward, giggling as usual. We demanded to know instantly what they had decided. Although she laughed, her brown eyes shining, she had an air of assurance as she said indifferently, "Well, he asked me to marry him, and I said I would; he'll help me raise my baby."

We scuttled around, getting a nice dress for Jessie and an outfit for the baby, and Miss Harmon corralled a minister, and they were married, right in the ward. When the minister said, "Henry, do you take this woman to be your lawful wedded wife?" we all felt solemn as owls. The ceremony occurred between feedings, and we went down the hall with them, saw Henry help Jessie and the baby into a taxi, waved good-by, turning back from the last glimpse of their smiling faces. We had been so lifted up, it was hard to return to the drab routine of the ward,—but that is life in a hospital.

A young Italian girl, mentally ill, was to be transferred to a hospital for the insane, and I was asked to use my own ingenuity in persuading her to go quietly. She was on the alert, suspicious of us all. I hated the job, but some one had to do it, so I told her we were going for a ride. Believing me sufficiently to dress and accompany me to the car, she drew back, asking where I was taking her. I lied, and she got in. When we reached the place, and drove along the extensive grounds, I told her that it was a private school; that we could go in, if she liked. Trusting me she got out, and we walked between rich blooming flowers under trees in full leaf, making dark cool shadows on green grass; the sky was blue and fleecy white clouds floated indolently. From the beautiful outdoors we entered a clean, cool hall where an attendant met us. As prearranged, he said, "Would you like to see the building?" and I said yes, feeling sick.

We followed him down the wide dark hall and through a door, where he signalled me to turn back, and as I turned she caught on. In rage and terror she screamed, "You dirty bastard! You've tricked me! How could you, when I trusted you? Oh, you rotten bastard!" Full of shame, I left, her sobbing ringing in my ears, and sat in a waiting room to weep. A nurse came in and said, "You mustn't feel like that. She'll be all right here. Let me show you around." Thinking that I should at least see to what sort of place I had brought her, I went with the nurse.

Seeing the place lessened my feeling of treachery, for it was the most cheerful hospital I had ever seen: sunny sitting rooms gay with chintz where patients sat happily reading or sewing. In a beautiful room a handsome girl was playing a piano. The nurse told me that they had sufficient talent, many of them well-known artists, to allow them to put on entire operas; that they had wonderful musical evenings. I wondered why so many musicians were there. I know now.

In a male ward, the nurse showed me a thing. It was, judging from the small black mustache, a man; in length about three feet, three-quarters of which seemed to be head. To a small body, tiny arms and legs with repulsive fingers and toes were attached. This thing had never spoken, though it made gruesome sounds. No consecutive thought had ever been generated within that skull, yet it had been bathed and fed, and kept comfortable, for forty years. It was horrible to look upon this travesty of a man, but the thought that stabbed and has never left me, was of the thousands upon thousands of children who are sensitive, aware, tuned as an instrument to the gentlest shadings of emotions, with undreamed of capacity for beauty, who are allowed to starve,—denied the first necessities that even an animal requires, not to speak of the mind and the spirit.

Toward the end of my training, I received this letter from Mrs. Bender:

Dear Miss Dan:

I am sorry for all the cruel things that I did to you, and am writing to ask you to come and be my assistant superintendent. This is a very fine hospital, and the salary is attractive, but most of all, it will give me an opportunity to show you that I regret my actions. I hope that you will accept my apology, and this job, sincerely yours,

Ida Bender.

In my reply I informed her that I did not trust her, and never would,— that rather than become her assistant, I would prefer not to be in the same State, town or country with her.

I had written and received many letters from Doctor Bleeker; he was always charming, encouraging, and friendly, but he had never asked me to come in and see him, and during my three months in New York, I had made no effort to see him. Now I wrote telling him that I was going to graduate, and that I wanted him to be there. He replied, saying that he wished very much that he could come, but that previous engagements made it impossible. Crushed because all the other girls had parents and friends coming, and I had no one, I wrote him a wildly rude letter, saying that if he did not come I would know that all his interest in me was only something to please himself; that if he did not come, I would never forgive him. I had returned to him the thirty-seven dollars he had spent on me, but I could not believe that he would not come. But he didn't.

The day actually came when we gathered in a church, and marched in line across the stage, where we each were handed a slender roll of white paper, signifying that now we were graduate nurses. That night there was a party, and the pain of standing against the wall was somewhat mitigated by the knowledge that tomorrow I was free.

Chapter 13

Phyllis Cromwell was one of the prettiest girls, and always had partners at the dances. She was lovely, like a deep pink carnation. Her soft cheeks were pink, her brown hair a cloud around her small sweet face. Her legs and feet were the most beautiful I have ever seen, and her character was quiet, gentle, honorable and true. She was timid, shy to an extent amounting to weakness, but her modesty overbalanced any defect she may have had. She and I accidentally finished our training the same day, and arranged to take a room together in the village.

The room was in a very nice-looking house, painted yellow with a large yard with tall trees. It was run as a rooming house by a slattern-looking woman of forty, who, by reason of the absence of her front teeth, her stringy faded hair and unkempt clothing, looked about sixty. Two long-legged children, a boy and a girl, possessing the incredible names of Love and Joy, sneaked slyly around the premises. The boy, Love, had the face of an incipient gunman; the little girl displayed none of the emotions implied by her name. Watchful, her small brown eyes alert, all-seeing, she aided and abetted Love in all his nefarious plots. Mrs. Drake, the mother, referred to them as her little flowers. The father, a long, thin gentleman sporting a drooping mustache, appeared at night, usually roaring drunk. Into this quiet restful household we brought our suitcases containing our worldly possessions. But our intangible assets were beyond calculation. We had youth, health, humor, and a curiosity to find out what made things happen. Deep inside, we hoped to find romance, and although we would have hooted at the inference, we still were naïve enough to look for a Prince Charming. Around any corner lay opportunity, excitement and love. We never spoke of such drivel, but there it was, nonetheless, and for Phyllis, why not? She had charm, innocence and beauty, all that a man could ask, and I knew that sooner or later she would find all that her young heart waited for.

Our second night was disturbed by the homecoming of the master, in his cups. We had gone to bed, and to sleep, when a great noise woke us; we sat up in bed, listening. Heavy objects were being interrupted in their flight through the air. Suddenly our door opened, and Mrs. Drake scuttled in, whispering, "Girls, it's only me, don't be frightened! Mr. Drake is in a frightful temper, poor man. If you don't mind, I'll conceal myself in your closet until his anger subsides; if he should make inquiries, will you say that I am not here?" We assured her that we would, and when Mr. Drake knocked, and suspicious of our denials, insisted upon looking for himself, Phyllis opened the door, turned on the light, and reassured he went away. Poor Mrs. Drake remained in the hot little closet far into the night.

Mrs. Drake, who spoke in a precise way, showed us photographs of herself as a young girl, and it made us sad to see how lovely she had been. She assured us in her careful English, that Mr. Drake was of a very fine family,—that when they were young, they enjoyed as she beautifully put it, "the advantages of an assured income, which alas, as the years have passed, has become dissipated." She begged us to excuse his "illness," saying that it was not his fault; trouble had driven him mad. Holding her faded calico wrapper around her meagre form, her pathetic wrecked face lighting up, she said, "Some day all will be well, and my little flowers will assume their rightful position in the world of culture and refinement!" We felt so sorry for her that we couldn't bear it, and made inquiries for another room.

This time we moved into a well-kept white cottage belonging to a Scotch woman named Boggs. She was about thirty, healthy, buxom, and stingy. She was clean and jolly, an all-round good soul whom we liked very much. Her red hair crinkled and her blue eyes twinkled, and laughter came comfortably and often to her lips. Her husband, of whom she seemed inordinately fond, was a cripple, due to an illness he had soon after she married him. He managed to get about with the aid of a crutch, his face twisting with pain at every step. He was a drunkard, and came home every night feeling high. Mrs. Boggs covered this up, saying, "Poor Harry! It's the medicine he takes for his pain that makes him act badly. He is a fine man, and it's only his illness that ruined him!" We suspected that his trouble was due to a slight touch of syphilis, contracted from a towel or washbasin, as it always is.

There was an older nurse rooming there, who looked down upon us with withering scorn. To her we were mere ignorant chits who couldn't possibly know anything about nursing. She wore black stockings, and clothes definitely reminiscent of Salvation Army lassies. Phyllis and I had other ideas, quite. We planned to get us some clothes with the first money we made, and go to New York and see the city. We had very little for several weeks, as our cases were of only a few days' duration, but I could sew, and Phyllis was so lovely that anything looked ravishing on her. We often bought the shape of a hat and divided it,—she taking the brim, and I the crown, and with the addition of a feather, or a ribbon, we made two hats. Some of our creations were startling, but to us they were beautiful. When we had, by a good deal of manipulations of our materials and finances, assembled two outfits sufficiently smart to please us, we went to New York. We didn't know what to do, once there, but we loved being there. We walked miles looking into shop windows, resting in the lobbies of hotels, observing the clothes and manners of people from Wichita, whom we thought to be of the élite of Fifth Avenue. We ate sparingly, but we loved the big city.

Phyllis was attractive to men, and always had a beau; I was not, and did not. But she would not go out without me, and her young man was obliged to bring a partner, however unwilling, and we went gayly forth. Just at this time a brother of one of our classmates was Phyllis's beau, and his name was Frank. He brought his friend, named Ernest, for me. They worked in the city, and we would come in on the train from Montrose, meet them and at some reasonably priced place, have dinner and dance as long as we possibly could, and still make the last train. The results of missing the last train were too horrible to contemplate.

Once we missed it, and returning by subway and slow rattling trolleys, arrived just as the virtuous citizens, bleary-eyed, were taking in the milk. Such a procedure would not be countenanced by the good Christians of the village, so we laid it to the lack of train connections, and got away with it once. The second time we offered no explanation, and were looked upon as lost. Miss Hanson, the old nurse, sniffed, and said to Mrs. Boggs, "That Miss Cromwell is a sweet girl, but as for Miss Dan, she will end in the gutter!" That remark became a standing joke with the girls, and frequently they would say, "Well, Linda, have you picked out a nice gutter yet?" I laughed it off, but away inside, I feared they spoke more truly than they recked.

But the nervous strain of making the last train, by tearing ourselves from the music and bright lights, was exhausting. Waiting in draughty subways and dismal junctions for phantom trolleys produced in us, perhaps illogically, a growing distaste for Frank and Ernest, and I imagine that we didn't look particularly attractive to them in the cold, ruthless light of dawn. We held a conference; I urged her to come to New York with me, to work there, but her timidity held her back. "Don't be silly, Linda; we wouldn't get work there where we are not known," she said, but I pointed out to her that we might do better where we weren't known; that we were not doing so well where we were. But she wouldn't go.

The weather was hot, and I was tired. Having lost weight, I didn't look so good with my height, at ninety-eight pounds, and I longed for some cool place, different surroundings and new faces. To Phyllis I said, "Let us go to Asbury Park and call on the doctors. Maybe they would give us work, and we'd have a change." She was afraid, but in this I prevailed.

The sun was a white-hot glare, the sidewalks like ovens as we walked from office to office. The doctors were all very polite, giving more than a passing glance to Phyllis, but explained that they had their own nurses, and that it was a very healthy place anyway. Our heels and spirits were blistered as we staggered into a cool restaurant and dropped upon green iron chairs. We couldn't afford real food, although we were hungry enough to gnaw the table legs, but we had two long cool lemonades. Phyllis was through and all for home, but I held out for just one more doctor. We selected him, as we had the others, from the telephone book. We chose Doctor James Parvula, and paying for our drinks, we hobbled out.

When we approached the address we beheld a green oasis in a red-hot world. A long low white house in the middle of green lawn, with trees and flowers in profusion; to our sun-glared hotdog-stand wearied eyes, it was a slice of heaven. Inside this beautiful cool place, I as usual did the talking, telling Doctor Parvula what we had hoped to do. He looked so calm and kind, and when he said to us, "I have a bungalow in Allenhurst you may have for nothing, if you want it," we exchanged glances. Our experiences had convinced us that one got nothing for nothing. He interpreted our glances correctly and laughed heartily.

"There's no nigger in the woodpile," he said. "It's a nice little house and I need someone in it. All I require is that you be there between the hours of one and two, in case I phone, or make an appointment with a patient up there instead of bringing them all the way to Asbury. Here is the key; my chauffeur will take you up; have a look, and if you want it, let me know." We went away in his car, feeling like queens, after having tramped the streets all day.

The low brown-shingled bungalow was the most heavenly place I had ever seen, and the possibility of having it for ourselves made me delirious. I couldn't wait to move in, but Phyllis held back, suspicious. She didn't believe that he'd let us have it for just being there for one hour. "Oh! Phyllis, let us take a chance! I think I'd allow more than that, if he lets us have this all for ourselves." Phyllis was firm, puritanical, and refused to be involved in a situation she could not understand. Angry, I said, "Very well; I'll take it alone!" Frightened, she said, "Linda, you wouldn't!" Determined, I replied, "You bet your life I will. Nothing like this has ever happened to me before,—I'd be afraid not to grab it."

We gave the key to the chauffeur, and at the station I telephoned to Doctor Parvula that I would take it, and asked him when I could come. He said, "Any time," and I said, "I'll be down in the morning." We returned to Montrose, and the following morning saw me on my way, suitcase in hand, bound for the Promised Land,—and about time, I said to myself.

When I got to the bungalow I phoned Doctor Parvula, and he sent his car up with bedding, and linen, dishes, pots and pans, and even a box of groceries. I could have wept, but had not time. When I had cleaned the place and arranged the sparse furniture, I had a lovely home. With flowers from the fields behind, I filled cheap bowls, and they were like friends. There was no bath but a pipe in back was a perfectly good shower. Doctor Parvula sent me a shovel—not without curiosity as to its purpose, with perhaps sinister suspicions of nocturnal concealment of dead bodies—I dug a deep hole in the ground, under the cherry tree, and in a wooden box kept all my vegetables and milk. They remained cool and beautiful, there in the earth. The tiny house was well built, and I longed for it to rain,—I wanted to be alone, to lie in quietness listening to the rain on the roof, and on the grass outside, and the cherry tree.

That night I lay in my narrow bed in the little house, alone for the first time in all my life. It was so beautiful that I ached,—with the joy of the silence, that seemed to pour over and around me, like a balm, curing my nerves of tension and tiredness. I lay awake for a long time, unable to know fully that such peace could be. I had been near the sea at Coney Island, but did not see it,—there were too many people. At Asbury Phyllis and I had glimpsed it at the end of long hot streets, but I had not really and actually seen it. Here it was close,—I could hear the waves pounding against a high stone wall at the end of my street. The waves came up and up, high towers of white flame, falling back into the green meadows of water. My first night I lay awake, just listening to the far-off sound of the sea, and the stillness in the tiny house. When I finally slept I dreamed horrible dreams, in which I was back at Olympia, running from Mrs. Bender.

Great fields lay to the north and east of my house, covered with flowers, wiry grass and blackberry vines, later on becoming sand dunes, and finally the beach on which the waves came and broke endlessly. I gathered black-berries by the pail and ate them ravenously, for I began to develop a ruin-ous appetite. I ate them stewed and raw until I could hold no more. I ate my breakfast under the cherry tree in the cool shade of the house,—my lunch from a paper on the beach, and at night I went to a small restaurant for my dinner.

For the first few weeks, many times I awakened cold with fear, back in the hospital with old Button eyes after me, feeling that I had been on the verge of administering a lethal dose to rows and rows of patients. Often I dreamed I was back in the wards at night, that Ippolito had fallen out of bed again, but with all my strength I could not get her back. Lifting and straining, in my dreams, I would wake wet with perspiration, and going behind the house, would let the cold water run over me, to drive the night-mares away. During the day I stared idiotically around me, unable to be-lieve that I could possibly be here in this heavenly place, alone. I wanted to take hold of something, to break some intangible wall that kept from me the complete realization of such a beautiful peace. I lay on the ground flat on my stomach, and for the first time in my whole life, really looked at a blade of grass. I saw it, and realized it, and the wonder of it shook me. Tiny flowers, buried deep in the grass and weeds, all unseen but perfect, lifted small faces to me. I could not see them enough, nor take in the amazing wonder of them. I lay on my back in the grass and looked at the sky, and felt that I had never seen it,—never had time to lie still and look into the endlessness of it, at the clouds drifting lazily. Heavenly to lie and know that no one could call for a bedpan,—no one could catch me out in some hor-rible mistake.

Some nights the fogs came in from the sea, covering everything with a veil, dimming the lights of the town, making wide streets glisten darkly mysterious. Standing in the damp salty mist, I watched the waves dash, not angrily, but majestically playful, against the stone wall, waves so high that only giants could play in them, rushing up and up, and falling back. My throat ached at the beauty and the smell of it,—so much that I had never seen, though it had always been there. The soft air damply laden with the penetrating odor of the sea, a smell that had been familiar to me a thousand years ago. Drenched with spray and sea damp, I returned to my cottage, closed out the night, knowing that it was still there, and that every day I would see it, and smell it and taste it. I lay down in the darkness to sleep deep, dreamless sleep.

On nights when the moon shone with a radiance that made every twig stand out clear, and the dark shade of the cherry tree blacker still, in my bathing suit I walked across the fields, skirting deep hollows in the sand, following a path through the blackberry briars, to the long sandy beach. I lay on the sand, looking up at the stars, for long hours, with no sound but the swishing, creeping of the waves that came and slid back. Sitting quiet, I saw small crabs that I never saw by day come out and walk tentatively about. Alone with the tiny crabs, and the deep dark sky full of stars, and the silvery yellow moon! I stayed on the beach until late at night, for it seemed that only by remaining could I realize the beauty of it, to know that I was alone, that no bell would ring for me. That no one would suspect me of evil if I came in after ten o'clock. When I returned I took a shower in the cool back yard, and went to bed by the paths of moonlight through the small windows.

I loved the sun and the sea, and every moment of it was a precious gift with which to part was pain, but when it rained, I loved it best. The rain on the sea was a surplus of joy, and to stand on the sandy beach, the rain pouring over me, to walk across the field enveloped in warm summer rain was joy deep in my soul. To lie in my cot listening to its caressing fingers on the shingled roof was the ultimate happiness.

When I had been there three weeks, I told Doctor Parvula that I had no more money for food, and asked him if he would give me a case. "Don't worry," he said, "I'll find something in the neighborhood in a few days. In the meantime, here is five dollars." I hesitated, and he said with annoyance in his voice, "Take it child,—you can return it when I give you a job." And the very next day a lady who lived quite near, fell down and broke her leg, and Doctor Parvula sent me to take care of her. I spent the days with her, except for the one hour that it was necessary for me to be in the bungalow, and I slept at home. For three weeks I made four dollars a day, and I was sorry when her sister came and they dispensed with my services. "I can't understand how I could have fallen down on a perfectly smooth sidewalk," she said to me. I thought to myself, it's an ill wind that blows nobody good.

During the summer I had many letters from Leonard Burke, with whom I had maintained a desultory correspondence since our Botany walks in college, and now he urged me to come south to Kingsville, saying that he could get me a good job. I hated the idea of going back to the South, and as I could barely recall his features, he was, of himself no inducement. But I knew that I must make some plans for the time when I would have to leave my darling house, and so far, I had no place to go.

When my money gave out, Doctor Parvula would give me a case near my house, and I saved some toward the end of the summer, in case I did decide to go to Kingsville. He came to the bungalow only a few times during the summer, and made appointments very seldom, but one day I asked him what he thought I might do in the fall,—telling him about the possibility of a job in Kingsville. He glanced at me and said, "Well, anyway, you look a little less like a beanpole than you did, but another ten pounds wouldn't hurt." That was all he ever said to me of a personal nature, but he had helped me more than any words of mine could tell. Helped me to build up my body and soul so that I could go refreshed for the fight that would surely face me at the end of the summer, wherever I went.

When I had saved enough money for my fare South, I stopped work, and kept carefully for myself the remainder of the summer. Leonard had written that he had been successful in securing an excellent position for me as head of a small private hospital; the salary was one hundred and twenty-five dollars, which was a million to me. I told him that I would take it, and made my plans accordingly.

The fields behind me now were gay with blue asters and yellow golden-rod, but sad too, for there was the first faint inkling of death; the death of long golden summer days. While I had the chance, I tasted to the full the feeling of richness in spendthrift hours, the luxury of sleeping when I pleased, and waking when my eyes chose. After eating to bells, sleeping to bells, praying to bells, thinking to bells, of having every waking minute of my life regulated by a bell, freedom was something to be taken in slowly, turned over on the tongue and savored with a keen palate; to be mulled over, almost held in the hands carefully for fear it might drop and break, shattered forever.

All summer I had had nothing to read except a few magazines a patient had given me, but I hadn't really thought about it much. Vaguely I knew that somewhere there were books, but aside from Mrs. Hall's library I had not seen them; some time I would find them, and read them all, but not this summer. My whole waking life was so filled with living and being happy that I couldn't bother just then. For the first time in my life I spent a summer with Belinda Dan, and on the whole I had found her companionable. At least I had not been bored for one minute, and I felt that given the opportunity, I might learn to like her.

The nights became cooler, the color of the sunlight changed almost imperceptibly; the last of the autumn flowers flaunted themselves defiantly in the fields behind, and clear to the sea. The first slight but unmistakable signs that summer had gone, came and found me unprepared, reluctant to go. I dallied with the idea of asking Doctor Parvula to let me stay forever, wondering how cold it would be in winter. I filled my bowls with blue asters, knowing in my soul that the end was upon me. Leaves changed colors, and many had already fallen, when I knew that I must face reality, the horrible reality of leaving. I left my Promised Land, setting out for one which might or might not be promising, for it was unknown and frightening.

Chapter 14

With a heavy heart I boarded a train for the South, unable to look forward with enthusiasm either to the job or to meeting Leonard Petit Burke. In his letters he had assumed a proprietary air that awakened in me no answering spark, but so far it was an intangible thing and I decided to bide my time and await developments. He had abandoned his idea of being a lawyer, which he had discussed with such determination on our walks in College, and had been studying for the Ministry. While I had no right to discourage him, if that was where his heart lay, still it seemed to me a bizarre occupation for a healthy man well over six feet tall.

He met me at the train, and for a moment I didn't recognize him, but he apparently had no difficulty in recognizing me, and rushed to me with cheerful greetings. With an efficient celerity he whisked my suitcase from my hand and piloted me quickly into a nice little restaurant where we had lunch. He looked well, and upon inspection, I was forced to admit that he had improved over my recollection of him. We talked a little of the girls and boys we had known in Troy, and then I asked him to tell me about the hospital, explaining to him my feeling of inadequacy. He dismissed that as inconsequential, saying, "Now don't you worry! The doctors here are keen on Northern-trained nurses, and they'll treat you all right. Just don't take it too seriously at first." That cheered me a little, and I said, "Well, Leonard, how are you? How is your work?" His face lighted up and he said, "Everything is fine; I'm going to my first charge in a few months; to a place called Boone Valley, about forty miles out in the country." I tried to display interest, and he continued, "The Lord's work takes time, Belinda, but I've got all my life to give to it, and I want to bring as many souls as I can, to God."

Embarrassed, I said, "How wonderful!" He continued with great fervor, "Yes, these farmers need the teachings of Jesus and it will be my privilege to do it!" His face was blazing with a flame of passionate sacrifice and love, but I felt miserable, ashamed. I didn't know just why. Turning to me, he took my hand in his and gazing fervently into my face, he said, "And for you too, Belinda, it will be a wonderful life! You will be my shield and buckler; together we will accomplish great things for God!" In sheer panic I cried out, "Now, now, just a minute, Leonard! I'm not good enough for that sort of life. Don't depend on me, for I'm no shield, and certainly no buckler, for any man!" He smiled happily, and privately I thought, maybe he is taking the great need of the farmers for granted, as he is me . . . but I didn't want to hurt his feelings, he was obviously so sincere. As he paid for our lunch, and picked up my suitcase, he said, "I'm not worrying about that, Belinda. I've always known you were the one girl who could help me in the Lord's work, and when you meet Doctor Simpson, my superior in the Field, you will feel just as I do, that it will be a good life for you and me." Wondering who this paragon was, who was going to make everything clear, I followed him out to a trolley.

At the hospital he introduced me to the young house physician, and left me to my fate. The doctor's name was Fitzhugh, and I learned later what should have been apparent at a glance, that he was one of The Fitzhughs. He was politely charming, and said, "I'll show you to your rooms and when you are ready, I'll show you over the hospital." He took me to the third floor rear, and said, "Now don't hurry; any time you're ready will be all right with me," and setting my suitcase down, he left me.

My rooms were comfortable, a bedroom, sitting room and bath looking out on a rather nice garden. I bathed and dressed in my best uniform, put on the freshest cap imaginable, and descended, looking about for Doctor Fitzhugh. A pretty young nurse said, "Ah rekon youah Miss Dan, ahn't you?" and when I said yes, that I was looking for Doctor Fitzhugh, she said casually, "Shuah, Ah'll show you his office."

He was seated calmly smoking, but rose at once, offering me a chair with real Southern courtesy. We talked, and he said, "It's so near supper now, we'll wait until afterwards to see the hospital." He took me to the dining room, and we watched the nurses come in, fifteen of them, with three head nurses. When they were all seated, he rose and with a great many flowery phrases, introduced me to them. My knees felt weak, and I could not think, but trembling, I stood up and managed to say, "I'm very happy to be here," and sat down. It was horrible, and I wished that I had died early that morning. I, a shield and buckler!

After supper Doctor Fitzhugh showed me all the hospital, and back in my room I felt completely sunk. I wished that I were older, more experienced. I thought, "Now I am in the same position that so many have held over me; how shall I conduct myself? How show the fairness and justice which so frequently is lacking in women over women?" I wished that I could run away, but necessity, and a certain pride and desire to succeed forced me to go on with what I had begun.

This hospital was different from any I had known, and for a week I observed, saying nothing. I met all the patients and read their charts. I was assistant in the operating room, but as there were rarely more than three cases a day, it was not difficult. What did worry me was the dirt, actual filth, everywhere I looked. That and the fact that there was a total absence of discipline. I had been trained so thoroughly in military tradition to stand when in the presence of a superior, that to see the nurses lolling casually before me, and the doctors as well, made me forget what I had in mind to say. Even the older physicians received no courtesy, and I went into a conference with myself.

I asked the three head nurses to come to my room one evening, and after a friendly talk, I came boldly out and asked them what they thought about discipline and dirt. I was anxious to hold my job, but not at the price of my conscience in regard to the technical side of nursing. They were charming, but emphatic in their rejection of discipline, and as for dirt, "Well, a little dirt wouldn't hurt anybody," and besides, they weren't maids. One fat blonde, as pretty as a picture, and good-natured to an astonishing degree drawled, "Honey, doan youah botha youah haid about it, we're foah youah anyway." The pronunciation sometimes left me in darkness as to their meaning, and I had been raised in the South. They left me in a charming good humor, and I was more puzzled than ever. Oh! If only Miss Merryweather were here to advise me! I felt completely alone, entirely futile, and I pulled the covers over my head and wept.

The uncleanness of the establishment gave me to pause. Not only were the semi-private wards dirty, but the private, paying patients had long dirty nails, and lay on bed linen gray and unwholesome-looking. The bathtubs were dingy from the accumulation of years. Practically nothing was ever sterilized, and instruments used on one patient were frequently used on another without being sterilized in the interim. In my bed at night I saw all the unclean articles marching before me; the fact that infection had not spread seemed to belie all that I had been taught. But the nurses were charming, and Doctor Fitzhugh was full of co-operation, on the surface; my experiences with young interns led me to reserve my opinion on that point.

On my afternoon off duty, Leonard came to take me out to see the town. He showed me a monument of a General on a horse, frozen forever in a state of constant parade, his iron coat tails blown forever back by iron winds. He took me to a cemetery and to the battlefields, pointing out historically important items. Exuding kindness and love, but infinitely boring. Carefully pontifical in his choice of words, he spoke already as he would in the pulpit. I told him of my difficulties, of the dirt, and lack of discipline, and he was amused in a fatherly way. "Don't take things too seriously; if they are dirty, they have a good record out there, so why should you worry?" I was surprised, as he went on casually, "Just let things ride, and take your salary. Do the best you can, and leave the rest to God!" That made me madder than a wet hen.

"But you can't expect God to wash the bathtubs, or can you? Or change the sheets, or would you? If you were ill, would you like that sort of thing done to you? Or me, if I were ill?" He looked pained, and said, "What you don't know won't hurt you; I advise you to drop the argument, do what they want, and take your salary." This from a man of God. He went on, "Besides, a great many wonderful people lived to ripe old ages before we ever heard of sterilization. God will look after His own." Obviously I was distinctly *not* one of His own.

As an experiment, I casually said to one of the younger nurses, "Miss Layton, will you please clean Mrs. Hill's finger nails this morning?" Her jaw dropped, and in an aggrieved drawl she said, "Why Miss Dan! Youah cain't expect me to do that sort of thing! Afta all, Ah'm no manicurist, ah'm a nurse!" I tried to talk to one of the older attending physicians, but I don't think he ever knew quite what I was talking about. He was a Southern Gentleman, and no Lady ever spoke of such things. I saw the nurses' bathtubs, and they also wore a band of deep mourning, and I wondered how they could put their ladylike bodies in them. I asked the head nurse who was supposed to clean the tubs, and she drawled from her sprawling position in a wicker chair near the desk, "Thuh Nigga maids," so I spoke to one of them about it, and a broad grin of the friendliest possible nature spread over her black face, and she said, "Lawd chile, Ah'll scrub dem ole tubs t'day; doan youah fret yousef anny moah." But they were elusive, and the tubs did not get scrubbed. I tried another doctor, and he said, "Ah, yes, tub.

Ummmm yes, now Ah, the bathtubs; well now, don't you botha yoouah haid about it; just let things take thair cose." Then I felt that I had a course to take and took it. Alone, confused, with no one to advise me, I took steps.

Calling a meeting of all the nurses except those necessary on the floors, I stood up and faced them and fought for my ideals, for my beliefs and my job. Honestly, simply, I told them how hard I had worked to learn to be a nurse, how I felt about dirt and discipline; how impossible it was for me to abandon all the technical skill I had acquired by years of effort because I believed from my experience that it was right. I told them that I was anxious to hold my job, that I needed it badly, but that if I could not run a hospital to which it was safe for a patient to come I would give it up. I made no sentimental plea, I simply told them how I felt, and wanting to burst into tears, I calmly asked them to think it over, and discuss it freely, and to give me their decision, one week from that night. I got away as quickly as possible, leaving some of them making voluble protestations against my suggested departure, and in my room I wept a little. With no one to advise me, I had to follow my nose, which might or might not have a mind behind it.

When Leonard met me on my day off, I told him exactly what I had done, and annoyed, impatiently he said, "You're very foolish to make an issue of it; if you had more patience you would accomplish more in the end, besides receiving a pretty good salary." A wee small voice told me that there was a modicum of common sense lurking somewhere in what he said, and at the same time I thought it a pretty worldly viewpoint from a man who was panting for righteousness. What I wanted terribly at that moment was tenderness and love. On our way to church, where we were going to meet the wonderful Doctor Simpson, we quarrelled vulgarly. Just before entering, I said, "Leonard, let us not quarrel; let us be friends," and he grinned as he used to when we walked in the fields at Troy.

Doctor Simpson was a plump man of forty with a pulpit voice. He spoke with vigor, complacency and reason, of the Parable of the Loaves and the Fishes. The rise and fall of his voice carried me back to scenes of my childhood, and I saw again the rain coming across the fields, and I found myself in that too familiar dazed, half-somnolent state. With a start, I snatched myself back, hoping Leonard had not noticed. We waited for the last hymn, my old *bête noire*, "Stand up, stand up for Jesus," and when the congregation had dispersed, Doctor Simpson came down to us. Leonard introduced us, and I rather liked his handclasp, and the casual way he said, "I'm starved; can't we find a bite somewheres?"

Seated in a little tea Shoppe, he asked me what I was doing and I told him of my difficulties. He listened and asked very sensible questions, showed intelligent sympathy, but offered no remedy, and abandoning me completely, he said to Leonard, "Well, Brother Burke, when do you take up the sword in the Battle of the Lord?" As when a child, I saw little lambs all covered with blood, and wondered why God was so militant. Leonard, his face beaming, said, "In the spring. Doctor, I'm being sent to Boone Valley, where I feel sure a great work awaits me!" Doctor Simpson buttered his bread and said, "That's good! The poor need the love of God brought to them, just as much as the rich!" Timidly I said, "But haven't they got it? Must it be brought to them?" He waggled a fat finger as to a naughty child and said, "We are discussing serious things, Miss Dan, and I must ask you to consider them seriously." I wanted to tell him that I was serious, but he turned again to Leonard. Brother Burke! I could hardly help laughing, I don't know why.

They continued their conversation and I heard the words Good and Evil, Love, and Hate, also salaries, and livings, with my mind really on the hospital until it was time for me to leave them. I went to bed with an aching head through which scuttled thoughts of Leonard, Simpson, bathtubs, my job, Stand up for Jesus, where to go next, until I slept.

The week passed quickly, and now I sat while their spokesman, a tall dark handsome girl named Missouri Ball, stood and read to me their resolutions, the gist of which was that although they liked me personally and appreciated my training, which undoubtedly was suitable for Northern nurses, they felt that it was unsuitable for Southern nurses. They deeply regretted their inability to accept my ideas, but as I had been honest with them, they could do no less. I thanked them, told them that I had enjoyed knowing them socially—at which they laughed good-naturedly—but that the situation settled itself. They argued, protesting that we could compromise, but I knew that it was the end. I told Doctor Fitzhugh that I would like to be relieved as soon as possible; dear old Doctor Muhlenberg, through his whiskers said, "Oh! Youth! Impatient! Cain't let well enough alone! Damned shame!"

As I had nowhere to go, when several doctors asked me to remain in the city and do private nursing, I decided to try it. They were all courteous, charming to the last gasp, but indifferent to the simplest rules of asepsis; casual toward the fact that enema tubes were used frequently and never boiled, that bed linen grew gray in the service, that the bathtubs got the stripes, that sterile gloves were a myth. Heigh Ho! So I packed my suitcase and left, amidst loud protestations of regret.

I found a cheap room and while I waited for a case, I walked around the city a lot. The leaves were falling and a dismal wind blew them disconsolately about,—sadness filled my heart. Leonard took me to prayer meetings and religious gatherings, where I met his friends. Some of them were young, and full of a passionate desire to be and do good, but the old ones looked awfully tired of being and doing good. Thin, sallow and dyspeptic, jealousies throve among them; envy of the richer appointments. The women were a sad lot; many of them buxom and gray, with pinched faces, with innumerable white-faced children oozing adenoids and prominent teeth. But I was determined to find good in them, not to question.

Perhaps the fact that Leonard wanted me and made it plain that he needed me, was the main factor in leading me more and more into something as foreign to my soul as China. When I was away from him the idea became fantastic; with him his zeal and sincerity acted as a hypnotic. Soon I was involved in an engagement and a life devoted to God laid out before me whether I willed it or no. Another thing that intrigued me was that by expressing a strong desire to become a missionary, I could go to school and be educated. I made careful inquiries, for my longing for education was only dormant and at the slightest encouragement sprung up overnight. I was even willing to become religious if by that method I could be educated.

We had one big fight which started after we left a meeting at which a famous missionary had spoken, and lasted well into the night. I said, "Leonard, why do they talk always of love, never of hate?" He stared at me and patiently explained, "Because love is the highest emotion of which we are capable, and the love of God is the highest manifestation of that capacity to love; hate is the most ignoble expression of which we are capable, and it must be crushed, stamped out!" His voice trembled with his passionate sincerity. "But Leonard," I said, "hate can be a grand and healthy emotion; it depends on what we hate, and why." He stopped, and with sorrow in his voice, he said, "Please, Belinda! Don't have such wicked thoughts. It is monstrous, blasphemous!" I didn't want to make him unhappy, but I still thought to myself, I hate many things: stupidity, lying, hypocrisy, dirty bathtubs, and cruelty,—above all cruelty. But I saw that it would not do to continue along that line, and edged over to the weather.

A Doctor Gillespie called me for a case, gave me the address and said that he would be along soon,—for me to go on over. I packed my bag for the night, and found the patient living in a four-roomed apartment opening immediately off the street, a down-at-the-heel thoroughfare. The family consisted of my patient, her husband, and two children. Questioning her, I made myself as useful as possible while we waited for Doctor Gillespie's arrival. He didn't come, so I put the children to bed, and the husband, a thin little runt of a man, came home tired from work, so I made up a couch for him in the one large room in which the patient lay.

Doctor Gillespie came about nine and gave me a few orders, and as he was leaving, I took him aside and said, "Do you want me to stay up with her tonight?" He said, "Oh no, it won't be necessary. You can go to bed as soon as you've done the things I've ordered," and I asked, "Where?" He looked annoyed and said, "With the patient, of course." I said nothing further, but I knew darn well that nothing would induce me to get in bed with any patient. I sat up all night in the bathroom, and as early as possible next morning I went to Doctor Gillespie's office. I told him that he would have to send another nurse, for I would not sleep with a patient. He looked astonished, and said, "Why, I never heard of such a thing; all my nurses sleep with the patient if it's a woman. She's a nice woman." I said I was sorry, but I wouldn't sleep with even a nice woman. His mouth twisted in a sneer and he said, "Perhaps you wouldn't object if the patient was a man, and a nice man." Angry, but wary, I said, "Is that your before-breakfast humor?" He smiled bitterly and said, "Not very nice, was it?" Tired and depressed, I said, "Oh, that's all right." He suddenly said, "Will you have dinner with me tonight?" and I said, "I'd love to."

I had been told that Doctor Gillespie was the best surgeon in the city, when he was sober, but unfortunately that was seldom. His clothes were shabby and his battered hat remained on his head by mystic persuasion, placed at an angle to tax one's belief. He looked lonely, driven, and his sharp brown eyes held a whipped look. When he called for me that evening, in a battered old gray, low-swung car, his hat was still perched at a perilous angle. Climbing in, I felt that I was taking my life in my hands, for I saw that he was distinctly drunk.

We rattled off, and he drove out of the city, past the battlefields, heading for open country, he singing loudly and dolefully, "For I lost my love in the Alamo!" Something in his voice made me want to cry, but then I wanted to cry anyway, so maybe it wasn't his voice at all. After a long time I said, "Where are we going?" He stopped his lament long enough to say, "Nevea you mind, sista," and drove on. Well, I didn't mind.

He drove into the yard of a farmhouse and parked his tin box. We went into a big room with an open fire. At first I couldn't see much but gradually a number of faces and figures became clear, as they called out, "Hi thar, Doc! Have a drink." Doctor Gillespie drawling, "Thanks, don't mind if I do," took a bottle from one of the men and poured a generous drink into a thick glass. They seemed to know each other well, and from their conversation I learned that they were railroad men. No one spoke to me, Doctor Gillespie said nothing to explain my presence, and when the negro, who could be seen in the back, cooking, brought food in, we all sat at the long table and ate. While they left me alone, I watched them and thought.

What I thought was what I had thought many times before, which was that men have the best of it. When they are blue, or rattled, or confused, they can get drunk, become rowdy, or go with a woman, and still be acceptable to society. But if I were in the same mood, I could go to prayer meeting with Leonard. Men are free to have women at any time they wish, but what is a woman going to do? Here I had been going about with a big six-foot of healthy man of God for three months, and had he kissed me? Once, meagrely. And would I marry him and help save the souls of farmers in Boone Valley, when I'd prefer saving their crops? Probably. And if I didn't, then what? Well, I could go on nursing . . . if I could bring myself to sleep with the patient, if any. If not why not? And why shouldn't I get drunk, as Doctor Gillespie could and did? Because by tomorrow I would be out on the street and not a doctor would give me work. A girl is not supposed to have the same desires that men have, for drink, or men. Says who? These things I pondered, as often before. When we had eaten, we all sat around the fire, and the men sang lustily, yet sadly. With no banging of steins literally or metaphorically. With a sadness that had some weird joy in it, they sang lugubrious songs like "The Wreck of the Old Ninety-Seven," their voices sadder than death.

> They gave him his orders in Monroe, Virginia,
> Saying Pete you're away behind time,
> This is not thirty-eight, but ole 97,
> You must put her in the centre on time . . .
> . . . .
> Ladies . . . you must take warning,
> From now and this time on,
> Never speak harsh words to a fond loving husband,
> He may leave you and never return.

They loved the sadness, and when Pete was scalded to death by the steam, tears rolled down their seamed, work-worn faces, due in part no doubt to the liquor. They were happy, and when they went on to tougher, bloodier songs, they wallowed in a sad sort of joy. I loved it too and sang with them, but their male voices sounded pitiful in the night, weighed down by horror, sadness, and death.

The fire burned down, flickered and died; two women came in, whether wives or otherwise, I didn't bother to wonder, for I was sleepy and, at twelve, Doctor Gillespie got up unsteadily, but with great dignity, gave a graceful, if jerky sweep of his battered old hat, stuck it at its perilous angle and said, "Good night, boys," and I followed him out, leaving those men sitting in the half-light, their weathered, unshaven faces picked out by the smoking oil lamp. When I came out the night was so beautiful that I hoped I would die instantly, without further worry. I saw my little house in Allenhurst, the paths of moonlight across the floor, and heard the sound of the waves swishing on the beach, and my heart was nigh to bursting. Looking up at the sky, a black velvet canopy so full of stars you couldn't put your finger down, I thought, Doctor Gillespie is drunk, and may smash us, but what of it? I hope he does.

He drove that old car so surely, almost unconsciously, around curves, over high hills, across long flat stretches of rough road, singing at the top of his power, "For I lost my love in the Alamo!" He handed me a coat, for the night was chilly; closing my eyes I wished that I could go on forever, and never have to face grim reality. The cool breeze was soothing, the stars close. He drove me right to my door, and I got out. He said, "Thanks," and with a great sputtering, continued on his lonely way. We had not exchanged a word all the way home, and it had been grand. As I dozed off, I wondered what Brother Burke would think of such doings . . . I needn't wonder; I knew. But I had loved it.

Leonard asked me when I would marry him, and I said, "Oh, I don't know. Let us wait a while." Looking hurt, he said, "I'd like to announce our engagement before I am sent to Boone Valley. Don't you want to come with me, then? We could be married, and go right into our work for the Lord." But I hedged, and said I would tell him in another week. In the meantime, his sister had been very nice to me, and his father, who had been a minister, but on account of his health had retired and ran a small real-estate office, was a dear, but I wanted to hear from my sister Adelaide.

She had married again, and was living in Carleton, so I wrote her of my difficulties in the hospital and all about Leonard, asking her advice. As usual, she wrote long friendly letters, in which she said, "Concerning marriage, don't rush. There is always another man; take your time. Personally I can't imagine you married to a minister." Everything seemed closing down on me; I saw no light, and felt almost indifferent. The doctors who had, with their well-known gallantry, urged me to remain, had with Southern reliability, given me no work, and my money was fast disappearing. I found myself afraid to face facts; either the Lord, or what? I didn't know.

The week passed, and Leonard came to take me to a party his great friend Doctor Simpson was giving, and on the way there he put his arms around me and said, "Cain't I tell them tonight that you are going to marry me? I want them to know what a great help I am going to have in my work." I wanted to scream and beat him, I pitied him so, and he was such an ass, really, and at the same time so appealing, which should be a legal offense. Why could I not say to him, "I will not marry you and be your helper! I'm *not* a good girl, and do not want to be!" I don't know unless it was the awful economic struggle that women face, that unconsciously drives them to run to any port in a storm. Calmly I said, "Yes, Leonard." He kissed me chastely on my brow. Twiddle de dee, twiddle de dum.

Doctor Simpson was still blondly fat, still charming with an eye to the main chance, here as well as in heaven. His meek wisp of a wife was fluttery in her duties as hostess, and the others exuded good fellowship. Leonard told them, his handsome face beaming, holding my hand proudly. I felt lower than the seaweed. They were effusive in their congratulations, all trying to say the right thing. Doctor Simpson made a point of telling me that I was getting a mighty fine boy in Brother Burke, as he consumed gingerbread and iced tea, "one of our young workers who will do great things for the Lord," munch munch, "yes sir, a fine young Christian." His complacency was exasperating, and I wanted to say, "Hey, listen, and I'll tell you what he is getting,—a girl who doesn't know her own mind, who is not one whit interested in saving souls, not even her own; a fool girl who is still hoping for something beautiful to happen to her; someone who will change the color of life, who will make every morning a joy, and every night a heaven to go to." And plenty more, but it was a nightmare, and I said, "Yes, Doctor Simpson, I know, and I'm very proud of him."

As we walked home, I felt a great desire to know Leonard, to somehow get in touch with him. He talked so beautifully about God, and I tried to react as he reacted, to feel as he felt, but my heart was still. "To know God, and to experience His great love is the most profound and satisfying experience that can come to man," he said. "But Leonard, what if I never feel as you do? How then can we ever really be married? How can I be a good wife to you?" I asked. He held my arm and laughed happily, saying, "I'm not worried about that! You pretend to be worse than you are, my dear Belinda! You are a fine girl, and you will soon come to see the beauty of a life of service to God." How little he knew! If I told him half the wicked thoughts I had, they would curdle his blood! As we walked along, under the stars, I said to him, "It seems to me that we are caught in some mysterious game of chance,—we are moved about like pawns, with no choice. Some of the moves are personal, ruthless, or kind, and glorious, but all chance!" Solemnly he answered me, "No, Belinda, we always have a choice. God gives us the capacity to choose; we may know heartaches, but to struggle against evil forces that destroy the world, to work for a good and glorious life is a fine thing, a choice that is offered to us by our heavenly Father."

His voice rang out strong and true and sure, in the silent night, and something inside me wept with loneliness. I thought, he is really good, and I am not. I wish I could be like him! But the night was lovely and I wanted to love some man as he loved God, and I couldn't switch from one to the other readily. He left me at my door with a firm handshake, and said, "Good night, Belinda. God keep you!" I wished that for once, just once, he would crush me to him, and kiss me and love me without thinking of God, but maybe that was the devil in me.

I went slowly up the stairs to my room, wondering why there was no joy in me. Undressing, I thought, "Is this what I have dreamed of? Am I looking for something that happens only in stories?" I wanted to want to sing and laugh with joy that I had found my mate! There should be, surely, real, deep, bounding joy in one's soul when one has found one's mate, and marries. "Where *is* this joy? Why am I like dead, my heart sad?" The word Mate stuck in my mind, and returned with redoubled force just as I slipped under the covers and lay quiet. The word held me and I allowed it to possess me wholly in its entire significance. Mate . . . married. I would get in bed with Leonard, lie close to him, close as are people who are in love. Stillness held the room, the street outside, and for the moment a stillness held my heart, from the impact of the knowledge of what marriage meant. An insignificant molecule, lying in the dark, yet somehow I reacted individually, when the enormity of the fact thoroughly possessed me.

Suddenly I got up and dressed, packed my suitcase, left a note with what

I owed her for the landlady, and crept quietly down the stairs and out to the street. Standing in the early morning light I felt that I was closing another door, a book, some past and unreal life which I could scarcely remember,— knew I must go on, make still another beginning, painful as rebirth, until I found some place where I felt at home; people with whom I could rest and be myself. The refrain of drunken Doctor Gillespie's song came to me, and I sang quietly to myself, "For I lost my love in the Alamo," as I hoofed it down the street, lugging my heavy suitcase. Free! I felt free, if only for that moment.

Near an all-night dog wagon I picked up a cab, and as the chauffeur started, he said, "Where to, Miss?" I was confused. Remembering my sister Adelaide, I said, "To the station." As we trundled along, the chauffeur joined me in a touching rendition of, "Oh, Ladies, from this take warning, from now and this time on," and in my joy at being free, I tipped him a whole quarter.

I found that no train left for Carleton for two hours, so when the chauffeur carried my suitcase in, I told him to check it, and have a cup of coffee with me. We went to a small place near the station, where railroad men and chauffeurs ate, and sitting on high stools, drinking coffee from thick mugs like old-fashioned shaving mugs, I inspected the funny little chauffeur. He was about thirty-five, with thin reddish hair, big ears and keen blue eyes. His nose was no more than a button holding the rest of his face together; his grin was infectious, a sort of idiotic giggle. But the most noticeable thing about him was his hands. They were unusually large, and beautifully made; strong, giving a feeling of steel, and yet very gentle,—alien entirely to the nondescript body. He caught me staring, and grinned. "Everybody stares at my hands," he said. "Ma says they're all I got from my famous ancestors." Interested, I asked, "Who were your famous ancestors?" He twisted shyly, and said, "A man named Beauregard; that's my name. But I tell Ma it don't do me no good," and he laughed his silly giggle. Turning on his stool, he bragged, "I can play a mouth organ fine. Want to hear me?" I said, "Yes, but not here; they'll put us out."

He paid for our coffee and I followed his bandy legs to the taxi, and got in the front with him. "We'll go where nobody can hear me," he said. He drove to a quiet spot beyond the straggling houses and stopped. Scratching around in his tool kit, he brought out a mouth organ; wiping it carefully with a grimy rag, he slowly raised it to his mouth, licking his lips; slowly, with reverence, he cupped his hands over it and began to play. He forgot about me and I forgot about my train; he made the most beautiful music imaginable. Unbelievable sounds came from that harmonica, and when I realized presently that I must return, I plucked at his sleeve reluctantly. "I'm sorry,—about my train," I said. He stopped, grinned his foolish grin and said, "How'd ya like it?" I told him I loved it.

At the station he retrieved my bag, and standing on the steps I thanked him for a lovely evening; he waved his beautiful hand and said, "Good-by and good luck!" and I called back, "I'm going to need a lot of it," and went into the day coach for Carleton. During the long night ride, I tried to focus my mind on what had been happening to me since I left Allenhurst, but nothing made sense. Figures floated around, and I found to my horror that I couldn't recall Leonard's face. I must be crazy!

Hungry, but not stopping for breakfast at the station in Carleton, I got on a trolley that took me to the Square,—the same square in which I had left my father thousands of years before, changed for another one, got off at Ashland Avenue and walked the five blocks to my sister's little house. It was heavenly to see her again, and while we had breakfast I told her everything. That is, all the obvious things, for I couldn't explain to her what had been going on inside me, important to me. My departure from Kingsville became funny, and it wasn't, really. I could not tell her why I had done what I had done; the wall of embarrassment that is strongest between relatives, even if they are friends, made it impossible.

Certain incidents in my life had taught me to conceal myself from my family: first, the remark that I had heard my mother make when I was playing on the floor. Another came from a remark Kingsland Mears had made to me as we sat on stools eating ice cream. He scolded me because I had not been home to see my father and mother; I said, "Why should I go? What have they ever done for me? They brought me into this world of their will,—I did not ask to come here" (that age-old cry of stupid youth, which is a lie, for in our hearts we are glad they did arrange for us to be here, and we wouldn't miss it for the world, in spite of our struggles). King looked sad and said, "What do you *want* from them? They are poor, and old!" Angrily I flung at him, "All that I want is a little love!" Hitching himself around on the stool, bringing his face close to mine, he said eagerly, "Linda, what you want, I got it!" I had foolishly told one of my sisters and for years, every opportunity was grasped to use that phrase, "What you want, I got it," accompanied by peals of laughter. I never told anything important again.

When I told Adelaide about Leonard she laughed and said, "I do think you are quite mad, but if you don't want to marry him, why do it? Forget it;

he will." But I felt a traitor to him, and wondered why things tore one in every direction at once, how I could ever know what to do?

My sister wanted me to stay in Carleton with her, as her husband, a long, loping, good-natured young man named Lawrence Lewis, a salesman of machinery, was frequently away. So I went to see a few of the doctors, many of whom had known my sisters Adelaide and Lucille for years. One of them, named Donald Martin, was young, unmarried, and the legitimate prey for all husband-seeking girls in the town. He had been in love with my beautiful sister Lucille for years, and no one knew why they had never married. He was very handsome,—a perfect type for a successful Society doctor. He was nice to me, and promised to give me the very first good case he had. Leaving my telephone number with many doctors, and having seen that my uniforms were in perfect order, I said to Adelaide, "I think I'll go visiting," and she thought it a grand idea. "You must go to see Celia," she said. Excitedly I said, "Is Celia here? But where? Gosh, I'm dying to see her!" And she told me that Celia had her house, and her babies, and was happy. I went there first.

Celia had a large old wooden house with a yard and trees, just as she had wanted it. I knew by her face that she had achieved her heart's desire. She had eighteen babies from six months to ten years, but the number varied she told me, as they got adopted, and some were sent on to other places, once she got them well. They were sent to her from different charities,—it seemed to be a sort of clearing house for children. With only a young country girl to help, Celia did all the work,—the cooking, bathing and feeding those too small to feed themselves. Her face shone with love and pride as she showed me over the house, and the children displayed their love for her, as she moved about smilingly among them. Sick ones and well ones, black ones and white ones, Celia loved them all.

Holding a tiny girl close, she said to me over her head, "This one leaves me next week; I hate it, but she's going to a good home, which makes it all right." She put the baby girl down in her crib, and as she smiled at me and laughed, her eyes were wet behind her glasses. "I'm a fool," she said, "I never want to part with them." In another room we met a sturdy boy of five, straight and strong, with roguish brown eyes, who held his hand behind his back and said, "Guess!" Celia said, "A ball!" He beamed and cried, "Nope, guess again!" Celia laughed and said pleadingly, "Oh, Tommy! You know I can never guess! You'll have to tell me!" He held out a dirty fist and slowly, slowly opened his fingers. On his palm lay a perfect acorn. We showed sufficient astonishment to satisfy him, his eyes sharp to see if we really were surprised. As we went on, Celia said, "Tommy goes tomorrow." In the kitchen we prepared food for them and I asked, "Where is Tommy going?" Celia carefully measured milk into a yellow bowl and said, "To a farm, a healthy country woman who has seven of her own and has adopted four besides Tommy." Appalled, I said, "But, Celia, she can never raise them all!" Celia broke an egg into the bowl and said, "She will,—you'd be surprised. They are poor, but they have good food and fresh air, and the older children all work and help her. Besides, they have love, and you know that makes up for an awful lot of other things." I thought of, "what you want, I got it," and I told her of my children's ward at Montrose,—that I had been happier there than in anything I had ever done.

Leaving, I said to Celia, "If I come back will you let me stay here with you?" and she smiled, "Any time! But you won't come back." Sad, I asked, "How do you know? I may be back tomorrow!" Thoughtfully she said, "I know you won't come back because you have not yet found something you are searching for,—and you'll never rest until you find it." Dear Celia, thus she spoke. "If you think that, do you think I ever will find it?" I asked. Her gentle, sweet face clouded and she hesitated, then said, "I don't know. You won't find it until you know what it is you're looking for,—and you don't know. And I don't know." We parted, and I didn't go back. As the years have passed, I have envied Celia. She alone of all my friends knew what she wanted and was happy when she got it. I was glad for her, but sad for me.

I visited Faith Charron and was shocked to see so great a change in her. From a petite beauty she had become an enormously fat woman, without her front teeth. Her hair still curled around her face, her eyes sparkled with health, and she laughed happily as she explained that the dentist had said that so many pregnancies had ruined her teeth; that she was having some made . . . she talked on, screaming above the noise of her children who were madly playing Indian. "How many are there?" I screamed as they raced past us. "Eight," she yelled back. "Six boys and two girls!" They were healthy, handsome children.

I saw the stairs that I used to polish until they shone like mirrors, now unrecognizable, for not a particle of paint remained; indeed, in places the wood itself was so worn that splinters came off. They were the emblem of all that I had worked for, fought for, in my life. What mattered it now that I had wept bitter tears on those steps? For what? I wanted to destroy them, and all the work that I had done to get an education . . . where was the good?

Faith told me that Mrs. Pierson had died, and many changes been made in the household. Our conversation was constantly interrupted by the sound of things falling or being thrown, and I soon left. The fine house I had known was now practically a ruin, filled to bursting with new life, which seemed more beautiful to me. On my way home I wondered how it was that these old friends of mine had found their places in life, where they were happy, and I could not? What was it I sought? With one part of me I could be Celia, and happy; with another part of me I could be Faith, and happy, but another part of me could be neither. I tried to think, but thoughts seemed useless for thinking.

I visited the Cartwrights, and they welcomed me as though I had never been away, with their enormous capacity for making one at once a part of their lives and their home. Etienne had become quieter, and when I asked where Diana was, she gave me a peculiar look, saying, "Later." The younger ones I had known as babies were big girls now, and demonstrated the same passionate reactions that had fascinated me in the older ones. Violet, who had been named so because of her eyes, had surprised them by changing into a dark child with black eyes. The home was the same casual hive I had known, minus the few pieces of beautiful furniture,—dropped probably en route; only the piano remained, older, more battered, but still the important part of the collection. I spent the night with them and experienced the well-remembered difficulty in finding pillow or blanket.

Breakfast proceeded along the familiar lines. When it became apparent that only one cup and saucer was intact, no apology was offered or thought of, as Doris poured and offered it to me first. Knowing the system, I drank as quickly as possible, and when Doris offered it next to Mr. Cartwright, he gave it to Etienne in a manner that somehow removed us to a beautiful scene, of richness and plenty. As the cup worked its way around, it finally became his, and with sharp eyes the children watched to see that his coffee was hot and the cup full. It was a noisy happy time and he made us laugh so we couldn't notice the absence of food. But Doris looked pale and tired,—perhaps too much charm had worn her down, unmixed with a few practical items like clothes and food. Borrowing a plate here, a fork there, time moved. Mr. Cartwright went to the piano for a moment, to illustrate some musical point he was elaborating with Etienne, returning in time to see Violet snatch his one piece of toast. He continued his discussion charmingly, unheeding the fight that immediately ensued. The three middle girls considered it their duty to rescue the toast, and loud yells and slapping became furious. The toast was torn in shreds, but finally offered to him with a stately air. Completely undisturbed, he said, "Thank you, darling." He imparted to the most grimy surroundings the feeling of spaciousness, luxury and ease; his personality colored drab everyday incidents with a glow of the unusual. I would erect a monument to him.

When the house was still, Etienne and I sat in the kitchen and talked. She was at that time training in the hospital in Rosedale. We compared notes on the malignancy of head nurses and doctors in general, laughing as much as we swore. When I said, "What of Diana?" her face became drawn and white, and she said tonelessly, "She is dead." Quietly she told me that Diana had become mentally ill, to such a degree it became necessary to place her in a sanitarium for the insane, and there, apparently, she merely pursued her main characteristics of self-effacement and shyness to a complete and final degree, and died. I had no words, nothing to offer Etienne. She knew that I had loved Diana,—it was not necessary to pretend.

After a long silence she said, "Did you know that Maurice was dead, too?" Stunned, I said, "How?" In a flat gray voice she said, "No one knows; he disappeared, and was found in the woods, shot. We never knew why." We looked at each other across the kitchen table. We wanted to know, to make things come out even, but every day our lives had proven that things don't make sense, ever. Etienne knew that I knew, and I knew that we both knew that nothing ever again could quite hurt as much as it used to hurt,— to that extent we were already dead. We had wanted an answer,—we knew now there was none.

One of the most picturesque personalities in Carleton was a doctor named Weldon Gallatin. He had been a friend of my sisters, and later, of mine, for many years. My sister Lucille had brought me to see him when I was a child in boarding school, and I had loved him ever after. He embodied for me all the requirements of a story-book father, and my admiration for him knew no bounds,—which sentiments were held by several hundred females in the town. He was at that time about sixty, tall and handsome, with a criminal amount of charm. He dressed differently from other men, in summer wearing beautiful white suits, his slender waist encircled by a crimson silk sash. That was enough to enthrall any woman, but the enchantment was made complete by the fact that he wore over his evening clothes a long, full, black cloak, which he threw over his shoulders like a Knight, and a high, shining silk hat.

He had always been wonderfully kind to me, and I loved him to distraction, off and on, when I saw him or thought about him. I had sat on his lap as a child, but he was a person from another world, above and beyond. Now he continued to treat me as a child; I wanted to be grown up. Frantic because people spoke of me as "that kid sister of the good-looking Dan girl," when I knew that what they meant was, "that homely" sister of the beautiful Dan girl, I went to him for comfort. Always there was something delicate in his manner, though God knows he was masculine enough. Now he said, "But my dear Belinda, you *are* a child. Don't wish to be grown up; it will be so too soon. Don't mind if you are not as beautiful as Lucille,—be happy and forget it. I love you very much, and if you please me, why bother about all the others?" I knew that he said those things to be kind, but I loved him for it, and told him so. As I was leaving, he held me close in his arms, and seriously said, "I want you to promise me that you will come to me, no matter what difficulties you encounter in this town. Will you?" I assured him that I would, anticipating no particular obstacles—not thinking that I would ever run to him—that I could easily take care of myself.

My sister Lucille had returned from Boston, and had a small apartment in a house run by a Mrs. Kendall. I was often there, and came to know many of the occupants, especially two girls named Dickery and Dockery Deane. Those were their names at this time; with what names they had begun life I never knew. Their mother had been an actress, and possibly they were duly christened so. Seventeen years old, very dark and devoted to each other, they toiled not; whether they spun or not I do not know. If they did, I never caught them at it. I liked them, and my interest was augmented rather than lessened by the opinion of the town that they were bad girls. Dying to know what made bad girls bad, I went about with them, accompanied by Senator Kenneth Bascombe, and his friend, Dave Reynolds, a salesman. So far I had found nothing different about Dickery and Dockery except that at some time in their varied careers, they had had some photographs of themselves made, in which they appeared nude. Their bodies were lovely enough to be photographed, goodness knows, and I saw nothing bad in that. But my sister Adelaide worried, and one day she said to me, "I'm going to tell you something for your own good. I know this town, and you don't. It's poison for any girl who makes one misstep. We're poor people; we've always worked for what we got, and if you spend your time with casual people who have no aims, no roots, you won't be able to make your living in this town. You'll have to watch your every step, every word, or they'll tear you limb from limb. Whether you believe me or not, I'm telling you the truth, as a friend." I knew enough to believe her, and I said, "I know; I won't see the Deane girls any more."

Lucille had written that she was returning, and now we heard that our oldest brother whom I could not recall ever having seen, was coming from Seattle. My sisters began the proverbial fatted-calf preparations, which sickened me. Lucille said, "You might show a little interest in a brother you've never seen!" Hating her sentimentality, I said, "Why? Has he ever shown any interest in me?" She made no reply, but when Adelaide asked me later, "Aren't you curious to see John?" I could not be rude to her, so I said, "No; I've managed to exist without having seen him, and I see no reason to pretend. He is no more to me than any man who might come from Seattle. I imagine there are thousands of them; because we happen purely accidentally to have the same parents doesn't get me all of a twitter." She couldn't understand, but said nothing.

The conquering hero from out of the West arrived. In his case Mr. Greeley should have said, "Take all the cash the old man has, and Go West Young Man, Go West!" When the slush of sentimentality had subsided, he pulled me down on his knees, this handsome stranger from Seattle, and said, "I've got a ticket to take you back with me! Yes sir, I'm going to take my baby sister back and show the fellers something!" Carefully removing myself from his stalwart knees, I said, "I have no intention of going to Seattle with a strange man." He turned to Lucille and angrily said, "Hard and unnatural! There's no feeling in the young folks today!" Furious, I said, "And was there more when you were young? What about your feelings when Father had to sell his mules and hogs to get you out of the Army? Because you whined. What about your leaving and never writing to him, not even to thank him? Oh! I was a baby, but I know all about it! And if I'm hard, what did you ever do to keep me soft? Or my other tall handsome brothers? Have you done anything to keep me from the streets? Have you ever wondered by what method I lived? Don't pull your rotten sentimental family stuff on me, for I'm not having any!" Flinging myself out, banging the door behind me, I walked the streets for hours, blind with rage and hate of everything, especially sentimentality and hypocrisy; sick and miserable, I walked the streets alone.

Doctor Martin, the nice young bachelor, called me for a case in one of the big hotels, and I went happily. The patient was a mild, gentle, thin young man with nose glasses and a straggly blond mustache, about thirty, whose name was Clement Rutherford. Doctor Martin had told me that he wanted terribly to be a drunkard, but his stomach didn't agree, so that he became very ill. He was the son of a very wealthy man who had a magnificent home outside Carleton. He got well much too soon to suit me, for he was so quiet and courteous it was a pleasure to be with him. He was known to have killed a man for some slight discourtesy to a lady, but it was difficult to believe it of so mild a man. In less than a week he was well, and I came home. He seemed lonely, and attached himself to my sister and me, in his shy way, and many nights we went out to dinner with him, or he ate with us at home. He couldn't bear being alone, and liked amusing company.

One night he said, "Let us get the Deane girls and drive to Eagle Rock for dinner." I was surprised that he knew them, but my sister said probably every man within fifty miles of Carleton knew them. I asked her, "Shall I go?" She thought, and said, "Well, I don't think anything bad can happen with Clement Rutherford,—I don't see why you shouldn't." I telephoned and Dockery shrieked, "Party? Did I hear you say Party? Where'll we meet? Shall I bring any men?" I explained about Mr. Rutherford, and that he had said to bring any one they wished. Senator Bascombe came, and Dave Reynolds; we drove twenty miles into the country where we had the usual fried chicken dinner. The men had a drink, but I had none. The Deane girls rarely drank. The night was beautiful, and on the way back we sang all the love songs and sad songs we could remember. Mr. Rutherford was quiet, as usual, but apparently very happy, as we all were.

Back in town the Deane girls said they were spending the night at the Langdon Hotel, and urged me to stay too. "It's after one, and your sister will be asleep," they argued. I was thinking of the expense, and hesitated. Mr. Rutherford said, "If you want to stay I'll be glad to pay for your room, Miss Dan." He had been in my home and certainly knew that I could not waste money, so I said, "Thank you; then I'll stay."

Alone in my room, I felt wide-awake, and wished for something to read. In anticipation of just such a situation no doubt, some religious sect had placed a Bible in the room, and I began to read it. As always I loved it, once I could forget the bitter memories connected with it, and I found myself remembering Kingsland. A knock on the door, and there was Mr. Rutherford, looking very ill. We were both fully dressed. I said, "What's the matter? Come in," and he entered, dropping into a chair. "Shall I phone for Doctor Martin?" I asked, and he said, "No; I don't want to bother him." As I looked at him, wondering what I could do for him, he suddenly rushed to the bathroom and was very ill. When he came out, he looked ghastly. In spite of his objection, I picked up the phone to call Doctor Martin, when there was a knock on the door. Before we could open it, an uncouth-looking fellow banged it open, and stood in the middle of the room, a sly, evil look on his ugly face. I didn't know who he was, but Mr. Rutherford did, and he said, "Well, Mike, what do you want?" The man from the side of his mouth said sneeringly, "You think you're purty smart, don't cha?" We didn't speak, and he went on, "Think ya can put one over on me, did ja? Well, ya may be a slick pair, but ya cain't fool me, so out ya git, Miss." Terrified, sensing what this would do to me, I said, "But you're making a mistake. I'm a nurse for Doctor Martin, and this is his patient, Mr. Rutherford." He smiled disagreeably and said, "Yeah? I've heard that one before, an' I know all the ansers, so git out!" Mr. Rutherford came close to him and said, "Listen, Mike, who put you up to this? How much are you getting? I'll pay you more to run along. How about a hundred? Two?" But that evil man only said, "Oh, no, ya cain't bribe me, Mr. Rutherford; I has my orders, an' I'm goin' to carry 'em out." Angry, I said to Mr. Rutherford, "Don't give him a penny,—that's all he wants," and to the man I said, "Why are you ordering me out, and not Mr. Rutherford? If I've done anything immoral, hasn't he too? Why do you say I've got to go, but not him?" He stood at the door and said, "Them's tha rules; wimmen goes, men stays, and I ain't goin' to waste any more time on ya; come on, hustle, an' git out."

I put my hat on and walked into the hall, sick with fear and sorrow for my sister to know about it. Mr. Rutherford got his coat and hat and we walked down the stairs and out into the street. As he left Mike, he said very quietly, "I wouldn't be surprised if you heard more about this," as we crossed the lobby, stinking with dead cigars. It was just two and the street was empty, our footsteps echoed as we walked along, not knowing just where to go. After a block or two in silence, I said, "Let's go home, where I should have gone in the first place. My sister will make us some coffee,—she'll be glad to see us."

While we drank hot coffee we told her about it, and she was angry and sick, for she knew what gossip would do to me. "Wait until I tell Tom Green what I think of his dirty hotel," she said. "Everybody knows where he got the money to build it!" Mr. Rutherford said, "How?" My sister said, "Of course I can't prove it, but it seems to be a fact that when Stickney and Daniels robbed the bank, they put the money in sacks, and into a suitcase, which they left with a stupid-looking farmer, telling him to keep it for them until they called for it. Unfortunately the farmer only looked stupid, and when they returned he had never seen them before, and had never had a suitcase to hold. So the stupid farmer came into town and built him a fine hotel, and now he is moral! Oh, damn his hotel!"

I appreciated her loyalty but something told me that she could do nothing. Without money one can do nothing, but what stuck in my mind was what happened to women, and what happened to men. I said, "Well, it's over; let us get some sleep." We went to bed, Mr. Rutherford on the couch in the living room, and when I got up next morning he had gone, leaving word that he would see me in a few days. Later in the day the Society Editor of the *Citizen* phoned, asking for details concerning my engagement to Clement Rutherford. I knew then why he had gone so early, and I said, "Don't publish anything until I see you; I'm on my way." In his office I told him the whole story, and that Mr. Rutherford had no desire to marry me nor I him; that he only did it to prevent people talking,—to forget it.

Then I went to see Doctor Martin and told him everything. I begged him to go to the manager of the hotel and explain that Mr. Rutherford was his patient. "What good will that do?" he asked. I said, "I don't know, but surely you won't let this ruin my chance of making a living here?" He smiled and slyly said, "How do I know what Clement was doing in your room?" Aghast, I said, "But I've told you; he was vomiting." He smiled and said, "I may believe you, but who else will?" And then I knew that he didn't believe me either. I got up to go and said, "I'm going to Doctor Gallatin." I knew that he feared and respected Doctor Gallatin, and looking worried, he said, "Don't tell him that I was unsympathetic, will you?" I wanted to slap his face, but I only said, "I'll tell him whatever I wish," and I left, knowing surely now that he was a worm; a pink one.

I told Doctor Gallatin everything, even to the exact words Doctor Martin had used. His beautiful face looked sad, and he said, "Poor boy! He too!" and he sighed. I said, "Doctor Gallatin, I'm thoroughly frightened now. What shall I do? How to live in a world where a girl is put out of a hotel, and a man is not? Where nothing happens to destroy men, but plenty to trip and throw a woman down?" He said seriously, "God help us, Belinda, that's the way the world is, and I'm sad because it is so. It will be difficult for you to understand . . ." I told him how apprehensive I had been, how aware of secret, horrible things in the town, which I could not understand, and he said, "Yes, it is true. I have lived here over twenty years, and I know that it is rotten at the core."

"What makes it so, Doctor Gallatin?" I asked. "Partly because it is a resort, and so many people will do things here they wouldn't in their home towns. Also because so many hundreds of tubercular people are here, who know that their lives are finished, and they are reckless, desperate. All this has infected the natives," he said. "But what am I to do? How hold on to nothing? Is there no beauty? I feel desperately lost! I don't suppose you'd care to marry me, would you, Doctor Gallatin? And let me live quietly with you? I'd be safe with you, and I crave safety. Besides, I trust you, and no other man. And I love you? Could you? Please?"

His face flushed, and he stood up, so beautiful, regal, and putting his arms around me, he kissed me many times. His voice trembled, and there were tears in his eyes when he said, "I'm so proud that you feel like this, to me!" I laughed shakily and said, "Now I've got you weeping too! Don't become an addict, like me!" He said quietly, "It is sweet of you to say what you have, Belinda, and you're so ignorant that you don't know what it means to me; how it touches my heart. I could so easily be a cad, and marry you, but I've got just enough sense left to not do it. You must help me to be decent now. I'm sixty years old, you are twenty-one!" I went to him, and put my arms around him, and said, "Don't you know that that doesn't matter?" He walked away from me, saying, "You think that now, but it will. I'm an old man, and you're still a child; I couldn't hurt you so."

He was so fine, and I loved him so much; I kissed him and said, "Don't think of it any more; don't bother. Darling Doctor Gallatin, I love you enough to marry you if you could manage it, but if you don't feel that you could, that's all right. We'll still be friends, shan't we? And you'll forgive me for whining? And for weeping all over your nice suit?"

He came to me and held me close for a long time, in silence. Then he said, "I wish to God I were a young man! Someday, Belinda, you'll find some one who will love you, and whom you will love. Keep brave,—don't give up your belief in beauty and decency, for it does exist. I swear it! All is not as grimy as this town, and the things that have touched you here. Go away! Take your youth and your courage to another market; it sells too cheaply here! And remember that as long as I live, I love you and am your friend. Come to me any time you need me, or let me know. Will you promise me that?" I said, "Yes, for I'll need a friend, I'm afraid." He kissed me good-by and I left him, healed of the bitter thoughts that had tortured my soul. I took his advice, and left Carleton.

I had very little money, but Adelaide loaned me some, and I again packed my suitcase and started North,—a sadder, if not wiser person than the one who accompanied Isiah. I had learned now that no one cared about me, that by no possible chance could I ever be educated. I could never save enough in nursing to go to school, not if I saved until I was rolled in in a wheel chair.

Having written to Phyllis Cromwell that I was returning, I immediately got a train for Montrose in the Grand Central. I was glad to see her and Martha again, and we sat up talking all night. I told them that I had decided to go into New York to work. Worried, Martha said, "But, Linda, the doctors there have their own nurses; they won't give work to an unknown nurse, from out of town!" and Phyllis said, "Remember the gutter!" Inwardly I felt that they were sound in their reasoning, but outwardly I was very brave and bold. "Well, I'll show you!" I said, "I'll go, and I will work only for famous doctors. Only the best will have the privilege of hiring me." They were extremely dubious, but I was determined.

Finding that no persuasion would induce Phyllis to go with me, we divided our last hat. I got the brim, which I put on my head, and set out for the big city. It was the most adventurous thing I had done, and I felt in my bones that it meant my life,—that here I stood, or fell. I was strong and would survive, or weak, and would go down. Without a friend to whom I could say Hello, I came to New York to establish myself as a nurse, and with the best doctors only.

The first thing I did before leaving the station was to look in the telephone book for a Nurse's Registry, and found one on Fifth Avenue. I chose that because I loved the sound of it, Fifth Avenue! Not knowing from the number that it was just south of Yonkers, well on the way to Boston. I went up by subway and arriving at a brownstone house, I saw Miss Hull, a nurse who managed the place. She was tiny, white-faced, and looked ill; she asked me where I had trained, and apparently believing me, she rented me a small room on the fourth floor back, for sixteen dollars a month.

The house contained about twenty rooms, chiefly occupied by living corpses,—or so they appeared from the faces that peered from different doors as Miss Hull took me up. And not peaceful corpses either, but sour ones. They were mostly, I found, addicted to religious practices, and looked upon anyone who was not of like mind, as suspicious characters. I felt that I had had enough religion to last me if I lived to be a hundred.

Giving Miss Hull twenty dollars of my hoard left me five, which I figured would last me at least two weeks, and then there would be four dollars change back, on which I could live for two weeks more. By that time I would have work and everything would be perfect. Which goes to show.

The first week I went to the offices of many well-known doctors, where I gave my name to charming secretaries, with but small hopes of beneficent results. Upon two occasions I had the privilege of talking to the doctor himself, but they didn't seem unduly impressed with the necessity of my having work. Every morning I went to a restaurant on One Hundred and Twenty-fifth Street for a cup of coffee and a roll, both of which they served for five cents. The coffee was good, and the place was clean and cheerful. Then I would walk for miles, covering a deal of territory in every direction. To the north lay Harlem with the negroes. There somehow I felt less lonely, even though I did not know them. How I wished that Mrs. Hall was still in her little house. I went to look at it, but found that it had been torn down and a street cut right through where we had sat under the tree.

I went to churches of denominations of which I had never heard; I went to museums, staring at things, but that I did not enjoy, for I knew nothing about such things, and I had an overwhelming desire to take each object and study it until I became an authority, which exhausted me. Besides, I didn't dare remain away from the registry, for fear I would miss a chance for work, but every day I walked the streets for at least three hours.

My five dollars soon became one, and I asked Miss Hull for my four dollars. She looked startled—still she always looked startled—and said, "Four dollars?" I said, "Yes, you know, from the twenty I gave you." Remembrance dawned. "Oh! Yes . . . well, I haven't the change today; I'll give it to you tomorrow." So the days passed and I didn't get it. Suddenly I realized I had only thirty cents, so I laid by a store of food for a siege. I bought a quart of milk and a box of soda crackers and peanut butter, thinking, "For two more days I'm safe." Walking that day was not so interesting, and the second day I climbed to my room like an old woman . . . with difficulty placing one foot before the other. I undressed and laid my body down, and lay very still. The house was quiet; even the street sounds came from afar. Behind the expressionless front of that house, identical with thousands of others, I lay alone in my small cell, and I sensed the thousands of others who at that moment, lay in other cells. I wondered if they were brave,—how they faced similar situations. I could lie here and die, I thought, and no one would know it for days. No one would really care except my sister Adelaide, and certainly I wouldn't mind particularly. It seemed such a small thing I asked . . . to be allowed to nurse sick people, and to earn enough to live simply.

My thoughts were interrupted by a knock, and surprised, I said, "Come in." A big, pink-cheeked woman came in, and held out her hand, saying,

"My name is Mary Gannet,—I live next door. I heard you weeping, and thought I'd see if there was anything I could do?" I said, "No, but it's nice of you to come in; won't you sit down?" She took the only chair in the room, a rickety one, and went on talking, showing her large false teeth as she filled the room with her healthy, jolly talk and laughter. She was a handsome woman of thirty, blond, blue-eyed, with a beautiful complexion. Casually she said, "I'm heating some soup for my supper,—I'll bring you some." Presently she returned with a bowl of soup, and a box of crackers, and sat on my bed while I ate; then she brought me a cup of good coffee. It tasted heavenly, and I consumed every drop, while she continued to talk. Presently she knew that I was alone, and worried; that I knew none of the good doctors, and when I told her of my boast that I would work for no others, she just stared at me, and said, "Now I want you to get up and dress. You may not know it, but you're coming out with me and my boyfriend. He has a car, and we'll go to the beach, so hurry up,—he'll be here any minute."

Her vitality was infectious; I was ready in no time. Her friend was a short, stocky, insignificant-looking man, with a kind face and a sweet smile. He took us to a shore, and gave us a good dinner, unbelievably tasty after my few days fast. The little man said little, but his smile conveyed perfectly his interest and amusement in our conversation. She was a wonderful woman; short on education perhaps, but long on humor, and kindness, and human sympathy and understanding. Every day we went, and often in the afternoon we bathed and had dinner, returning in the beautiful warm night.

One night she and I sat up for a long time, just talking. She asked me point-blank what I wanted to do,—what aim I had in life? Embarrassed, I hesitated. Faltering, stumbling, I said, "I want above all to know distinguished people; grand, glorious people who are simple and kind, intelligent and well educated." She looked puzzled and said, "I don't know where you're going to find them! You'll never find more than one at a time, and you can't get them all together,—so you can never hope to make a life with them." Discouraged, I said, "I know I won't find many, and that one of them may be a garbage man, one a laundress, and one perhaps a millionaire, but there must be some locality where they collect, where one could live without fear always. There must be some sign by which one can recognize them—that sets them apart from others, from the stupid and cruel. I want to know great people; I want to be great myself! I want to understand human beings, and live a useful, beautiful life!" She got up and strode around the room, and said, "Don't let me wake you up from a crazy dream! But while you're looking for your great people, what are you planning to eat?" I felt stupid and ashamed. She continued, "If you don't put some food in your stomach you're not going to look so great when you do find them, let me tell you!"

I had to admit that the doctors in New York were not clamoring for my services, in fact that I had not found anyone, so far, who considered me an asset, and that I didn't know what I was going to do. Torn between sympathy and irritation she said, "I guess I'll have to take you in hand, and tell you what life is all about, for with all your experiences, you don't seem to have grasped many essential facts! First off, you take the very next case that is offered to you, even if it's from Doctor Popoloupis, located in Hell's Kitchen; second, move from this nunnery. I'm leaving, and I can't bear leaving you at the mercy of the Hatchet Brigade. Those old harpies with prayer books in their hands! They'll tear you limb from limb before you can say scat!" I protested that although they had shown no great friendliness, still they could do me no harm. "Good God!" she exclaimed. "You're dumber than I thought! Don't you know they hate any one under thirty, and if you happen to look human, they hate your guts? Unless you do exactly as they do, go to church regularly, and wear frightful clothes, they'll pan you behind your back, and prevent Miss Hull giving you work?" Appalled, I said, "But Miss Hull told me that cases were given in rotation!" At that she burst into tears, and through her sobs said, "Oh! My God! I didn't know they still grew as ignorant as you!" and staring at me she said more quietly, "What do you think of me? Don't you think that I had great hopes at your age? Starting out with stars in my eyes, believing that things would work out right for me? Well, has it? Like hell it has! Well, what am I now? I'll tell you; I'm what the occupants of this nunnery call a Prostitute!" Unconsciously, I started. She laughed and said, "I see you still react normally to that word!"

Afraid I had hurt her I said, "Listen, I don't care what you are, you've been good to me, and I'll never forget it! I think you are one of my grand people, and you see I've found you! We'll find others, give us time!" She laughed bitterly and said, "Time? We've already been given time; thirty years at hard labor!" She walked around the room, wiping her nose, and continued. "Why do you think I am living with this little man? He's a fine man, but God knows he's no woman's dream hero! But he's kind to me, and he's human. If I stay in this house I'll begin to be like the others, and I'd rather be dead. I don't really want to marry him, but I would if he was free." I said, "Oh, is he married?" She stared at me and said, "Yep, that's what they call it. He supports a wife and two daughters in a fine home in the Bronx. They're ashamed of him because he's small and not smart-looking. They don't give a hoot for him, only for what they get from him, and they get plenty! He's lonely, and so am I. If we can make this rotten world a little happier for each other, it's O.K. with me. I nursed her; that's how I got to know him, and the family. I know what they are. Anyway, we're friends, and I care a lot for him, and he does for me." Not knowing what to say, I kept silent, and she continued. "But don't kid yourself that you can win, barring a stroke of luck! It's not possible for you, with no money, to help yourself out of the kind of life you're in. Your only chance is to marry, and I've seen plenty of those back asking for work. Maybe you'll have better luck than I've had. No decent man ever asked me to marry him, and I have to be grateful for my half-pint little feller, even to live in sin! But he's kind, and I appreciate that!"

She had been half weeping all the time, and I wept too out of sympathy. Suddenly she wiped her nose noisily, laughed, and said, "What a fool I am! Forget it; tomorrow's a new day, and we'll get up early and go to a place I used to have a room. I know the woman who runs it and you can get one real cheap. Good night! I'll see you in the morning." That night, in my little hard bed, the gutter didn't seem more than a hand's breadth from the end of my nose. I lay awake a long time thinking over all that Mary Gannet had said. I liked her very much.

Next morning was sunny, and we had a cheerful breakfast after which she took me to an apartment house on One Hundred and Twenty-eighth Street, near Fifth Avenue, run as a rooming-house by a Mrs. Gregg, a thin, blond little woman. She took us up in a rickety elevator, to the fifth floor and showed us the smallest room I had ever seen. It was absolutely without daylight, and with the one gas jet lighted, it still presented a doleful appearance. Its one window was flush against the brick wall of an adjoining house, but I took it because it was cheap—only two dollars a week. We came back to the registry and got my four dollars from Miss Hull, and between us, carried my suitcase back to my new room. Then we had lunch. Mary made me take ten dollars, and with the four I had, I felt safe for at least three weeks. She said, "This afternoon I'll take you to some doctors who know me," and to all of them she said, "This is an old friend of mine, a good nurse, and I want you to give her a chance." Oh! She was a grand woman! When we'd seen three, and left my name with four others, she said, "Let's have a soda," and in the drug store, sitting on stools, she said, "Listen, Belinda! I'm going away for about ten days, with my boyfriend, so don't move until I get back. You'll find Mrs. Gregg all right, and later maybe we can get a nice light room together." I said, "Thank you a thousand times for your kindness, Mary! I hope you have a good time, and I'll be waiting for you."

I never saw her again. She didn't come back, she didn't write me; I had no address, and even the name of her boyfriend, I had forgotten, besides, she had told me it wasn't his real name. I went many times to the registry, hoping she would write, or that someone would know her address. I went to all the doctors to whom she had taken me, and none of them had any address except the registry. Now indeed I was alone, and the mystery of it made me afraid of what could easily happen to me. The horror of what can happen to people with no money or friends! Rubbed out, leaving no trace! Something in me revolted, and I was afraid to go on living, and I thought it would be simpler, more intelligent to die without waiting for the claw-like monster to nab me and crush me. One should have at least the dignity of dying by one's own hand, not by torture of the haphazard whims of chance! Things that had seemed trivial to me, now appeared as signs pointing to my own complete annihilation; hardships through which I had lived almost casually, now in retrospect frightened me beyond bearing. Alone in my tiny dark room, one of millions in a teeming city, I asked myself, "With what will you face life?" and I had no answer. My soul was sick, my heart like lead.

When I got down to my last five dollars, I began to read the Want Ads, looking for any sort of work I felt capable of doing. One, for a Personal Maid, I answered, although I had only the foggiest notion of the duties of a personal maid. The address was on Park Avenue, and a charming woman questioned me. I told her that I had never done that particular type of work, but that if it included sewing, I was an expert. I gave her a fictitious name, and when she asked me for references, I had to admit that I had none. Finally I told her that I was a graduate nurse, and that I felt ashamed that I could not make my living by my own trade. She was really nice, and said, "Well, but you can see I must know something about you, can't you?" and I said yes. To keep from bursting into tears before her, I left hurriedly, saying, "I'm sorry to have bothered you." Once outside, I wanted to die. Oh! I thought, if any of my classmates should ever know that I had come to such a pass!

Then I answered an ad for models, at Wanamakers department store, and waited with dozens of well-dressed, stylish, beautiful girls, thinking,

"I'll never in the world get a job, when there are so many lovely looking girls." But I did. I was hired to wear riding habits, and I loved it. They were mostly woolen, and hot, but so beautifully made, and the accessories so lovely and I looked, I thought, so wonderful in them, that I'd have worn them just for my food, if they'd only known it. At first they paid me twenty dollars a week, but after two weeks, they gave me thirty, which was a large sum of money. Later they asked me to model underwear, but I didn't think I had the requirements for that. However, they tried me, and I passed. Anyway, I thought, it will be cooler. I wore all sorts of things, lovelier than I had ever imagined underwear could be. It paid less than riding habits, but it was so beautiful I hated to take them off at closing time. Before I left, I got at a great reduction, a beautiful tweed suit, and when I had a hat, and shoes, and bag to go with it, I looked wonderful, and I was so happy!

I still lived in my tiny room in Harlem, and now that I had some money, and a job, I got two cans of paint and a brush, and painted the entire room, walls, ceiling, chair, and bed. It was all white except a wide band of yellow around the top, to make myself think it was sunshine. In one corner I had a shelf that held my few books; in another, one that held a pot of ivy that grew long luxuriant tendrils down the wall. It was a fool plant, and didn't seem to know it had no sun and air! We weren't supposed to cook, but I had a little stove that burned alcohol, and often cooked an egg for my supper. My room was really cheerful now, and I didn't feel so lonely when I got home at night. But I missed Mary Gannet.

In between jobs I continued calling on doctors, and never gave up hope that sooner or later I would get a case with a good doctor, and show him that I was an excellent nurse. When my work at the store ended, I began going systematically to offices, but soon my money began to dwindle, eat as little as I might. One of my biggest expenses was for soap and Lysol with which I scrubbed the bathtub. It was used by dozens of people on my floor, and I had a horror of catching something. Just when my rent was due, and I was avoiding Mrs. Gregg, I got a job as waitress at Child's, because I could honestly say that I had had experience. It wasn't bad at all; one got tips, and best of all they allowed us to eat plenty.

When I'd been there two months, and saved my tips, I decided to quit, and to get work as a nurse or die trying. I walked the streets at night, looking at the crowds, wondering where they came from, where they were going, and Why? But I didn't have the hope, the enthusiasm I used to have. Why bother? I thought. Suppose you *do* get work as a nurse, then what? I laughed at myself for ever having thought to make myself important in a world so full of millions who were well occupied without me, from among whom I would be missed no more than a drop would be missed from the ocean. I walked miles, and one night stood outside a big house that I had discovered belonged to Anne Morgan, and I looked, wondering why she should have so much, and I so little. I saw people and houses until I was exhausted, and in my small bed slept soundly.

But the time came when I knew I must settle once and for all whether or not I would give up, or continue trying. I had relinquished, painfully, my hopes of an education; now it seemed that I could not even be a nurse, but must let that go, too, and perhaps become a waitress. For surely I was competent enough for that. Well, then, I thought, I'll be a good waitress! But suddenly I saw the faces of the girls who had worked with me in Maple Inn, the dead shells of drab, weak, work-worn bodies, and something inside me said, "*No*! I'll die first!"

I decided to make a continuous drive on all doctors, all hospitals, all registries, until I got work. But if I spent too much time out, I stood to miss a call when it did come. In fact, while I had been on my other jobs, I had had calls from two doctors. This made it more difficult. I went back to Miss Hull, humbled myself, begged her to give me work. She looked startled, as usual, and said, "I'm sorry, but I can only give work to the nurses in the house . . . if you want to come back, I will let you have your old room, if you pay me in advance. Leaving here with Miss Gannet, you see, is against you." Furious, I said, "Don't you dare knock her, to me!" and that settled that.

That night I counted my money,—sixty-three cents I had. I sat up, thinking harder than I had ever thought in my life, trying to see where I was going, and what I would do when I got there. It seemed almost as though I had arrived, only I couldn't realize it. It all seemed silly, but I arrived at a conclusion; I would go out next day, see some more doctors, and if nothing came of it, I would take it as a sign that I was through. Finished. Having arrived at this simple solution, I went to bed and slept instantly.

Next morning I got up early, scrubbed the tub, bathed and dressed in my beautiful tweed suit, and set out. It was a beautiful day, and I couldn't help feeling hopeful. Something wonderful *must* happen, when the sun shone in such glory. At my little restaurant I had my coffee and roll, and went downtown. I went to a great many offices, some new ones I had never tried, and as there seemed to be thousands and thousands of doctors in New York, if the law of averages worked, I surely would get work. At noon

I went to an automat, ate a bite, and rested. As the afternoon wore on, I got more and more discouraged. Surely something will happen, I thought. But it didn't. Hoping that some doctor would like my looks, or be short of nurses, maybe an epidemic start, or all the nurses fall ill, and I alone would be available, then I'd have a break! My mind occupied with such fantastic imaginings, I found myself standing at Seventy-second Street and Madison Avenue. Hesitating, wondering what direction I would take, I made a solemn pact with myself. I would see *one* more doctor, the very first name on the north side of the street. If he was kind, all right: if nothing came of it, I would end my life within the hour. Calm, sure of myself, I felt glad that it was settled.

I crossed the avenue, going east, and in the middle of the block I saw a sign, "Dr. James Alexander." I walked up the steps almost with indifference, for by this time I didn't care if good came of it or not. A maid opened the door and took me back a darkish hall to the secretary, a lovely blond girl with a sweet face, who said, "What can I do for you?" I said, "I want to see Doctor Alexander. I'm a nurse, and I need work." She smiled in a friendly way, and said, "I'm afraid you can't see him, as he's just leaving for the day." I looked at her long and steadily, and my heart seemed turned to stone. Without a word, I walked back to the front door, opened it and went out. I was not aware of having done so . . . my feet moved of themselves, and a lightness and unreality possessed me. I wondered what method would be best, most neat, when I heard footsteps behind me, running footsteps. I vaguely noted them, but when they stopped, I felt a hand on my arm. Surprised, I turned and saw that it was the lovely secretary, and she seemed breathless, frightened, as she said, "Please come back! Doctor Alexander will see you." Dazed, my mind still confused by my previous anguish and pain, I walked back with her. She knocked on a door, opened it and said, "Doctor Alexander, here is Miss Dan." I stood in a long, quiet, restful room, lined with books, and in one corner near the window sat a noble figure,— a man with a kind, gentle, beautiful face. I looked for a long moment, afraid it couldn't be true. He smiled, and said, "Come over and have a chair." Slowly I crossed the room and sat down in a chair near his desk.

He sat so still, unhurried, as though he had time to hear me, to know that I was there. He asked me my name, and hospital, and I told him. He asked me why I wanted to work in New York, and I told him everything. But how I told him! I told him how I had boasted that I would work for only famous physicians, and he smiled, saying, "Well, I guess that leaves me out!" But I knew his name, and that he was one of the really well-known doctors, so that under ordinary circumstances I would hardly have had the courage to ask him for work. I told him of all the jobs I had had while waiting to be called on a case, and all the time he listened, sometimes laughing so hard he shook all over, and once he wiped a tear surreptitiously from his eye. But I knew that he was fair, and just. I spoke freely to him; I told him my hopes, my aims, and he was patient, kind. For two hours and more he listened, and I did wonder where it was he had been going, but I was so anxious to work for him that I just had to make him understand, and I selfishly held his attention. I wanted him to give me a chance! And he did. He was the finest friend anyone ever had. If only the world could be filled with people as simple and honest and really kind as Doctor Alexander! So everything changed for me! I had work!

I went home happy because I had absolute faith in Doctor Alexander. I knew that I had found one of the good people I had been looking for,—it was written in his face. Having only sixty-two cents, I hoped he would call me real soon, which he did. Two days later, while I still had two eggs, his charming secretary called me to say that Doctor Alexander wanted me to report to a hospital on the West Side immediately. I knew that this hospital was for the care and treatment of alcoholics and drug addicts, and I was nervous as I dressed as quickly as possible. This was my big chance,—I must prove to Doctor Alexander that I was a good nurse or all would be lost.

When I reached the hospital and went in, I liked the place at once. The atmosphere seemed more friendly than any hospital I had ever been in. The doctor in charge, a very fat, very handsome man named Dewey, asked me to sit down, while he told me about the patient. "His name is David Graham Roude," he said, "and he is one of the richest men in the country. He is going to take the cure for alcoholism, and is in a very irritable mood and difficult to handle. You'll have your hands full, but don't mind his temper,—you'll have a good night nurse, as Doctor Alexander wants you on day duty." All the time he'd been talking I was occupied with trying to look intelligent and competent, but I was scared stiff. I absolutely had to make good on this case, no matter what the obstacles were.

Doctor Dewey took me up in the elevator to the third floor, and walked toward the front of the hospital, knocked on a door, and we heard a bored voice call irritably, "Come in, damn you!" We went in, and I saw a large man sitting quietly with a relaxed, discouraged look, yet a certain litheness in his body seemed to suggest that instantly he might spring up and change his whole environment. He looked into space as though unwilling to admit our existence, then slowly turned his gaze back to us, with indifference bordering on distaste, his brown eyes sad and cynical.

Doctor Dewey said, "Mr. Roude, this is Miss Dan, your nurse. Doctor Alexander sent her to take care of you." I was so nervous I could only manage to say, "How do you do, Mr. Roude." He gave me a nasty look and said, "I do as I damn well please, how do *you* do?" Without thinking, I said, "I do as I'm told." Regretting my words, I waited to hear him fire me, but he smiled a little and said, "That's good; for if you're going to be around me I want you to do what I tell you, not what these stupid doctors tell you. When I tell you to give me a drink, by God, I want action, and no shilly-shallying! D'you understand?" I said, "Yes, Mr. Roude, I understand, but still I have to do what Doctor Alexander tells me."

He glowered at me and stood up, towering above me and Doctor Dewey, teetering ever so slightly on his feet, and said, "Well, you're a damned fool, and I might as well begin now to teach you a few things! Let me see your teeth!" Startled, I looked at Doctor Dewey, but his face was expressionless, so I said, "Mr. Roude, you're only hiring me, not buying me." But I grinned, pulling back my lips so he could see my teeth. He gave them a careful scrutiny and said, "Not buck teeth, anyway! But have you got any brains?" Feeling a little safer, I said, "I doubt it." He grunted, and said, "So do I."

During this conversation Doctor Dewey had said nothing, and now he said, "I'll leave you in good hands, Mr. Roude. If there is anything you want, just have Miss Dan telephone the office, sir." As he turned to go, Mr. Roude said, "I don't want a damned thing, except for you to take your damned fat ass out . . . it makes me tired just to look at your behind." When the door closed behind Doctor Dewey, he turned to me with an unhappy look and said, "That doctor is all right; I'm a son of a bitch to talk so to him! He can't help being stupid, but I wish I hadn't said it!" And then frantically, angry that the situation had forced him into a state of regret, he said, "But I don't care! Damn him, he is stupid! God Almighty! I'm the only man alive with brains, and I'm lonely! I'm as lonely as Hell!"

He sank again into a brooding sadness, his dark eyes sad, beaten. Just when I was feeling sorry for him he lifted his eyes to me questioningly and said, "Well, what are *you* going to do? Stand there like a wooden Indian?" I said, "No, I'm going to change into my uniform, and do anything you like me to." He yelled at me, "Damn the uniform! I hate 'em! Don't bother about that now. I want you to earn your money, so go ahead and entertain me! Do you do tricks? Are you a good talker? Or a good listener? For if you're one of those damned females only good at giving little pink pills, you won't be any use to me!"

Watching his face, not wishing to be fired I said, "I don't know what I'm good at, Mr. Roude, but if you'll give me a chance, maybe I'm not so dumb as I look." He glanced at me and said, "You don't look so dumb, but that's no sign in a woman. I've seen some awfully pretty ones who didn't have the sense God gave geese." He got up and walked around the room, restlessly, continuing, "I don't need any regular nursing. I'm only going to take the goddam cure they give here. I'm not sick,—only bored. And I'm bored because everybody around me is dumb. You wouldn't know how lonely that can make a man with brains."

While I was putting my hat and coat into a closet, a young man came in whom I took to be a servant. When he said, "Mr. Roude, shall I undress you now?" I knew he was a valet, although I had never actually seen one. Mr. Roude said, "Larkin, this is Miss Dan, my nurse. Will you see that they treat her right around this dump?" And Larkin said, in a very polite way, "Yes, Mr. Roude." I didn't trust his face. To me, Mr. Roude said, "Take yourself for a walk or something for half an hour, and come back. D'you hear? I said, Come back!" as I left the room. I was glad he hadn't fired me yet.

When I returned Mrs. Roude was there, and from his bed he introduced us. She spoke politely, indifferently. She was slight, exquisitely beautiful, with a babyish face, and was, apparently not so bright. But I thought to myself, "You never can tell; nothing is the way it seems," and watched my step. Mr. Roude said, "Now Maggie, I want you to go home. I'll have my nurses, and I don't want a crowd around," and she answered docilely, plaintively, "All right, David," and left the room. She couldn't have been said to walk,—it was a peculiar feat of getting from one place to another with no visible muscular movements. She was dressed extremely simply, but expensively. Her French maid, a woman of fortyish, angular, sour, had apparently eaten something that hadn't agreed with her, and smelled something offensive to her. An altogether strange person to me, and ever was. When they'd gone, the rooms were quiet, and Mr. Roude less irritable.

The regular twin beds were too short and narrow for Mr. Roude, and they had been pulled together, so that he lay at an angle. On the extra space he kept his two small dogs, the like of which I had never seen. He said they were Griffons, and their names were Peace and Quiet. He never petted them, nor talked foolishly to them, and yet there was a gentle tenderness in his consideration for those two small dogs that was astonishing and touching. When he was dressed, and carried one under his arm, it was ludicrous.

Doctor Alexander came in at five o'clock and talked to Mr. Roude and me for a while, and left a few orders for me. His simple kindness made me feel somehow safe, less tense, and seemed to affect Mr. Roude much the same. At six Larkin came to take the dogs for a walk, and to get his orders for the night and the following day. I gave Mr. Roude his supper, of which he ate little, and at seven the night nurse came on. Mr. Roude whispered to me, "See if she has buck teeth." She was short and squat, but she had no buck teeth, I told him. He had a deep hatred of false teeth, and that is what he called them. When I had given her the orders for the night, I put on my hat and coat to leave. Mr. Roude gave me a sharp, evil look, saying, "Try and drag your old bones back here tomorrow, will you? And don't come creeping in here around noon,—remember I expect you to earn your money." But I knew that he wanted me back, and was happy. I was exhausted by excitement and tension, and slept instantly.

At seven next morning I was in his room, considerably fortified by a stiffly starched uniform and cap, which later on he begged me to abandon. I gave him his breakfast, Larkin came in to dress him, the barber to shave him, and Mr. Roude said to me, "Can you imagine this fellow? All he does for a living is to shave my face once a day! He's been doing it for years!" Brooding a moment he said thoughtfully, "How he can keep from slitting my throat, just for a change, I don't understand. Shaving the same face every day! Good God, for twelve years! He must know personally every hair, every wrinkle! It beats me!" But I learned later that the barber didn't mind at all,—he got a good income and lived very nicely, thank you, on shaving that one face. Besides, it was such a good-looking one.

When Mr. Roude was bathed, shaved and dressed in the most beautiful clothes, he looked wonderful. He was over six feet tall, broad, but well built with small hands and feet. His swarthy skin and dark brown hair and eyes gave him at times the appearance of an Italian, but his features were a combination of Scotch and Irish. His expression in repose was quiet and brooding, sad, weary, but in conversation or anger, his whole body became tense and vibrant, flame-like.

"Well, can you read? Or did you go to night school?" he asked me. "I didn't go to school much night or day, Mr. Roude, but I can read simple words—not big ones," I told him. He wanted me to read only the headlines of the papers, which I did, but that was a joke. He knew beforehand exactly what I was going to read, and could go on with the entire article, in complete detail. In all the years I knew him, I never saw him look at a book, paper or magazine, and yet he knew everything. He told me that when he was young he had no time to read, and that later, it was not necessary. He would tell me about writers, and poets—when they lived, and why they wrote certain things—and of historical events, and would discuss engineering achievements in foreign countries, in a truly amazing way. This made entertaining him difficult. Without glancing at the stock market he could tell me to the smallest fraction how much almost any given stock would rise or fall during the next twenty-four hours. Many times I have tried to catch him out in some local event, but I was never able to do so. Events of national importance he would frequently tell me beforehand, saying, "This will happen so, on Friday, and he will say this," and it would be just as he had said. Living in that atmosphere gave me a peculiarly fatalistic feeling.

Every afternoon his huge Rolls would wait for us in front of the hospital, while Mr. Roude moved about in a slow, haphazard way around the room, following a method all his own, by which suddenly he was ready and expected everyone else to be ready to go. Larkin handed him his hat and gloves, his cane, and Peace, and we moved down the hall; Mr. Roude very straight and dignified in front, I following, followed in turn by Larkin carrying Quiet. At the car stood a chauffeur who had been with Mr. Roude so long language was not necessary. We settled in the enormous car, a rich robe tucked around us, Peace on his right, Quiet on his lap, when the car moved silently away.

Sometimes Mr. Roude sat wrapped in dark silence for the entire ride; on others he talked constantly and interestingly on every subject under the sun. His thoughts were often of his childhood, and his poverty; of his mother, and of his first great wealth. He asked me about my life, and I told all. We became real friends on those rides, and usually he returned laughing, happier, than when we had set out.

The days passed rapidly, and I came to know some of the nurses on regular hospital duty, and many, who like me, were specials. They interested me deeply, for in them I saw myself in a very few years, and I wanted to know what their lives were like,—if they were happy, and if they had been able to save anything for their old age. Some things I learned frightened me; tragedy, futility, and disillusion had walked with many of them. They lived on the fringe between reality and unreality,—touching the lives of other people so intimately, knowing the truth behind the facade that was presented to the world, all of which they carefully placed in a compartment labelled, "None of my business," until they had become automatons, with a wall of indifference to protect them. They lived for weeks or months in luxury, were thrust back suddenly into drab, dull surroundings of poverty, to be again jerked into a luxury which was in no way a part of their lives.

The great gulf between the material ease while on a case, and great poverty when idle, was conditioned by apparently unavoidable circumstances which are these: to be able to afford a nice room in pleasant surroundings, it is necessary for a nurse to be busy constantly, in which case naturally she doesn't need a nice room; and if one is off duty a lot, and could use and enjoy a nice room, it is impossible to afford it. After trying to figure this out for a few years, one becomes resigned, and forgets about it, if possible. Nurses learn to return to their shabby rooms with stoicism, and indifference, hoping soon to be on another case, constantly adapting themselves to contrasting environment, which tends in the end to destroy all identity, all personality. It was this that frightened me most.

A few of the nurses were very beautiful, and I learned that their lives had held adventure, love, joy, sadness and change, and in some cases great material advancement, only in the end to be thrust back into the same job they had left with faith and hope in the future. By marrying a rich husband—and among the professions of women, there is no more propitious field for matrimonial possibilities—they had experienced all the emotions of ease and security, only to awaken at his death to find themselves back on their own; taking up a difficult life made more difficult by the release, later in life. Sometimes this was due to the fact that the husband had spent or lost all his money, but more often it was because the man had in his will, left his property to his family. It is a fact that men look upon trained nurses as peculiarly different from other women. They are expected to be self-reliant, self-supporting, and not to require the same tenderness and love, and material protection that other women automatically call forth. I cannot explain this, but I know what brings it about.

Some of these nurses had children in school whom it was necessary for them to support and educate. As it was obviously impossible to do this on their salary, they added to it whatever they could get from men. Many of them drank, not to excess, just enough perhaps to dull the edge of reality, and a few of them took drugs. Looking at them I wondered which one I would follow; where my life would end. Most of all I feared losing my own personality; that feeling of being myself, however unimportant to the world, and of becoming indifferent, unresponsive, an efficient machine.

I discovered that many of them, when they were off duty, and lonely, went to the lobbies of hotels and picked up men, sometimes achieving a dinner in that way. What they gave in return I did not ask. So once, when I was in a similar situation, I thought to try their scheme, feeling sure that I could escape without Paying the Price. I chose the Waldorf, and sat, feeling horribly embarrassed, not quite sure of the technique. Once I got up and walked around, as though impatient at the failure in punctuality on the part of a friend. When I sat down again, I saw a man who reminded me of Felix Worth, and I remembered the cotton fields of Oklahoma. While I thought of my life at that time, I glanced up, and he was coming directly toward me. I smiled. He hesitated, stopped, saying, "Pardon me, but you remind me of a girl I knew once . . ." and as I continued to smile, he said, impatiently, "I know that sounds like a 'line' but it happens to be true." I said, "That's all right," for I knew then that it was Felix Worth indeed; "what was her name?" He said, slowly, "Belinda Dan." The heat, the melons, the heavy bags of cotton were clear in my mind, and I said, "Was she a nice girl?" Thoughtfully he said, "I suppose so,—but she was more than that. Not pretty, but something . . . I couldn't tell you what, that I loved. She had freckles, and bare feet."

I moved, making room for him beside me, and when he sat down, I said, "You interest me; won't you tell me all about her? Why didn't you marry her?" He sat, holding his hat in his two hands, and I saw that he had grown heavier, was well dressed, the picture of success. He looked sharply at me and said, "I made a big mistake, but I didn't know it until later. She had a fool determination to go to school, to be educated, and I could have helped her; I was a fool to try to make her marry me, to get me to help her. I should have done it anyway." He was so serious, I laughed and said, "Why bother now? You've probably found some one else much better!" He said, "Yes, I suppose so,—but I've never forgotten that girl. My wife is jealous of every woman I speak to and if she only knew it, that's the only one she has any reason to mind, and she's never heard of her. That funny, freckled, barefoot girl I picked cotton with! I've made money, like I told her I would,— I could educate her now, but I don't even know where she is. You remind me of her, though you haven't got such big freckles."

He moved impatiently and spoke irritably. "But why talk of it now? Excuse me for speaking of my personal affairs, but it's because it all came over me . . . you look so like her." I laid my hand on his and said, "Felix, have you still got the little silk bag?" His face turned deathly white, and he said, "Oh! My God! Belinda, it's you!" and quickly he pulled me to my feet, and with his arm around my shoulders he walked rapidly toward the door, saying, "Let's get out of here, quick. They know me here." He signalled for a taxi, and once inside, he told the man to drive to the Park. He put his arms around me and kissed me many times, and I let him. For I loved him, as I had before, in my own way.

Then he began asking questions, finding out everything I had done since we picked cotton together, and I told him almost all. My pride would not allow me to confess my extreme poverty. He became very businesslike, saying, "Listen, Belinda! I've got a million, and you can have anything you want. You've got to let me help you; we've got to be friends. Never again will I be a fool, and don't you believe it!" And all the time I thought that I must not see him again, that it would be wrong; it would be too great a temptation. He said, "Belinda, I've got three children; and they could have been ours!" He covered his face with his hands, and was silent for a long time; I could say nothing. After a long ride, we went to a quiet little restaurant for dinner and talked over everything again. He told me how he had made his million in cotton, and meant to make more.

We arranged to meet next day for lunch, and when he asked me where I lived, I said West Forty-seventh Street, and we walked along. I stopped at a brownstone house that looked like a very nice rooming house, and told him good-by. I went up the steps and waited in the vestibule until he had gone, then came quickly down and got in the subway for home. I never saw him again. Incredible stupidity! Any girl with a modicum of awareness of reality would instantly have removed him, and his million, from his jealous wife, the probability of doing him a favor clinched by the certainty of doing herself one. The years of Youth, cluttered up with sentimental tripe called Honor, Ideals! In a world keyed to rugged individualism, go-getters! Those who can't see the light should be, and damned well are, discarded, like the piles of old junked automobiles outside every small town.

After three weeks Doctor Alexander said that Mr. Roude could go home, and arrangements were made for him to leave the following day. While I didn't want him to remain ill, or drunk, still I hated terribly to leave him and return to my dark little room in Harlem. There was color and life in all that he said, or did,—a tension that made one know they were alive, and ready for whatever might happen, and plenty did. When I left at seven, he was asleep, and I asked the night nurse to tell him good-by for me. On my way home I began to see why a nurse would take drugs,—the change is so sudden; constantly adapting oneself to totally different situations was a shock. From associating with a vibrant, amusing personality, a brilliant mind and security of work, suddenly I found myself back in my room, alone, with only sufficient money to live for a few weeks at best,—for I had received twenty-one dollars a week for three weeks.

The next morning I got up early and after thoroughly scrubbing the general tub, I washed my hair. While it was still wet the elevator man came up to say that I was wanted on the phone, and with a towel around my head, I went down. When I said "Hello," I heard the voice of Doctor Dewey, troubled, hurried, speaking: "Is that you, Miss Dan?" I said, "Yes, of course," thinking that I had made some horrible mistake, which they had only now discovered. He went on, "Will you come down here right away? Mr. Roude is raising Hell, and if you don't get here soon I'm afraid he'll tear the place down and murder the lot of us!" Thinking of my wet head, I said, "But Doctor Dewey, I've just washed my hair; what'll I do?" Impatiently he said, "I don't care a hoot what you do, only get down here quick; your hair will dry in the heat around here. You'll be lucky if it doesn't burn!" and hung up on me.

Pinning up my wet hair, I hurried down. Outside I saw the familiar car, with an imperturbable Jennings at the wheel, and I wondered what had happened. Seeing no one in the front office, I took the elevator to the third floor, where I found the very air tense and the nurses scuttling to cover. Doctor Dewey, standing helpless in the hall, said nothing, only waved his hand toward the door of Mr. Roude's room, giving it to me gladly. Afraid to hesitate, I went boldly to the door and walked in, to see a very funny sight.

In the middle of the room, his old-fashioned nightshirt flapping around his shins, stood Mr. Roude. His brown eyes blazing, his cheeks pink, he towered over Larkin who stood meekly holding out a pair of drawers. Mrs. Roude and her horse-faced maid huddled in a corner for self-protection; the air was dynamic, and I wondered where the next head would fall. Giving me a baleful look, Mr. Roude said, "So you thought you'd pull a fast one on me, eh? A dirty trick, I calls it, leaving me here with these pimps and whores! But you won't get away with it! You're not so smart, my girl; I'm on to all the tricks of doctors and nurses! Now we'll get out of this joint! Larkin, where's my *pants*?" Larkin moved quickly toward him with the drawers, and Mr. Roude turned to Mrs. Roude and yelled, "For God's sakes, go home, woman! A pack of snivelling women gives me the creeps!

You're as much help to me as a sore thumb. Go on home,—I'll come when I get damned ready, and by God, I'll choose my own company, and don't forget that My Lady!"

The two women left with celerity, and while I collected and packed the personal articles, Larkin got Mr. Roude dressed and we were soon marching out quietly as though nothing had disturbed him at all. I didn't know then why he was so mad, and once in the car, with Peace and Quiet, Mr. Roude didn't tell me; I was afraid to ask. We rode through the city, across the bridge and headed for Long Island. Not a word was spoken as we drove for miles through villages, and finally between beautiful estates. I vaguely knew that Mr. Roude had a home out there, but I didn't know where. After a long time we came to a pair of magnificent iron gates, a man came out of a stone house and opened them and we drove through, and for several miles between beautiful trees and flowers, a lawn like green velvet, finally ascending a sharp rise to the top of a hill. The car stopped before the entrance of an imposing building, that to me was a castle. Not in Spain, but a castle just the same.

Walking with Mr. Roude, I had always the feeling that he wanted some one near, but not too near in case he should need assistance, while his height and health precluded the possibility of such an occasion arising. He was, for all his profanity and temper, austere, dignified and daring. We got out of the car, and I walked by his side to a great door opened by an enormous man in uniform. The enormous hall was gloomy near the front, but opened up in the middle where the ceiling rose four full floors above us. A disagreeable, unnatural light was diffused through stained glass at the top of this well, from which rose a wide stairway. Far to the back I could see that the hall opened onto verandas, and farther on, to beautiful flower gardens, in which I caught a glimpse of water. I observed everything I could, as we proceeded slowly down the hall and started to ascend the wide curving stairs.

No one came to greet Mr. Roude, and I felt very lonely for him. On the second floor we turned sharply to the right, walked down a long hall to his bedroom, where Larkin took his hat, stick and gloves, saying, "I'm glad to see you home, sir," to receive the reply, "Like Hell you are!" He walked across the room, which I later learned was fifty-nine by seventy-two feet, and stepped out on a wide, luxuriously furnished balcony, extending the full length of the house.

He sank into a comfortable chair, and said nothing. I looked with awe at the beauty of the scene. The balcony looked straight into a rose garden, in full bloom; to the right could be seen the corner of another more formal garden, with a small lake. To the left the blue waters of the Sound, and straight across in front we looked smack into the surprised face of a clock, which I learned was in the top of the stable tower. The air was sweet with the odor of roses and new-mown hay; the birds were singing like mad. Otherwise there was no sound; a silence almost of death lay over the house and grounds.

After a long silence, Mr. Roude said, "Do you know why I was so mad this morning?" I said, "No, but I'm dying to know." He chuckled and said, "Well, I'll tell you. The Missus didn't want me to bring you home with me, and I said I wouldn't come without you. I said it to annoy her, for between you and me, although I like you all right, I liked some of the others just as much. But I thought you needed a vacation." He thought it a great joke, but my heart sank. Obviously, with all his experiences he had no conception of what one woman could do to another, when one has all the power on her side.

Although I had no desire to go back to my dark room, I said, "Mr. Roude, I don't think you need a nurse at all, and that I should go home right now. Besides, my hair is all wet, and I want to dry it." From a jolly friendly person he became instantly hard, cruel, and dominating. "Well, it so happens, my dear Miss Dan, that you are not here to think. Only to do what you're told, and I'm telling you that I need a nurse, and you are hired. Now if you will just attend to my orders, with less chit-chat, we'll get along just fine." Dignified, determined, relentlessly, he spoke, and I said, "Right; you're the captain!" As I left him to go to my room, I thought to myself, "Dark clouds are gathering in the northwest, the barometer is falling,—I'll batten down my hatches and lie low."

When I returned, our lunch was being served by two tall butlers, and I watched them with great interest. They did it much more cleverly than I had learned as a waitress, and I admired their noiseless performance. The linen and silver was more beautiful than any I had ever seen or imagined, and the thought went through my mind that just what lay on our small table, would have sent me to college for a whole year, without washing pots either. The food was much too good to be eaten; I don't know what should have been done with it, but merely eating it didn't seem enough. Mr. Roude told me that practically everything served in the house was raised on his own farm.

After lunch he moved about in his perfectly organized haphazard way that achieved his aim with the expenditure of the smallest amount of energy, and suddenly he was ready to go for a walk. "Let's go see the dogs,

Miss Dan," he said, and with his hat at a certain angle, he marched sedately toward the clock tower. In kennels and wire enclosures he had a great many dogs, of which he was inordinately fond. From mongrels to thoroughbreds, he knew them all, and they knew him. Some were old and moth-eaten, wabbling about on bandy old legs, half or wholly blind, some of them deaf, but he loved those old dogs. He was very proud of one that was appallingly large and stupid-looking, and explained that it was a mongrel he had found somewhere when it was a wee pup, very starved and miserable, and now look at the damned thing. With good care and food it not only lived, but began to grow, and continued to do so, perched high up on strong legs, his muscles rippling as he lumbered around. He laughed heartily, and said, "I just want to see how big the darn thing will get!"

When he returned, he said he wanted to take a nap, and suggested that I do the same, for he wanted me to sit up late with him, so Larkin brought my bag and I went to the third floor room to which I had been shown before. It was an octagonal room, with a wonderful view of fields spread out, and the blue Sound in the distance. I let down my damp hair, hoping it would dry while I slept. A nice old Irish maid named Mary had charge of that room, and she came around six o'clock to tell me where I was to have my dinner. This had, apparently, presented a nice problem to the housekeeper, for although I was not a servant, neither was I a guest. Some one had neatly settled the problem by having me eat in the library, an enormous room in which there was not a book. I never did find out why it was called the library, since it adjoined a small, practical theatre, completely equipped with dressing rooms and footlights. Mr. Roude told me he had built it for his second wife, who had been an actress, and during her lifetime he frequently had entire casts down from New York to give a performance for her and her friends.

My dinner was beautifully served by the third butler, which showed plainly my rating. His name was Thorpe, a pale, gentle young boy whom I came to know and like very much. I remember the day he left for the war; he was killed. I asked him how many clocks were in the house, as I had already counted twenty-three, and he said he thought there were over a hundred; that one man did nothing but wind the clocks. All day long he wound the clocks, and when they all struck together, they made a wonderful sound. While I didn't question Thorpe exactly, I managed to extract quite a little information from him,—things I thought it best to know, as forewarned is forearmed, or something.

Mr. Roude had his dinner in a very formal, gloomy, tapestry-hung dining room, with Mrs. Roude. I did not see her for several days, and when I did, she practically ignored me. When I came up, I found Mr. Roude sitting alone on the balcony. The sun had gone down, and the evening air was heavy with sweet country odors. We sat in silence for a long time, and somehow he didn't seem a great financier, but a lonely little boy. With all his millions, I felt great sympathy for him. The moon came up, bathing the trees and flowers and the lake like a mirror, in a peace more beautiful even than death. A longing that was a keen pain, filled my heart,—a searing nostalgia for something I had never had, and could not name. The marble seat shown white against black shadows. I got up, walking restlessly to the end of the balcony, and leaning against the balustrade, I tried to find some way to realize fully the beauty; to bear the pain of such beauty, but I could not. After a long time, Mr. Roude called to me, "What are you thinking about, Miss Dan?"

I came back and sat down, wondering how to answer him. He was unpredictable in his reactions,—he might laugh, or he might be understanding. I told him how I suddenly had seen as in the distance, the whole round world riding high, rhythmically, in the moonlight; not whirling like mad, as I had read in a book that it did. I much preferred a slow, rhythmic progress, and he agreed with me there. That I saw this world drenched in moonlight, entirely without people, and it was a heaven for the plants and animals. Without the slums, and black stinking dives in which human beings fought, sickened, and died; without injustice, and cruelty, and I thought it would be more beautiful. He listened, and said, "Yes, I think so too, often. We are a rotten lot, and the world would be a cleaner, saner place without us. We fight, and kill, lust and envy, destroying what we cannot understand." I said, "Why do we, Mr. Roude?" and he lighted another cigar, saying, "I never went to school much; I've never studied philosophy, but I think it is because of fear. No human being has within himself the capacity actually to see and thoroughly realize the beauty of a night like this. If one takes the time to sit, and let the wonder seep into his soul, maybe, but it makes one feel small, insignificant, futile. It is a shock to our pride, and we are afraid. Fear and awe of something greater than our capacity to understand. Maybe that's why I drink; I wouldn't know." He walked up and down the balcony, and said, "It's midnight, and I think I can sleep. Run on to bed."

Days of happiness followed for me, and I think, to a certain extent, for him. He began going into the city every day, leaving me alone. No one spoke to me except Thorpe and old Mary, but I was at liberty to wander all over the grounds, and farther to the chickens and vegetable garden. I love passionately a vegetable garden, and here was one beyond anything I could have imagined. In the evenings we sat on the balcony and mostly he talked; I listened, answering questions when I could. I had good food and sweet sleep, and for the time, I was happy. At the end of two weeks he thanked me for my kindness, paid me, and my heart was filled with gratitude to him. We shook hands, I got in the car and once on the train, I wasn't sure I hadn't imagined the whole thing.

Back in the hot town, with no friends, I had plenty to do. My room to clean, uniforms to mend for the laundry, clothes to make. I bought me a hand Singer sewing machine for five dollars, on which I made all my clothes; incredibly small, astoundingly efficient, it saved me much money. For ten days I was quite happy, for I had enough money to live on for a while, and something told me that my luck had changed,—that now I would always have work.

One night at one o'clock, Mrs. Gregg climbed the five flights because there was no elevator man after midnight, to tell me that I was wanted on the phone. I hurried down, and said "Hello." I heard Mr. Roude's voice, almost whispering, saying, "Is that you, Miss Dan?" I said, "Yes, Mr. Roude." He was quite drunk, I thought, and he said, "Listen, I want you to come and get me out of this place; I don't like it. I sneaked away, told them I had to go to the toilet, so they don't know I'm phoning. Now listen, call my house, but don't let the Missus know. Get Larkin and tell him to come with you, and hurry up, for I don't like this place for a cent!" I said, "Certainly, but what is the address?" He laughed and said, "Yep, I guess you'd need that," and he gave me a number on Gramercy Park. "Now shake a leg my fair damsel, for I want to leave here damned quick!" I said, "All right, captain!"

I got Larkin on the phone but he didn't seem eager to accompany me. Angry, I said, "Very well, Larkin, I'll go alone. But you know I don't think Mr. Roude will like that, do you?" Afraid not to, he agreed to meet me at Fifty-seventh Street and Fifth Avenue, where we would take a taxi down. Larkin looked a mixture of sleepiness, fear, and annoyance, as he said, "You're too green to know what scrapes you can get into, getting Mr. Roude out of places where they don't want him to leave!" That scared me, but I said, "Why bring that up? If Mr. Roude wants me to get him out I'll do it or die trying!" Larkin looked bored by the whole proceeding, but to me it was an adventure. I wanted to match my wits with someone, and I did want to do something for Mr. Roude.

Larkin made no move to pay the fare, when we got to Gramercy Park. He reminded me of what my father used to say of Uncle Fate, "He'd skin a flea for the hide and tallow." We found the number, a fine-looking house with a dim light showing in the vestibule. It was well after two, and the streets almost deserted—the silent dark house had a sinister air, but I motioned for Larkin to come on. He hung back, saying, "How are you going to get him out?" I didn't know myself, but I wouldn't admit it, so I said, "I'm going to ring the bell and say I'm Mrs. Roude." He looked dashed at that, and said, "Maybe he won't like that." But I didn't wait to ponder over it—I pushed the button, a colored maid opened the door, and in a very decided tone I said, "I want to speak to Mr. Roude." Her face was absolutely innocent as she said, "He ain't heah." Quickly, before she suspected my intention, I gave her a shove in the stomach and got past her into the front hall. Indignant, she said, "What yo' comin' like dat foah, Miss? Mistah Roude ain't heah!" Giving her a haughty look I said, "Go at once and tell Mr. Roude that Mrs. Roude is here!" Her eyes bulged in surprise and fear as she started up the stairs, I following her.

Hesitating on the first landing, she knocked on a door and listened; someone said, "Come in," and she slid past me, unwilling to be further involved. I opened the door and saw three people in a large, well-furnished sitting room. A tall blonde girl in a beautiful evening gown was sitting near Mr. Roude, and a heavy, thick-set, Swedish-looking man stood near the fireplace, one elbow on the mantel, one hand in his coat pocket. For an instant his face held my eyes, for it was brutal, ruthless. I wasted no time on either of the blondes, but looked straight into Mr. Roude's brown eyes and said, "David, I've come to take you home," trying to make him understand that I didn't know what to say, hoping that he would give me some sign. He smiled quietly and said, "Why that's real sweet of you, Maggie," and I knew that he had twigged.

He got up casually, put his glass down and said, "Well, it's kinda late— I guess we'll run along," and the blonde woman rang for the maid, who brought his hat and stick. Mr. Roude adjusted his hat at a nice angle and said to me carelessly, "Did the men come with you, Maggie?" I said, "Yes, David; all six of them. They're waiting outside," and he said indifferently, "That's good." He said good-by to the two blondes, politely, and as we stepped through the door he turned and gave them a long, direct look and said, "It's been a pleasure to see you both; I'll be down again, real soon," and as we went down the stairs, I felt sure we'd get a bullet in the back or a club over the head.

The door closed behind us and we stood in the fresh morning air. The light was cool and shivery gray; the street quiet. I looked back at the front of the silent house, and felt that there was something sinister in it. Mr. Roude stood so straight, so unconcerned, and said, "Where's the brave Larkin?" Larkin emerged from near the iron railing and said, "Yes, sir!" very brave now that the worst was over. Mr. Roude said, "Brave fellow! Rustle me a taxi and do it quick, you damned white-livered rat!"

From the taxi he said to Larkin, "Get home the best way you can, me brave boy," and to the chauffeur he said, "Plaza Hotel." All the way uptown he said nothing, nor did I. At the Plaza we got out, he paid the man, and stood on the sidewalk until the car had disappeared, then we walked around the hotel, got into another cab, and he gave his home address. Arriving there, he got out, gave me a ten-dollar bill and said, "Take this taxi home and snatch yourself some sleep, Miss Dan; something tells me I'm going to need you before this time tomorrow. Thank you for coming, and good night!"

At my street miles uptown, the first signs of the day's activities were beginning—a few shutters were being opened, pedestrians hurrying to work, the pall of sleep not yet exhausted. I went to bed and lay with the dead, until late afternoon. My hunger awoke me, drove me to find food, and upon my return I found a message from Mr. Roude, asking me to call his private number, which I did. By his voice I knew he was half-seas over, as he said, articulating carefully, "Listen, Miss Dan! I'll send Jennings for you some time this evening, so don't go out please. I'm as drunk as a lord, and I want you to come to the country; will you?" I said, "Right, Captain, any time you say."

Jennings came at eight, and drove me to the beautiful country, up the hill to the gloomy, but beautiful house I had so recently left. The impassive butler opened the door and said that I was to go straight up to Mr. Roude. As I went, I saw no one, heard no sound, as though a plague had decimated the occupants. The door to his enormous room was open, and away in the distance I saw him sitting alone, gazing into space; brooding, silent, lonely looking. He smiled and said, "Hello, friend! It's damned nice of you to come," and I said, "It's damned nice of you to have me, Mr. Roude." He looked around helplessly and said, "The Missus has gone, and so have a lot of the servants. We'll be alone and in peace for a while, anyway!" I said, "I'll go up and change my clothes, and be right down, Mr. Roude."

For weeks I was practically alone with him, for the servants came only when I rang for them, and Larkin lurked around in a servile, mistrustful manner. The man came every day to shave Mr. Roude, but aside from those few, I was alone and spent hours on end listening to him talk, or talking to him. He wouldn't let me send for Doctor Alexander, and I didn't dare do it on my own, but I was afraid that Mrs. Roude had left me there for some ulterior purpose. I made up my mind that I would remain until Mr. Roude was in safe hands, and bided my time. I slept short catnaps, while he was being bathed, and shaved, and often when he was talking, I learned by practice to answer him with sufficient coherency, while I dozed in a deep chair.

He talked almost constantly, eating very little, sleeping not at all. Never before, nor have I since, seen a person remain awake day and night, continuously, for interminable periods. He was quietly drinking, but not drunk. He made no demands on me other than to be wide-awake, and listen to him talk, or talk to him. He said to me, "Miss Dan, when I was a kid, my mother used to take in washing, and I delivered it for her." As he spoke those words, there was in them a challenge to my credulity, asking me to try and grasp the enormity of such a cruel, footless calamity! That the mother of David Graham Roude, had borne such indignities! His eyes implored me to sympathize with his inability to believe a thing so incredible! He never said it in words, but always in speaking of it, there was the pain and wonder of a child that has been brutally slapped, stunned by something too overwhelming to cry out. The pain and sorrow in his voice tore me in twain, as after a long silence he quietly continued. "When I was twelve, I got a job sweeping out a bank, and washing the windows. I rode an old white horse there, six miles, and back at night, for twelve years. All the time my life went past me damned quick, but all the time I was learning." Relaxed, quiet, he sat, the painful recollection of the past possessing him. I wanted to cry out, to strike at something that hurt him, but I only said, "And then?" Shifting his great body around in his chair, he said, "Well, finally they offered me the presidency of the bank. Poor Bramwell! I'll never forget his face when I told him that I would be unable to accept it! You see, they'd discussed it for months, and they thought they were offering me something beyond anything I had imagined, a prize for which I would give my life! The poor old coots! By that time I had enough money to buy their dinky little bank, and five more like it! I had to explain that I couldn't accept the great honor they were offering me, and why." He drew a few puffs on his cigar, and said sadly, "I hated to hurt their feelings; they were fine men, and had been fair to me; the trouble was they hadn't really noticed that for years I hadn't been sweeping the floor nor washing the windows. I told them that I had more responsibilities than I could well carry, and would be forced to refuse!" After the fourth puff, he threw his cigar away. They cost one dollar each, and he spoiled at least ten a day. I often wished that I could collect them and sell them, or do something with them. He went on, "You see, you poor ignorant girl, in the meantime I had become interested in Tin Plate, and Steel, and a few railroads, and had plenty on my mind, without a dinky bank. By God, they were surprised! I tell you they were!" Looking sharply at me, he said, "Do you want to know why I wanted to make so much money?" and I said, "Yes." Quietly, solemnly, he said, "I wanted to make my mother a queen!" He got up, saying, "Come, I'll show you her picture." And that big man, big in every human quality as well as body, took my arm like a child, and we walked down the hall and stairs to the wide front hall, to stand before a large painting of his mother. The painting was of a gentle, beautiful woman, whose eyes, dark and brooding like her son's, looked straight into your own. Eyes that had seen and known all the ills to which human beings are familiar, all the frailties with which we are cursed; had seen also the great beauty inherent, the capacities for good suppressed. They had seen, understood, and loved nonetheless. Wise, tolerant, kind, and luminous, her eyes looked into ours, and Mr. Roude put his two hands over his eyes, his body shaking with sobs. Her quiet pose reflected, just as his, an alertness of mind and muscle, and it seemed that at any moment, one of her quiet hands resting in her lap, would reach out and lie on his bowed head. I couldn't bear that his pain should tear him so, but there was nothing I could say or do. There was a physical austerity enveloping him always that precluded sentimentality. I think in his whole life, he did not acquire a physical casualness.

He wept for a long time, and I wished that I could put my arms around him and comfort him, but he somehow stood alone. After a while I said, "But, Mr. Roude, don't weep! She can't bear it. Can't you see she can't?" He stopped, gradually, wiped his nose noisily, and we retraced our steps to his room. Back on the balcony, in the moonlight, the beauty of the night seemed filled with his loneliness and sadness. I suggested another nurse, for I was groggy for sleep, and urged him to see Doctor Alexander, but he always said, "Not now; later." He went on with his story, telling me how he had married his first wife when he had very little money, and how she had first a baby girl, and later a boy. She became ill with tuberculosis, and he borrowed money to send her away, hoping that she would be cured. She wasn't.

And how later, his son died. Looking straight at me, and through me, he said bitterly, "I lost my only son, when he was just a little feller." By this time he had made a lot of money, and, he said, "I chartered a ship to take my mother back to Scotland." An extravagant gesture, but knowing him as I came to, entirely consistent. A hurt, whipped look was in his eyes as he said, "Just when we were ready to go, my mother died." His eyes pleaded for me to try and match that for a rotten break. All these things he told me, and sometimes he would break off, and say, "Where were you born? How did you happen to become a trained nurse? It's a rotten job for a young girl; you shouldn't do it. Isn't there something else you can do?" I told him how hard I had worked, trying to make enough money to go to school, of how miserably I had failed. He said, "It's not too late; I'll help you. You must not spend your life nursing drunken old sots like me." I said, "Listen, Mr. Roude! No matter how much you drink, you're the finest man I've ever known, and I'm happy with you. Don't call yourself a drunkard, for drunk though you may be, you're a grand person, a fine, kind, brilliant man, and you know it. I don't want you to drink, but if you do, I prefer being with you. If you'll stop, I'll learn another trade. Is that a bargain?" He laughed, and said, "Oh, no, you don't trap me that way. I'm going to get drunk whenever I like, as long as I live, but I'll help you to learn something else, for it's a shame for you to be shut up here with a man like me."

Later he referred again to the matter of education, saying, "I don't think too damned much of this college business. The ones I've met were dumb as hell; can't figure, can't even add." And he asked me to bring him a pad and pencil, to write down a row of eight figures, and to continue until I had ten rows. Under those rows he drew a line and instantly wrote down the sum of their addition, from the left to right. Unable to believe my eyes, I worked laboriously over it for hours, counting on my fingers, only to find that it was absolutely correct. We spent hours doing sums in arithmetic, and he could at a glance, add a phenomenal number of figures, or subtract, or multiply them. He did it by one glance, and always correct. Fearing that I was mistaken, I had others later, go over them, but found no mistakes.

Often in the middle of the night or early morning, he would get up, saying, "Come, let us prowl," and we would go down to the veranda, out into the garden and sit on a stone seat by the small lake. The whole scene bathed in white moonlight, no sounds except that of small insects, the odor of flowers and hay filling the summer night. When he had sat in silence for a long time, he'd say, "Beautiful, isn't it?" Then he would go to the pantries, where enormous ice boxes were filled with food such as I had never known existed, were opened, and scorned. Great bunches of grapes on beds of cotton, and peaches, apricots, with their heavenly odors. Melons, too, and cold meats he viewed with distaste, saying, "Oh! for God's sakes! Wake up Betsy and have her make me some scrambled eggs and bacon!" Betsy was an elderly woman who had been with him for a long time, and when she hustled her great bulk around to please him, he would say, "Look in my wallet and give her fifty dollars." She never seemed to mind getting up to cook for him. I think that he had lived in luxury so long that he craved simplicity; something he had as a child. He was lonely, hungry, for the things of the past, and didn't know it.

After eating the ham and eggs, or baked beans, as the case might be, he would begin again to tell me of his life. "Well, then I married my second wife. She was an actress named Alice Wimple. A lovelier woman never lived, Miss Dan. She was as sweet as a morning in the country when the dew is on the grass, and the birds twittering. And fun! Why that girl was full of fun! She'd come into this room, not like ordinary mortals like you and me, my girl. But no! She'd start up the hall, and turn cartwheels all the way down the hall, straight into this room, and right across my bed, quick as a flash of light. Then she'd laugh with joy, just because she was happy. And good-hearted! Do you know what she'd do?" And I would say, "No, Mr. Roude, what would she do?" Eyeing me to see that I was properly awake, he continued, "I'll tell you what that girl did! She had every damned down-and-out chorus girl and actress in New York down here, and fed them, and bought them clothes, helped them get jobs! Some nights they'd get all dressed up in costumes and put on a show for me, or play games. The house was alive, and gay then! She was the loveliest woman I have ever known!" He would remain silent so long, I'd think he had dropped off to sleep, but he never did, for he went on with his thinking aloud.

"We were married for only four years!" he said, with great sadness in his voice. "What happened?" I asked. His face became bitter, and cruel lines shaped themselves around his mouth, and he spoke venomously, "Some god-damned doctor decided that she needed an operation! Well, maybe she did, I wouldn't know. Anyhow, he did it, and charged me ten thousand dollars for doing it! If he'd saved her life I'd have given him a million. But he didn't. No, damn him, he didn't. She died. Only seven minutes did she live after she came out of the ether. And do you know what her last words were to me?" I said, "No, Mr. Roude. What were her last words to you?"

He gave me a long curious look, and said, "I'll tell you what her last words were. She held my hand, and looked at me and said, 'Thank you, David, for all you've done for me; all the sweet things, all the beautiful things you've given me. Thank you for everything, David. You are a king! David, you are a king!' and with those words, she died." He rested his head on his hands, and tears ran down his cheeks. "Why does God do such cruel things, Dan? I don't understand! When the world is full of the god-damnedest lousiest females, and to kill off one like that! Can you understand that? I ask you, *can* you understand that?" And my heart was torn, I wept with him and said, "No, I damned well can't, Mr. Roude."

So, he told me of his first wife, and of his second wife, of his daughter, of whom he was inordinately proud, praising her head for figures, but he never mentioned his third wife, his current one. I said nothing, for I thought likely he knew I didn't admire her, nor she me, and that was his effort at fairness and consideration. With all his drinking and temper, he was always kind and considerate. No matter what he said, or did, I know that his heart was as kind as God is supposed to be. He was a mixture of hardness and generosity, of egotism, and simplicity, even gentle humbleness. The kindness of his heart was at times hidden under a layer of distrust and suspicion, due probably to the hard years of his youth, and as I learned in time, to the falseness of many so-called friends, of many who got money from him under false pretenses. Among the people, many of high worldly positions, some of great wealth, I knew only one man who was his true and loyal friend. For me, he was a great man, born perhaps at the wrong time; if he had been in the gutter, I would have got him out, and held him up. How any one could fail to see him as he really was, always remained a mystery to me.

After two weeks, Mrs. Roude returned, bringing with her a doctor and nurse. I was in my room at the time, and Thorpe sneaked up to warn me. I went quietly down to see what was going on, and I heard loud voices coming not only from Mr. Roude's room, but from Mr. Roude himself. I listened, and heard him say, angrily, "You'll not force that cutthroat doctor on me, and as for that hatchet-faced old horse with buck teeth, I say No! I have a nurse, and by God, I'll keep her! I say *no*, and I mean No! She's got buck teeth, and you damned well know it!" There was a murmur of persuasive conversation, then Mr. Roude again, "If she dares to come near my room, I'll shoot her! I may be drunk, but not drunk enough to stand that awful face! Get out, before I get mad! The whole lot of you." I slipped back to my room, and soon Larkin came to say that Mr. Roude wanted me to come down.

When I came down, he was fit to be tied. "Can you beat that for a dirty trick! Bring that cheap thug, that nasty-nosed squirt of a doctor in on me, and that old spavined warhorse with buck teeth! Tripe! I've kicked them out!" When I could get a word in edgewise, I said, "But, Mr. Roude, maybe he's not so bad as he looks. You don't know him; give him a chance!" He stared at me, and burst into howls of laughter. He laughed as I had never known he could. I was glad to hear him, no matter what the cause. When he could get his breath, he said, "Oh! My God! Don't know him! The dirty bastard is my own cousin, and I've paid him out of many a jam. Do I know that son of a bitch? I'll say I know him! He's the lowest snivelling pimp in the world!" and he went off again into snorts of laughter.

From being quiet, and a bit lonely, the situation took on another color. There was the tension of armed, though silent, battle in the house. A strange feeling of waiting, of hatred, exuded from every corner, and I watched my step, for I knew that on my side I had only Thorpe and Mr. Roude, while Mrs. Roude had her entire entourage. Larkin played safe, remaining neutral, but he didn't like me I knew, for I had caught him rifling Mr. Roude's pockets once. He knew I had his number. Added to this charming situation, Thorpe told me that the grimy doctor Mrs. Roude had brought was in love with the horse-faced nurse, and that he was jealous because she spent her nights with Mrs. Roude. The dark, dirty tattling going on around in that house like a fog of evil gas, and Mr. Roude knew nothing of it, really.

Mrs. Roude began to entertain, and almost every night ten or twelve guests dressed in beautiful evening clothes, dined in the outdoor dining room, served in great style by the three butlers. They made the night ring with their talk and laughter, but not one of them ever came to enquire how Mr. Roude was. They ignored him completely. The nurse and doctor remained as guests; they never spoke to me, nor came near Mr. Roude. There they stayed, eating Mr. Roude's food, drinking his wine, and showing him no courtesy whatever. I hated them for it,—I could have killed them every one. Mr. Roude said nothing, but I knew he felt it,—that he was hurt and lonely. Often I wished that I could go to Mrs. Roude and say, "Look now, this is a job, and I'm trying to earn my money. I have to make a living, so let us be friends," but I couldn't. Her manner was inimical; I abandoned the idea.

Things came to a climax as I knew they must, one evening when they were at dinner. Mr. Roude was quiet, but seething inside, quite drunk. Pulling himself erect, he said, "Come, we will descend and gaze upon the pimps and whores and crooks who are dining with me this evening." I tried in vain to dissuade him, for I knew no good would come of it, but he walked fairly steadily down the hall, laying his hand on my shoulder at the stairs. He was just unsteady enough to make negotiation of the turns a precarious proposition, and I realized that dexterity would be required to make the landing safely, right side up. He leaned more and more on me, and his weight increased, so that at the bottom step I was panting for breath, and relaxed for one instant. He fell, flat on his back, in the hall. There was something about his being in that helpless, ignoble position that I could not bear, and I began to scream as loud as I could, "Help! Come and help me!" They all came running in and stood looking at me, as I tried to lift him up, but not one of them came to help. Releasing my hold on him, and letting his head gently down on the floor, I ran at them, striking out at them as they backed away from me. I screamed at them, for I saw on their faces an amused, tolerant, satisfied look, when they saw his helpless position. "Go away," I screamed. "You lousy, filthy swine! Don't you dare touch him, nor sneer at him! You've eaten his food, and drunk his wine, slept in his beds, and I tell you to your faces you are rotten cowards not fit to tie his shoes! And you, Mrs. Roude! His wife! A hell of a wife you are; you haven't been to see him, nor ask about him, for a week! Go away! Go away!" I yelled at them, and they retreated.

Suddenly I had finished with them, and went back to Mr. Roude. Perhaps my noisy yelling brought him to, for he was making an effort to rise. I helped him up, and we went slowly up the stairs and to his room. Knowing my goose was cooked anyway, I said, "Now, Mr. Roude, I'm going to call Doctor Alexander," and I didn't wait for him to say no. Doctor Alexander said he would come right up, when I told him the hole I was in, what I'd said and done. He came and talked to Mr. Roude, and to me, and we somehow felt better.

I expected to have to go next day, but nothing happened at all, except that Mrs. Roude and her guests were as meek as mice, and showed by various small courtesies that they wished to placate me. That was all right, but I wouldn't have trusted one of them further than I could throw a cow by the tail, but I was polite, letting sleeping dogs, and I mean dogs, lie. How I wished that his daughter, a Mrs. de Witt would come, and that I might show her what an unhappy household it was. I never understood why she left her wonderful father alone with a cheap bunch of people, but already I was putting things in my compartment labelled, "None of my business."

With Doctor Alexander on the job, Mr. Roude began to improve, and although he was nervous and irritable he was making a great effort to be calm, and give up alcohol. When we went to see the pigs, in our walks over the farm, he told me of a very rich man he knew, who had married a young and beautiful wife. Becoming suspicious that she had married him only for his money, he sought to prove her love, which he did by moving into the pigpen where they lived for one year. At the end of that time he decided that she loved him for himself alone, and they moved into his great mansion. Naturally I didn't believe it, but he conceded that the pigpen was a very nice cottage, with cement floors, and troughs in it; a pigpen *de luxe*. Mr. Roude said that he visited them while they lived in the pigpen, and the whole thing amused him greatly. He was so well, and I loved seeing the farm with him. He told me that every egg cost him one dollar, and every strawberry fifty cents, every pea a quarter.

Although Mrs. Roude and her guests were more polite to both me and Mr. Roude, after my fit, they still were not genuine, and I knew it. They came in to see him, but itched to get away, for they really feared him. Mrs. Roude was certainly beautiful, with skin like pearl, her eyes bright and starry, a golden brown, but she was dumb. But how dumb! In her slinking, creeping way, she would come in when he was having his lunch, and say in a high, nasal, plaintive drawl, "Having your lunch, Davie?" He would lay down his fork with a puzzled expression, as though maybe he hadn't heard correctly; just look, shake his head, and say quietly, "No, I'm riding a bicycle." Sometimes it would be that Mr. Roude sat in his big barber chair, his face lathered, the man with razor poised, when she would creep in, smiling like a child, and say, "Getting a shave, David?" Almost springing from his chair with nervousness, he would jerk the towel from around his neck, and bellow, "No, by God! Can't you *see* I'm taking a ride down Fifth Avenue?"

I was forced to ask her not to come in, unless she could think of some more sensible remark to make. The doctor and nurse she had brought finally left, and the house began faintly to resemble a home; not a happy home, but a home. I learned a lot from Thorpe about the rules governing servants in an establishment of that size. I had never seen nor imagined a house with thirty-five servants. He showed me their rooms, their sitting rooms, which were lovely, and the dining room and billiard room, great oak-paneled rooms with beautiful and valuable paintings, luxurious chairs and rugs. He told me that Mr. Cromer, the head butler, sat at the head of the table, that he entered the dining room first, followed by the second butler; then the valets and ladies' maids, then the third butler, followed by the upstairs parlor maids; below these came the kitchen maids and laundresses. I suppose the stable men didn't get in at all. They entered and took their seats according to immutable rules, no one daring to step out of their proper place. Their castes seemed more rigid than those above stairs. No doubt it is a practical plan, but to me it seemed somehow grotesque.

Mr. Roude was soon perfectly well, for he had a strong, healthy body, good nerves, perfect eyes and teeth. He was fifty years old. Aside from his periodic bouts, he was in perfect physical condition. He often said to me, "Miss Dan, I'll live to a ripe old age, if I can keep out of the hands of the doctors. They're the babies that can polish you off." That made me sore, and I spoke up, out of turn. "Mr. Roude, that's not fair. There are doctors who will polish you off, and there are those who will help you to live long and healthy lives. It depends on the doctor you choose. But you're like most rich people; you want a doctor who will grovel to you, and soft soap you, and a good doctor won't do it. That's why rich people have such crummy doctors, so don't blame the profession. It's your fault for wanting that sort of incompetent crook. Nurses laugh at the type of doctor a rich person will pay thousands for. You stick to Doctor Alexander, and you'll live to be a hundred, likely. But you won't. Within a year you'll be in the hands of one of those birds you scorn." He just laughed.

I left the beautiful country reluctantly, and I hated most leaving Mr. Roude, for he certainly didn't seem too happy, for all his money. I'd have been a drunkard too, I expect, in his situation. He let me ride in with him, and near his office I got out, said good-by, took the subway, and was back in my dark, hot little room. Having no friends, I might easily have been lonely, but there was always so much to do, what with sewing and mending, and reading, that I didn't have time. And then I got a call from Doctor James Havemeyer to come to his office. I had left my name with little hope that he would call me, for he was a very famous man, so I went immediately. He was a tall, rangy, ugly man, outside, but inside kind and good. He said, "I've got a devil of a patient for you if you want to try him, Miss Dan. He has fired four of my best nurses in the last three days. Do you want to try him?" I said, "Yes, Doctor Havemeyer." He smiled and said, "I'll make you a present of him, with one understanding. If he fires you, you're not to mind. Promise?" I said, "It's a promise." He told me the name of the patient, Joseph Brevia, who had fallen from a tree, into which some friend's pet kitten had climbed, and broken his arm. He was in a hospital on the West Side, and I was to report at seven the next morning.

That night I was so nervous I couldn't sleep well, and I got up early, took a cold bath to give me courage, and at seven, stood at the head nurse's desk. Before she took me in, she explained that he was a most difficult patient. We stood in his room, and I saw lying in bed, a handsome man of fortyish, with a spoiled, petulant expression. His coloring was dark, his eyes large and melting brown, his tiny teeth white, rodent-like. The nurse said, "This is Miss Dan, Mr. Brevia. I know you're going to like her!" He smiled sardonically and said, "Are you? Charming!" The nurse made no effort to conceal her pleasure at being able to leave the room, and there I was, alone with a spoiled, mean man.

Knowing that Doctor Havemeyer would understand, no matter what happened, I proceeded with my work, just as though he was a patient being used for demonstration purposes. I bathed his face and hands, handed him his toothbrush nicely wet, with a ribbon of paste laid neatly on the bristles, with a cup of water. When he'd finished, I removed the basin and served his breakfast. I did not speak, nor did he. After his breakfast, I got towels and hot water and gave him a nice bed bath, and when I'd finished, I handed him a washcloth, squeezed to the right moisture soaped, and said, "Now you can finish." His face expressed astonishment and helplessness, and he said, "Finish what?" Calmly I said, "I wonder?" and left the room. I don't know what the other nurses had done about it, but I had never bathed a man completely and I didn't intend to begin now.

Many times I have been embarrassed by the display of vulgar minds, not always masculine either, concerning the intimate details a nurse is supposed to encounter in the practice of her profession. To cover their own dirty minds, men will say sly things, and will say, "Oh, you're a nurse; you know all about those things!" I often wished to kill them. How and why explain to that sort of man that at no time in my entire hospital experiences did I see a nude man? That there are orderlies always to carry out treatments of an intimate nature? It is not that I do not know how, or that it would in any way embarrass me to do anything that is needed to be done for a sick man. There is nothing about it to excite vulgar remarks, except from peculiarly vulgar people. A sick man, to a good nurse, is a patient, and sex is not the point. He is a human being whom it is her duty to help if possible. It has always seemed to me that a certain type of person experiences a secret pleasure from the wild imaginings of all sorts of familiarities indulged in by nurses, which must be due to some lack of healthy sexual adjustment in themselves.

In this particular instance, I simply left the room, and upon my return, proceeded on the assumption that he had done the only intelligent thing. I changed all his linen, put his clean pajamas on him, then I said, "Now I'm going to give you a shave." He drew back in horror, and said decisively, "You are not!" Calmly I said, "I am so," and got ready. "You're much too handsome a man to go on looking like a tramp, and I'm certainly not going to remain on an Island with Robinson Crusoe." By this time I had my old-fashioned razor in hand, and stricken with fear, he screamed, "You're *not* going to use that museum piece, are you?" I ran my finger along its edge, and said, "sure; why not? It's a good razor." I gave him my watch and said, "Now you time me. I'll bet you a nickel I can give you a perfectly grand shave in four minutes flat." He eyed the watch, and when I whisked the towel away, and bathed his face, it was just over the four minutes. He almost smiled, forgetting his rôle of tyrant.

He looked lovely when I'd finished with him, and like an undertaker, I surveyed my work with pride, thinking how human he looked, almost as if he were alive. I arranged his flowers, of which there were far too many. He was perfect, his room was perfect, and I thought I myself wasn't so bad, so I took one of his books and sat down to read. He lay quiet for a while, then said indignantly, "Put down that book!" I turned from the book long enough to give him a straight look right in the eye, and said, "I will not. I've done everything for you, you're comfortable, and I'm tired. Just you lie still and think. Or can you?" And I went on reading, wondering what he would do next. He made no reply, and I thought "That is probably the end of this case," but I knew Doctor Havemeyer would understand.

When the doctor came, I waited in the hall, and on his way out he stopped and said, "Congratulations! He says he'll go home if you will go with him!" I was as proud as Punch, for I wanted Doctor Havemeyer to give me more work, and I saw that he was pleased. "Keep him here a few days longer, for I want to get some pictures of the break before he goes home," and I said, "Yes, Doctor Havemeyer." Oh! I did so want him to believe I was a good nurse, for I liked working for him.

Mr. Brevia got along splendidly after that, and the days flew by. Every day women came to see him, bringing more flowers than he could look at, more cigarettes than he would ever smoke, more books than he would ever read, and handkerchiefs, pajamas, and socks. I had never seen so many beautiful women, and when I heard their names, I was thrilled, because there before me moved and talked, women whose names I had seen in the papers, with pictures. Women from the Opera, the Theatre, Society; artists, actresses and writers cluttered his room and the halls. I'd never seen so many famous people, and I observed with interest his technique. He rarely allowed two admissions at a time, except when he wanted to play one against the other; their excessive politeness, covering sharp claws, I think, amused him. It puzzled me somewhat, but that was pigeonholed in my N.O.M.B. department.

They were all polite to me, as they did not consider me a competitor, but I had no conversation with any of them until one day as I waited in the hall, one of them stopped, on her way out and said, "I'll bet you have a good time when you're off duty!" For an instant I visualized my tiny dark room, and said, "Good time? Doing what?" Impatiently she tapped her beautifully shod foot and said, "Going out with men, dancing." I wanted to smack her, but after all what could she know about it? I said, "I don't know any men, and if I did, I have no clothes to wear to dance." Surprised, she opened her blue eyes wide, and said, "No clothes? That's ridiculous! I'll send you some." Surprised, I said, "That is kind of you, but what of the other requirements?" Puzzled, she asked, "What? Oh, yes, the man! Don't worry about that; if you have the clothes, you'll get the man!" and she went down the hall, singing happily to herself. What a lovely woman, I thought!

The next day an enormous box came for me, and I was so excited I could hardly wait to open it. Mr. Brevia was, too, and when I found, between layers of tissue paper, five of the most beautiful dresses that could be imagined, we were both speechless; one after the other I laid them on his bed, first a plain morning dress, then two day dresses, and two beautiful evening gowns! Mr. Brevia became so excited that I was worried about his health. Placing them all carefully back in the box, I said, "Now, Mr. Brevia, let us discuss this calmly. It is wonderful of her to send them, but I must return them." At that he became violently argumentative. "Return them? You will not! Why should you?" he demanded. "Now, now, Mr. Brevia, be quiet, and I'll explain. First off, I have not the accessories to go with such clothes,—it would cost a hundred dollars to get them,—and even if I had them, where would I wear them? I can't use them, therefore I must return them." But he begged, and demanded, until in the end I said, "All right, I'll keep them."

When she came next day, I thanked her for them. She waved her hand carelessly, and said, "Oh, that's nothing!" Nothing, I thought. Those dresses cost at least five hundred dollars; enough for me to go to school a whole year, and for the matter of that, to allow me to have a room with daylight for years. Nothing, thinks I to myself! At last I got them to my small room, where I pushed the box under my bed—that was the only place it fitted—and wondered what to do with them. Then I remembered a tall lovely girl I had met in the hospital where I had first met Mr. Roude, and decided to give them to her. Her name was Carol Prince, and I knew that she had boyfriends, and could use them. She couldn't believe her eyes when she saw them. I kept the plain one, which was made of the finest blue wool material I had ever seen, with white linen collar and cuffs. It was cut so cleverly that I planned to copy it one day.

When I had been with Mr. Brevia for ten days, he said, "I can go home today. Will you go with me?" I said I'd be glad to. He was worried, and asked, "You're sure you won't mind being in my apartment alone except for my sour old Scotch housekeeper?" I said, "No, why should I mind?" He didn't answer.

His lady friends fought a silent battle as to which one could have the honor of taking him home, and in the end, the Lady of the Dresses won, carrying him off in her big limousine, while I followed with a disgruntled loser and all the loot he had received in the hospital. He was the most popular man I had ever known, and to save my life I couldn't, and never did, find out in what lay his fatal charm. When we reached his apartment, a charming one on Washington Square, the ladies fussed about, each trying to make herself more indispensable than the other, until I said I thought he should be left to rest. They scuttled off, each proudly in her big car, and he said with fervor, "Thank God they've gone!" and I said, "You don't have to have them unless you wish, and you know it; you love having them make fools of themselves over you."

He had his dinner on a tray, while I had mine in the sweetest little dining room, opening right into a lovely garden. His old maid cook showed plainly her opinion of a woman who would remain alone with a man, but when I mentioned it to Mr. Brevia he said, "Don't mind her; she's that way to every woman who comes here. Jealous!" Even the sour Scotch woman had the disease all the other women had, and I wondered.

Mr. Brevia was an interior decorator, and he showed me pieces of wonderful materials, of which he had hundreds in an old chest. He gave me a piece, which I kept for years; the shabbiest room looked cheerful with that in view. We had a quiet, peaceful time except for the afternoons when his lady friends came. He read books to me, and discussed them interestingly. He never asked me personal questions, neither did he discuss his own, and he was always kind, courteous, and charming. When he got really well, his lady friends came and took him to the theatres, and to the opera, and on those evenings I usually went to my room for mail and clean clothes.

One afternoon the Lady of the Dresses came, and as Mr. Brevia had already a lady with him, I took her into the little garden, hoping to entertain her until the other had gone. She was jolly and friendly, and asked me why I was a trained nurse. I asked her, "Why not?" She said that somehow it didn't seem the right sort of work for me. I didn't tell her of my disappointments concerning education, for it was obvious that she had always had everything and wouldn't understand. She said, "Why don't you do something else? Be a secretary, for instance." I said that Doctor Alexander had told me that if I would take a secretarial course, it would be a good idea, because no secretaries know anything of medicine, and that I had dallied with the idea until I discovered that a good course would cost a hundred and fifty dollars, during which time I would also have to eat, else the training would be wasted. She said, "That's fine! Any time you want to do it, let me know, and I'll be glad to help you, for I think you're a grand girl. You'd make a good social secretary—I might need you myself!" I thanked her, and she said, "Nonsense! Now don't forget; you know my name and address. Let me know if you ever decide to do it, and need any help." I said that I certainly would remember. And like a poor sap, I trusted her!

When he became so well there was no possible excuse for my remaining, I said I thought I would go. He looked annoyed, like a spoiled child, and he said, "Why don't you remain here with me always?" I laughed and said, "Why, Mr. Brevia, you don't need a nurse. I do sort of hate to go for I've been very happy with you, but you know I must." He said, petulantly, "I'll even marry you to get you to stay!" That made me angry, and I said, "You'll do nothing of the kind! I don't want to marry you, and you know darn well you don't want to marry me. If you really want me to stay, all you have to do is pay me twenty-one dollars a week; you'll find it cheaper too!" I pretended the whole thing was a joke, which indeed it was. I thanked him for the most restful time I had ever had with a patient, and he repeated many times, "I do wish you'd stay! I'll miss you terribly!" I laughed at him, and said, "Miss me! With all your lady friends, in a week you won't remember my name!"

Following my usual plan, I got my clothes ready for my next case. One of the most maddening things about being a nurse is that of having to remain in all day, day after day, for fear of missing a call. I have remained indoors until in sheer desperation I have gone for a short walk, only to find on my return that I had missed two calls. The reason is that naturally, when a doctor wants a nurse, he wants her at once. If one is out, it's just too bad. Two weeks went by, and I kept thinking over some plan for learning something that would be more certain than nursing. I liked it, it was exciting and interesting, but frightfully uncertain. I wrote a letter, a simple, straightforward letter, to the Lady of the Dresses, reminding her of our conversation, and her offer to help me, and said that I believed her suggestion was a good one. I had no reply, and two days later I was called to the phone, to hear Mr. Brevia's voice. Happy to hear from him, I said, "How are you, Mr. Brevia?" His reply was curt, cutting, cold. "I'm calling to tell you that you must stop annoying my friends, ladies whom you were fortunate enough to meet at my house, and unless you do stop it at once, I will take legal steps to see that you do." His words were like a knife in my heart. I was stunned. I gasped, and said, "Mr. Brevia, what on earth are you talking about? I have not, intentionally, annoyed your friends!" By this time I was weeping hysterically, and he said, "Oh, yes you have, and I warn you now, if you do it again, I'll have you arrested," and he hung up. I'm not the fainting kind of female, but I wished at that moment I could simply pass out, lose all consciousness of a world in which such things could be. I wanted to obliterate all feeling, all sense of sound, but nothing so comfortable happened. I remained acutely aware of every word he had said, and in my room I cried in rage and despair, and terror. I knew that that woman had told him of my letter, and that they had talked of me like that! I had no redress, there was nothing I could do, and the knowledge of my helplessness drove me mad. I wanted to kill them, or myself, and the night was long in passing. His words repeated themselves over and over until my head ached with the repetition. "I'll have you arrested . . . annoying my friends . . . fortunate enough to meet." Over and over I heard those words until I could bear them no longer. Then I remembered the dresses! And I had worn her dress! Oh! God damn her! I dressed very early and went to the hospital, determined to find Carol Prince, explain to her, and to return all the dresses to the devil from Hell.

At the hospital they gave me an address in New Jersey. After the long ride to that place, I was told that she was in Brooklyn. I went there, only to find that she had left that address, and no one knew where she had gone. All day long, without food or rest, I looked for her, almost like a mad woman, filled with seething hate and despair. And in the end, I could not find her! I wondered if I could possibly kill them both, but could think of no way. I wanted to torture them, as they had me. Tired, half crazy, I returned to my room late that night, too distraught to sleep. I packed up the one dress I had, and wrote her a letter, explaining why I could not return the others; that I would undertake to pay for them, and to that end, enclosed five dollars. I was so mixed up in my mind I didn't realize that all that I might make for years would be required to pay for them, but I had somehow, to make myself free from her evil, so that is how I tried. I carried the box with the one dress, and handed it to the butler and ran from the neighborhood, ashamed, and full of hate. That woman has constantly received great adulation and publicity in all the New York papers from that day to this, and whenever I see her name, I remember what she did to me. And no evil has fallen on her; she is in the pink.

The whole episode did something to me that I could not properly evaluate at the time. I became afraid, and suspicious of everything and everybody; I didn't trust myself anymore, neither my eyes nor my intuition. For I had believed that those two people were kind, and natural; now I was forced to see that they were utterly cruel and base. All my pain and anguish concerning my personal appearance, which I had forgotten for years, returned to me, and with such force that I could not walk along the street, without wishing to cover my face. If a passerby glanced at me, I felt that they were horrified at my ugliness. Because I could not sit in a restaurant, I bought supplies that I could eat in my room, and there I sat hour after hour, weeping bitterly. I bought a thick black veil, and hurrying to the store, bought my food, hanging my head if anyone looked at me, and suffering agony until I was back in my room. Great boils came on my face and neck, increasing daily until my whole appearance was horrible to see. Afraid to look at myself in the glass, I could not prevent myself looking. I was glad when I became really repulsive, for now I couldn't go to see the doctors; naturally they could not give work to a nurse who looked like that. Days and nights passed, and I sat as though paralyzed, knowing that my savings were dwindling and I did not care. For all my hard work, my ambitions and my naïve belief in myself, my great desire to know distinguished people, here I was at the end. Alone in a small room in Harlem I sat and thought over and over every word that he had said, "I'll have you arrested." I thought of my sister Adelaide, and wondered if she too had experienced such unbearable pain.

I tried to retrace my steps, to see where I had blundered, what move on my part had brought me to where I was, but I could not understand; everything seemed fantastic, unreal. The qualities I had taken for granted as part of the makeup of decent human beings were, evidently, entirely lacking in certain specimens. Well then, how was I to know them when I saw them? How make the things I had been taught to believe fit with facts which were entirely different? The most cruel and arrogant, the really bad, flourished as the bay tree, and around me I saw quite decent specimens being destroyed by the strong, destructive kind. They were well fed, comfortably housed, beautifully dressed, respected before men. They were not even constipated. They would destroy with a smile, nothing could hurt them, while I had not even the power to keep out from my heart the pain that hurt beyond bearing. I had been taught to believe that it was stupid to hate; what then must one feel, upon witnessing vileness rampant, vulgarity and cruelty protected and admired? I knew that this was only one slight gesture on their part, that they had always done that sort of thing until they were adepts at it. I wished that I could be with the others and say, "I too know about this; you must not let it kill you." I remembered how shocked Leonard was when I said, "It is good to hate, so long as you hate the right thing." Now I thought, I hate. If it is a wrong emotion, then something must tell me why,—and there was no answer.

Thinking until my head was a huge ball of fire, I came to the conclusion that I was a very poor specimen, and likely should be destroyed. On the farm when I was a child, the best and strongest plants and animals were preserved; the others abandoned or destroyed. Then why not me? I said to myself, if I am not strong enough to exist in these natural surroundings, then I should expect and accept the same principle as that applied to plants and animals. That was the only line of thinking that made sense, and somehow comforted me.

After about two weeks, I telephoned to Doctor Williams and said that I had a slight rash on my face, making light of it, and asked him if he knew a good skin specialist. He did, and gave me the name and address. I went next day, and I explained to the nurse that I was also a nurse, and could not pay much, but she was very nice about it. This doctor, a rather pompous affair, examined me and asked a few questions. After pondering deeply, he said, "What you need, young lady, is to get married." Half in anger, half in astonishment, at such naïveté, I said, "Well, will you marry me?" He drew back, annoyed, and I went on, "Well, it's your idea. Don't you like it? If that's your prescription, you should be willing to see that it is carried out." I got up to go, and as he still had not answered, as a parting shot I said, "Who do you think would marry a girl with a face like mine? Thank you for nothing on earth." Science is wonderful.

Now I was curious to know what other famous skin specialists would advise, so I telephoned to Doctor Alexander's nice secretary, and she sent me to Doctor John Fordyce, and my meeting with him was one of the many things I have to be thankful for in this foolish life. He was short-spoken, but a great man, a commanding personality. He examined my face, gave me lotions to use, soap for my hair, and told me to come back in one week. He was so alive, vital, that just seeing him for a few minutes, made me want to get well at once. I carried out his instructions meticulously, and in two days my face was so improved that I went out without my black veil. I went downtown on the subway, and from Forty-second Street, I walked up Broadway, with all the hundreds from New Jersey and the Bronx. I had been in my room so long that everything looked lovely, the lights brighter, and I was happy just to be alive. For some fool reason I wanted to sing and shout for joy. Doctor Fordyce had given me back my courage and without saying ten words to me. Just something he had of health.

As I walked along with the crowd, I saw a young man smiling, and at me. I smiled at him. He elbowed his way through the mob and we found ourselves in a quiet eddy near the stores. He said Hello, and I said Hello, and there we stood, embarrassed, unable to continue. Then we both laughed, and he said, "Won't you come with me to some place we can have a drink, and maybe a dance?" and I said I'd love to. He took me nicely in his care, and I thought my face couldn't be so bad, or such a nice young man wouldn't have chosen me out of all the mob.

We went to a place where the music was good, and we had a drink, and danced for hours. He told me his name was Reuben Rosenthal, and I told him mine. He was a marvellous dancer, and it was heavenly to dance as much as I liked, for the first time in my life. He seemed happy too, and when he took me uptown on the subway at one o'clock, we exchanged small bits of information about ourselves. He told me that he had an older brother who was married, and a small sister. I told him of my work, and a little of my life. He seemed surprised to find that I lived in Harlem, but asked me to meet him the next night for dinner. I rushed to my mirror as soon as I got in, and I thought I didn't look so bad. I went to sleep thinking, "Now I've got me a nice boyfriend!"

For three evenings we met and had dinner and danced, and we had such a good time. He was twenty-five, a graduate of Harvard, which made me remember Judge Reeves. He was good-looking, and I couldn't believe that he really liked being with me, but so it was. At the end of the week I went back to see Doctor Fordyce, and he was amazed at the improvement in my face. He ascribed it entirely to the efficacy of his prescriptions, and maybe rightly; how was I to tell him that I had a friend, a lovely, beautiful young man who made me forget my face, who made me laugh, and that just possibly that helped somewhat.

And then Mr. Roude's secretary phoned to say that Mr. Roude wanted me to come down at once. I telephoned Reuben, and told him where I was going, and he said, "But you'll be back soon? And you'll let me hear from you, won't you?" and I said, "Of course!" Oh! It was wonderful to have someone want to know where I was, and to hear from me!

When I reached Mr. Roude's house, I found that he had a brand-new physician,—a contribution of Mrs. Roude, of whom I suspected the worst beforehand. He was dapper, and suave, and Oh, so jovial. I waited to see what method he would pursue. Through Thorpe, I discovered that he had moved in, bag and baggage,—was indeed living in the house, his beautiful car and chauffeur being splendidly cared for. Apparently he had no other patients,—he had, he explained to me, such a profound interest in Mr. Roude's case that he had turned all his patients over to his assistant. "I shouldn't have thought a case of alcoholism so engrossing," I said, but he only tried to look important, muttering sagely, "Very, very interesting case!" And I knew why; just another crook, I thought.

Mr. Roude seemed glad to see me, and my usual routine began. He was in an excited, active phase, not drinking too much to attend to many things, including a great deal of entertaining. I soon learned from the names of the men who came, Governors, Senators, and politicians of lesser prominence, and from their conversation, that they were deeply engrossed in politics. Different men came, and long conferences ensued, during which I usually tried to sneak a nap, or go for a walk, but one day when Mr. Roude had lunched with six men, out on the balcony, I gathered that they were going to decide who the next President would be. I harbored a certain curiosity myself, on that point, so I hung around, listening. After a long argument between them Mr. Roude said, "Oh! Hell, make it ——————. The men all looked relieved, and said, "Just as you say, Mr. Roude." I waited, and sure enough that man was our next President.

No matter how much he drank, he seemed always to know what the market was doing, and every day some one would phone to ask him what to buy, or when to sell. He would call them every low name imaginable, ending by giving them the advice they wanted, and returning to me, describe the person to me in no uncertain terms, including his near and remote ancestors, his progeny legitimate and otherwise. The next day this same person would phone to say that he had followed the advice, and made a killing, offering Mr. Roude part of his winnings. That made him wild, and he would yell into the phone, "To Hell with your lousy chicken feed, you dirty bastard!" and to me he would mutter, "As though I want his pennies! A miserable forty thousand dollars! And the poor fool thinks he's made money!"

And always, in spite of his great wealth, reputed to be anywhere from fifty to a hundred millions, but in reality probably about twenty millions, which is a nice round sum too, he was lonely. Often he said to me, "I wish my grandsons would climb on my knees, put their arms around my neck and give me a hug and a kiss. But they won't. You watch, and you'll see what they do. They'll come in and shriek, 'Grandad, where's my air gun you promised me?' and the other one will say, 'You promised me a pony!' That's all they care about, just what they get. If only I'd had a granddaughter, she'd have been different!" I watched, and the grandsons did say exactly what he said they would; said the very words.

Although at times his generosity amounted to vulgarity, such as, once he took me to a night club, and to the head waiter, and the table men, and the hat-check girl, he gave a one-hundred-dollar bill, each, and another time a tip of fifty dollars to a manicurist, he never gave me a penny above my exact salary. I sometimes wondered why, and Mrs. Roude, who was quite decent to me now, said to him, "David, why don't you do something nice for Miss Dan? You give so much to other people!" Her whining voice stopped, and he turned from her, giving me a strange look, then back to her, and answered, slowly, "Because I want to keep one friend." Long years later I knew better what he meant.

Many things he said to me I have had reasons to recall. One day we went for a ride in his car, and stopped near a place where he had fifty men, Italians and Irish Americans chiefly, he told me, digging to enlarge a small pond. All around stood cars in which they had driven to work. He silently observed them for a while, and said, "Listen, Miss Dan. I want to tell you something important, only you won't know that it is. I tell you that it is, and I know." I said, "Yes, Mr. Roude." He looked again toward the laborers and the cars, and said, "You see those men digging, and you see the cars. I pay those men eighteen dollars a day to dig a ditch, and they drive to work in expensive cars, wearing silk shirts. Well, I won't be here to see it, but you will, and my daughter and my grandchildren will. This country will be so busted in ten or fifteen years, that men like those down there will be in the breadline. Hunger will march over the land, and Want go to bed with millions. We pay as high as sixty-eight dollars a day in the steel mills, and they too drive to work in limousines. The whole world will know hunger and want." He was silent, and I asked, "Why will this be, Mr. Roude?" His eyes were deep and dark, and he was more serious than I had ever seen him. He spoke quietly, decisively, answering my question. "Because it's against Nature! It's against Nature for laborers to drive to work in silk shirts and in limousines. It's against Nature, and it won't, it cannot last!"

Having grown up a poor boy who worked hard, and developed with the country at a period of great expansion, at a time when fortunes were quickly made, during the great development of many of the natural resources of the country, I could understand his line of thinking, his wonder at the changes in labor conditions, and I had a strong suspicion that he knew of what he spoke.

When I'd been there a week, during which Mr. Roude had been very active, and not very intoxicated, I noticed a change in him. He became lethargic, moody, slow in his movements, and although he still tried to make a joke, and to laugh, his efforts were forced. I told Mrs. Roude that there was something distinctly wrong with him, and she said, "I'll have Doctor Pinckney Marshall come down to see him." This doctor's name was familiar to me, for he was extremely successful, with a very rich clientele. So I awaited his arrival with suppressed curiosity. Mr. Roude was up, sitting broodingly in his chair, patently bored with the whole idea. The Great Man made his appearance, attired in perfectly fitting striped trousers and cut-a-way coat bound with braid, his vest outlined with virgin white, a red carnation in his buttonhole. Tailored to perfection, his coat accentuated his slender, graceful figure. I didn't see his hat, but I fervently hoped that it was silk, and high, and shiny. He was a picture of Something, but I couldn't think what . . .

He made a cursory examination of Mr. Roude, and standing before us in all his magnificence, announced in pontifical tones, "Why, Mr. Roude, you're not going to die!" Silently Mr. Roude raised his brooding eyes, up the striped trousers, past the slender waist with the platinum watch chain, past the white edging of his waistcoat, and reached the pale blue eyes behind their shining nose glasses. Quietly, wearily, he said in disgust, "Who the Hell said I was?" The two learned gentlemen laughed ingratiatingly, as though he had said something amazingly witty, and Mr. Roude gave me a pained, puzzled look, but said no more. The two charming men, after many expressions of cordial interest and assurances of his ultimate recovery, left the room.

Mr. Roude said, "Well, what do you think of the Ambassador?" I said, "What country?" He thought a while and said, "Maybe Norway?" and I said, "I have a good friend from there," and he said, "My apologies; maybe Sweden . . . still, they are right nice people too . . ." he hesitated, and angrily I said, "Ambassador from Hell!" He said, still speaking seriously, "Yes, it might be, at that. What do you think of his diagnosis?" I said, "Just what you deserve for having any other doctor than Doctor Alexander, whom you know to be honest, and efficient. I think it's a damned shame!" He just smiled. In a few days he received a bill for the visit, which he showed me, laughingly. It was a horrible travesty on the Medical Profession, and angrily I said, "You laugh, and you'll pay that fake a thousand dollars, which is more than you've ever paid Doctor Alexander for a dozen visits, and I would have to work twenty-four hours a day for a year, I imagine, to get that much! No wonder honest nurses and good doctors laugh at the rich . . . you do such funny things!" He didn't answer, but he sent his check for one thousand dollars!

One afternoon when Mr. Roude seemed all right, I came into town for clean clothes. When I returned at six, I found him desperately ill, lying in his bed, completely unconscious. The suave doctor was fluttering helplessly about. I asked him what had happened, what was wrong, and he said anxiously, "I don't know!" Exasperated at the whole farce, and indifferent to his precious dignity, I said, "You wouldn't! If you don't know, you'd better find out damned quick!" He drew his stupid head back like a reptile and said, "No nurse can talk to me like that!" Driven past discretion, knowing that Mr. Roude needed attention, I fairly hissed at him, "Oh, for God's sakes! No self-respecting nurse would speak to you except under necessity! Take your filthy pride and stick it in your pocket! You don't know anything, but by God, I'll get someone who does!" He made a menacing gesture toward me and I said quite calmly to him, "If you try to stop me, I'll slap you down."

I called Doctor Alexander, and asked him to come just as quick as he could. I remained with Mr. Roude, who lay absolutely inert, his breathing slow and labored, his pulse barely discernible. Doctor Avery crept around, utterly useless in an emergency; probably the flower of efficiency with a teacup in his hand. I said, "Look here, Doctor Avery, if anything happens to Mr. Roude, you're responsible. You were here, you've been living off him for weeks,—you should know what happened while I was away. You know I don't care a fig for you,—my patient comes first, which obviously is not the case with you." He made no reply, but looked scared stiff.

Doctor Alexander came, and remained with Mr. Roude for five hours, doing everything that could be done for him. He said that he suspected someone of having given him some drug, probably morphine. Mr. Roude hated any kind of drugs, and would never take them knowingly. He asked me to keep careful watch, that perhaps we might find out who did it. Whoever it was, I saw that it didn't happen again, and in a week he was on the mend. He was curious about what he called his "spell," but he made no inquiries of me, and I said nothing. He could control his liquor with comparative ease, stopping whenever he made up his mind, and usually made a quick comeback. I felt in my bones that when I'd gone, some one would do him in,—some one wished him dead. That also went into my N.O.M.B. compartment, for I could do nothing.

He brought me in town with him, when I left, and on the way he said, "Listen Miss Dan. I've told you before, and I tell you again, this nursing is not a nice job for you, and I wish you'd learn something else." I said, "And you listen to me, Mr. Roude! I've been kicked about for so long that when I've found one entirely decent person, I want to hold on to him. Drunk or sober, you're the finest man I've ever met, and I like being with you. I hate to see you drink too much, but if you're going to do it, I want to see that some damned doctor doesn't polish you off. You know you've got to be protected, and who is going to do it? Besides, I like being with you enormously; you're a wonderful person." He looked embarrassed, for he hated anything that savored of compliments or sentimentality, and he said, "To Hell with that bologny! What can you learn that would be better than this rotten job?" I told him that I had thought of learning to be a secretary to a doctor, at Doctor Alexander's suggestion. "All right, do that. I'll give you a hundred dollars a month to live on until you do it." Touched by his kindness, I said, "But Mr. Roude, it takes six months, and that would be six hundred dollars; more than I could allow you to spend on something problematical." He gave me a sharp look and said, "You do your part, and don't worry about the money." Silence between us for several miles, and I said, "But, Mr. Roude, what will you do the next time you go on a bender? Let some quack come in and kill you? Then where would I get my hundred

dollars?" He laughed, then looked serious and said, "Can't you do both? I'll
not get lit so often, and you can always take two weeks off from pot hooks
and typing; won't hurt." I said, "No, Mr. Roude, that won't work I think; I
must do one or the other; you must decide." Enthusiastically he said, "All
right. You learn to be a secretary, and if you don't like it you can always
come back to the Old Soak."

So I went to Miss Conklin's Secretarial School, on West Thirty-ninth
Street. I knew at a glance at banking and double entries that I couldn't learn
them, not if I studied for a thousand years, so I concentrated on typing and
shorthand, finding them difficult enough. It was an excellent school, Miss
Conklin and the teachers were fine women, and I worked very hard, and
learned fairly well. My check from Mr. Roude was always a little late, and
one month it hadn't come on the fifteenth, so I went to an advertising agency
for which I had worked once, and got a job modelling stockings and underwear. When my check came, I returned to typing. I wondered if Mr. Roude
was sorry he'd started it, but I didn't communicate with him at all.

By this time I was terribly in love with Reuben, and he with me. Every
day was welcome because it held so much happiness. The knowledge that I
would either speak to him on the phone, or see him, perhaps have supper
with him and dance with him made everything beautiful and good. Nothing distressed me as it used to, for I lived in the complete assurance that I
had a real friend; some one who loved me. I had never known a Jew before,
but I never gave it a thought; I only knew that he was gentle, thoughtful,
and sweet to me; that I loved him, and thereby life became colorful, stimulating, delightful. For many things I loved him—because he helped me
hunt a room closer to school, and helped me put up my little bookshelf—
but most of all I loved him because he called me his "lovely girl." When he
said, "How is my Lovely Girl?" my knees trembled, a faint nausea of happiness almost made me dizzy. I pinched myself, unable to believe that such a
charming man called me his lovely girl, making my life a blissful joy. My
heart was filled with gratitude to him—nothing I could do seemed sufficient
return for the joy he brought to me.

Four months went by, and Mr. Roude's secretary asked me to come
down to the office. I had never been there, but when I saw him in his large
comfortable private office, so well and handsome, so full of fun, it seemed
that things were breaking too well for me, and I was filled with dread. I
knew that it couldn't last . . . couldn't possibly be true. He motioned me to
a chair that resembled somewhat an old-fashioned rocker gone modern, in

some mongrel way, and as we talked the chair moved, so that presently I found my knees knocking against his. Embarrassed, I pushed away, but in a short time there I was again, too close proximity for me. I stood up, and he said, "Take this chair, Miss Dan, you'll find it more comfortable." After a few minutes in that chair, I found myself almost half across the room, raising my voice to reach him. He laughed so hard, and told me that he had those two chairs for good and sufficient reasons, the one offered depending upon the person. He loved them.

He asked me about the school, and general subjects, and as I was saying good-by, at the door, he said, "Oh, by the way. Have you any beaus?" I felt my face burn, and said, "One." He said, "When you think of getting married, let me know, and I'll look him up,—see if he's worth a damn. And don't do it without letting me know, will you? Besides, I might break down and be big-hearted and give you a present!" He was a good man, and I said, "You've already done so much for me, Mr. Roude." His face became a cold mask, as always at any reference to a kindness on his part, and he said good-by in a way to preclude further remarks.

But he had put an idea into my head,—a wonderful idea. I wanted instantly to marry Reuben and have a baby, a lot of them. I wanted some one to love, and to love me; a home, however small,—I wanted Reuben. He had told me that he worked for his father, a contractor, who paid him twenty-five dollars a week; that he was a graduate lawyer. Thrilled with the idea, I could hardly wait to see him, and when we met I told him that I had seen Mr. Roude, and what he had said about my ever marrying; how I had suddenly known that I wanted to marry him. I was happy, and excited, for it seemed such a good idea at the time, that I failed to notice his lack of enthusiasm. "You see, Reuben, I love you and you love me, therefore let us wed." I laughed, but he didn't. He looked embarrassed, his face white. Puzzled, I said, "What's the matter? Why do you look so funny? Is it the thought of marrying me that gives you that sick look? Don't you love me? What is the trouble? Please, please tell me!"

He looked ghastly and said slowly, "I want very much to marry you; I love you more than any one in the world. But I cannot; it is impossible." A small voice inside me said, "You see; I told you all the time it wouldn't last; that there was sure to be something hideous in it; nothing is the way it seems." I just looked at him, sick to the pit of me. After a moment I said, "But I don't understand! What do you mean by 'Cannot?' If you say to me, 'I do not wish to marry you,' I can understand; those are simple words, and make sense. I don't want you to do anything that you don't in your heart want to do more than anything else. But, cannot,—I simply don't understand. I'm sorry, but I must know what you mean."

He found it hard to speak, and stammered, words, broken sentences, and gradually I understood that he was telling me that his family were orthodox Jews,—that they would never allow him to marry a Gentile. I had never realized before that I was a Gentile. It was difficult for me to grasp the idea, for I had no feeling that we were in any way different. I had been brought up so thoroughly free from prejudices that I couldn't believe that ordinary people, living in New York City, could be bound by dead beliefs, mouldy superstitions. From a personal problem it became a principle which I must understand, a stupidity I personally must eradicate. How live in a world where such cruel barriers of medieval origin were allowed to destroy people? I told him how evil and destructive such ideas were to me, how horrible; he just listened and all he could say was that his family would never allow it. "But you knew this all the time? Why then did you make me love you? Why?" He bowed his head and whispered, "I know,—I shouldn't have." But I loved him and said, "Listen, Reuben! You're a grown man, and free; I'm free. We can work, we can work together, and make a beautiful life! Let us be free!" He could only say, "You don't understand." And he was right.

We parted, not exactly in anger, but miserable and unhappy. I felt that I had been trying to force a man to marry me against his will, and the thought was nauseating. After a sleepless night, I got up early to carry out a plan which I had evolved, which was to go and see his mother; to ask her what she found objectionable in me. For I determined to get at the bottom of so much that eluded me, that I obviously lacked the capacity to see and understand. And also, to fight for my love.

In their apartment, I waited for his mother, who was out. I could formulate no opening sentence, beforehand, but trusted to luck and her attitude. She came in, a short, plump, intelligent-looking Jewish woman who met my stare with one equally curious. She was possessed of a simplicity and poise that communicated itself to me, somehow extracting from our meeting any sense of strain, of anything unusual. Almost as if we had both been through this exact scene a thousand years ago. We spoke politely, she asked me to sit down, and said, "Well, vat can I do for you?" I stood up to answer her. "I've come to ask you why you will not let your son marry me. What is wrong with me? Do you think that I am not an honorable person?" She listened quite calmly and said, "Sit down, and ve vill speak about it." I seated myself, and she spoke to me.

"Vell, you ask me straight, I tell you in de same vay. I speak my mind, the truth, to you. Vell, first, you are a fool! I know mine son better than you do, and I tell you plain out, he is not worth it. He iss lazy, he iss no goot. Ve vurk hard so he should be educated; by collitch ve send him yet, und to Yurrup, fur vat? He von't vurk; he iss dancing too much! Ve are Jews, and it is no goot dot Jews marry Gentiles! It von't vurk!" I listened, preparing my answer; she gave me a very direct appraisal, and went on. "You are a nice-lookink girl,—I don't know how he efer got sooch a girl! You're too goot for him. Go and marry one of your own kind, and leave him to his kind! For vy should you vant to marry mine Reuben? Phuy! You're crazy! I'm tellink you!" She paused for breath, and I broke in impatiently. "But, Mrs. Rosenthal! I love your son, and he loves me! We are decent young people,— why shouldn't we marry like any one else? What harm can it do to you, or any one?" She moved her foot impatiently, and made a sound of exaspera- tion in her throat, saying scornfully, "Lof? Lof? Vat do you know of lof? Vat does *he* know of Lof? Dun't make me laf! If you vant, go ahead and marry him, but I varn you now, I vill nefer speak mit him, nor vill his father. Reuben vill not like dat, and vat he vill not like more is dat ve vill gif him not vun penny! And he vill not vurk for you, beleaf me, I know! I know mine son, and I tell you dat he vill not vurk for you! Take my adwise, and forget him! Marry a man of your own kind, leaf mine son to his. It is best!" She saw that I was weeping, and became softer, more friendly, but still said, "Trust me; I am your friend! Veep if you vant, but you will tank me vun day dat I haf been honest miet you!"

When she stopped, I tried to talk to her about the stupidity of being ruled by old customs, evil beliefs, which only hurt people, for what? I asked her to explain how she could hold to such stupid superstitions, but she only smiled and said, as Reuben had said, "You don't understand; you nefer will!" I realized that I had lost, and I didn't understand, not really. I stood up and held out my hand, which she took in an embarrassed pitiful way, and said good-by. In spite of my unhappiness, I could not dislike her. Some- how I knew she had been honest, and that it had not been easy for her.

Dazed, overcome by futility, my incapacity to grasp properly what it all meant, I got off the elevated at Fiftieth and Sixth, and wandered along the street, hardly aware of my direction. At Forty-second Street, I went into a drug store, thinking, "I'll call him, and tell him that it's all over."

When he answered, just the sound of his voice made my knees weak, I said, "Hello, Reuben! I've just been to see your mother." I heard his gasp of astonishment, mixed with fear, as he said, "Whatever for?" Simply, I said, "To ask her why they will not allow you to marry me." I heard him kick a door closed, heard his voice speaking tensely, hurried, "Listen, Belinda! Please listen! I'm alone just now, but some one may come in any minute, so I've got to speak fast. This is the last time we'll ever speak together, ever, do you hear? Whatever you think of me now, I love you. You can't believe this now, but someday you will. Please listen to what I'm saying." I heard every word, or felt them like a knife cutting slices off my heart, and he could hear me weeping. Against the sounds of my sobs he persisted, talking against the fear of interruption, against everything, he went on. "Belinda, my lovely girl, I love you more than anything in the world; you're the loveliest thing that has ever happened to me, and to give you up the decentest thing I've ever done. I love enough to hurt you,—it's the only way I can prove my love for you . . . anything else would be betraying you. Listen, Belinda! I'm going to ring off any minute, and I want you to know what I'm saying. I love you, I love you, I'll always love you! All my life I'll love you, and sometime you'll know how much I love you; that I have to do what I'm doing. I cannot help being what I am; I'm caught, I'm not free, as you think,—but, Oh! My lovely girl, I love you." I heard the receiver click; he was gone. I hung on to the phone to keep from falling. For a long time I remained in the booth, crying as I didn't know one could.

When I could compose my face so that people wouldn't stare, I came out and walked up Sixth Avenue to Forty-ninth Street, to my little room Reuben had helped me find, and arrange. I climbed the steps of an old brownstone house, up the three flights to my room, in a dazed way; nothing seemed real, not the house, nor the room. I took off my clothes, putting them carefully away, and went to bed, to lie still; to let things go over my head. This, I thought, is death. Nothing more can happen to me now; life had surely run out of tricks, and from now on I would be free. Everything that could be done to finish me had been neatly attended to,—there would, in the future be no need for apprehension, for wariness. And I didn't give a good goddamn.

The Jewish woman who owned the house where I had my room, understood in a very touching way, that something horrible had happened to me. She never intruded, never talked, which I thought was heavenly of her. Occasionally she brought me a cup of coffee, and begged me to drink it.

Sometimes I did, often I couldn't. I lay quiet, getting up only to bathe, for days and days. Shut off from life, waiting. I was waiting for a sign, for something to show me the way, since I couldn't find it for myself. I went over every aspect of my life, trying to see why a blindness prevented me seeing ordinary signposts which even the most stupid must see clearly, else they would have all been destroyed.

Completely unable to fathom the mysterious forces that seemed to enfold me, so much of which was inimical to me, I was afraid to venture out again. Time and again I had faced difficulties, had been out, and had got up, staggering, but up, and on my feet; this time I had no desire to fight. It was all so useless, and extremely uninteresting. For weeks I lay in quietness, seeing only my landlady with the food which she urged upon me. Inert, indifferent, almost happy, for there was a peace in accepting the fact that I was completely finished. Nothing could ever hurt again.

One bright sunny day my landlady came and with such a tender, understanding small voice, urged me to go out for a walk. Such beautiful sensitivity must, I thought vaguely, be rewarded, so I dressed myself carelessly and went toward the Park. I dropped weakly on the first bench I reached, too indifferent even to look at people passing. I just sat. Soon I returned, climbed the stairs to my small room, a haven, a safe place, where if I just stayed nothing could get at me, ever again. I loved the very walls of my room, because no one could see in; they surrounded me with a nice protection, for which I was enormously grateful.

After a few days my landlady again urged me to go out, and again I tried, to please her. Idly looking over odd bits of papers and cards on my bureau, I saw the name of a very famous doctor; the card had been given me by a nurse in the hospital where I had first met Mr. Roude. She had told me that he was one of the most famous Neurologists, and that he had somewhat unusual ideas concerning the treatment of nervous and mental diseases. I had kept it, intending one day to go and ask him to give me work; I had liked so much the name,—Doctor Stuart Ellery Jerrold.

As I looked at the card, I thought, "Well, maybe I'm mentally ill. Perhaps I should be locked up." The consideration did not dismay me; in fact it seemed a pleasant suggestion. Locked up. In that case, nothing could get me . . . I'd be safe forever. That would be one way to beat life, when it was too bitter to be borne. I telephoned to his office, and his secretary put me on to him at once. His voice came over the wire with a pleasing resonance; a healthy, buoyant, musical voice, with deep tones. He gave me an appointment for the following day, at one o'clock. I had a presentiment, which increased over the night, that this appointment was more important to me than it appeared at first glance. I thought, "Perhaps he will help me get a job as secretary; perhaps he will lock me up. We'll see." I liked his name,— it had a dependable, straight-forward sound to it that had remained with me. I wondered if he looked like the Great Physician who had so pontifically assured Mr. Roude that he was not going to die?

I put on my nicest suit, making myself look like a secretary, I thought, and set out for my appointment at his office, on East Sixty-seventh Street. It was an old-fashioned brownstone house, and the maid showed me into the reception room,—a long, badly lighted cavernous affair, but somehow impressive. Two pairs of dark mahogany doors, one at the side, the other at the end, intrigued me. They went up and up, almost to the high ceiling, and had rounded tops, presenting a strong, citadel-like feeling. Some faint premonition came to me then that this was to be my home.

When I had waited about ten minutes, the tall doors at the end slid back, with a squeak, and Doctor Jerrold came toward me. I saw a tall, but fat man, who moved quickly, lightly, on small feet; his head was large and imposing; his hair thinnish, fair, and inclined to curl. He needed a shave, and irrelevantly I saw Mr. Brevia's face as he drew back in horror upon seeing my old-fashioned razor. Doctor Jerrold seemed unaware of his appearance, even uninterested. He smiled, and asked me to come with him back to his office. His manner was casual, friendly, reassuring, and I became more at ease, during the short distance that I preceded him into his office.

As I walked back I thought, "He probably knows the why and wherefore of all the things that drive me mad; the unexplainable, unbelievable incidents that happen only to me." He motioned to a small chair near his desk, and he sat in a chair with a high, carved back, facing me. He picked up his pen, and I saw that he had before him the usual history sheet for patients. That annoyed me, and I said, "I'm not a patient, Doctor Jerrold. I've really come to ask you to help me get a job as secretary to a doctor." He smiled a little, and said, "I know, but I'll take a little information for my record, just the same." He asked my name, and age, and where I was born, and carefully wrote them down. Frantic at what seemed to me stupid, I protested again that I was not a patient. He ignored my remark and said, "Were your father and mother any relation?" Impatiently, I said, "None whatever!" He laughed, and I said, "Why do you laugh? What's funny about that?" He smiled and said, "Most people fumble the question, trying to think quickly whether or not marriage makes them related." He laid down his pen and turned to me so casually, and said, "What would you like?" I stared at him, and with no warning, no awareness of what was going to come out of my mouth, I answered him, my voice loud, vehement.

"I want a steak, a huge one; a steak smothered with mushrooms; I want a cup of coffee every morning, and an apple every night! I want my rent paid from now until the day I die; I want, I *demand* that some one believe that I am decent; that I pay my bills, and cheat nobody! I want some one to know that I am not really mad, only that I don't understand things, that nothing makes sense, and puzzles me so! I want some one who knows to tell me why there is so much cruelty in the world. I want some one to love, and to be loved! I want never to have to think again, Will I eat next week, or not? I want some one to read to me,—poetry, brave, singing poetry, and poetry of pain, and anguish! All these things I want, and I have no hope." My voice, grown louder, almost shrill, startled me when suddenly I heard it, and found myself wiping my nose, weeping bitterly. When I realized where I was, and what I'd said, I thought, "Now he *will* lock me up, but what the Hell?" I had got up, unknowingly, while I was screaming at him, and now I sat meekly down, quite calm and completely indifferent as to the next move.

He sat perfectly still, his face inscrutable; the huge bulk of him so still; the room still, and we sat for a long moment like that. Very quietly he said, "If you want a steak, will you have dinner with me tonight?" Surprised, not expecting quite that, I glanced at him, trying to decipher what was going on in his mind. Thinks I to myself, "Ah Ha! The villain appears! He's going to lead me astray! Well, let him, I'm astray as it is." I looked directly at him, laughed, and said, "I'd be glad to." There was a sharp little twinkle in his light blue eyes as he got quickly up, walked lightly to the door, which he held open, and in a charming, polite voice said, "Will you meet me at the Plaza at eight?" I said, "With pleasure."

He held out his hand, I put mine in it, and said good-by. As I left his house, I said to myself, "Now I am walking into the biggest and most difficult job I have ever had,—but it will be worth it, for I have found some one who understands, and is a friend."

Short Stories

My Mother-in-Law

My mother-in-law was a wonderful little old lady. She was seventy-five years old when I first knew her. Small and wrinkled she was, but lively, with sharp, small, wise, old eyes, like those of an elephant. Although the difference in our ages was enormous, I felt more at home with her than with any of the younger members of my husband's family. She told me that at no time in her life had she been pretty; that her eyes, now a pale but keen blue-gray, had never been different; that her hair, now white, had been an ugly shade of red. But a beautiful body she must always have had, for even now it was rounded and supple, supported by a pair of seductive legs. She went about the business of living with an alert, casual eagerness. She told me that she had seen the arrival of gas, electricity, trolley cars, bicycles, automobiles, ocean liners, submarines and airplanes; telephones and telegraph, motion pictures, silent and noisy, and radio. I think that she observed all these phenomena with a certain amount of nonchalance,—almost as though she had expected them and would have been mightily surprised if they had not come. All these she incorporated into her awareness of life with little astonishment, and I think that she sensed the many things to come, regretting her inability to be here and to see and use them. Her casual, So What? in exactly the tone used by her grandchildren, seemed somehow natural; it was very difficult to remember that she was old.

Her husband, a school teacher in Brooklyn, had died when she was fifty, leaving her a small amount of money and a house well protected by a mortgage, but she displayed sufficient perspicacity concerning investments as to enable her to live independently all her life. I think that was one reason she was so well and happy,—she never had to live about with her children, as so many tired old people are forced to do. Instead, hers came to live with her, which is quite different.

From the very first I loved her and felt at home with her. She was the only member of her family before whom I could swear freely and smoke a cigarette enjoyably. She even tried one herself, giggling like a girl, saying, "I wouldn't have Sarah catch me for the world." Sarah was one of her daughters, whose manner gave one the feeling that whatever one had done, one really shouldn't have. Madame was quite different; I could and did talk to her about anything and everything that came to my mind, and she responded with more enthusiasm and understanding than any young friend I had. Once she said to me, "Deborah, I've been thinking about it, and I've decided that my son didn't do so badly in marrying you for a second wife; it could well have been worse." Curious, I said, "In what way?" She laughed, her small face full of wrinkles, and said, "Well, I've noticed that men of Robert's age, left free to marry again after a conservative life, usually go to extremes and end up by marrying a chorus girl; at least you are a trained nurse, which is much safer." I thought she might very well be mistaken in that conclusion, but let it pass. We laughed, a secret between us.

She never coddled herself and made short shrift of subterfuges, but once when she was visiting me she had a pain in her right knee, and upon my insistence that she let my doctor see it, she grudgingly consented. When he had made his examination, she said, "Well, Doctor, what's the matter with it?" Benignly he smiled and said, twirling his glasses the while, "You DEAR little old lady, it's old age!" She observed him none too tolerantly with her small elephant eyes, and said coolly, "Is THAT so? That other one is just as old, and IT's alright!"

I begged her often to come and stay with me for always, but she said, "No. I like visiting you and Robert, but I like my own home best." Once when she was visiting me I had a new cook, a very old lady named Mary, whom I had taken instead of many young ones who applied, because I could not possibly not take her. I thought with fear in my heart, "What if she were MY mother, or Madame?" and hired her at once. One night Mary served a very dark colored ginger bread with apple sauce, for dessert. Madame tried it and made a wry face, whispering to me, "I don't like this,—I can't eat it." It did taste rather peculiar, but I said, "Don't be so fussy; if we don't eat it poor Mary will feel hurt. Be a sport,—you can manage one small piece if you try." She tried, chewing courageously, but with such loathing on her face that I said, "Don't bother; I'll eat both pieces,—it's not so bad if you put butter on it." She pushed hers toward me with alacrity. Later upstairs, I wondered where Mary had got molasses for it, as I had not ordered any, and didn't think we had any, so I went down and enquired. Tremulously hoping for my approval, Mary showed me the can from which the molasses had come. Unfortunately it was the can in which I had prepared a rich mixture of varnish and paint for the woodwork in the halls. Anxious, I went up and told Madame that we had been poisoned and would probably die in the night. She pursed her lips thoughtfully, her glasses far down on her little nose, and said, "Now I'll tell you what you do; have your doctor's telephone number right where you can get it, and we'll wait and see what happens." Not a bit flustered. We read until late, went to bed and slept soundly. Nothing happened.

Once my husband and I, like all married people, had a bitter fight, and I went to her, white with rage. Grasping her shoulders, shaking her a little, I hissed, "Madame! I'm going to murder your son!" She stared at me, then looked all around the room for possible eavesdroppers, put her lips close to my ear and whispered, "Today, or tomorrow?" We burst into peals of laughter, which forced me to abandon the project, at least temporarily. She was a darling.

Madam's youngest son had gone away from home, as is often the way of youth, and had remained away for eighteen years, not writing to her at all. I wanted to ask her about him, but could not. She talked of all her family, but never of him. Of Robert, my husband, she said, "It is odd to have so famous a son! When he was little we called him Pinky, because his cheeks were so pink, and his hair so fine and blond that he looked all pink. He was a good child, and very wise. He was always the brightest in his class, and when he was a grown young man he thought he knew Everything! The annoying thing about it was that he almost did. The things that boy knew! And now he is a famous psychiatrist! My little Pinky!" She laughed gaily; it was difficult to realize that she, so tiny, had carried within her so tall and big a man.

We often talked until late at night, she against her pillows, I sitting on her bed. She stood clear and strong because her wants were simple. A bewildering desire for material things had never walled her in. In her I found sanctuary from crowded unbelievable things, events which swept me from one day into another with no time for appraisal,—a refuge in a world as foreign to me as darkest Africa. She was rain on a field of corn, natural, as life should be. One night I came into her room without knocking, and seeing that she was undressing, I turned to go, but she said, "Don't go;

come in." I sat on her little rocker while she quickly and gracefully removed her clothes, placing them neatly across a chair until she stood nude before me. She displayed none of the self-consciousness that would, I know, have been inevitable in her daughters or even her granddaughters. She noticed that I was staring at her knees, and laughed when I said, "Madame, do you know that your knees are dimpled? It's wicked of you!" She examined them, looked up at me with an elfish grin and said, "So they are! Imagine!" and with her small wrinkled hands she touched her smooth round abdomen and said, "Isn't it odd that I have no marks to show that I carried four babies? And my breasts are firm, at my age,—but such a wrinkled old face!" She went to her bureau and studied her face for a long moment, turned, picked up her nightdress, slipped it over her head, and stood like a child, her bare toes showing below it. Passionately she said, "Oh, Deborah! Life is a puzzle! I can't FEEL that I am seventy-six! That I've lived my life,— that it is over! I've played my little part and now it is done. With one part of me I know this, but another part says no,—that I've not used up all the time due me. It has gone so quickly, unexpectedly. It seems last week that I was a girl and William came courting me. Where has all that time gone? I've been busy, and mostly happy too; I've worked hard, but it was a joy for I had a wonderful husband and nice children. We had very little money to do with, but it didn't matter. It is hard to realize that I had my children, and yet it is clear too; I don't remember the pain at all, yet I can see clearly the little sprigs on a dress I had when I was six! And the attic where we played when it rained, and a stone, and a certain blue hair ribbon,—all such trivial things. Arthur is more real than the others,—maybe because he caused me more pain . . ."

I remained silent, hoping that she would tell me of him, hating memories that made her sad. I stood up and began to brush her wisp of hair, and for a long time she said nothing. As if to herself, she said, "There's a part of me that feels so young! I CAN'T be the person that has done all the things I SEEM to have done, and who has not done those I meant so to do. My handful of dreams . . . poems I meant to read . . . words I had on the tip of my tongue . . . where are they? Always there was something Practical I had to do, and now the time is running short! I can feel the breeze blowing my hair back when I was five, and seven, and ten,—my first long dress . . . Oh, the things I've meant to do, that I've been too busy living to get done. We think we're cheating time, but all the same, time is cheating us."

The rhythm of life was in her small body, and the present and the future,—fused, continuous; and outside a summer night pregnant with the memories of a thousand yesterdays. Her life, so attuned to her time that her flame had not flickered nor been trampled down, ever. She had held it unconsciously, bravely in her hands, had given it to her children; it would go on in them, forever. Reverent in the presence of something sublime, held in suspense by the surging breath of the scented night, I was speechless. She gave the lie to the generally accepted belief that we leave behind us the garden of childhood, never to return. We must return when the confusion of being adult leaves us lost, short of breath for the fight. Then we return, if only for a moment,—or perhaps never to leave it. Crowded by the caprices of life, we think we are grown up, but we are not.

I laid down her comb and said, "Instead of the poems you meant to read, you have written one of your own. Finer things you have done than you ever planned; you bring courage and beauty with you, and give it without thought. And now you can begin to catch up on those things you think you have not done. You'll have at least twenty years more." She laughed and replied, "I might, at that, barring accident. My mother wanted a monument erected to a friend whom she felt had not received the recognition he deserved—an astronomer, I think he was—and having no money, she wrote a book and sold it and caused the monument to be established, all after she was ninety years old! But I'm not so energetic, nor bright enough for that."

She slipped her arms into a light wool jacket and holding it together at the throat, she said, "Deborah, the only unbearable pain I've had was when Arthur left me and didn't write. For eighteen years I never went to sleep at night without weeping and wondering where he was,—if he was well, or sick. Oh! The anguish of the awful not knowing! I can't even now believe that he would do it,—not because I was his mother, but because one simply can't do that to another human being! It is unreal,—yet the pain was real." She laid her hand on my arm and looked into my face, seeking, demanding an answer to puzzles beyond her. As though I could answer! She went on, "Deborah, how can it be that all these things happened to some one I knew, intimately, but not really to ME?" Troubled, not able to bear her to suffer, I said, "I don't know; maybe we are all like that,—leading one life on top while another underneath flows apart, with no awareness of the other."

Thoughtfully she said, "I have not felt things keenly enough; it is not possible, perhaps, at the moment, and only later have I felt them deeply.

Rain on the roof, and green vegetables. At the time one only sees them, but looking back it is sharp pain and pleasure." One hand still held the little jacket together, the other smoothed the cover lying flat on the bureau, and she went on, "But the greatest puzzle of all, the one that I CANNOT solve, that I will go down to my grave never understanding, is this: WHY have I loved Arthur more than my other children? WHY? Could it be because he gave me more pain and anguish? No,— is not that, for I always loved him more, from the very beginning. A mother shouldn't be like that,—yet I am like that, and I don't know why. What do you think?" I put my arm around her, holding here close, and giving her a little shake I said, "Listen, my good woman! You're going to bed; we'll get up early in the morning and get our wondering out of the way well before noon, for you've got to go to the Church supper, and you know it." She sighed, and obediently crept between the sheets. I tucked her in and kissed her goodnight; with my finger on the switch to turn out the light, I saw her small face against the big pillow, her bright elephant eyes twinkling as she said, "I DO like you, Deborah!" I loved my mother-in-law.

Agnes Island

The quiet of Sunday afternoon held no hint of tragedy. The Lake was a blue expanse reflecting the mountains that high, abrupt and wild, rose straight from the water's edge. Deer's Leap, its sheer face of rock softened somewhat by tenacious shrubs grasping a life among gray boulders broken loose by weight of years, rose to a great height, standing clear in the bright sunlight. From the old Mansion of the highest point of the Jerrold place, came the sounds of children's voices.

In the Jerrold kitchen of sophisticated nickel and porcelain, Olga, the efficient Norwegian maid, shelled peas for dinner. Next she made ice cream, filled a tray and deposited it in the Frigidaire; these preparations completed, she went into her cool room, came out ready for her swim. She walked majestically along the veranda down the steps, where she started to run. The length of the dock and her swift movement gave her momentum for a clean dive, her large well-shaped body cutting the water like a knife, leaving hardly a ripple. Swimming about easily, casually, for ten minutes, she climbed the ladder and returned to her room, from which she emerged dressed in crisp gingham. Clean, efficient, happy, her whole mechanism functioning like a well-oiled machine, she presented a sense of well-being like the hum of a perfect motor.

Mrs. Jerrold came from the garden, handing long-stemmed phlox to Olga, yawning lazily as she said, "I'm going to bathe. If any one should be inconsiderate enough to call, I am not home; I never have been home . . . if they prove uncomfortably insistent, say that I am dead." Olga understood and secretly approved of Mrs. Jerrold, but she answered noncommittally, "Yes, Mrs. Jerrold," and proceeded to arrange the flowers in tall vases. Soon, with the corner of her eye, she saw Mrs. Jerrold, a bright spot of movement in a brilliant scarlet suit, climbing down the ladder, for un-like Olga, she could never learn to dive, to her sorrow and chagrin. Once in the water, however, she swam about with ease and pleasure, came out to lie in cool pyjamas in the patio.

Dr. Jerrold, a pink-cheeked blond man of fifty, came over from his study in the boat house, and in a few minutes was sitting, his feet dangling over the extreme end of the dock, while he shaved, after which he dived off as casually as he walked. Later, in fresh flannel slacks he arranged himself in an enormous chair on the front veranda, under which the water gurgled and slapped the rocks. He rather carefully went through the avalanche of printed matter called the *Times*; on the other side of the house, Mrs. Jerrold equally carefully, persistently, worked her way through the *Tribune*.

Life moved peacefully through the haze of hot sun, deep, cool shade, lapping water and soft, light breezes. While clouds drifted across a theatri-cally blue sky,—cicadas kept up a continuous sound, not unrestful. From Agnes Island, which lay off the point beyond the boathouse, came sounds of loud voices, faintly irritating to Mrs. Jerrold. She dismissed them, with a half thought of the annoyance of campers, and continued her book reviews. Olga the Efficient heard the calls from the Island, but exercising her enormous capacity for seeing, hearing, and above all, saying nothing about things that in no way impinged upon her own work, ignored them superbly. Dr. Jerrold, frowning over the financial page, did not even hear them.

The dining room, painted lemon yellow with black trim, was filled with a pale golden later sun when they came in to supper. Olga served delectable food imperturbably. Having been married a sufficient length of time to have achieved complete understanding without boredom, conversation was desultory,—vague references to items in the papers, the state of the lawn due to lack of rain. Dinner over, Dr. Jerrold went out on the veranda and looked across the almost enclosed bay towards a boat which moved about in an aimless fashion, then succumbed to his easy chair and the paper. Mrs. Jerrold talked for a moment with Olga and trailed lazily back to her deck chair in the stone patio. Olga carried out the dishes and proceeded me-thodically to put in order again that which the cooking, serving and con-suming of dinner had barely disarranged. Peace settled down like a cloak,—the shadows grew longer across the grass, the birds twittered in the hedge of arborvitae, and crickets began their delicate chirping tweet. All the natural sounds of quiet country were heard, but so a part of the air and trees and water as to be almost unnoticed.

Silence was broken into rough bits by Charles, the fifteen-year-old son of the house on the hill, who came rapidly, breathlessly down the path, and asked for Dr. Jerrold. Mrs. Jerrold said, "He's on the veranda, Charles," and he left her with such haste and tension that she followed him. Standing before Dr. Jerrold, he said, "Please sir; two men have drowned off Agnes; Uncle Don is on his way to the boat house. Will you come sir?" Flushed, the serious dignity of fifteen disturbed by anxiety and desire to be moving, he spoke with suppressed excitement. Dr. Jerrold was on his feet instantly and they disappeared over the hill running, and Mrs. Jerrold, following quickly behind them, saw the two large motor boats, *Dragon Fly* and *Ducky*, rocking in their slips; she heard their engines coughing before settling down to a steady purr as they backed out and headed for the Island. She walked slowly back, shaken and afraid. Waiting to know what had happened was difficult, but compulsory.

She came swiftly through the patio and stopped in the enormous room, gay, cheerful, lined with books on all four sides, from floor to ceiling. The green rug was almost covered by Indian rugs in primitive colors, and above the mantle of the huge stone fireplace, a caribou with wide antlers gazed with sad gentle unseeing eyes. Slender finger-like rays of the last sunlight came through the Virginia creepers that clung to the top of the west window, festooning it as though with garlands. Tense, her heart beating rapidly, she felt the room strange, as if she had never been in it before. The silence was like a roaring in her ears, and unable to remain alone, she went out, her sandals clicking on the boards of the deck-like veranda that connected the three separate buildings.

She found Olga and said, "Come! Let us go out on the Point! A man has been drowned!" They went across the low hill to the boathouse, through tall grass, following an indistinct trail clear to the Point. They could hear voices on the Island, and saw other boats come around Turtle Rock, which lay like some prehistoric animal, nearer to the mainland than to the Island, frightening in the dark shadow laid across it by the high mountain behind. After listening for a little while Olga said, "Let us go back, Mrs. Jerrold. I'll make some coffee,—someone might want it later." In the tall grass small insects made happy, evening sounds, and across the bay a bullfrog croaked lugubriously. Near the house a screech owl gave a call like the sound of a lost soul, and as they topped the rise a whip-poor-will called, so close they could hear him cluck, at the finish. Sadness like a weight enveloped her heart, and in the patio, she bade Olga make the coffee.

Walking restlessly up and down the deck-like veranda became unbearable, and when the whispering, lapping water seemed laughing, she went through the enormous room to the patio. Faintly the voices on the Island came across the still water, and she forced herself to sit quietly in her deck chair, still surrounded by the Sunday paper. Resting her head against the high chair back, she closed her eyes, hearing the mixture of all small evening sounds, trying to separate them, one from the other. The light faded and twilight almost imperceptibly arrived; stars began to appear in the deep night sky. Leaves on the great oak moved like gently moving fingers as a soft restless breeze touched them casually; tree frogs were making their hollow-reed-like sounds, and a new moon was faintly discernible over the trees that loomed dark behind the kitchen. Mrs. Jerrold had an almost uncontrollable desire to weep, but at the sound of the *Dragon Fly* returning, she raced across to the boathouse.

She stood well down on the dock, squatting to catch the tie-rope her husband threw to her, tied it firmly to the cleat, ran quickly to the other side to repeat the motion. Dr. Jerrold assisted a woman from the boat, and in the pale light her face was luminous, beautiful, as she sprang lightly to the dock. Dr. Jerrold said, "Alice, this is Mrs. Randolph. She wants to use the phone,—will you take her over?" With a few polite phrases, the two women went up the stone steps that led to the road, Mrs. Jerrold cautioning the stranger as the darkness by now made the way uncertain to unfamiliar feet. On the top of the hill, Mrs. Randolph stopped and looked around her,—at the Lake lying mysterious and still before them, silver in the middle, darker towards the land, lapping gently the stones just below them. A chipmunk scuttled across their path, and the crickets chirped in a tornado of sound. "This is too beautiful!" she said, and Mrs. Jerrold in a flat voice replied, "Yes. At first I couldn't bear it. Even now, after years, it hurts," and they went on to the kitchen.

Mrs. Jerrold showed her the telephone and left the kitchen as she heard her ask for Western Union. From the veranda off the kitchen, under which the water slid up and over, receded and covering again the large, solid rock, Mrs. Jerrold could hear without listening, "Will you take a message please? Isadore Blomburg, Barret Lake, Canada. Yes, Canada. Harvey and John drowned. Come. Clarice." Silence as the operator read the message back, and the clear voice of Mrs. Randolph as she said, "Right. Thank you." Olga came to say that she had served coffee in the dining room, and the two women went in. Mrs. Jerrold asked politely about cream and sugar, wondering whether to mention the accident, or to leave it to her guest. Something in the manner, attitude, of Mrs. Randolph made her uncertain.

When she had finished her coffee, Mrs. Randolph walked around the small dining room, admiring the color and arrangements volubly, and became particularly enthusiastic over a small interior carved in wood. "My!" she said, "That is lovely! I wish I had one to take to my little girl!" Mrs. Jerrold said, "I bought it in the Semmering—up in the mountains of Austria—the peasants carve them in the winter to sell to the tourists in the summer!" Examining all the small details and laughing like a child, she went on, "My daughter would love that, and Bob, my nine-year-old son, would be crazy about it!" Unable to join in her enthusiasm, and determinedly ignoring the hint that she give her the plaque, Mrs. Jerrold flatly said, "Would he?" and went on with her coffee, her mind still on what happened at the Island.

Afterward they went out and stood on the veranda, then into the big room, Mrs. Jerrold tense, uneasy and Mrs. Randolph smiling happily. "What a lovely room!" she said, her beauty emphasized by the background of books, her happy smile. "How odd to be here like this; for years I have wondered what Dr. Jerrold was like, for I have read his books and wanted to know him. And here I am in his house!" She spoke with what might be referred to as "bated breath." Mrs. Jerrold had become inured to similar outbursts during her married life, from women of all ages and kind, but this at least was the first time she had heard it from a woman whose husband had just been drowned. Usually she smiled and felt embarrassed for them, but now it only bored her, irritated her beyond endurance, for she did not yet know how the tragedy had happened. She was on the point of interrupting the happy exuberance by asking plain out, but was prevented by the arrival of Dr. Jerrold.

He stopped for a moment and said, "I've phoned for the coroner and the undertaker, Mrs. Randolph." She said, "Thank you Dr. Jerrold," and he continued his light, quick steps through the room and out onto the veranda. Mrs. Jerrold wondered how long this weird, uncanny situation would continue, puzzled by her own tension which was completely unlike her natural reaction to incidents great or small. She hated the detached air of this woman, yet was able to ask herself why she bothered to care that much. Mrs. Randolph walked slowly around the room, reading titles, carelessly humming to herself. She came at length to the piano and said, "Oh, may I play? I'd love to play in this huge room!" Mrs. Jerrold answered without turning her head, "Go ahead; look sharp for the two keys that stay down,—the mice get in it." Half expecting a light waltz, or a jolly hunting song, Mrs. Jerrold toyed with the idea of suggesting the *Marche Funèbre*. The room seemed filled with sound that poured out upon the water, filling the night, closing off all other sounds, and clinching her hands, she said to herself, "I cannot BEAR it!" and wondered what it was she could not bear.

Olga came to say that Mrs. Randolph was wanted on the phone, and as she left the room, Dr. Jerrold came in from the patio. Standing quite near his wife, he said, "What's the matter?" She whispered desperately, "Robert! Tell me at once! What happened?" He patted her hand, looking at her curiously and said, "Why her husband and another man, a friend, drowned off Agnes Island; why are you so tense?" Ignoring his question she asked, "But how?" Patiently he answered, "I don't exactly know,—things like that can happen so quickly!" He sat down and went on, "Charles and John Squires brought the bodies up,—finest physical specimens I've seen for a long time, and expert swimmers, Mrs. Randolph tells me." Mrs. Jerrold wanted to scream, but quietly, almost timidly she said, "But Robert, expert swimmers don't drown in a calm lake on Sunday." He smiled wryly and said, "Maybe they didn't know it was Sunday!" but she seriously answered, "Yes, she told me the friend was a minister."

A car drove in and Dr. Jerrold went out, saying, "It's the men from Walton," and she saw them talk together, then go across the hill to the boathouse. The old bullfrog across the bay began his evening t-r-r-o-n-k, t-r-r-o-n-k, and a cool breeze ruffled the hair on her damp forehead. The very air seemed pregnant with something unseen, inexplicable, almost sinister,—she caught a glimpse, an evanescent thought, but concrete surmise eluded her. Her tension carried her to the threshold of mystery, for the space of a second she was aware, but the time was too short. It was like opening the mouth to speak a familiar name, and suddenly finding it gone. Her thoughts stammered, hesitated, and continuity ceased. Definitely she knew now with some part of her that she had for a long time, too long, carried the thought of the water, warm, bright and pure water, as a refuge to which one could always come at the end. The thought of cool green water closing over her was seductive, pleasing and tempting,—this she knew. But those two men having experienced it,—somehow destroyed her hold on that knowledge,—in some mysterious way suddenly it was no longer her refuge, and she was lost, completely lost.

The bare fact that they were gone, silenced forever, brought to her forcibly the realization of her dependence upon that way out. Mrs. Randolph's surprising aplomb also presented her with the undoubted fact that Robert would meet any emergency of that nature with the same calm detached efficiency; she did not know why this fact should so disturb her,—why this tension, accompanied by a profound inertia. Alone on the veranda she felt free in the dark to let her thoughts follow any lead, to any conclusion, and the weird hoot of an owl in the upper garden represented stark, spacious twilight and all the unsatisfying thoughts, unfinished, unrelated, incoherent, that raced pell-mell through her brain. Her head, she suddenly realized, ached horribly. The evening star made a silver line like a dagger across the water, and she tried to be calm, to be soothed by the beauty of the night, but when she heard the *Dragon Fly* returning, she went quickly through the big room and waited, expectant of she knew not what, in the patio.

She went up the stone steps, faint white blurred spots in the dusk, and met Charles at the top, who said, "Dr. Jerrold sent me to ask if Mrs. Randolph will come." Mrs. Jerrold held her voice to a dead level as she asked, "Why?" Charles, flushed and solemn, obviously awed by the whole experience, but with the beautiful dignity of fifteen, replied, "The police dog will not allow anyone near the bodies; she will have to take him away." Mrs. Jerrold said, "I'll tell her." *Will not allow* . . . the words repeated themselves in her mind.

The night was filled with boats, lights, telephone calls, motorcars and movement until after two, and Mrs. Jerrold, exhausted, went to bed, in which she lay awake, the sound of the water under the veranda caressing, sibilant, at times dropping to an intimate whisper, telling her that something important had touched her, brushed lightly by, that she was unable to stay or understand. Finally she slept, but her dreams were nothing to be desired, and at six she went for her swim, to make a pale appearance in the dining room at seven. Mrs. Randolph was ahead of her, looking as fresh as a new blown peony, enjoying a hearty breakfast of bacon and eggs with a few pancakes for good measure. Wanly Mrs. Jerrold gave Olga a pleading look as she asked for black coffee, inwardly wondering if drowned husbands gave one that high color and sound appetite.

Having finished her breakfast, Mrs. Randolph smiled and said, "Perhaps you are wondering why I'm not weeping hysterically?" and Mrs. Jerrold vaguely, "Yes, something like that," intently watching a gray spider energetically spinning its web between a vase and the edge of the table and across to the diamond-paned window below the grapevines. Mrs. Randolph laughed showing perfect teeth, and said, "It's because I don't BELIEVE it. I know my husband and one of our old friends are dead,—I saw their bodies in the water; I actually poked them with a stick, and I saw them brought up out of the water, but I don't believe a word of it. Can you understand that at all?" Mrs. Jerrold supported her cup with both hands, her elbows squarely on the table, looked across at the questioning face, and answered slowly, "Yes, I can understand that. So many things happen to me, that go on happening, that I KNOW absolutely cannot be, and that I do not believe at all . . . perhaps the part of me that handles Believing, is out of order,— glands maybe. Or we might be mad,—more likely."

Mrs. Randolph, facing the water that was a gray blue, almost exactly the color of her eyes, said, "All my life I have wanted to be on an island, in the middle of a lake,—that's why we came here. In my dreams I've seen it, all my life. We left the car on the other side of the lake and got a man to row us over to the island. We put up our tents and ate our lunch, and I lay on the ground, looking up at the blue sky and told them that I was happy; this was my dream come true,—we had come to my island of Dreams. They laughed at me, but I laughed too, for I was absolutely happy." Mrs. Jerrold put down her cup and asked, "Who is Dr. Trevor?" not with the curiosity of one who knows nothing, but with an almost indifferent manner of one who feared to know too much. "He and his wife are very old friends of mine; she hates camping, he loves it, and that is why he came alone." She stood up, slim and tall, and Mrs. Jerrold said, "Then what happened,— after you told them you were happy?" Walking around the room, Mrs. Randolph went on, "We got into our suits and went in the water. Harvey and John are good swimmers, but I am not; but I was not afraid, with them near me. When we'd been in the water for perhaps five minutes, I heard John gasp and start towards the shore; Harvey swam quickly to him. John was gasping and struggling; I saw Harvey take hold of him and almost instantly they went down. Naturally I expected any moment to see them come up; when they didn't, I was terrified, and felt myself sinking. Some- thing, instinct perhaps, told me to straighten out, and I did, stiffening my body and swimming a few strokes. I reached the rocks, and clambered out and ran to the edge nearest the spot I had last seen them. I could see their bodies, the water was so clear. Frantic, scarcely knowing what I did, I found a long pole with which I could almost touch their bodies, but I saw that that was useless and gave it up. Then I began screaming for help. I screamed until my throat was dry, and all the time Belge, Harvey's police dog, was whimpering piteously. Boats went by but did not stop, although I called with all my might. It became like a horrible nightmare; people couldn't just go by like that! At moments I felt that I had imagined the whole thing, then the bare facts would stun me, and I would call again for help. Finally a boat did turn and come back; then your husband came, and others. The boys brought their bodies up, and poor Belge cried in fear and rage."

After a long silence, Mrs. Jerrold asked, "Who is Isador Blomburg?" Mrs. Randolph said, "He is my oldest and best friend; he married my best woman friend, a friend from childhood days. Do you think I should have my child come down for the funeral, or do you think I should leave her up there with Jane?" Her voice was troubled, and Mrs. Jerrold thoughtfully answered, "I wouldn't know. If you don't, she may later come to feel that you should. I always proceed on the theory that whatever you do will not have been the right thing anyway."

At the sound of a car, Mrs. Randolph looked through the grapevines and said, "That's my car,—they've brought it around the lake. I'll go out and arrange our luggage, then I'll be ready to go as soon as Isador comes." Mrs. Jerrold followed her slowly; some peculiar apathy held her, making it difficult to move about with a reasonable degree of interest. She watched Mrs. Randolph who, with an efficiency nauseating to behold, removed all blankets and camping articles, spread them on the grass, methodically separating them as she said, "I'll put all John's things together and I can just drop them off as I go through Hartford. Save time." Mrs. Jerrold wanted to strike her, to say something bitterly annihilating, but couldn't. She only thought, "Is HER husband dead, or mine?"

The car satisfactorily arranged, they came back toward the kitchen, and through the window they saw Olga placidly ironing. Mrs. Randolph stepped in and said, "May I iron something, Olga?" Olga wordlessly left the ironing board, and Mrs. Randolph said to Mrs. Jerrold, "I'm restless, impatient to get started, so if I can be busy I'll be less bother to you. Isador should be here soon, surely." Mrs. Jerrold watched the neatness and dispatch with which the napkins and pillowcases were impartially smoothed and folded. As she ironed, she talked almost constantly. "Harvey and I have been married almost fifteen years," she said. "He was in the war, you know, the one that was going to make the world safe for democracy, wasn't it? Well, it didn't do much for him, or me. It was a long time before he could earn enough to get married, so I told him I would marry him anyway. I was a music teacher, and made a small income,—enough and more than I needed, so I helped him, and ever since he got a good job in the International Insurance Company, we have been all right. I've been absolutely happy, and I'm grateful for that. Now I've got to support myself and raise my little girl." Mrs. Jerrold asked, "Did your husband carry insurance for you?" Mrs. Randolph shook out a towel, spread it on the board as she said, "Not much,—and there's a mortgage on our house. I'll manage, but I can't decide anything until Isador comes. He will know exactly what to do."

The ironing finished, Mrs. Randolph said, "I'm hungry! Could we have some lunch?" Olga came from her room and the two women walked up and down the veranda while she laid the table. Dr. Jerrold came over from the boathouse, and in the dining room they found cold meat, crisp salad and iced tea. "If Mr. Blomburg doesn't come soon, I'm going," Mrs. Randolph said. "You have been wonderfully kind and I appreciate it, but I am anxious to get home. If he comes after I've gone, will you tell him that I couldn't wait?" Dr. Jerrold said that he would explain fully. They left the table, and stood on the veranda where goodbyes were exchanged. At that moment a gray haired, elderly man came from the main road, around the corner of the kitchen, and hesitated on the steps. Mrs. Jerrold was looking at Mrs. Randolph, and saw her blue-gray eyes widen with indescribable joy, her face radiant with child-like trust, with complete faith, as she walked swiftly to him. Mrs. Jerrold had a moment of faintness from the impact of the vision of beauty, of the simple love and trust so openly displayed, and turned her eyes away.

The elderly man, obviously tired and travel-worn, stumbled on a stone that lay half embedded in the lawn, as Mrs. Randolph reached him, put her arms around his neck, laid her face against his breast; he put his arms around her, kissed her forehead, neither of them having spoken one word. For a moment they stood, then turned as one person and slowly started up the path toward the car. Suddenly they stopped, and Mrs. Randolph looked back, laughing happily, confusedly, and said, "Oh, goodbye!" Dr. and Mrs. Jerrold said, "Goodbye," and watched them get into the car and drive away. They heard the boards of the bridge near the main road rattle, and turned to walk along the veranda, silent. When the sound of the departing car had sunk, or become mingled with the trees and the lapping water, Mrs. Jerrold felt an enormous, overwhelming lassitude, which she had no desire to combat. "Robert, I'm going to lie down," she said. She went to her room, knowing that there was something, some problem, fact or illusion that constantly eluded her, on which she could not focus her mind.

Lying between cool sheets in her darkened room, hearing the sound of the waves, gentle, persuasive, reminiscent, the cicadas keen in the hot sun shut out, she saw again, too clearly, the rapt, radiant face of Mrs. Randolph when she first saw her friend. There was something painful, like a knife thrust in it, which she thought tiredly might be due to its evanescent rarity. There is no such faith and trust, she thought; it is a mirage, and she wanted again, as she had always wanted, to lie down in the cool green water; to sleep as the two men now slept. The beautiful face again came before her closed eyes, and her last struggle for the right word to describe it was, As though God had come . . .

Unable to further pursue intangibles, she slept.